The Golden Labyrinth

By

Steve Earles

Noir Publishing
10 Spinney Grove
Hereford
Herefordshire
HR1 1AY
UK
www.noirpublishing.co.uk
email:noirpub@dsl.pipex.com

WITHDRAWN

SWINDON COLLEGE

LEARNING RESOURCE CENTRE

The Golden Labyrinth

By
Steve Earles

SWINDON COLLEGE

LEARNING RESOURCE CENTRE

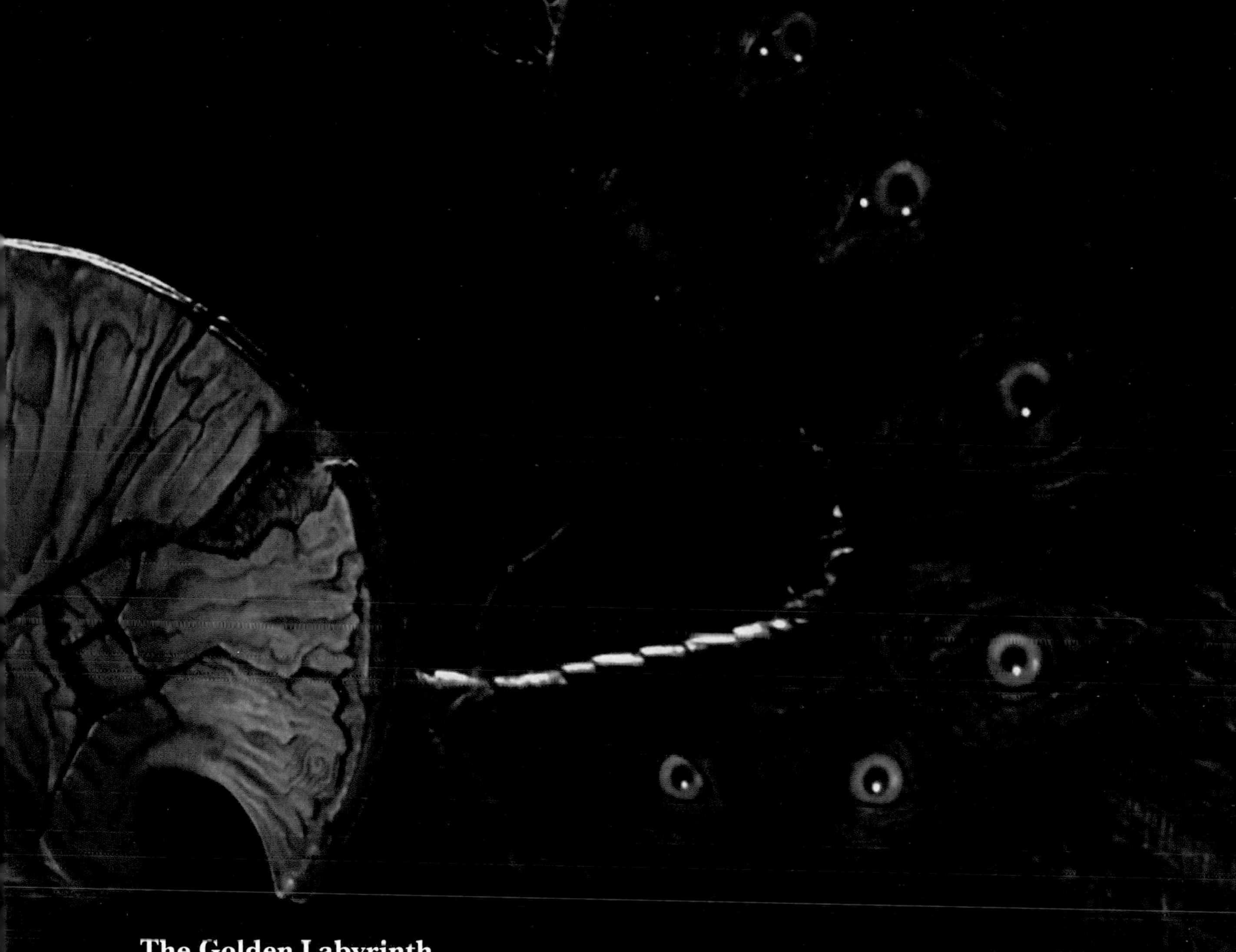

The Golden Labyrinth
By Steve Earles
ISBN 9780953656493
© Steve Earles 2009, all rights reserved
First published 2009 by:
Noir Publishing www.noirpublishing.co.uk
Copyright © Noir Publishing 2009

Photographs taken from the Noir Publishing Collection & reproduced in the spirit of publicity - any omissions to be corrected in future editions.
Cover Photos: Hellboy II - The Golden Army , Pan's Labyrinth & The Devil's Backbone
Author Acknowledgements:
Many an individual has aided the production of this volume but special mention goes to Optimum Releasing.
Steve Earles would like to thank Andy Black for his fantastic book design, and for being everything a good editor and publisher should be, supportive without being intrusive, a gentleman. Thanks also to my dog Rusty.

SWINDON COLLEGE
2nd March 2010
LEARNING RESOURCE CENTRE

Steve Earles would like to dedicate this book with love and respect to his parents Eileen and Gerry.

Contents

SWINDON COLLEGE

LEARNING RESOURCE CENTRE

Introduction

"Guillermo's interested in parables, he's interested in parallel universes and he interested in telling a story in a fantastical world."
RON PERLMAN

Guillermo del Toro is producing what I believe will one day be viewed as one of the most comprehensive bodies of fantasy films in cinematic history. He is also showing that hard work, self-belief, and most importantly, a true heart, can still work in the cynical 21st century. Guillermo makes his films by combining art with innocence. He has done this by, since an early age, following his own muse, something that takes great courage.

The majority of people in life are what other people have decided they are. They go through life wearing the false face placed upon them like an unwanted crown by people who don't care, wheras a theme in both Guillermo's art and life is that you can be what you believe you are. A man that can go from making Super-8 films with his family and friends to directing *The Hobbit*, has more than proved his point.

Speaking from a personal point of view I find that extremely inspirational, and he's done it by making his visions come to life by love and sheer hard graft and self-belief, rather than by committee (The sources of so much forgettable celluloid in the last couple of decades.)

While Guillermo's experience of so many aspects of film-making is vast, and his hunger for more cinematic knowledge seemingly insatiable, it is true to say his greatest strength is that he is a story-teller first and foremost, his craft stretches back beyond the history of cinema to a tradition of story-telling in homes over the centuries lit only by hearth-fire and candle light. These tales and fables, historical and fantastic didn't serve only as a distraction from life's worries and fears, they served also as a way of comprehending them, in much the same way as Guillermo's films do in the 21st century.

While they appeal to our inner-child, they are anything but childish. They are not escapist fare, rather they serve to greater comprehend and understand the world around us. He is very like the alchemists who inspire him, searching to transform the world that has inspired him into celluloid gold. He is driven by his love of the characters and story, not the cheque at the end of the production (indeed, as you read *The Golden Labyrinth* you will see Guillermo literally does put his money where his mouth us, often taking serious financial risks to commit inner vision to film).

His vast knowledge, not just of film though it is extensive, but also the incredible amount of literature he's read also set him apart from the glut of generic cookie-cutter directors whose 'work' (they would call it 'product', a more appropriate term). His films work on the principle, 'As Above, So Below', on the surface they function as entertainment, but what lies beneath is frequently surprising and astounding.

This is a man to whom animation is not an effect, it is a performance. He is a director that serves his inner muse rather than a franchise (a cursory glance at the films he turned down to direct *Pan's Labyrinth* confirms this. These include *I Am Legend* (now that would have been something, a Guillermo del Toro film of Richard Matheson's classic novel.), *One Missed Call* , *Halo*, *The Chronicles of Narnia: The Lion*, *The Witch and the Wardrobe*, and *Harry Potter and the Half-Blood Prince*).

His films demand the same loyalty and commitment that he does from his cast and crew, 100%! But it's a commitment that rewards itself 100%. The most exciting thing of all is, he hasn't peaked yet, he would probably have to live several lifetimes to produce all the films he envisions. So rather than celebrating an artist whose best work is behind him, Guillermo's future seems to be just as bright as his past and present. His very strong work

Guillermo del Toro living the dream with Selma Blair in Hellboy II - The Golden Army

ethic bears this out, in Guillermo's world the easy way is not the better way, hence his desire to be personally responsible for as much of his films as possible. Guillermo has also seen a world where the outsider, the so-called monster, is actually a worthy person, wheras those that are perceived as good (because of superficial things like appearance, which is ridiculous but responsible for so much misery in the world. We badly need to start seeing each other with our inner eyes, our hearts, if the world is ever going to be a better place to live). In his universe, the real monsters, like Captain Vidal in *Pan's Labyrinth* are considered to be very acceptable parts of society, for this brave truism alone,

I salute Guillermo as a person and as an artist. On a personal level, while researching this book, I came to enjoy and appreciate the man and his work more than ever (something that doesn't always happen working on a project, sometimes the exact opposite occurs). He is also courageous in putting aspects of his upbringing in Mexico, his personal experiences, his Catholic upbringing, his personal philosophies, all feature in his films, large and small, and are there for those who know where to look. In fact, his films are like a labyrinth, you have to be willing to explore to find the hidden treasures within. In the last few years he has begun to draw more and more inspiration from painters and illustrators, Arthur Rackham, Hieronymous Bosch, Salvador Dali, the Surrealists, the Symbolists, Goya and even medieval engraving. This is increasingly responsible for the ever more original look of his films

To watch Guillermo's films is to uncover some of the most amazing influences, from history, cinema, literature, art, and alchemy, all of which are explored in *The Golden Labyrinth*...it's a fantastic journey, one well worth taking!

Biography

Guillermo del Toro was born 9 October 1964 in Guadalajara; Mexico. Growing up in Mexico influenced him in his early exposure to death, seeing his first dead body at the age of four, a road accident with a decapitated head. And, of course, Mexico is awash with gory religious images. He lived with his grandmother for many weeks in a row, where he slept in a bedroom at the end of a long corridor and at night he would see a hand come from behind a closet and a ghost's visage.

He was, and still is, very influenced by reading, as can be seen many times throughout the text of *The Golden Labyrinth*. As a child he read a book a day, and it shows, his work is littered with literary references that add further depth to an already deep body of work. "I think the gothic spirit of the novel *Wuthering Heights*, in a way, marked me for the rest of my life. It wasn't a horror film, but its tone! *Wuthering Heights* is a hardcore gothic novel, with a ghost, whether imagined or not, a curse, the whole feeling of fate, and so on." He was also exposed to the magic of cinema at an early age, which is as it should be!

"My earliest cinematic memory is of a version of *Wuthering Heights* with Laurence Olivier. I saw it in a cinema called Cine Park. Normally they screened horror movies and children's film in the morning and afternoon. So, to me, Disney was just the same as Italian and Japanese horror films...From a very young age, I was a fan of genre film...horror, horror on TV. Gradually I came to recognise different actors, first it was actors then directors, Japanese, Italian horror films, Mario Bava."

Guillermo studied scriptwriting with famed Mexican director Jaime Humberto Hemosillo and was a founding member of the Film Studies Centre and was a founding member of the film studies centre and the Muestra del Cine Mexicano (Mexican Film Festival) in his home town.

Of his numerous shorts (Shot on Super Eight, 16mm and 35mm), 'Dona Lupe' and 'Geometry' were selected in a dozen international films festivals. "I started with films you could buy to project, a bit like DVDs nowadays. But they were in cut-down versions. So the *Curse of the Crimson Altar* with Boris Karloff began with a scene from the start, then the house was on fire and he was dying, they were very short! They were Super 8s which condensed film in10 minutes. It was like *Reader's Digest*. So that's how it started.

My dad had a camera, the same make as the projector, a Canon or a Xenon, one of those from the old days. I took my dad's camera and a couple of rolls of film he had and started making my own films with my toys. I started to like it more and more...and when I saw them projected! I took the rolls of film to the pharmacy in a kind of ecstasy...I took them to be developed and they were ready a week later. The roll would come back, and when you projected it, for me it captured the magic of making film on Super 8, which you don't get on video, It's very immediate. Seeing those images, real cinema, and saying 'I made that', was addictive. And to this day, the search for that pleasure is what makes me carry on making movies."

His first efforts were pretty primitive. "I made them with dolls and they were actually quite violent. Mainly, I used toys from *Planet of the Apes*, and I had a few monsters from Universal. So there were battles between fantastic creatures, with lots of ketchup and no much production." It started to get serious when Guillermo realised he had to do credit sequences, and do short films with actors and plot. "I started to think, okay, it starts, then you get the title....So I started later, when I was about 15 years old...I started to organised a group of friends. There were complex productions which we called two-afternoons, and less complex productions which were an afternoon or half an afternoon."

He didn't have to look far for cast and crew. "My friends and my family! My mother was my actress in two short films. One was *Geometria*, which was in the 1980s. She suffered a brutal death at the hands of a zombie. It cost $2,500, a considerable amount of money. Before that she acted in an even more bizarre short called *Matilde*."

In many respects, the approach he took back then, is the same approach he has now, albeit on a massive scale. "The weird thing is that between making Super 8 films and now...my attitude to my own film making hasn't changed that much in the sense that I always saw the money I heard about or earned in other ways...in terms of how much do I need to make a ten minute short, five minutes, twenty minutes...and I still think the same way. When I have the money, I think...that'll fund two days shooting. In that sense, I've never had a professional attitude. I became professional in terms of discipline, organisation. But because I did my training as an assistant, I began to special effects for friend's short films, acting as an assistant director on friend's features, doing anything on other people's short films and features.

I started getting involved in what the structure of a film set is without realising it. I remember very clearly in 1986 or 1985, I asked myself what can I do to get the film of *Cronos* made. I was planning it back then. It was called 'Vampire of the Grey Dawn'. I thought I should look for a professional angle, which no one else had, which I alone could exploit, to ask for favours, to win favours, and that was special effects make-up. That was the start of everything, but it was in parallel. I did my own short films and special effects and make up for other people."

He went on to studied special effects and makeup with legendary SFX artist Dick Smith (*The Godfather*, *The Exorcist*, *Altered States*, *Amadeus*).For ten years he was dedicated to this work through his Necropia company where he supervised special effects make up for several films, including *Bandidos*, *Caitia*, *Cabeza De Vaca*, *Mentrira Piadosas*, *Dollar Mambo* and more than twenty episodes of the TV series *La Hora Marcada*, three of which he wrote and directed. It was through his Necropia company that Guillermo met leading producer Bertha Navarro, with whom, alongside Laura Esquivel and Rossa Bosch, he formed Mexico City based production company Tequilla Gang. He has also gone on to form Cha Cha Cha Producciones, with Alfonso Cuaron and Alejandro González Inarritu (sometime called The Three Amigos!). They produced the well received *Rudo Y Cursi* directed by Carlos Cuaron, Alfonso's brother.

He has taught and headed film workshops since the age of 15, and has served as a juror on the selection committee of the Mexican Film Institute, Sundance Institute and the Spirit Awards. His commitment to film also extends to production, a commitment which has culminated in the creation of Tequila Gang, together with Bertha Navarro, Laura Esquível and Rosa Bosch. As a promoter of Latin American cinema he was selected as one of the fifty young leaders for the coming millennium by both *Time Magazine* and CNN. As a writer, he has been published in several newspapers and magazines, including *Sight and Sound* and *Village Voice*. His book on Alfred Hitchcock and his script for *Cronos* have been published in Mexico.

Cronos won the Critics Week Award at the Cannes Film Festival in 1993, nine Ariedes from the Mexican Academy Awards, and twenty other international awards.

In development at various points

over the years were such films Guillermo has scripted as *Down There*, *Riding Shotgun*, *Montecristo* with Francis Ford Coppola, *Mephisto's Bridge* (Based on Christopher Fowler's fine novel 'Spanky') with Martin Scorsese, *Within The Walls* with Miramax, and *Domu* with Disney.

With *The Hobbit*, the years of development hell are over forever for Guillermo, and the only hell he will have to deal with is that of the tyranny of choice. He once wished he could have made double the films he has, be careful what you wish! "I wish I could have done double the movies I've done, but that's the way it is. Between *Cronos* and *Mimic*, I wrote six screenplays. All of them went unproduced so far. Between *Mimic* and *The Devil's Backbone*, I wrote three screenplays, all unproduced. So I have eight to ten screenplays, all unproduced. So I have eight to ten screenplays, all written and unproduced. And frankly, some of them are my favourite stories. I have a western version of *The Count Of Monte Cristo*, where the count has a clockwork hand. I have a screenplay called *Mephisto's Bridge* about a Faustian deal with the devil. I love them all. And I'm always peddling them."

His fascination with horror films began when he stayed up late without his parent's permission to watch *The Outer Limits* episode *The Mutant*. He got terrified by the make-up that was created for Warren Oates in that episode, and he went to bed really scared. His older brother put two plastic fried eggs over his face and his mother's stocking over his head and crept into Guillermo's room, further scaring him.

After that he began waking up at night and would see monsters in his room. The patterns in a shaggy sixties carpet would morph into a waving ocean of green fingers. He ended up being too sacred to go to the toilet, which got him into trouble, so he made a deal with the monsters if they allowed him to go to the toilet at night he would be their friend since then he has been on good terms with the monsters.

It was also in his childhood that Guillermo started his love affair with film music. "My first record, my first LP was the

Images this page & opposite: Rudo Y Cursi - one of the films from del Toro's Cha Cha cha Producciones

Jaws soundtrack by John Williams. My second was *The Godfather*. And since then my music collection, what I listen to...is film music."

As we shall see as we explore *The Golden Labyrinth*, the child truly is the father of the man, and in Guillermo's case, all these formative experiences and influences have served as the raw material for him to transform into cinematic gold.

Chapter One
Cronos

Cronos begins with the sound of clocks ticking, which is apt because... it's all about time.

An alchemist is hard at work in his workshop of wonders (It's like a look into Guillermo's head, full of wondrous mechanical devices, clocks, mechanical insects and automata.) We see an alchemist hard at work on his magnum opus, his hand bears the brand of the Inquisition. A statue of an archangel watches over him.

The narrator (Jorge Martinez des Hoyos) tells us: "In fifteen hundred and thirty-six, fleeing from the Inquisition, the Alchemist Umberto Fulcanelli disembarked in Vera Cruz, Mexico. Appointed official watchmaker to the viceroy, Fulcanelli was determined to perfect an invention which would provide him with the key to eternal life. He was to name it... The Cronos Device."

"Four hundred years later, one night in nineteen-hundred-and-thirty-seven, part of the vault in a building collapsed. Among the victims was a man of strange skin, the colour of marble in moonlight, his chest mortally pierced. His last words 'suo tempore'. This was the alchemist. The authorities located the residence of the dead man. What they found there was never fully revealed to the public".

The authorities found a dead man hanging from the alchemist's ceiling, his blood dripping into a bowl below him.

"After a brief investigation, the mansion and its contents were sold at public auction. Never on any list or inventory was the Cronos Device mentioned, as far as anyone knew, it never existed."

In the present day, it's Christmas time. An elderly antique dealer, Jesús Gris (Federico Luppi), is with his granddaughter, Aurora (Tamara Shanath), in his antique shop. As Gris unwraps a recent acquisition, a statue of an archangel, a man comes into shop, observes Gris unwrap the statue, and then leaves. It's the statue we saw in the alchemist's workshop.

Gris is clearly devoted to Aurora, he does a puzzle with her, as he sings her a song; "Early in the morning when the sun rises. You open your little eyes, a window of God." In a masterful contrast by Guillermo, we next see the opposite of an innocent eye, as cockroaches crawl from the statue's black empty eye. It's a warning, whatever the statue's empty eye socket is a window to...it isn't God.

Engrossed in their puzzle, they are unaware of their invited cockroach guests. Gris tells Aurora. "You still have to finish this part. Sort them by size and shape." Suddenly she spots the insects as they crawl onto the table, she tries to swat one of them but is chastised by her grandfather. "It's worse if you provoke them, Aurora."

Realising that the cockroaches have come from his new acquisition, Gris investigates the statue, removing it from its base. Within the base, wrapped in a cloth, Gris rediscovers the Cronos Device.

Looking out the window, he sees the man who was in his shop earlier, talking on a mobile phone. He has phoned the De La Guardia Corporation, where his phone call is taken by Angel de la Guardia (Ron Perlman, in the first of his roles for Guillermo), the nephew, and general dogsbody of the owner. "What did you find? Another statue. I'll tell him."

He walks through an oppressive looking factory floor and takes a lift to his uncle's surgically sealed headquarters. Wearing a face mask, surgical gloves and slippers, Angel enters a bizarre room, full of suspended statues of archangels wrapped in plastic (clearly his uncle has been searching for a particular archangel for a long time. He wheels in a breakfast tray for his uncle, Dieter de la Guardia (Claudio Brook). A breakfast of pills.

Angel tells him. "Ah, lovely day for breakfast, reds, yellows, blues and the new draft of your will?" The booming of his huge voice irritates his uncle. "Why do you always have to be so noisy?" "Just sign the new draft of your will, and I have news for you. Our buyer just called." "Now, tell me, what did our buyer have to say to you?" "Same old thing...another archangel." "So what are you waiting for?" "No, not this time. This time you get someone else to pick up your garbage!" "Not everything is garbage." Dieter takes an

Jesus Gris makes a Faustian pact in Cronos

ancient object out of a drawer. Angel has seen it too many times. "Oh no, not the little book again" Dieter shows him an aged parchment with a drawing of the Cronos Device. "This is not garbage." "You know, they all look the same to me." "That's my problem. Open your eyes. Look! This is different. This one will be mine."

Angel visits Gris's antique shop and purchases the statue. Gris tells Angel. "It's one of a kind." Angel cynically, wearily (after all he's been on this particular search for the proverbial needle in the haystack many times) replies. "They all are. But then, it's not my money. Keep the change." Gris goes to wrap the statue up, while Angel amuses Aurora. Angel asks Gris and Aurora their opinion on a series of pictures of noses which he holds up to his face. The two of them pick the one that suits him most. He takes the now wrapped statue, thanking Gris and telling him he doesn't know how important this is (But he soon will do). He gives Aurora a candy bar and leaves with his uncle's purchase.

When Angel leaves, Gris examines the Cronos Device, cleaning it with a brush, telling Aurora. "No, sweetheart, it's not made of chocolate. You come across something like this once in lifetime." Once cleaned, the scarab-shaped Cronos Device resembles a golden egg, covered in carvings, with a little winding lever. After winding the device, it begins to tick and a dial rotates (we see another variation on this in the character of Kroenen in *Hellboy*, a self-winding clockwork cyborg). For a moment nothing happens. "It's so strange, what do you make of it? A toy, maybe?" The Cronos Device is no toy. Then...the device extends six metal legs, now it looks like a golden scarab beetle (the Egyptian symbol of transformation, rebirth, and immortality). The legs stab into his hand, clamping there, drawing blood, like a clockwork vampire. Painfully he tears it off and places it upside down on his desk, like an overturned insect. The legs retract back into the device, and Gris gets the frightened Aurora to fetch a box for his bizarre find.

Gris and Aurora go to his wife Mercedes (Margarita Isobelle), she is teaching a man called Mauelito (Farnesio de Bernal) to dance as part of the class she is teaching. She goes to dress her husband's wound. "And where did you say you fell?" "On a pile of broken glass." "You won't need any stitches. Blood is always frightening. Remember when Grandma died. Everybody was covered with blood. She was all clean. But dead for good." Mercedes is obsessed by death, and her 'blood is always frightening' warning will prove prophetic. Being married to an older man may be her attempt an eternity, to eternally always be the younger part of the couple. He pulls a sharp object from his wound. It looks like the barbed sting of an insect.

That night, Gris opens his fridge. He's

dehydrated, taking huge gulps of water from a jug, a plate of raw meat seems to beckon to him. The cold light of the fridge highlighting the red of the blood. He's burning up, opening the window for air. His hand is irritating him too, and he cuts at the bandage on his hand. Aurora, drawing pictures in her bedroom, can hear her grandfather up. She goes to observe him. He has descended the stairs and removed the Cronos Device from its box. He addresses the alchemical creation, this strange philosopher's stone of eternity. "Please. Please. Please. Be careful with my soul. I beg you." He winds the Cronos Device and lets it sting him again. He prays for redemption while the Cronos Device does what it was built to do. "Our father who art in heaven...Thy kingdom come...Forgive us our trespasses. He collapses as the Device extends its grip.

Inside the Cronos Device we see an intricate internal mechanism of cogs and wheels with a living insect meshed into it. Its work done, the Device releases itself. Gris tells his granddaughter there is nothing wrong. It's a theme of Guillermo's work that adults don't listen to or tell the truth to children. Aurora is all too aware everything is far from alright. (This scene is also being significant for keeping Guillermo's interest for the entire eight years it took him to conceive and film *Cronos*).

The following morning, Gris examines himself in the mirror, he's looking noticeably younger. Entering the kitchen, he draws the blind, the light is hurting his eyes (his glasses are gone too), an indication of his vampirism. His wife is pontificating on death ,her favourite subject. "It's unbelievable, really. That Vizcaya woman died at 92." She notices Gris has shaved off his moustache. "You look different. Much younger." He's delighted at her reaction. "That's why I did it. I feel younger." There romance is being rekindled, but Gris has already reached the point of no return, he just doesn't know it. The warmth of Gris's home is in marked contrast to the sterile cold of the factory that makes a 'home' for Angel and Dieter, two men living in self-made antiseptic slavery. (Interestingly, the factory was being demolished as they shot, adding a sense of urgency to the proceedings).

When Gris goes to open his shop, he discovers the padlock on the door has been cut, and his premises ransacked. He picks up a card from his desk that reads. "De La Guardia Corporation. Angel De La Guardia", on the back of the card, in handwriting, it says-"We are open all night." He realises they want the Cronos Device.

Gris goes to the De La Guardia Corporation where he confronts Angel. "You destroyed my store." "I'm not the one you want to talk to,"

Gris is brought to meet Dieter, who offers him his sterile hospitality. "The red ones are especially good...You don't know what you are getting into" He throws Gris

Jesus Gris beholds the alchemical insect – immortality and damnation

the decapitated head of the archangel he had Angel purchase from him. A mute metatron. A silent warning. Dieter produces the alchemist's notes. "Almost forty years ago...I came upon that manuscript. Forty years ago. These are the notes...the secret diary of a 16th-century alchemist. It's a fascinating text. It's written backwards in Latin. It describes a very singular device. An invention that prolongs the life of its user. But it also contains some rules, very precise and strict rules, about the way it should be used."

Dieter folds out an age-stained diagram of a scarab beetle, the light of madness in his eyes. Gris asks. "An insect?" "That's the genius of it. The insect is trapped in the device, acting like sort of a living filter." "Do you think so? I mean, after all these years?" That's not what the dying Dieter wishes to hear, the Cronos Device is the chimera all his hopes rest on, he takes the book back. "Who knows? Maybe insects are God's favourite creatures? Christ walked on water, just like a mosquito does. And as for resurrection, it's not a strange concept to ants, to spiders. They can remain inside a rock for hundreds of years, until someone some one comes and sets them free." "I find it very educational, but what are you telling me this?" Dieter gets up, hobbling along, aided by an ornate cane. "I'm dying, Mr Gris. I'm going to show you something. Scalpels have been slicing me up bit by bit. Chemotherapy, radiotherapy, psychotherapy. Look carefully, my friend. Half my body is in here, in this glass case. And the other half...is one the menu. Or being chewed up right now, as we talk."

The irony of Dieter wanting to live forever is unbelievable, he never leaves his room, he enjoys nothing, he is a cruel mean bully, what good is the Cronos Device to him? He makes a grab for the box he believes Gris brought the Cronos Device in. Gris doesn't want him to have it, and Dieter realises Gris has already felt its sting of eternity. "Did you use it?" "Just by accident?" "Imbecile!" He calls for Angel, who brings Gris his shoes. As Gris leaves, he turns. "De la Guardia. We both lose something." And he leaves Dieter with his box. Angel comments sarcastically. "So, you finally got your...whatever it is." But inside the box is the broken padlock from the antique shop. Dieter shouts after Gris. "You may continue the game. After all, you have the toy, but , but I'm keeping the instructions, and I'm open all night."

When he gets home, Gris takes a box from beneath his bed. "This can't be possible." The box is empty and he craves the device's sanguinary kiss. "Where did I put the damn thing" Aurora!" He goes to Aurora's playroom on top of the roof of their apartment. Entering the playroom, he announces. "Aurora. I know you've got it." He looks in her toy box, then spots Aurora hiding behind a blanket. "Are you scared? You think something bad may happen to me?" If you love someone, you will quickly spot any changes in them. He notices Aurora has set a table for tea, complete with tiny child-sized cups. He begins to pour tea. "Are you comfortable back there? This happened to me once, with your dad. Do you remember him? A little, at least." Her small hand comes out from behind the blanket to take the cup. He sees the look on her face as he drops a sugar cube into the tea. "Yes, I guess you do. When he was about your age, he heard somebody talk about people dying from lung cancer." She puts back the now empty cup as her grandfather continues his tale, little realising the precious memory it will one day become.

"When I came home from work, all my cigarettes had disappeared. After searching all day, I went to the bathroom and found lots of bits of tobacco floating in the toilet. Just little pieces. I think he understood later that destroying my cigarettes wouldn't do any good. But at least I realised he was worried about me. And he knew that I knew. You know..." He takes a tiny cup, rendered even more tiny by his grown-up hand. "...I don't know what's happening to me..." He drops a sugar cube into the cup. "...but its best if we're together." He no more wants to be alone than she does (It's surprising more horror films haven't touched on the fear of loneliness, it's sadly far more common than a lunatic in a hockey mask, and a much slower killer).

She comes out from behind the blanket and gives him her teddy bear (which has the Cronos Device hidden inside it, Guillermo's homage to Charles Laughton's masterful *Night of The Hunter* (1955). Laughton (1899-1962) a fine actor in such films as *The Private Life of Henry VIII* (1933), *The Hunchback of Notre Dame* (1939), and *Jamaica Inn* (1939), sadly his single directorial effort was a commercial failure on release, and he never directed again, robbing the cinematic world of who knows what masterpieces, yet at least today the film is now regarded as a classic. Let us hope today we are able to recognise a fine film and encourage its auteur), and gives him a hug.

She doesn't judge her grandfather, she simply loves him, and knowing he loves her is enough. There are few directors who would put so tender and moving scene in a horror film, and even more bravely Guillermo has drawn on his childhood relationship with his grandmother, giving the scene added truth and meaning. Guillermo's films, while they are a feast for the eyes, they also need to be watched with the inner eyes, the soul.

In his bathroom, Gris uses the Cronos Device again, this time on his chest where the marks won't be as noticeable. He's like a junkie craving a fix. There's a knock on the door, as the Cronos Device's dial turns. Mercedes and Aurora want him, they are going to a New Years Eve ball. (It's amusing the way Aurora imitates Mercedes' shrug of her shoulders). Gris asks the Cronos Device, in a blackly humorous 'Hamlet' moment. "Who are you, little one? A god?" Inside the Cronos Device, cogs turn. "You're so good for me." Those are the words of an addict. He puts it back into the cotton bowels of the teddy bear." He pulls a barb out of his chest, he is clearly getting younger. I like the contrast between the ordinary events outside the bathroom and the extraordinary ones inside. (This a theme we will see again in Guillermo's films, such as *Pan's Labyrinth*)

Outside the bathroom, his wife frets about her weight. "Why doesn't this dress fit me now? How could I change in such a short time." (Another example of the film's themes of time, she is obsessed by death and the passing of time).

At the ball, Mercedes can subconsciously sense her husband's increased energy and vigour. She asks him if he can remember the first time he saw her. He replies. "How could I forget. I do remember. The first time I saw you, I thought you'd never notice me." She's delighted with his renewed attention, it conversely makes her feel young. Aurora notices this sudden change, and feels left out, no longer her grandfather's confidant. Adults often don't see (or ignore) the fear and loneliness in others, particularly children. A child who's already lost her father, fears she may lose her surrogate father.

As if to further emphasise the theme of time, a mime wanders the ballroom, dressed as a clock, his hands counting down the midnight, and the dawn of the New Year.

At dinner, Gris sees someone at a nearby table get up with a nosebleed. He heads to the bathroom Gris cannot help himself. Telling Mercedes truthfully that he's going to get a drink, he gets up to follow the bleeding man.

By the time Gris reaches the bathroom, the man he followed has cleaned himself up. He comments to Gris. "It's too hot in here. This always happens to me." When he leaves, Gris gathers together the spilt blood, like a junkie sorting a line of cocaine. He's interrupted by another party goer coming out of a toilet cubicle. He comments to Gris. "We've been coming here since I was a boy. Damn, what an awful party." He spots the blood , and to Gris's silent horror begins to clear up , washing the precious liquid down the sink, commenting angrily. "Animals, look what they've done here. Probably some uninvited Argentinian or Peruvian. You work hard all year for just one decent party." Then the partygoer leaves in disgust. Gris spots drop of blood on the floor, and goes to lick it up like a cat with a saucer of milk (licking blood from such a disgusting source, you couldn't be further from the clichéd Hollywood vampire film), but he's kicked unconscious. As the partygoers count down the New Year, Mercedes and Aurora wonder where Gris could be.

Gris has been dragged away and regains consciousness in Angel's car, as the radio in the car broadcasts directly from the party Gris has been rudely removed from...

'happy new year' indeed.

Angel parks on a cliff top overlooking the lights of the city below, and tries beating the location of the Cronos Device out of Gris. "Tell me where it is or my uncle won't leave me alone." Here, despite his brutal behaviour, we have some sympathy for Angel, he is enslaved to his uncle as much as Gris is enslaved to the Cronos Device. Gris asks Angel what Dieter wants the Cronos Device for. Angel tells him. "You all think I'm stupid, don't you? He thinks it'll help him live longer!" Something that amuses Angel greatly, his uncle has no quality of life as it is and he still wants to prolong it. Angel beats Gris unconscious and places Gris into his car and pushes it over the cliff.

In the wreckage below, Gris recites to himself. "So much silence. So much blood, my God. All that blood is mine. I'm dying. My, my! Everything is upside down...and I am dying. Alone. Alone! Don't let me die today. It hurts so much but I can stand much more, much more. Oh, Aurora." There are sirens in the background, back home, Aurora hears them too. That Cronos takes place at Christmas, traditionally the celebration of the birth of Christ is no accident, and that Gris dies and is reborn on New Years Day fits this mythos perfectly. Gris's words are heartbreaking, coming from an inner well-spring of despair and loneliness, the same cry for redemption everybody stifles inside.

Later, in a mortuary, the undertaker (Daniel Gimenez Cacho) sews Gris's lips together and staples his forehead. The funeral director (Juan Carlos Columbo) is impressed. "Wonderful. Tito. Wonderful. The forehead's beginning to look perfect. As if nothing had happened. It's your best work." Tito agrees. "It requires a lot of technique. I'm giving him shape...texture...I'm giving him colour. You've got to be a damn artist!" "Yes. But don't work too hard, he's being cremated." "What!? I wouldn't have done him up so beautifully... May he rest in peace. Nobody respects my work here! Why didn't somebody tell me?" "The widow changed her mind. Apparently the guy had no arrangements. He had no cemetery plot, no planning." He doesn't notice Gris's eyes start to open. (Guillermo drew from personal experience once again for this scene, giving it added authenticity. It's also very true for any artist to feel that way, that their work isn't appreciated).

Angel's uncle is furious with him, and doesn't believe his story about his car skidding. He breaks Angel's nose with his cane, the part of his body he's most sensitive about. He asks him if anything happened to Gris's heart. Angel is puzzled by his question and wonders what difference it makes, he's dead after all. "It makes all the difference, you clumsy beast. Can't you do anything right? After all these years I thought they'd still be hope for you." Dieter is an unpleasant bully, a nasty piece of work, and has obviously always put down and abused Angel, making him what he is. He has never fully explained what the Cronos Device does to him, a further sign of his contempt, he knows while Angel waits to inherit his fortune, he has him under a short leash, their relationship as Vampiric as that of Gris and the Cronos Device.

Clutching his bleeding nose, Angel asks. "How could somebody be deader than dead?" "You know nothing about dying." "I don't understand?" "You will remain that way. But there's one last thing you still have to do, and you'd better do it right. Because I'm not going to rest till I have what's rightfully mine and neither are you."

Angel goes to Gris's wake. He opens a piece of gum, disrespectfully putting the wrapper in the pocket of the suit Gris has been laid out in. Experimentally, he pinches Gris's nostrils shut.

After the wake. Gris is returned to the morgue, where Tito prepares him for cremation. The oven isn't working properly. He goes to the basement to see if he can get the gas to flow properly. This done, he returns to try again. He doesn't see the coffin is now empty, and lights the oven successfully this time, cremating an empty coffin.

The deed supposedly done, Tito nonchalantly eats a banana. The unctuous funeral director brings in Angel. "Tito, Mr De la Guardia. He is...he was a friend of the deceased. He wants to see the body one last time. "Sure, medium rare or well done?"

Meanwhile, a worse for wear Gris has made his way to some waste ground. He

is beginning to resemble the alchemist that built the Cronos Device, becoming remade in his maker's image. He removes a shard of glass from his foot and uses it to cut the stitches from his note. Scavenging through some bins, he finds his own memorial notice in the paper. It reads, "He is not dead. He just left before his time." How true!

At that moment, his wife prepares to cut out the same memorial notice, her compulsive habit even extending to her own husband. The phone rings, it's Gris. He finally manages to speak her name but she puts the phone down. Aurora has been listening on the extension phone. Gris beats the payphone in frustration, and walks off forlornly into the rainy night. He makes his way home to Aurora's den, where she is waiting her him with a towel. There is a link between grandfather and granddaughter that transcends physical death. Gris retrieves the Cronos Device. Aurora finds him a pillow. "Is that for me?" She nods, but as the sun rises, its rays come through the holes in the room and burn Gris. He uses her toy box as a coffin. As she's about to close the lid, we see she has tucked him up with a doll and her teddy bear. It is both amusing and sad, bitter sweet. The way a child makes sense of the madness of the world of adults.

Later, as Aurora paints pictures, the lid of the toy box opens like Dracula's coffin. Gris tries to write to his wife (who's playing mournfully at her piano, expressing her grief in music, while he tries to express his in words with hands hardened with rigor mortis), but it's hard, he's deteriorating rapidly, Aurora is filling a tray with his failed previous attempts at writing the letter (In *Hellboy*, *Hellboy* will try and write a letter to Liz in much the same fashion).

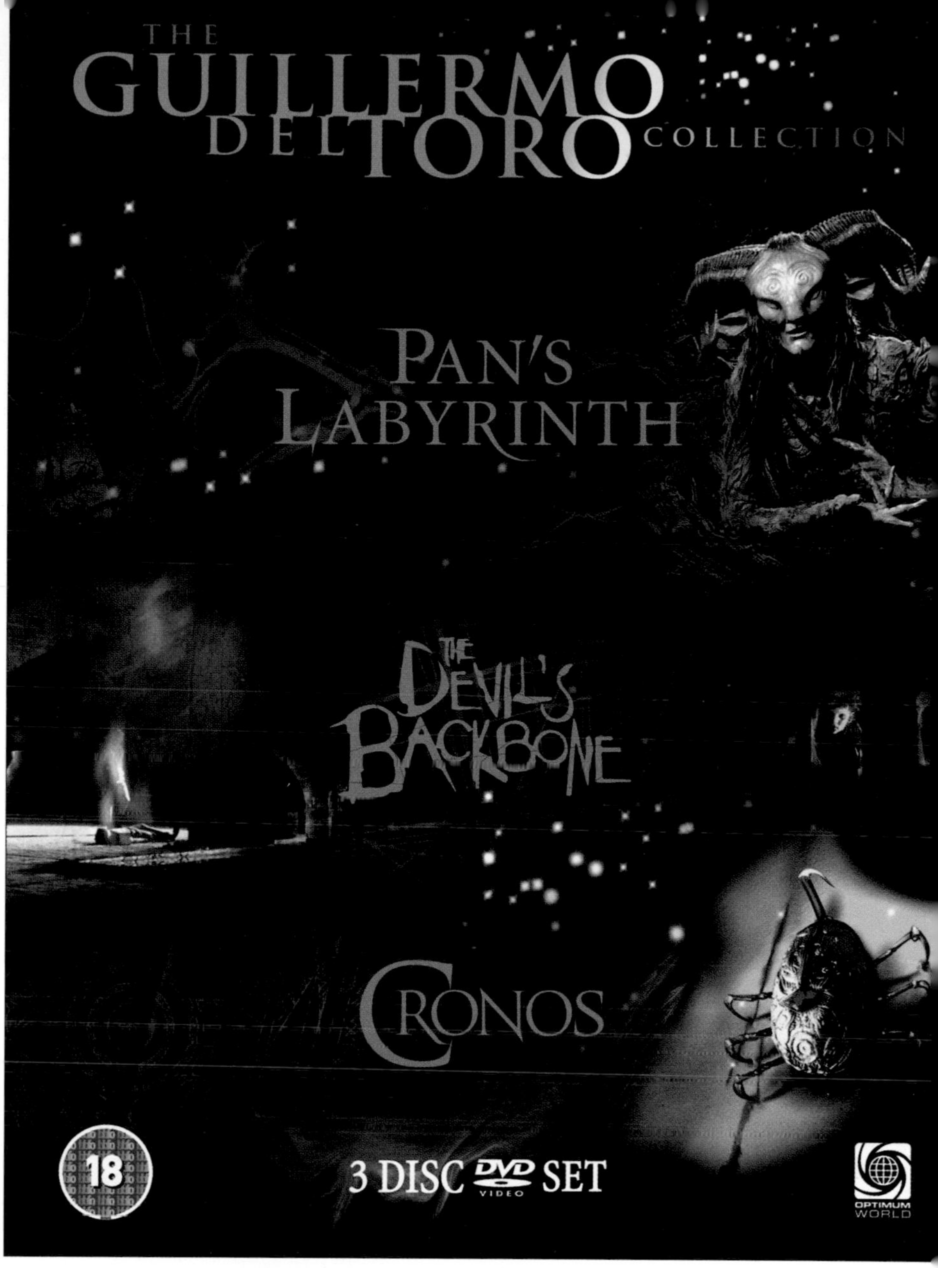

Sleeve art for Guillermo del Toro box set

"Dear Mer...cedes. I write to you with much effort. I want you to know that, in some way, for some reason, I'm still alive. And it's so painful to be alive. This thirst is consuming me. And I feel like I don't belong at all, to daylight, to this house and to you. Aurora will stay with you. She will give you this letter. By the time you read it, I'll have already left for a sort of rendezvous, something I need to finish. If I've lost everything, I want at least to

know why. I'm beginning to realise how much I miss you. I hope you're here when I return and want to see me, regardless of what I look like, I love you-Jesús."

And as he writes the last word, she forlornly closes the piano, a sad coda to their married life, only at the end do they realise how much they mean to each other, as is so often the way in life when it's too late. You never miss what you have until it's gone.

Once night falls, Gris goes to La Guardia's factory, only to discover when he gets there that Aurora has followed him. He realises that he has endangered the life of the person he loves most in this world. "My God, what are you doing here? I told you not to come." She's brought the Cronos Device. "Put that away! Don't you realise they can kill us? That we're in danger." She merely smiles. Gris lets her into Dieter's apartment through the food hatch, and she lets Gris in. Gris goes in search of answers while Aurora look fascinated at the jars containing Dieter's wasted and discarded organs.

Aurora finds the box containing the alchemist's notes but Dieter hears her. He's delighted to see Gris. "It works! I knew you'd be back. If you're looking for the missing pages... you're wasting your time. I ate them! Best meal I had in years." Gris's body is changing, he's like a chrysalis. "My skin is rotting away, its falling part." "Peel it off." Dieter pulls at Gris's skin, telling Gris to look in a mirror, he's moulting like an insect. "You've been reborn." Distracted, Gris doesn't see Dieter signal for Angel, he asks. "But why this? Why this new skin? And don't answer me in riddles! You talk about insects, alchemists, devices...but what do I really need?" "Blood." "Human blood?" "But of course, you can't gain eternity with a cow or a pig." "I can destroy the device, smash it to pieces!" "As you wish, if the device goes, you go. But, we can share eternity." "I don't give a damn. I don't want to be eternal. I just want a way out." "That's even better. There is a way out. But first the device." Gris shakes his head. "I don't trust you."

And the idea of sharing eternity with a monster like Dieter isn't appealing either. "I don't think you have a lot of options." Gris offers Dieter the Cronos Device in return for a way out. Dieter agrees and stabs Gris with a knife. "You don't even bleed right!" He goes to

stab Gris in the heart but Angel clubs Dieter with his own cane, giving Gris a chance to recover. He goes to leave but cannot resist the fallen Dieter's blood, and drinks hungrily. Aurora looks on non-judgementally, she has no point of reference for this whatsoever. Hearing the lift carrying Angel to Dieter's apartment, Gris and Aurora hide.

When Angel arrives, he is delighted to see the fallen Dieter. "Merry Christmas! Mine, mine, everything is mine!" Dieter isn't dead though, he raises his arm, Angel snaps his neck. "Enough! You kept me waiting long enough." In turn, he is clubbed in the face by Gris, who breaks a window so he and Aurora can escape. Angel is close behind. "Not my nose again! Ah, Mr Gris, now I have to kill you again." He finds Gris on the roof of the factory, where he's placed Aurora on the huge neon sign that adorns the building. All Gris cares about is saving Aurora, he tells Angel. "You stand to lose more than I do. For me, it's only pain." Pain is something Angel will be delighted to provide. "Get ready for some more." Gris grabs Angel, and together hurls the two of them off the building to crash through a skylight into the factory below. Aurora comes for him. He activates the Cronos Device and places it on his chest where it stings him.

Impaled with glass, Gris gets to his feet. He places his hand into his chest, and peels off the skin. He approaches Aurora, it's clear he's considering taking her blood, such is the Faustian pact he's inadvertently made with the Cronos Device. Aurora speaks for the first time, the only word she speaks, and thus it carries the weight of mountains. "Grandfather." Horrified, hearing her speak his name, he realises what he has become, and what she means to him. "No!" He tears off the Cronos Device and smashes it. "I am Jesús Gris." In condemning himself, he has redeemed himself.

Back home, his old skin shed, Gris dies for the second and final time. This time, at least he's not alone, his beloved Aurora and Mercedes are with him. Mercedes kisses his hand. In a story where many of the characters are struggling with the effects of time, we see that you only achieve true freedom from time when you accept your own mortality, then the fear goes, it no longer has power over you. Jesús Gris has found his way out. His only way out, and at the end he was loved. That's all anyone can hope for, if they're lucky. That's the only eternity that matters.

SCARAB

"The idea for the front of the Cronos Device, the shape was the egg which is a symbol of eternity and immortality...the Scarab, another symbol of immortality..."
GUILLERMO DEL TORO

That the Cronos Device greatly resembles a clockwork scarab beetle is purely intentional on Guillermo's part (It combines his love of insects and clockwork mechanisms). The scarab was held sacred by the ancient Egyptians. In fact, all species of Dung Beetle belong to the family named after the scarab: Scarabaeodea. Scarabs are dung beetles. Like many other dung beetles, they breed in dung. One species of dung beetle navigates by using polarization patterns in moonlight. They sometimes roll this dung into small pellets, which they then move to their underground burrows as food for their larvae. Eggs are laid in the pellets. Egyptians regarded the pellets as symbols of the world, and believed that the antennae projecting on the heads of the beetles were emblems of the sun's rays.

For Egyptians, the scarab also symbolised the resurrection and immortality, especially Scarabaeus Sacer, more commonly known as The Sacred Scarab. They carved figures of the insects out of stone or metal, and used them as charms. The hieroglyphic image of the beetle literally translates as "to transform", which fits in well with the themes in Cronos. The scarab was linked to the God Khepri (which translates as "he who has come into being"), the god of the rising sun. The assumed self-creation of the beetle, parallels that of the god Khepri, who creates himself out of nothing (the ancient Egyptians observed the sun vanish as night fell, and emerge again as the dawn broke). They also considered the dung balls rolled by the beetle to represent the sun. They thought that Khepri renewed the sun everyday before rolling it above the horizon, then bringing it to the other world after sunset and renewing it all over again the following day. In fact, the scarab was often used in tombs as a symbol of the morning sun. Usually, Egyptians removed the heart of a dead person, and put a large carved scarab in its place when the body was embalmed (The most famous example of the heart-scarab is the yellow green pectoral scarab found with the possession of Tutankhamen. It had been carved from a piece of Libyan desert glass.)

The reason for placing the heart-scarab was so that the heart would not bear witness of the sins of the body to the 42 gods against the deceased during the judgement in the after life. It also ties in with concepts of transformation after death. . A small spell from the Book of the Dead was written on the underside of the scarab. Other scarabs were smaller, and bore a small hole to allow them to be worn on a necklace, with the base baring a cartouche, an inscription. Other scarabs served as seals. The scarabs were created from a variety of materials, ivory, bone, stone (particularly green stone), and precious metal and jewels, but their purpose remained the same, to convey the concepts of transformation, renewal, and resurrection. They are a fundamental part of Egyptian funerary and religious art. They remained a part of Egyptian culture from the Sixth Dynasty to the period of Roman domination. Great sculptures of scarabs can be seen at the Serpahim in Alexandria, Luxor Temple, and other locations in Egypt.

Cronos Analysis

Cronos, when Guillermo made it, was one of the highest budgeted films made in the history of Mexican cinema. It was budgeted at $1.5 million, but ended up costing $2 million. Not much by Hollywood standards, where higher sums are invested in advertising the latest toy-tie-in commercials, but a fortune for Mexico. It is also a good example of fearing your first movie is going to be your last and throwing in the proverbial kitchen sink. Guillermo describes the making of the film as "incredibly ambitious for the genre in Mexico.

The idea was to combine insect mythology, alchemy, and vampire mythology, all into one. The idea of combining Christian mythology, Catholic imagery, vampirism, with insects and so forth comes from observation... I always thought that alchemy, Catholicism, and vampirism, were somewhat linked. I think there are a lot vampiric elements to some rites in the Catholic Church, including of course drinking the blood of Christ, but there's also a very interesting alchemical link in the fact that both the church, vampirism and alchemy are ultimately about transforming into something more sublime, something eternal."

Of course the insect trapped inside the Cronos Device as a living filter is both the ultimate vampire and ultimate victim. An unusual trend Guillermo witnessed a child inspired it's creation. "In Mexico, one of the things that came to my attention when I was a kid, in the seventies, was many women started wearing some really strange jewellery...living jewellery it was called! They were large scarabs, large beetles. Some sadistic mind had fastened some jewellery to them. They were living brooches. So women were walking around with living insects on their chests." This made a huge impression on the young Guillermo.

"I've always been a fan of entomology. I collected insects as a kid and observed them carefully, and was always in awe of how beautiful and mechanical they look." He was a fan of *The Gold Bug* by Edgar Allan Poe,

which had 'such a beautiful title', obviously an influence on the title of the second *Hellboy* film. He wondered, "what if an insect existed in the real world that created a disease, that would create a thirst for blood, longevity, lower metabolism, and ultimately an inexplicable change of skin, and the renewal of cells...so the idea of *Cronos* was born, and in turn transformed into some kind of vampire." This meshed with another of Guillermo's passions. "Then my second big love in life is clockwork mechanisms and ancient machinery. I hate digital technology. I love it as a user but I just don't see the ingenuity in it...So the movie combined all that and I decided the only way to preserve this mythical insect was to encase him alive. So the insect was vampirising the victim...the mechanism was vampirising the insect. In turn the industrialists are vampirising Mexico. I wanted to create an ever-growing chain of vampirism in the movie. That's why you see all the signs on the streets and the newspapers being in several languages because the movie was made in a pre-NAFTA Mexico. NAFTA was seen by me as essentially a form of vampirism."

In the scene where the cockroaches crawl from the statue of the archangel's eye socket, Guillermo was the insect wrangler.

The Cronos Device was designed by Guillermo's friend, Jose Forest, and built by his special effect company, Necropia Incorporated (Necropia created the special effects for several movies and 24 episodes of a TV series. Often doing favours for friends, the company existed for love not money). It was to be Guillermo's last special effects job and Necropia was wound down like the Cronos Device itself. The Cronos Device is covered in alchemical symbols, to indicate eternity, such as the worm Ouroboros biting its own tail creating an ever-lasting cycle. The shape of the egg as a symbol also represents birth, as does the Cronos Device when it's legs extend, resembling a scarab. Guillermo explains. "It's full of little symbols like fire, water and shapes that remind you of all the elements that are used in the alchemical process. The alchemical process enunciates four essences, air, water, fire, earth, which if you notice in the movie, are all present at different stages of the character's vampirism. The device also incorporates below a phrase in Latin-'Suo Temporae', which means everything in its own time. I think that's why the idea of vampirism is not a desirable trait for me. When it's time to die, it's time to die. You should live life to the fullest. So you encounter a character, Jesús Gris, 'Grey Jesus', who is basically not living his life, and he becomes more 'alive', and becomes aware of what his good fortune was."

Guillermo had thirteen versions of the Cronos Device constructed. "Each one of them was highly specialised. One of them opened its legs, one of them closed them, one of them ejected the seventh talon that goes into the skin, all of them were mechanised, they were constructed by a jewellery expert that was working for Necropia. Then again, they were mechanised by my father-in-law, who was quite a genius at mechanics, and we used to work every day at his workshop, creating little mechanisms that were operated by guitar strings and little pulleys on levers, miniature Lilliputian levers and gears...back then you couldn't retouch anything digitally, so you had to do everything on camera, in front of the lens and it had to work for practical."

That Angel is obsessed with his nose, and wants to change it, is no accident. "The nose is in many cultures, the portal to the soul...the hole in the face. There are seven holes in the human body and the nose is supposedly representing the one, in certain cultures, where the soul enters and leaves the body, and I wanted this guy to have a deformed nose, not only as a little thing that obsesses a big guy, and makes him somewhat fragile, but also symbolically, because the guy has had his soul crushed by his uncle, through the years, again and again and again."

Cronos is the antithesis of the bland CGI dependent horror so prevalent today. "Right now, genre and horror movies are supposed to be so full of effects, that this movie tries to showcase the imagination, of the myth and idea of the device, than to make it an effects heavy film, nevertheless, for Mexico it was considered very effects heavy."

The alchemical symbolism goes beyond the markings on the Cronos Device.

"I wanted the characters to have different hair colours...because the three colour hairs of the wife, the girl and the husband, black, white and red, were again colour codes that correspond to alchemy" Red for instance in alchemy, symbolises making future potential a present reality.

In most vampire films, the vampires are young and attractive, yet in *Cronos* the 'gift' of immortality is given to an old man, "a character who doesn't care about living or dying that much, and nevertheless, he is given the gift of eternal life...The idea is take genre movies and twist them, this doesn't necessarily make them more popular but I'm very happy about experimenting within the genre, with different sorts of mixtures." This is refreshing, as it raises more questions than a typical Hollywood vampire film. Our society is obsessed with youth and beauty, and the elderly are an inconvenience, to be hidden and put aside, not matter what wisdom they have gained. We live in a society where women are considered old at 30! The world has gone crazy, in it's obsession with youth and cosmetic artificial beauty. It has forgotten that youth is not always 'beautiful', far more often it is ugly and cruel. We associate vampirism with youth, yet whether it's visible or not, vampirism is always about age, and here we have an OAP vampire to prove it. It's not glamorous, it's not Christopher Lee biting Barbara Shelley, its someone feeding from the bathroom floor.

The alchemist's diary is an inspired idea that gives great authenticity and weight to the Cronos Device, it is also semi-autobiographical on Guillermo's part as he constantly carries around a diary to write his own fantastical ideas in, and indeed many that feature in his films have evolved from there. A case of life imitating art! "I had the idea for the diary for the alchemist because I've always been fascinated by antique documents. It would be great to have the machine but give the manual of the machine to someone else. Thus would in turn create a big problem for the main character but also create a puzzle for the audience that is good. If someone keeps the instructions and just gives you enough hints that the machine will give you eternal life. That the bug is inside. It will create the sensation of a complete mythology...Its better to hint at explanations than to fully try to rationalise a mythology like this because then you kill it. If you explain everything , and this will unfortunately happen if you put a movie through a focus group, and through testing in the American system. If you explain everything there will be no mystery. Mystery and fetish and so many things that give us our kinks in daily life, have to be enshrouded in mystery, have to be about concealing or repressing some of the logical things and surrounding them with mystery."

The genesis of Dieter de la Guardia's character is fascinating, like so much of *Cronos*, it is drawn from real life. "The idea of this sort of Howard Hughes character that in interpreted by Claudio Brook , also came from him to me from a real life incident. A friend of mine inherited a house from an uncle and when he went there to open it, the uncle had been living there for thirty years alone and he had put all his fingernails and nail clippings and, unfortunately, bowel functions, in little jars and he had kept them for thirty years and organised them with the date on them, and when they opened the house...literally thousands and thousands of jars. He told this anecdote and I thought, yes, that's the essence of capitalism, this character is such a rich man, he wants to preserve everything, he wants life, he wants money. He doesn't know what to do with either of them, but he wants them and he wants them all, and therefore the character would be into a kind of S&M thing by putting himself through many operations, removing parts of his body which is a thing that obsesses me too (think of Kroenen in *Hellboy*, very different character to the one in the comics), but this character will want to keep them, that and Howard Hughes are the genesis of this old man's character."

While the clichéd vampire film present eternal life as something wonderful (Why? To outlive all those you love, to become an anachronism-a person out of time, would surely be a fate worse than death, a living hell, particularly in our youth-obsessed society). Age is not a bad thing, but our society fears it, like it fears illness, grief, depression, loneliness,

fear, bereavement, any of the myriad things that life brings, it's our fear of them that makes our life difficult. Society ignorantly shuns the old instead of making them a part of society, yet we will all grow old, and die. We learn and grow from these experience, living for ever, watching our loved ones die before us, living in a world that we don't belong to, does not bare thinking about, it is the ultimate horror. To belong is all in society, to be outside is to exist rather than live. The message *Cronos* has is, be careful what you wish. "You embrace the fact that you are going to die sometime. Your warranty is going to run out, and you're going to slowly unwind and stop. That's what makes the ticking so much fun, if we didn't have death ahead of us, it would be a very drab perspective."

Alchemy is a very important part of *Cronos*, and it is important to understand, that while on the surface, alchemical texts may speak of the transmutation of base metals to gold, this is often a coded way of describing personal transformation (presented thus to protect the alchemist). "When alchemy is taken more seriously, we realise that the quest is not so much for gold as it is for eternity." Gris goes through the alchemical process of transformation: "...going through, water, fire and air. He is 'burned'[by the sunlight], which is one of the processes of alchemy. He is reborn and he has to peel off his skin revealing new layers. Gives his own life to save those he loves."

Running concurrent with this theme are the religious analogies in *Cronos*, ironic when you consider the church's attitude to alchemy, but *Cronos* is a film with many hidden depths. Not for nothing is the central character, an old man, called Jesús Gris-the 'Grey Jesus." (And his granddaughter, Aurora, 'The Dawn'). The alpha and omega, one at the end of their life, the other at the beginning, and then suddenly the natural order is reversed, and chaos ensues. There are many comparisons between Gris and the biblical Christ. "He dies and resurrects on the third day. He has stigmata, both from the device, on his hand and on his chest, on his feet from pieces of glass. He wears a red cape like Christ had in his passion. The way he ultimately behaves is like a saviour, he's like a messiah for the girl. There is some very heavy Catholic feel of redemption through pain through out the movie, and throughout, frankly, most of the things I do."

The eternal vigilance of the self-damned – Cronos

While we in West believe we must avoid pain, tragedy, death, disappointment, all the negative things of life, as part of our unhealthy media fear driven pseudo-world, in the Spanish speaking world the attitude is much healthier than our unbalanced lives (which leaves us ill-prepared for the negative parts of life). This is another distinct aspect of both *Cronos* and Guillermo's work as a whole.

"We spend too much time avoiding pain. I think that the value of the horror genre is that it puts us back in touch with pain and puts us back in touch with the nasty side of life...the dark side of life. Most people spend their lives after thirty trying to look younger, trying to achieve perpetual teenage years, but frankly I'm thankful for aging, and I'm thankful for pain. I have learned much more from pain than I have ever learned from success...This movie was such a nightmare to make from an economic standpoint and a personal standpoint because when you're producing one of your own movies, it's difficult to deal with the day-to-day problems. Those problems taught me more than awards, good reviews, and so forth."

Cronos is also a piece of cinema inspired by cinema. "It's a movie that's been done by a guy that loves movies so much! I still do to this day. I am first a film fan and then a film maker. I still get teary-eyed with a good movie...and the movie is full of homages to that. There's homages to Christopher Lee in the Hammer movies and Terrance Fisher."

What makes *Cronos* all the more of a triumph, are the sheer difficulties a young filmmaker (particularly a genre filmmaker) has to surmount. The project in the beginning was called The Cronos Device. It was not seen 'with good eyes'. Guillermo was told repeatedly a vampire movie could not be an art movie, an art movie could not contain vampirism. "The movie was done against the grain because in Mexico, most of the films were financed by the Mexican Government...

The film industry in Mexico is sadly very corrupt in its own way. There are little mafias, and the older generation filmmakers, all on fifth, tenth, eleventh, or more films, keep shooting movies, and it is very hard for young generations to take a bow and jump into the scene. So all my generation had years of internship, working for free or almost free on each other's movies. You have film makers that only made one or no film. The Mexican government was not very supportive of our generation..." *Cronos* was hard to make even by these draconian standards.

"Frankly, no one wanted to help us. Normally, a film is put through the process at the Mexican Film Institute in a year of two. But then there are the cursed projects which take four, five, ten years. Mine was in the midrange, they didn't like it, but year after year I kept coming back. I put all my efforts, all my money into creating the Cronos Device to show them, to show it could be made. I had the storyboards. I had designs, documents on the look of the movie...They gave me the runaround for four years and finally, I guess, they couldn't stomach me anymore, they allowed me to do the movie. Once it was made and it was shown to them, one of the heads of the Mexican Institute Of Film told us in no uncertain terms the movie would fade into obscurity very fast and make no money, and win no awards in Mexico, right after that I really believed them, you tend to believe the worst always. The movie was nominated for 11 Mexican Academy Awards. People just liked it, and recognised it as a really nice effort in creating a different type of genre film... usually horror film in Mexico means cheap rubber suits and masked wrestlers fighting creatures. I love those movies and I revere them, but I wanted to do something slightly different. The movie came out and won 9 of the 11 Academy Awards and then went to participate at the Cannes Film Festival which was a huge honour and then to win the critic's week first prize. Back then being a filmmaker in Mexico was not very prestigious, it was the equivalent of saying you were unemployed. The doors are now open, but still under extreme duress from the lack of support by the Mexican government." As an example of what Guillermo is saying here, the promotional budget for promoting *Cronos* at Cannes was 10 posters and a roll of scotch tape.

For the crucial character of Tito in the morgue, Guillermo actually went to work in a morgue to get the details right. "This and a dark sense of humour is what makes the movie ultimately Mexican...Can you imagine any other vampire movie in any other country where you have a scene like this...the sense of irreverence about dying this movie has."

Another Mexican touch Guillermo brings to *Cronos* is the reversal of the way Mexicans are usually portrayed in Hollywood movies, with Ron Perlman playing the American thug Angel, though he's got far more depth than the usual bruiser, his life is sad, living in a cramped apartment, at his uncle's beck and call. Perlman and Guillermo forged a strong friendship on *Cronos*. When, at one point the money ran out, Perlman agreed to keep working. His kind deed was rewarded many times over. Jean-Perre Jeunet and Marc Caro cast Perlman in *The City Of Lost Children* after seeing him in Cronos in their capacity as jurors at a film festival, and of course he would go on star in other films Guillermo would make including *Blade II* and the *Hellboy* movies

The house Gris is laid out in (complete with crucifix, of course, there has to be one somewhere in Guillermo's films) came with real-life production horrors. "Until I explored the sewers in Prague for *Blade II*, I had never smelt anything as foul as this house...a family of about 11 squatters had been living in it, with 30 or 40 stray dogs."

Aurora, who swaps roles with her grandfather (the scene where he hides in her toy box with her teddy bear and dolly, shows he has clearly descended to the level of a much-loved pet), is immune to the concept of death (A great performance from both actors, they act as though they really are related). When you are a child you accept crazy situations as normal in a way you would never accept as an adult. "The child that has no prejudice, that has no preconceived notions of what normalcy should be, is actually the healthiest character in the movie."

The scene where Gris reads his own obituary is inspired by a real-life experience of Guillermo's where a man with the same name died, people actually phoned his parents to express sympathy. Guillermo was to cut out the obituary and put it in his family album, thinking one day to use the event in a movie .While all his films have an element of autobiography in them, none more so than the Spanish language ones.

Guillermo had written *The Devil's Backbone* with the purpose of using the script as his thesis for his three year screen-writing class with Humberto Hermosillo, but Hermosillo was very strict on presentation and did not like the way the script was formatted. Back in those days there were no computers, it was the start of the Corona word processor and only very rich writers had it. He had typed his screenplay on an IBM electric typewriter and taken it to Hermosillo for him to read. Hermosillo put it aside, telling Guillermo that he would not read it until he had learnt to present his work more clearly. Guillermo was somewhat deflated at this so rather than go back and re-write the same script because the layout wasn't correct, he would start afresh.

Looking back, he does not regret this because *The Devil's Backbone* evolved into a better movie. He told Hermosillo that he was going to write a story in which a young girl gives her granddad a vampire as a pet. The idea came from a treatise on vampires where they say in Europe that the vampire first comes to the house to vampirise the family and then goes out to the world. His first idea, which doesn't really remain in the finished movie, was to make it a critique of the Mexican family where the father figure returns, but he found this too overwhelming.

So he made it a story of acceptance between the granddaughter and grandfather. At that time his grandmother was slowly dying and they had come to accept and love each other despite their differences and the fear she had put in Guillermo as a child. *Cronos* is actually dedicated to her: 'Dedicada a la memoria de Josefina Camberos'. He used the movie to heal his grief and found it had a cathartic effect. "*Cronos* is sentimentally a very autobiographical movie for me, because I lived as a kid with my grandmother, who was a staunch Catholic woman and actually made me wear upside down bottle caps in my shoes, when I was six or seven or eight. She told me you should do that to mortify your flesh and offer your suffering to Christ, so you had this seven- year-old going through hell physically because he was so afraid of Purgatory. I was so afraid of burning in the eternal fires of Hell, or even transitional fires of Purgatory. All those fears are in this movie and are in my movies. At the same time, the way I felt about her was very unprejudiced, I felt that she loved me in an imperfect way, but she loved me nevertheless, and much like the girl in the movie, at the end of our lives together, when I was a young adult and she was dying, we made peace. We made peace with all this, and imperfect love is as much a form of love as perfect love, and that you cannot qualify it, you just have to take it the way it is."

So many times in life, we love people

who are flawed, (as we are ourselves, if we could but see our own behaviour. That's one of the sad ironies of life, we're the first to feel the effects other's actions have on us, but we seldom have enough empathy to feel the effects out behaviour has on others), and I feel it's because we identify with them, that their flaws might compliment our flaws, cancelling out their effects. Whatever the reason, we would all be better off accepting it, doing so would make us much more tolerant and bring a great deal of happiness back into our lives.

The difficulties that Guillermo had to surmount to make *Cronos* are an inspiration to all those of us who refuse to be ground down by others and follow our dreams and inner muse. "The gulf between your dreams and your potential has to be bridged solely by effort and not by pride."

As to his own attitude to life, Guillermo describes himself as "a sceptic...but a hopeful sceptic. I always look for the Fortean in life." A good attitude! It's always nice to be pleasantly surprised, and life is nothing if not surprising.

Fortean is a term that could certainly be used to describe the myriad of influences on *Cronos*, its origins very different to the sources usually mined for a typical vampire movie. The earliest draft of the script was entitled *The Vampire Of The Grey Dawn*. "It came from various sources, from the idea of a sort of autobiography, my relationship with my grandmother, which was very difficult but very full of love, in which we both forgave each other our imperfections. So from that came the idea of a movie about vampires, which starts like an American movie where the first three minutes are spectacular. Then it becomes a melodrama with for characters at breakfast. From there, if you add to it the idea of an addiction to an insect...if the juice of an insect injected into your flesh could become addictive."

"But it comes from an obsession with alchemy...with reinventing vampirism. A modest aim for a first film, isn't it? How can I create vampire characters without the usual origins?"

"In the first script for *Cronos*, he was transformed with a bite. The guy was a watchmaker. He was working late, he came out of the workshop and he met a tramp who said to him, 'help me, for the love of God'. He went over to him, the tramp pulled him into an alleyway and bit him, and it was the same process. That was the first script, which I must have written in 1984 at the latest. I finished a first version for scriptwriting school. I wrote two scripts for my thesis, *Vampire Of The Grey Dawn* and *The Devil's Backbone*. *The Devil's Backbone* at that stage took place during the Mexican Revolution, and then *Vampire Of The Grey Dawn*, the story was quite different. There were a lot more plot twists in the third act. The version that ended up in the film is much better. It was the second or third version. I did it over eight or nine year, re-writing the script almost every day. An American producer came along and he said, 'we need to translate the script into English'. When I saw the English translation, I didn't like it. So I said, 'I'll rewrite it and I'll translate it back into Spanish'. So the script has a structure, which you could say is more American, if you like. Its bit more first, second, third act, and so on. Of course, the American money never materialised. Now that I work in Hollywood, I know exactly why it didn't. In those days I knew nothing and I thought, 'they're gonna love a story about a vampire grandfather, with a granddaughter who loves him."

On *Cronos*, Guillermo began a habit that still serves him well today. "I draw, not brilliantly, but I draw well. Saying where to put the camera, the angle, the composition, the lens, that was fairly simple, just natural. I started then doing something I still do, which is carrying a notebook, and making visual notes in it for the film. So what I did was the morning before shooting, I would draw the storyboard very loosely. It's more alive than a storyboard that's beautifully finished. To this day, I only storyboard sequences with special effects. Then in the morning, I scribble my doodles and I go on set happy."

The Universal horror film of the thirties were a great influence on Guillermo when it came to creating *Cronos*. "I really liked Universal movies. In fact, I grew up watching Universal movies as a kid. Because traditionally,

Sunday movies on Mexican TV consisted mainly of movies made by Universal. So they influenced me a lot...the most powerful scene in horror cinema from the beginning...for me is *Frankenstein* with Maria, throwing the flowers...all the films I made are no more than an aspiration to one day achieve what I felt when I saw that scene...which is how terrible the monster is...The marvellous thing about Frankenstein's monster is the absence of conscience. I'm talking about Whale's version, not Mary Shelley's. There is an absence of conscience at that moment. It's a storm or an earthquake. It's a force of nature. It doesn't know the difference between life and death...and that's the idea in *Cronos*. The idea is more fully realised in the script, you realise that no one ever told the girl that her parents died. There are letters which the grandfather writes and so on. But the idea is that the only real immortality in the film is the girl's. All of the characters are marked by flesh or mortality. La Guardia wants to live forever but he lives locked away, which to me is the essence of the USA to some extent. The nephew is obsessed with the shape of his face. The woman says, 'oh no, I'm getting fat, I'm getting old'. She's obsessed with beauty. The guy who's not interested in anything has become a vampire. And the girl, who can't distinguish between life and death is the only one who's really immortal. So, that's in the scene from Whale's *Frankenstein*, and in essence, it's in *Cronos*."

Cronos is also influenced by expressionist cinema. "The straight lines, the lightning, very deep shadows. Watch the film, you see it's full of the diagonal lines of Expressionist cinema."

Finding the right actor for the central role of Jesús Gris was essential. "To me, the perfect movie has no dialogue. Movies shouldn't have dialogue, but they do. I saw this film in which an actor sustains the screen, the camera, for the whole of the film, with very little dialogue. I said, 'that actor has to do the film'. And the fates decreed that Federico Luppi should come to Mexico to make a film. I knocked on the door of his dressing room and gave him the script. Luckily, I had the money to pay him, otherwise..."

Cronos is also significant for being the beginning of Guillermo's relationship with Ron Perlman. "I wanted them [Dieter and Angel La Guardia] to be Nazis who'd gone into hiding in Mexico. So I was thinking of Max Von Sydow and Klaus Maria Brandauer, some really weird casting. And suddenly, this American investor said, 'can we get an American actor?', and I said, 'great, I'll make the baddies Americans'. I thought it would be perfect revenge for all the Mexican baddies like Satipo in *Raiders of the Lost Ark*...all those baddies who are a bit dumb and so on, so I re-wrote it. And I thought, 'who is the perfect actor for the brute? For a nice brute with a heart?', and I thought 'Ron Perlman', I loved him in *Name of the Rose* and in *Quest For Fire*...the film which comes closest to my idea of perfection in cinema. There's no dialogue in the sense of , 'coffee, please. Two sugars'...which annoys me a bit."

Cronos was also important for establishing Guillermo's relationship with cinematographer Guillermo Navarro, and his producer sister Bertha. "Guillermo Navarro introduced me to his sister Bertha, who is one of the greatest producers in the history of Mexican cinema. From the start, she said we had to aim for a certain level of quality in terms of cast and crew. Bertha became, to some extent, a second mother to me. We've made three films together, *The Devil's Backbone*, *Cronos*, and *Pan's Labyrinth*, as director and producer, and a few others as producers. We're very close. It's essentially for a director to find a producer who understands the size of the movie. In other words, the normal producer in Mexico, as in Spain I imagine, is someone who says, 'why five horses? Make it two'. Bertha has always been someone who understands that the size of the film is important and should be made as well as possible."

Federico Luppi's character was very deliberately called Gris (meaning Grey). "The idea of making an involuntary Jesus, a 'grey' Jesus... The idea was that the film takes place at Christmas time which is when Christ is born. So this specific Christ is born at Christmas time. He dies, he's resurrected on the third day, he wears a red cloak, he has the stigmata...So

this Jesus has to be heralded. So I though the statue of the archangel heralds him. But the person who really watches over him and helps him to fulfil his manifest destiny is this character who in theory is evil, Angel de La Guardia. Without this character, there would be no death or resurrection, there would be no moment of doubt. So it's certainly a very pagan and very strange reinterpretation, but the idea for me is that Jesús has to choose between his life and the child's, between staying alive as a vampire and breaking the device and dying. And the person who brings all this about is Angel, the film's is a state of grace. I've been fascinated since childhood with the idea of the state of grace in Catholic cosmology. It is represented by Aurora, who is the beginning, dawn, the start of the day..."

Guillermo's plan has also been to cross-pollinate, not just different genres of film, but other aspects of art and philosophy. "My idea has always been to combine elements in films instinctively. In other words, if a painter can say, 'I feel that a certain colour, shape, texture or symbol should go here.' There are two schools of painting which I'm influenced by. The Surrealists, who work by instinct, and the Symbolists who used a method. I tend more towards the Surrealists. The idea here was that in order to deconstruct the Catholic mythology, alchemy would be useful. There are elements of vampirism in the Catholic communion, alchemical elements in the idea of transfiguration, the transformation of flesh into spirit. There are elements in all of that which I found very interesting. There were great monks who were great alchemists. There was one I like in particular called Aurillac, who constructed a metal head, made of bronze which answered certain questions asked of it. That influenced *Cronos*, the idea of the mechanical apparatus. The symbols on the device I designed with a friend of mine José Forest. I designed the inside, he designed the front part. And the back of it was designed by me and by a jeweller. A guy called Ruben Rivera. The idea for the front of the Cronos Device, the shape was the egg, which is a symbol of eternity and immortality. The serpent [ourobourus] swallowing its own tail in the coil which starts the device, another symbol of immortality. The design was to have elements which go down and go back up. Basically, a Mobius strip drawn around the egg, giving you immortality...It's all there in code. And I will be so bold as to say, with great enthusiasm, that *Cronos* and all the films I've made, contain many things which perhaps only have symbolic meaning for me. But they're hidden away in there for anyone who wants to see them."

"There are repetitions. In alchemy, and in symbolism, repetition is important. It's important to return to the same element, to illuminate its meaning in the previous sentence or page, in fact coded language is always based on repetition, so if anyone wants to watch them again, all of them in one afternoon, they'll see new stuff. That's what's nice about watching them again."

A good example of Guillermo's dedication to getting *Cronos* made, are his literally putting his money where his mouth was when financial difficulties occurred. Apart from Ron Perlman agreeing to finish the film for nothing, which is why as Guillermo says, they are "friends for life", he also made many personal sacrifices. "So I took out a loan on my house. I sold my car, a whole lot of things. We also asked the bank for a huge loan. Interest in those days was running at something like 110% a year. The movie cost $1.5 million and another $0.5 million in interest. I never got my money back. I got my house back but it took four years to pay back what I owed. I finished off paying my debts on *Cronos* in 1997 with *Mimic*. I used my director's salary to finally pay off my debts from *Cronos*...I still make movies the same way. On *Hellboy*, I put half of my salary into making the film. On *Blade II*, I offered to pay for some special effects. On *Mimic*, I paid about $120,000 for effects, which the studio later paid back because the shots I'd wanted stayed in...The spirit will remain the same, which is, 'I have to make films...how much will it cost to make it the way I want it?'. Not, 'how much will it earn?'"

These financial difficulties only make Guillermo's achievements with *Cronos* seem all the more impressive. "It was strange because *Cronos* was made in the face of opposition.

The financial institutions didn't want it made. They said it was a vampire movie...that Mexican films receiving state funding had to be artistic. Lots of people didn't want it to be made...The Mexican critics gave it the worst reception of all time."

This began to change when *Cronos* won a Mexican film competition. "We had entered the only honest competition in Mexican history...That's the only time in my life that I've cried on receiving an award. The cheque arrived and I was crying my eyes out. It was partly the relief of receiving recognition."

Guillermo knows that his unique vision is not easily for Hollywood to sell and market. "I don't think that I'm a brand. I'm not someone who people can say like Steven Spielberg or James Cameron. I'm an acquired taste. I'm not a brand of food. I'm an acquired taste. Someone who says, 'I like oysters with peanut butter and tabasco'. That's who I am. I'm something weird, which some people like. And fortunately, it seems that this film was the start of all that."

The original cut of *Cronos* was 27 minutes longer. "I made a basic mistake, which did affect the film. I had a difference of opinion with an actor who was going in a direction I didn't like and I cut out a lot of his part. What I should have done was to work with what I had. I wasn't as flexible. A director is not someone who gets his own way but who allows the material to yield as much as it can. That character shrank a great deal between the script and the screen. I would have liked to have worked more with that person and got more out of him."

Wheras many directors see fantasy and horror as rigid genres with strict rules to be followed, Guillermo sees them in a completely different light, and puts it in his own unique way. "I always saw fantasy as a genre that was so diverse that it allows for a lot of different registers...If you bring me four tortillas, I won't eat one, I'll eat all four. The same thing happens with genres. I'm so anxious to do the things I want to do. So I thought, and I still believe that, the funniest thing in the world is to switch from tragedy to comedy, by cutting from one to the other. In *Hellboy*, there's a scene which is pretty heavy for the audience. Hellboy's father is killed, the guy's dead, a great tragedy. Cut to *Hellboy* with a glass of milk talking to a boy on the terrace about his jealousy over the girl...It's a desire to experiment, its desire to have fun with genres."

Guillermo's own special effects company played a significant part in the genesis of *Cronos*. "A very good friend of mine, Rigoberto Mora and I, started that great company Necropia S.A. Out idea was to make animated films with plasticine figures, stop-motion special effects make-up, and we did all that. We set it up mainly because I said we'll do everything...So that when I make *Cronos*, we can make the device. In those days, nobody was doing special effects make-up. Shortly after that, a few people started to appear. We took everything on, as a company, we grew and grew. Rigo, who's anagram as Rigo Mora is Igor, we were Dr Frankenstein and Igor, 'yes, master'...My wife, Lorenza, her father made the mechanisms for the machines. It was a family business. When we made *Cronos*, we had a staff of about 15, more or less...After a while, I closed the company to concentrate on what I was doing. Even today, I get involved on every film I make. I get deeply involved in how the characters are sculpted...Knowing the language of special effects, whether in terms of optics, make-up or mechanical effects, has helped me make the genre of films I like."

Finally, the following anecdote about *Cronos* is worth repeating. "There are lots of stories about *Cronos*. Some of them I can't tell you, in order to protect the innocent... We were filming the interior of the Cronos Device and part of the make up for the insect was made up of cow's livers, intestines, and that kind of stuff. We shot , as I said, against the clock, we filmed it, and closed it up. The last shot is when the camera enters the eye of the archangel, which was filmed in my make-up lab without the proper backdrop or anything. The camera goes down inside, you see the device, the titles, and the inside of the machine. We finished all that, closed it up. The last shot is when the camera enters the eye of the archangel, which was filmed in my make-up lab without the proper backdrop or anything. The camera goes down inside, you see the device, the titles and the inside of the machine. We finished off all that, closed my lab on the fourth floor of a block of accountants offices and so on. We sent to the US and two weeks later, they call me and say "The police want to enter and search your offices. I said, 'why?', 'because there are flies everywhere, it smells like a dead body'. Then I said, 'we forgot to get rid of the intestines.'

In conclusion, *Cronos* is an outstanding debut, as big in heart as it is in scope, in it we see the elements that continue to bloom through Guillermo's body of work. It's a unique fusion of Mexican cinema, the fine work of Terence Fisher, but most of all, it represents the experiences of its creator. Guillermo del Toro is the beating heart of *Cronos*. A film in which Guillermo was a cinematic alchemist. It's a film that continually rewards viewing, even all these years after seeing an imported VHS copy of *Cronos*, I'm still amazed by its textures and layers, and that surely is truly the aim of alchemy, to transform elements that already exist into something new and wonderful!

ALCHEMY

"The real quest of alchemy is the quest for the divine essence...for divine knowledge, for the achievement of eternity."
GUILLERMO DEL TORO

"The most common form of alchemy is changing metal in to gold. At some point in the process you are meant to transform vile matter into the most beautiful pure substance in the world...gold. Gold was considered the ultimate expression of matter...into eternity."
GUILLERMO DEL TORO

"There are repetitions. In alchemy, and in symbolism, repetition is important. It's important. It's important to return to the same element, to illuminate it's meaning in the previous sentence or page. In fact, coded language is always based on repetition, so if anyone wants to watch them again, all of them in one afternoon, they'll see new stuff. That's what's nice about watching them again."
GUILLERMO DEL TORO

Extraordinary as the alchemist in *Cronos* and his creation, the Cronos Device, seem to be, the true historical alchemical influences that Guillermo drew from in creating *Cronos*, are even more incredible. (It is also fair to say that filmmaking is like alchemy, mixing ideas with base substances and creating something new). Science itself resulted from alchemy. Occult in the sense of alchemy means hidden, it is a quest for truth, a quest to understand the world.

Alchemy is a blend of magic, science and religion. Its name derives from the Arabic al-ḳima. An important part of the occult tradition, it is both a practice and a philosophy. One that was as much about improving and transforming the alchemist as it was about improving and refining metal. A search for ultimate wisdom. The practical side of alchemy created some of the basic procedures and equipment of modern inorganic chemistry, and included the identification of many substances in use today. It was popular from the time of early Christianity until around 1700. Alchemists attempted to transform less costly metals into silver and gold (known as chrysopoeia). They also endeavoured to discover the elixir of life (a substance that would cure disease and lengthen life, also known as The Philosopher's Stone).

Much effort was devoted to this task, as this substance was thought to mystically amplify the user's knowledge of alchemy to a great degree. Their work in preparing and studying chemical substances helped the development of the science of chemistry, so in many ways alchemy is alive and well in the 21st century. Alchemists made great contributions to the production of gunpowder, metalworking, dyes, ink, paints, cosmetics, ceramics, leather tanning, and the manufacture of glass.

Some alchemists were merely charlatans, separating the gullible from their gold, and selling quack medicines in the manner of a 19th century snake oil

salesman.

However, others were learned people who had a far more philosophical goal. They believed that if they learned how to make gold from lesser metals, they could also perfect other things. They considered gold the perfect metal because of its beautiful appearance and resistance to rusting. In other words, the quest to turn lead into gold, was as much a quest to turn disease into health, to turn mortality into immortality, to understand the un-understandable. Put yourselves in their boots, and contemplate their courage, they lived in a time of dark ignorance and superstition, where church dogma (such as the age of the Earth, or the idea that the planets revolved around the Earth, making it the centre of the universe) was absolute.

Thus, the alchemists had to be secretive and work in codes and symbols. It is no exaggeration to say their quest for knowledge illuminated many of the facts and discoveries that we take for granted today, one could easily say they helped build the modern world as we comprehend it and take it for granted today. The transmutation of base metals into gold, and the search for the philosophers stone, were also symbolic of a desire to move away from an imperfect, corrupted and diseased state to a healthy, harmonised and perfect state, the Philosopher's Stone being the key that would open the lock of this enigma.

They could see the world was broken, there was hatred, violence, famine, poverty, disease and insecurity, they knew in their hearts, as all men do, that this was wrong, that there must be a better way, from ignorance to enlightenment, the philosopher's stone represented that hidden spiritual truth (the psychology behind the quest for the Holy Grail, comes from a similar symbolic subconscious desire to heal the world). As an example of how seriously alchemy was taken. The English Crown was afraid of the devaluation of gold should the Philosopher's Stone be discovered, and made penalties for unauthorised alchemy severe, including the public execution of an offending alchemist.

Some alchemy was practiced in China and India before the birth of Christ. In the case of China, this included the development of gunpowder, for many years a component of harmless fireworks, but man being man eventually applied it to slaughtering his fellows, (another example of alchemy changing the world that can be sadly be seen on the news any night of the week). But it developed into a major system in Egypt during the next 300 years. The Greek-speaking scholars of Alexandria used it in trying to explain how Egyptian artisans made things. The Greek philosophers theorised that there were the four classical elements, Earth, Air, Fire, and Water. These philosophers would burn a log, the log was the earth, the flames burning it were fire, the smoke thus released was air, and the smouldering soot was bubbling water. Greek-Egyptian alchemy spread through Syria and Persia to the Arabs. It spread to Western Europe during the 1100's and 1200's.

Thus we see that the knowledge the alchemists discovered through painstaking hard work, repetition and experiment (often dangerous experiments), would be like a living creature, a virus of knowledge if you will, infecting people slowly and driving away ignorance.

Alchemists believed that all matter was made up of a single formless substance. They thought this substance became the four elements-earth, air, fire, and water, when combined with hot or cold and wet or dry. They thought they could change one substance into another merely by changing the balance of these elements, a process called transmutation. This theory led them to try producing gold from other metals. In the early 1500s', Swiss alchemist Paracelsus tried to substitute three elements, sulphur, mercury and salt-for earth, air, fire and water. Alchemists also searched for the Philosopher's Stone (a magical substance that was supposed to make the transmutation process easier). Gold's lasting quality led many persons to

believe that they would find the secret of long life or even immortality if they could discover how to make gold from lesser substances. The Chinese once believed that eating from golden dishes prolonged life.

Alchemy was associated with many religious beliefs. It is both an art and a science, examining the relationship of humanity to the universe, a puzzle that could be solved by fermentation, transmutation and procreation, a cosmic lock that could be opened by the alchemist clever and diligent enough to discover the key. It was believed that the technique used to make gold were symbolically related to death, corruption, regeneration and resurrection. Alchemy and astrology became closely related because of the belief that each heavenly represented and controlled a certain metal. Some thought the sun represented gold; the moon, silver; Mars, iron; Venus, copper; Jupiter, tin; Saturn, lead; and Mercury, the metal mercury, also called quicksilver.

Alchemists believed that the positions of these bodies influenced the success or failure of their work. Chemistry, a science that probes the elements by experimentation and logic derives from this. Alchemy thrived on secrecy (so it's fair to say alchemy would not thrive in the 21st century where secrecy is becoming as outmoded a concept as privacy). The alchemists held ancient texts and ancient wisdom in high regard. They also adopted Latinate pseudonyms and circulated secret manuscripts, a practice also followed by Christian theologians

Sir Isaac Newton was an alchemist, sometimes described as "one of the greatest names in the history of human thought." Newton famously said, truth was "the offspring of silence and meditation" and that "all is flux, nothing stays still, Nothing endures but change." He would also reveal the secrets of light and colour and how the universe is held together through his theory of gravitation. He invented a branch of mathematics called calculus, and most significantly, he made all these discoveries within 18 months from 1665 to 1667, though it would be some years before he publicised his findings, and it would not be realised until centuries later, when Newton's papers were finally reassembled, that the extent of his alchemical knowledge was revealed.

It would be fair to say that on the strength of these papers, that Newton was one of Europe's foremost alchemists. After studying Newton's alchemical writings in the 1940s, John Maynard Keynes said: "Newton was not the first of the age of reason, he was the last of the magicians."

One day in 1684, Edmund Halley, an English astronomer, Robert Hooke, an English alchemist, and Christopher Wren, the architect were discussing what law of force produced the visible motion of the planets around the sun. They could not solve this problem. Halley went to Cambridge to ask Newton about it. He found Newton in possession of complete proof of the law of gravity. Halley persuaded Newton to publish his findings. Halley paid all the expenses, corrected the proofs, and laid aside his own work to publish Newton's discoveries.

Newton's discoveries on the laws of motion and theories of gravitation were published in 1687 in Philosophaie Mathematica (Mathematic Principles of Natural Philosophy). This work, usually called Principia or Principia Mathematica, is considered one of the single greatest contributions in the history of science. It includes Newton's laws of motion and theory of gravitation. It was the first book to contain a unified system of scientific principles explaining what happens on earth and in the heavens. But while he was a mathematician and a mechanist, he did not believe in a nature without spirit. He did not believe a purely mechanical theory could for the universe could be derived. In his garden, he built a laboratory, where the fire burned continually as he carried out his experiments. To the alchemist, nature was alive and active, as was fire. So the alchemist was continually experimenting with calcination and melting, distilling and subliming, and Newton was no exception.

In sublimation, vapours rise from the ashes of burned earth and condensed again upon cooling, while in calcination, fire converted solids to dust. Alchemists had a saying: "Be you not weary of calcination, calcination is the treasure of a thing."

When a crimson-tinged earth, cinnabar, was heated, a substance emerged called 'silvery water' or 'chaotic water': Quicksilver. Cinnabar was red mercuric sulphide, which painters knew as vermillion. Alchemists knew it was a sublimation of quicksilver (mercury) and brimstone (Sulphur). Alchemists linked the metal mercury with a 'philosophic mercury'. The fact that mercury was both a liquid and metal led alchemists to believe it had special powers. Some thought a wheel rimmed with mercury would turn by perpetual motion. In their secret writing, alchemists referred to quicksilvers as 'the serpents'. Newton once wrote 'the two serpents ferment well'. One of the reasons that mercury held such fascination to alchemists was its ability to react to other metals. It could form soft amalgams with lead, silver, copper and gold. It could also be used to purify metal. However, the alchemists suffered in the health department, mercury, over a prolonged period of exposure causes tremors, insomnia, neurological damage and paranoid delusions (something that also affected hat-makers, who also used mercury as part of their work, hence the phrase 'mad as a hatter'.)

Newton believed that it would one day be possible to create alchemical gold, but that such knowledge would have it's dangers, he thought that the basic substance of matter was the safe everywhere, which meant the transmutation of metal (as almost a side-effect of this more important knowledge) should be possible

Newton's discoveries in optics were equally spectacular. He published the results of his experiments and studies in Opticks (1704). Newton's discoveries explained why bodies appear to be coloured. This laid the foundation for the science of spectrum analysis. This science allows us to determine the chemical composition, temperature, and even the speed of such hot, glowing bodies as a distant star or an object heated in a laboratory.

Newton discovered that sunlight is a mixture of light of all colours. He passed a beam of sunlight through a glass prism and studied the colours that were produced. A green sweater illuminated by sunlight looks green, because it largely reflects the green light in the sun and absorbs most of the other colours. If the greet sweater were lighted by a red light or any colour light not containing green, it would not appear green.

Newton was born at Woolsthorpe, Lincolnshire, on December 25, 1642. He attended Grantham grammar school. As a boy, he was more interested in making mechanical devices than studying. He was considered a poor student. His youthful inventions included a small windmill that could grind wheat and corn, a water clock, run by the force of dropping water, and a sundial. He left school when he was 14 to help his widowed mother manage her farm. But he spent so much time reading, he was sent back to school. He entered Trinity College, Cambridge University, in 1661. He showed no exceptional ability during his college career, and was graduated in 1665 without any particular distinction. He retuned to Cambridge as a fellow of Trinity College in 1667.

Newton became professor of mathematics at Cambridge in 1669. He lectured once a week on geometry, astronomy, optics, arithmetic, or other mathematical subjects. He was elected a fellow of the Royal Society in 1672.

He became active in public life after the publication of Principia. He became the Cambridge University Member of Parliament in 1689 and held his seat until Parliament in dissolved the following year. He became warden of the mint in 1699, a position he held until his death.

In 1699, he also became a member of the Royal Society council and an associate of the French Academy. He was

elected to Parliament again from the university in 1701. He left Cambridge and settled permanently in London in 1701. He became president of the Royal Society in 1703 and was re-elected annually until his death. Queen Anne knighted Newton in 1705. He died in 1727 and was buried in Westminster Abbey.

Newton did not enjoy the scientific arguments that arose from his discoveries. Many new scientific theories are opposed violently when they are first announced, and Newton's did not escape criticism. He was so sensitive to such criticism that his friends had to plead with him to publish his most valuable discoveries.

He also spent a great deal of his time on questions of theology and Biblical chronology. For the alchemist, the transformation of metal was a spiritual purification. They believed it was God who breathed life into matter. Theology would join alchemy as the chief preoccupation of Newton's middle decades. "I do not know what I may appear to the world, but to myself I seem to have been only like a boy playing on the seashore and diverting myself in mow and then finding a smoother pebble or a prettier shell than ordinary, whilst the great ocean of truth lay undiscovered before me."

Paracelsus (1493-1541), A Swiss alchemist, was a pioneer in the application of chemistry to medicine and introduced the use of many drugs. He sharply attacked the foundations of modern medicine, but everywhere he went he met with opposition to his theories. However, some of his theories foreshadowed modern medical practices. Paracelsus was the first to point out the relation between goiter in the parent and a condition called cretinism in the child.

Paraselsus was born near Einsiedeln, Switzerland. His real name was Theophrastus Bombastus von Hohenheim. He received his early education from his father, a physician and chemist. He invented an alphabet called the Alphabet of the Magi, for engraving names upon talismans. His motto was 'alterius non sitqui suus esse potest'-let no man that can belong to himself be of another', a fine motto in this age as well as Paracelsus's. He certainly practiced what he preached, upsetting Kings and Queens, doctors and priests. All this in a time, where even more so than today, to go against engrained thinking could literally be fatal. Remember he was a free thinking, argumentative man. His unique philosophy of the universe was difficult for people to comprehend, in a time that was the dawning of the modern age. A world where magic was real and accepted. Witches flew at night, demons waited to tempt men's immortal souls from their bodies in return for material wealth, goblins lurked for victims in the forests, ghouls haunted graveyards, and portents of doom, pestilence and destruction filled the sky.

With this background of superstition to contend with, Paracelsus was bound to cause controversy. An old folk tale tells how he communed with the Devil to achieve the secret of eternal life. Certainly, he believed in the influence of the heavenly bodies upon the Earth. "The stars have their own nature and properties just as men have upon the earth. They change within themselves...Sometimes better...Sometimes worse...Sometimes sweeter...Sometimes sourer, and so on. When they are good in themselves, no evil comes from them, but infection proceeds from them when they are evil."

He believed the cosmos was fashioned from three spiritual substances, the tria prima of Mercury, Sulfur and Salt. Sulfur embodied the soul (the emotions and desires), Salt represented the body. Mercury epitomized the spirit (imagination, moral judgement, and the higher metal faculties). In Transylvania, they believed he had a horse presented to him by the Devil. Sometimes he is called Teofrastus, or Frastikus, or Faustus, which brings us to Faustus whose name Paracelsus has been linked to, who sold his soul for arcane knowledge.

Or else Paracelsus takes the nickname Alpenus-a man from the Alpine

slopes, which becomes corrupted to Arpenus or Aprina. From which it is a short step to Orpina and then Orpheus, a central character in the great tradition of natural magic, who gained victory over death. He summed up his character best in his own words. "I cannot boast of any rhetoric of subtleties. I speak the language of my birth and my country, for I am from Einsiedeln, of Swiss nationality, and let no one find fault with me for my rough speech. My writings must not be judged by my language, but by art and experience, which I offer to the whole world, and which I hope will be useful to the whole world."

Doctor John Dee (born 13 July 1527, died 1608/1609). His name derives from the Welsh 'du', meaning black. A close confidante of Queen Elizabeth, it was he who chose her coronation date (interestingly, Ian Fleming's stepson, Sir John Morgan, believed his stepfather got the idea of '007' prefix for James Bond from Dee, who designed the 007 code for his correspondence with the Queen. The two zeros indicated 'for your eyes only'.). Dee promoted the idea of maths as the basis of science, anticipated the invention of the telescope, charted the New World and created one of the most magnificent libraries in Europe Curiously, many of his effects would survive the Great Fire and ended up in the possession of Elias Ashmole).

He also seemed to possess the power of magic, as he interpreted ancient mystical texts, created potent compound using alchemy, performed miracles with machines and saw the future. His experiments led him to pledge everything in a Faustain pact in return for a chance to explore the spirit world. He was disappointed with our world (who can blame him?), and his desperate obsessive search to understand how the universe functioned would grow to steadily dominate his entire life. Dee's most treasured book was *Liber Mysteriorum*-his book of mysteries-Dee said they contained the secrets of the universe. Dee owes much of his occult reputation to the construction of a mechanical beetle, (shades of the Cronos Device), that amazed onlookers when it was displayed at Trinity College, Cambridge. Dee himself wrote: "A greate wonder arose among the beholders, than of my Aristophanes Scarabeus [the dung beetle] mounting up to the top of Trinity Hall in Cambridge." Unfortunately mud, has a way of sticking, especially when the mud has the stench of brimstone, Dee would partially inspire Christopher Marlowe.

"When Faustus had with pleasure ta'en the view
Of rarest things, and royal courts of Kings.
He stayed his course, and so returned home,
Where such as bear his absence, but with grief,
I mean his friends and nearest companions,
Did gratulate his safety with kind words,
And in their conference of what befell,
Touching his journey through the world and air,
They put forth questions of astrology,
Which Faustus answered with such learned skill,
As they admired and wondered at his wit.
Now is his face spread forth in every land;
Among the rest the Emperor is one,
Carolus the fifth, at whose palace now
Faustus is feasted 'mongst his noblemen.
What there he did in trial of his art,
I leave untold-your eyes shall see perform'd

Christopher Marlowe
'The Tragedie of Dr Faustus'

It was a great shame that this reputation would attach itself to John Dee, for he was an extraordinary man by the standards of his, and indeed any time. Dee was a serious scholar and one of the most learned men in Europe. He was one of England's most noted English mathematicians, and also an astronomer, astrologer, geographer, occultist and consultant to Queen Elizabeth I, devoting much of his life to alchemy, divination and Hermetic philosophy. In his lifetime, he possessed the largest library

in England, and indeed, he suggested the concept of founding a National Library. An expert in Navigation and trained many of those who would conduct England's voyages of discovery, and did much to encourage English voyages of exploration. In 1577, Dee published General and Rare Memorials pertaining to the Perfect Art of Navigation, which set out his vision of a maritime empire for England.

He introduced the term "British Empire" into print. He wanted top know what lay beneath what he could see, and became impatient and he attempted to communicate with Angels to learn the universal language of creation. In 1564, Dee wrote the Hermetic work *Monas Hieroglyphica/'The Hieroglphic Monad;)* an extensive Cabalistic interpretation of a glyph of his own design, meant to express the physical unity of all creation. He travelled to Hungary to present a copy personally to Maximilian II, Holy Roman Emperor. By this time Dee had seriously turned towards the supernatural to acquire knowledge.

Dee took Irishman Edward Kelly into his service as scryer. Dee said the angels dictated a language known as Enochian through Kelly to him. He believed, like Newton would also, that number was the basis of all things and the key to knowledge, that God's creation was an act of numbering (There is a nice reference to this in Gregory Widen's fine film *The Prophecy* (1995), when Christopher Walken's Gabriel sarcastically tells a group of grade school kids to 'Study your math... Key to the Universe"). From Hermeticism, he drew the belief that man had divine power, and he believed this divine power could be exercised through mathematics. His Cabalistic angel magic (which was heavily numerological) and his work on practical mathematics, were one and the same to him. His ultimate goal was to help bring forth a unified world religion through the healing of the breech in the Protestant and Catholic churches and the recapture of the pure theology of the ancients (the Bible is often said to be a primal source of ancient magic and lore). Eventually Dee and Kelly parted ways. Dee returned to England to find his library looted and eventually died in poverty.

Dee has however achieved a kind in literature and film. Prospero in *The Tempest* by William Shakespeare may be modelled on him. The Irish Gothic novelist Charles Maturin refers to Dee and Kelley in his novel *Melmouth the Wanderer* (1820). Dee appears in *Elizabeth-The Golden Age* (2007).

The alchemists and their works are a fascinating subjects, and film makers like Guillermo have only just begun to scratch the surface, greater depths wait to be plumbed for inspiration for future films.

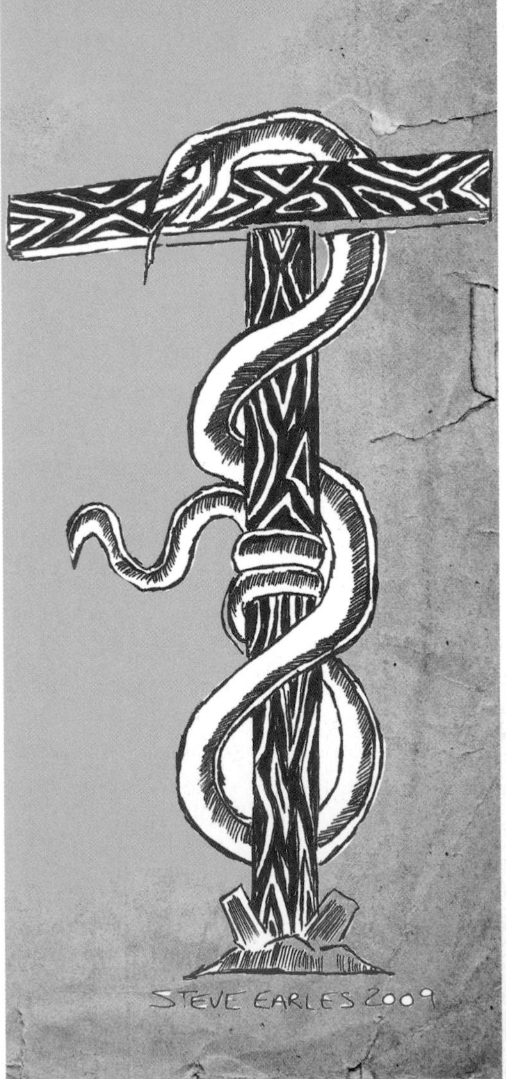

Chapter Two
Mimic

"By believing passionately in something that still does not exist, we create it. The nonexistent is whatever we have not sufficiently desired."
Franz Kafka

Mimic opens by establishing its Manhattan location, then by telling it's back-story over a collage of press-cuttings and images of insects. A news reporter tells us, "an eight-year old boy from Manhattan was delivered dead on arrival today." Headlines read. "Death toll reaches 1000." "Epidemic spreads in NY." "Desperate search for a cure." A voice montage tells us the Centre for Disease control has been called in. We see a frozen, empty playground, ribbons and wreaths tied to its railings (similar to the ribbons tied to the bomb in *The Devil's Backbone*). The voice-over continues. "Strickler's Disease was first diagnosed two years ago. We're no better off now."

Inside a hospital isolation ward, sick and dying children are quarantined, a doctor named Peter Mann (Jeremy Northam), who is deputy director of the Centre for Disease Control, explains the situation to Dr Susan Tyler (Mira Sorvino), Professor of Entomology at the New York State University. "I needed you to see this for yourself, Dr Tyler. It's the same at every hospital in the city. For the lucky ones, it's a lifetime in leg braces...Most of these children won't make it. We need your help."

In a sewer beneath Manhattan, scientists in bio-hazard suits are carrying boxes like miniature coffins. From these they release large black cockroaches, the Judas Breed. The suited Dr Tyler observes them attack the regular cockroaches, destroying them all.

Some time later, Susan is being introduced at a press conference by Peter. "Strickler's disease came to New York like a thief in the night, threatening to steal an entire generation of our children from before our eyes. The killer was cunning. It was deadly. Neither a cure nor a vaccine could be found. We at the CDC had to contain it before it could spread beyond Manhattan Island. So we went after the carrier, the common cockroach. Or rather she did. Dr Susan Tyler is the reason that there hasn't been a new case of Strickler's Disease in this city for six months." Susan takes the stand. "I don't need to tell you New Yorkers just how resilient the common cockroach is. Since it has proven to be virtually immune to chemical control, we had to find a new avenue of attack. So, with the aid of genetic labs across the country, we recombined termite and mantid DNA to create a biological counteragent. A new species to be our six-legged ally in wiping out the roach population. We call it the Judas Breed. Once in contact with the Judas's secretions, the common roaches were infected with an enzyme that caused their metabolism to go into overdrive. No matter what the roaches ate, every last member of the nest starved to death in a matter of hours." Peter happily tells the crowd. "This announcements been a long time coming. The Strickler's outbreak has officially been contained. The epidemic is over."

As he leaves the building, Peter is questioned by reporters. "Dr. Mann, what did this victory mean to you personally?" "I can move on to other projects, and personally, it's where I met my wife."

Peter and Susan fell in love and married during the course of their work together. Watching themselves on television later, she expresses doubts about the introduction of the Judas Breed. "Our fifteen minutes are gone." Peter asks. "What is this? Is this some kind of Catholic guilt thing?" "We don't even know what the impact is of what we did." "The impact is that a lot of kids will be running around next year because of you. Maybe if we get lucky, a couple of them will be ours someday." "Oh, a couple, huh? Oh, okay. We're not rushing things." I didn't want to overtax you. It's been a hard year." "It's been a great year."

THREE YEARS LATER

An elderly Chinese preacher (Pak-Kwong Ho) stumbles onto the roof of an apartment building, clearly terrified, his crucifix glittering in the neon glow. He just manages to lock the door behind him, which begins to buckle, something is trying to break through. Terrified, he runs, the door bucking from ferocious

blows, he knows it won't take much more. The only escape offered from the rooftop is a painter's platform suspended over a neon cross that bears the electric legend: 'Jesus Saves'. As the door breaks, the preacher jumps onto the platform. The impact of his landing snaps the ropes on one side, leaving him hanging, suspended precariously over the street below. He's observed by what looks like the sinister silhouette of a man in a trenchcoat. Terrifyingly, the preacher slides off the crane to crash onto the paint cans that have already fallen onto the rain-swept street below. From the apartment building facing the 'Jesus Saves' sign, a young boy named Chuy (Alexander Goodwin) has emotionlessly observed all that has occurred. Looking at the preacher's shoes, he comments. "Seven and a half. Black. Leather soles."

The shadowy creature that pursued the preacher to his death approaches the corpse, making an insectile clicking as it does so, which the boy imitates perfectly with two spoons. Arms outstretched in a pose mirroring the neon crucifix flashing above, the preacher is dragged into a nearby sewer culvert. The beating of the spoons, the clicking of the creature, and the soundtrack all combine masterfully to create terror, as the rain washing the spilt white paint after the body. Impassively, Chuy starts unravelling a ball of wire wool, murmuring to himself. "Funny, funny shoes."

The following day the crane is raised over the neon crucifix, the area is has been cordoned off the CDC. Peter turns up, to be greeted by one of his staff, Josh (Josh Brolin). "Hey. Boss, welcome to disease land." "Are you sure this is yellow fever?" "Are you ignoring your pages now? These two cops saw the broken scaffold and then the paint here, and then they looked through that cellar." A clearly infected person pushes against the cellar window. Josh continues. "Pleasant, isn't it. Couldn't let 'em out until you gave me the okay."

Inside the cellar is a chapel. Josh explains. "There were three dozen people trapped in here. Bacterial samples reading off the scale, though nothing is airborne. We got a Reverend Harry Ping, preacher, if you can imagine that. He ran this place. There's no sign of him. Oh, have you had lunch? Try to keep it down when you see this, OK?" Josh leads Peter into a tunnel that connects with a subway, one that's covered with unknown excrement of which samples are taken. "This is what I love about my job. I get to travel, see the world and meet new exotic cultures." They are being watched from below as Peter orders. "Board up every exit. If this leads to the subways, I don't want anything to spread. Quarantine everything."

Back at New York State University, Susan finds her friend Remmy (Alix Koromzay) crying and taking a Polaroid of herself. "What's going on, Remmy?" She's commemorating a sad moment, he date tried to spike her drink. "This city is full of perverts. You don't know who anybody is anymore." She has no idea how right she is.

Two boys, Ricky and Davis, are waiting outside Susan's office. Davis (Jason Barnwell) asks Susan. "You the bug-lady,

Going Underground – Susan enters the belly of the beast in Mimic

right?" Ricky (James Costa), holding a cornflake box announces. "We're here to deal."

Inside her office, Susan goes through the insects the boys have brought her, a multitude of butterflies, some of them with broken wings. She tells the boys. "When you pick them up, you should pick them up by this front vein on the wing because it's the strongest part of the wing, that way you don't break it." Davis asks her. "How come you like bugs so much?"

By way of answer, Susan shows him a termite mound in a glass case (the idea of combing Termite DNA is not as far fetched as it sounds. Termites are related to cockroaches and share many traits in common). "Just imagine that you're one of them." "Eating furniture and stuff? That's gotta suck." "Don't judge them too quickly. These guys were building castles while dinosaurs were still wimpy little lizards." She zooms in with a camera and indicates on a screen. "Now, say you're him. He's what we call a soldier. Now, there is no way you would ever quit fighting, no matter how badly injured you were. I would be a battle to the death. But most insects don't kill unless their territory is invaded. You'd just stun your prey up here..."She indicates a tunnel with a laser spot. "...and then they'd drag it all the way down through here to there, into what is a kind of pantry." "They eat it alive?" "Yeah. They're not really squeamish about those kind of things." Susan shows them the largest chamber of the termite colony. "This is the nest. It's the heart of the colony, the big enchilada." "Why?" "If anything happened to the nest, the entire colony would die out." "I'd just bail and start my own." "Well, you couldn't do that. See that big guy here? Next to the queen?...He's the king. And out of all the nest, he's the only fertile male." "He got a good deal." "It's a simple structure designed for their survival, perfectly balanced and it's very beautiful."

Ricky isn't impressed by her entomology lesson. "Whatever peels your banana, lady. You wanna buy the butterflies, or what?" "You guys have done a really good job, so how about five bucks." Davis is equally unimpressed by her financial offer. "That's your best?" Ricky decides to show his trump card. "I'm gonna show her the weird bug." Davis says. "Costs a dollar just to look." Ricky pleads. "It's really big bug, got it on the subway. We kind of broke it a little." Susan gives in. "Okay, my best offer. Ten bucks for everything, plus specimen jars, tweezers and mounts." Davis still isn't impressed. "Are you crazy? This is the best. This is our meal ticket." Ricky is more pragmatic something is better than nothing at all. "Come on. Bug's almost dead anyway." Davis hands it to her. "It's yours."

Myra can't believe what she's just witnessed, telling Susan. "You gave them ten bucks." Susan doesn't consider the money wasted. "They're from alphabet city. There's much worse things they could be selling." A breeze blows the papers in Susan's office and they both go to shut the window. The insect in the box begins to vibrate in response to a shadowy figure outside.

Back at the scene the CDC have

cordoned off, Peter is explaining why he's put the two policemen who discovered the infected people in quarantine. "Listen to me, Captain. Those two, they go home, they kiss their wives, they kiss their kids and I'm the one with the full blown epidemic." An elderly man, Manny Gaviola (Giancarlo Gianni) passes by, with Chuy, the child who watched the preacher die. He tells the boy. "Don't stare. People look back if you stare. It's not polite."

Peter tells Josh. "I can't believe this. I spend an hour in the field. I get a weekend's worth of crap." "Oh, speaking of that, that turd that I took to the lab..." He holds up an evidence bag."...they found these in it." "What are they?" "Buttons...maybe they needed fibre."

As Myra gets her bike to leave the university, she's started by what appears to be a man in a trenchcoat. Inside her lab, Susan opens the box to find a big cockroach. "Oh my God, you're just a baby." A vicious baby that immediately bites her hand, only her glove protecting her from it's penetrating her skin. She pins the cockroach down and it immediately begins secreting an enzyme, and she recognises it as one of the Judas Breed. While the shadowy figure in the trenchcoat watches from outside, she inserts a cassette tape marked 'Judas Breed' into a player. As she works, she listens to the sound of her own voice. "The transfer of recombinant genetic material from termites and mantids into Judas Breed will allow rapid enzymatic change ensuring 100% sterility in all Judas females...utilisation of suicide gene, leading to a life expectancy of 120 to 180 days." The figure in the trenchcoat enters the room while she's working and takes the insect. (It's interesting to note the mantid is the greediest of all insects, and will eat anything it can including other mantids).

While, in their small apartment, the little boy, Chuy is playing with a toy by the window, while his grandfather Manny tries to teach him how to polish shoes. "Not too little and not too much. You rub it in. Around and around. Like this. Let the leather take it." The boy hears the creature before he sees it. "Funny shoes. Mr Funny Shoes." Manny comes to the window. "No one is there. Is empty. Chuy, listen to me. They have Jesus on the cross but that is not a holy place."

Back at her apartment, Susan's husband has reported the theft of her specimen to the police. "I'm sorry about you losing a specimen." He doesn't understand the significance of this particular specimen, she explains. "This is not just a specimen, Peter. I did a pH test and there are only two species that match what I found. Now, one of them is a leafcutter ant in the Amazon. The other one we released here three years ago." "You said the ones we released only had a lifespan of six months." "We engineered them to be sterile adults, the Judas was not supposed to last past one generation." "So what happened?" "The one I examined today was a baby. They were designed to die. They are breeding."

In the subway, the following day, Chuy is sitting with Manny at his shoeshine stand. While he polishes the shoes of a transport cop named Leonard (Charles S. Dutton), he tells Chuy. "I shine them good, Chuy, Black Lincoln." Chuy is in a world of his own. "Chuy, Black Lincoln. This one. Pay attention. Please."

Peter and Susan are there too, he's with Ricky and Davis, the kids who found the Judas cockroach. Peter tries to force the lock leading to where they found the insect but

it's being changed. Susan shows the boys a picture of an ootheca, an eggcase, but they haven't seen one. But it does spark in the idea in their minds that if they find one, there will be a reward in it.

Peter finally gets the lock to open and leads Susan in. They find themselves in a foul disused locker room. Susan discovers a crawl space under a locker and wonders. "How deep does this go?" "Let's see."

Inside the crawl space is one of the Judas Breed. Peter drops his torch into the crawlspace. There is a nail-biting moment while he tries to retrieve it. He can't reach it, and with her smaller hands, Susan volunteers to try. The creature watches her hand clutch for the torch, just as it's about to grab her, Leonard, the cop who was getting his shoes shined investigates.

Meanwhile the two boys have gone down the subway tracks in search of the eggcase.

Peter is trying to explain what they're doing there to Leonard. "Look, I already told you, this is CDC business." "And I'm telling you those lockers are MTA business." "All we want to se is..." "See what? That's the old maintenance bridge." "...this insect we're looking for." "Look, your lady wants a bug or its eggs or whatever she wants, that's fine by me. But it's like Swiss cheese down there. Tunnels in, tunnels out, old tracks. You go messing around, break your neck and it's my ass on the line."

Leaving them to it, hearing Chuy play the spoons, she goes over to talk to the boy, fascinated. Chuy is able to identify the size and make of ever shoe he sees. She compliments Manny. "he's really good at that." "Oh, yes, he imitates anything." "Doesn't he go to school?" "He doesn't need school. He's special." Chuy has been making a wire sculpture of the creature that killed the preacher. One with six limbs. Susan asks him. "What are you making there? Is that a superhero?" He answers. "Mr Funny Shoes." "He knows everything about shoes." Says his grandfather proudly.

Meanwhile Peter has gotten nowhere with Leonard, who tells him. "You come back with the proper permits, maybe we'll have a conversation." "Great, we'll do lunch." "Yeah, I'll look forward to it."

Susan asks Peter how he went. He replies laconically. "Napoleon is alive and well and working for the MTA." "We have to get down there." "He wants a permit? I'll give him a special one."

Meanwhile Davis and Ricky have found an eggcase. They tap it and the creature within makes a noise. "She's gotta give us at least 40 bucks." They hear a noise and see what they think is a man watching them. They quickly realise it's anything but a man. Davis gets caught on some wire, and the creature kills him and Ricky.

At the university, Susan is listening to a lecture by Dr. Gates (F. Murray Abraham). "A philosopher named Hobbes once wrote that 'Life, by its very nature, is nasty, brutish and short.' An ant would put it more succinctly: 'Can I eat it or will it eat me?' It's this kind of simplicity that governs the phylum Insecta."

Peter phones Susan to tell her he's go the necessary permits, and that they're going down first thing tomorrow. After his lecture, Susa goes to talk to Dr. Gates, who asks her. "So, you think your little Frankenstein has got the better of you?" "I was hoping you could tell me. I really need to find some

Leonard discovers the Mimics do not respect his authority

answers, Walter." "Dear Susan, is it answers you want from me, or is it absolution?" "You still think making the Judases was wrong?" "Three years ago, I would have called it unforgivable. But I have two grandchildren who are alive today probably because of you. It would be a tad hypocritical for me to pass judgement." "That's not an answer, Walter." "It's not an easy question. But as to the Judases, I think it's likely that some survived. Evolution has a way of keeping things alive." "But they all died in the lab." "yes, Susan. But you let them out...into the world...The world's a much bigger lab."

Chuy is looking out of his bedroom window. Behind him, on his wall, a simple but sincerely meant crucifix, unlike the neon monstrosity on the building opposite. Hearing the Judases, he goes out on the fire escape, and down to ground level, and into the area the CDC cordoned off. Inside, he sees the head of a statue of Christ on the floor. The symbolism is clear. God is not watching over this place. (The statues wrapped in plastic bring to mind Dieter de la Guardia's apartment in *Cronos*). The crucifix the head belonged to lies toppled on the ground. It's as eerie and gothic as any of the scenes in *Cronos* or *The Devil's Backbone*. Chuy clicks his spoons, imitating the sound of the Judases, as though he's communicating with them. Sure enough, two of the creatures appear, and we see no more of Chuy's fate.

Remmy calls Susan's apartment. Susan is taking a pregnancy test. Her greatest wish is to have a child, but alas the test is negative. Remmy wants Susan to meet her at the city's sewage filtration plant.

At the sewage filtration plant, they meet a friend of Remmy's, Jeremy (Norman Reedus, who would go on to play Scud in *Blade II*), who plays in her band, he's found a huge decomposing insect, telling them. "I remember Remy said to me, 'if it's got more than four legs, it's not a mammal'." The creature is sent to Dr. Gates to perform an autopsy.

Chuy's grandfather, Manny, is preparing the boy's breakfast. "My father saw me stay in bed, he go get the pitcher of cold water and whoosh. I tell you, that's some alarm clock." To his horror, he discovers Chuy is missing.

Peter and Josh use their permit to get permission to investigate the tunnel beneath the locker room. A reluctant Leonard has to come with them. "We've got burrows going down seven storeys there."

Manny has reported Chuy's disappearance to the police, but they won't help him until the boy has been missing for 48 hours. He sees one of Chuy's wire sculptures on the window sill facing the cordoned off building, and realises where Chuy has gone. "Mr Funny Shoes." He goes to the cordoned off building, and finds another of Chuy's sculptures there. He knows he's on the right track. (Interestingly, like both Professor Broom and Hellboy, he has a crucifix wrapped around his arm).

As they explore the disused subway tunnels, Peter asks Leonard. "People actually live down here?" "Yeah, man. The 'Mole People'. This section was pretty popular all the way to Fulton Street...then suddenly all gone. Rumours got started. Someone found a couple of stiffs. And they make up some crap about a killer. Overcoat Slim. Down here is the land of talk. The wildest version goes furthest." (The name mole people refers to reports of groups of people living beneath New York City, such tales have inspired books like *The Reliquary* by Douglas Preston and *Lincoln Child* [the sequel to *The Relic*], and films like *C.H.U.D.* An author named Jennifer Toth has written an interesting book on the subject called *The Mole People*).

In a scene reminiscent of Hammer's *Quatermass And The Pit* (1967), Dr. Gates performs an autopsy on the large insect. He reports. "This thing is not just some random mutation. It's highly evolved soldier caste. It couldn't have developed in a vacuum. It's part of a colony."

Meanwhile, Susan has followed Peter to the subway station, which is closing in five minutes. Susan makes the connection that the Judases can mimic humans. Finding herself alone in the station, she investigates a shadowy figure, one of the Judases that burst into flight and grabs her.

Leonard tells Peter and Josh that

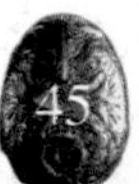

he's never been down this deep. "This is the old armoury station. They built it around the turn of the century. It's been closed for decades." Peter tells Josh he wants a full team in there by six. Leonard stamps on a insect, collapsing the ancient walkway he and Peter and standing on, sending the two crashing below. They send Josh for help.

Susan regains consciousness in the creature's lair. She retrieves a metal pipe from a decomposing human body to use as a weapon (It's reminiscent of the way she pinned her specimen in her laboratory). She passes the body of the priest, his crucifix glowing against the background of his blood-stained body. One of the creatures attacks her and she rams the pipe into it, sending it crashing into a sewer, giving her a chance to run away before it gets to its feet. She descends even deeper to escape. Manny witnesses her being pursued

Josh is trying to make his way back to the station, and finds a chamber full of unhatched eggs. He attempts to climb to the next level but one of the creatures kills him

Leonard comments to Peter. "This is really weird. We should have seen some 'track-bunnies' by now." "What are they?" "Track bunnies...Rats. They're usually around." "They big?" "You damn right." They come across Manny, who helps them Susan needs help. They pull Susan up just in time as a Judas break through a manhole cover. They make their way to an old railway car. The attacking Judas, despite being shot and cut in two, in a scene very reminiscent of John Carpenter's classic remake of *The Thing* (1982), which always shared the genius of creature designer Rob Bottin, part of it crawls away to fight another day, leaving it's severed half behind. The severed half manages to sting Leonard, who finishes it off with his pistol. Peter tries to hush the screaming Leonard. "If you keep on screaming like that, we're gonna meet the rest of its family."

Susan has discovered the dead Judas has lungs. Peter can't believe it. "Biology 101. You know, insects don't have lungs. That's what limits their size." "When I increased the Judases metabolism, I must have sped up its breeding cycle. We're talking tens, hundred of thousands of generations...who knows how many mutations." "How could the Judas evolve into this?" "Think generations, not years. It took only 40,000 generations for apes to turn into humans." Leonard can't believe it. "If that thing has been around, how come nobody has ever seen it." Susan has an answer, she starts to put the parts of Judas's human camouflage together as she speaks. "I think we have. Sometimes an insect will evolve to mimic it's predator. A fly can look like a spider. A caterpillar can look like a snake. The Judas evolved to mimic its predator. Us." Peter realises. "Nobody out there knows about this." "Nobody would until it's too late. These things can imitate us, they can infiltrate us and breed a legion before anyone would even notice." Manny is disgusted. "How could you do this? You take something and you make it like a man. A man who's not a man. He's a thing, that steals my child." Leonard agrees. "Manny, you tell her, cos she don't give a damn. Your kid's gone. My leg is chewed up! And they're both talking about insects with lungs."

He's interrupted by the Judases attacking the railcar. Susan realises they're being driven crazy by the smell of Leonard's blood. She takes some glands from the dead insect and hands them to Manny, telling him to rub it on the windows and anywhere there are cracks. "Scent glands. Insects use them to identify themselves. Rub it all over yourself. They won't attack you if they think that you're one of them."

It works, the insects withdraw. Leonard examines a map of the tunnels. "This is where we are. These tunnels may leads to the surface. If we can get this car moving, we might be able to make it." Peter is sceptical. "This thing's been down here rotting half a century. How do you know it'll move." "Listen to me. This car is a CR-17 from Cony Island. Believe me, it was made to last...Now, Manny, there's a track relay switch in this room here. Switch the tracks. That'll get us going." "Yes, I'll try." "There's a fusebox down the tracks. If I can rewire it, I can juice up the whole system."

But he can't do it with his wounded leg. Susan volunteers, but Peter won't let her. With her specialist knowledge she has to make it back to the surface. Manny and Peter volunteer in her place. Susan covers Peter and Manny with the remaining scent glands. "They mimic us. We mimic them."

Outside, Manny hears what he assumes to be Chuy playing his spoons.

Peter tries to rewire the fusebox only to find he's sharing space with a Mimic, its pseudo-human features open back like a door to reveal the true insect face beneath. The scent glands work and the creature leaves him alone. While, Manny finds Chuy

Susan asks Leonard. "Do these subway tracks lead to the regular train tunnels at Grand Central and Penn Station." "Yeah." "Well, they'll use them to migrate out of the city. After that, they'll set up colonies anywhere they can...Every specimen we've seen has been female. Because a male would be a lighter colour and would have no wings. If they're holding true to the Judases spawning pattern, the nest will have only one fertile male. Now if we could catch that male and kill him, then the females won't be able to breed and the whole generation could die out." "Where the hell is the male?"

The Judases kill Manny. Susan goes out to investigate, telling Leonarad. "Listen, if the car starts, I'll meet you at the end of path."

Peter gets the power back on (there's a beautiful shot of the station as its chandeliers come back on. It's a magical moment, they really knew how to building a train station in those days.

Susan finds Manny's crucifix in a pool of blood and then finds Chuy. She wraps the crucifix around her arm, exactly the same way Manny wore it. A tribute to the unfortunate man? A good luck talisman? (albeit one that ironically brought no luck to it's previous owner). Perhaps a bit of both. Leonard gets the railcar started, re-opening his wound in the process.

Peter goes for Susan and Chuy. He has found a hand-cranked restaurant service lift, a 'dumb waiter', that leads to the service.

Leonard, leaving a trail of blood, leads the Judases away and is killed.

Peter hoists Susan and Chuy to the surface. He finds himself in the Judas Breed's egg chamber, the new generation looking even more human. The creatures are using a series of pipes, some carrying gas for warmth to incubate the eggs. Seeing a chance to stop the creatures once and for all, Peter ruptures a pipe and ignites the gas, barely escaping with his life.

Susan encounters the sole surviving Mimic, the male. It goes for Chuy. To save him she cuts her hand with Manny's crucifix. Holding up a stigmata-like wound, the creature turns it's attention to her. She leads it into the path of an oncoming train, destroying it.

On the surface, its turmoil, flames burst from manholes, cars are overturned. A reporter announces. "Police and emergency crews continue to work in the aftermath of tonight's explosion on the lower East Side."

There is no sign of Peter. Dr Gates tells her the Judas Breed is finished. "We swept the area twice. It's burnt. Nothing could have survived down there." "What about one of us?" "I'm sorry, Susan, I really am."

Just as she's about to despair, peter emerges from the devastated station to embrace her, and Chuy embraces them both, hinting that their wish to have a family may finally come true.

Josh finds out the hard way that the Mimics won't leave him alone

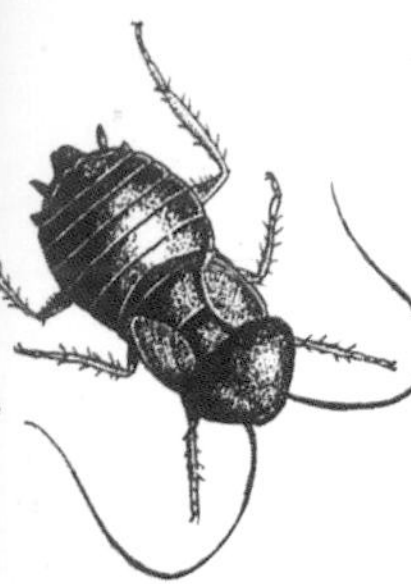

COCKROACHES

"By believing passionately in something that still does not exist, we create it. The nonexistent is whatever we have not sufficiently desired."
FRANZ KAFKA

"I love cockroaches! I'm not afraid of them!"
GUILLERMO DEL TORO

While in reality not as dangerous as the Judas Breed found in Mimic, the cockroach is an annoying, destructive and filthy insect with a worldwide distribution. It is closely related to the more popular grasshoppers and crickets. There are over 4,000 species of cockroaches, of which thirty species are closely associated with human habitations.

The cockroach can easily be identified by a flattened, slippery body, covered with a shiny, leathery casing, and long antennae. It has long legs covered with bristles. The strong legs permit the cockroach to run rapidly, thus escaping the wrath of irate householders distressed to find they are not alone! The cockroach is one of the fastest runners among insects, as Guillermo discovered shooting both *Cronos* and *Mimic*.

Cockroaches eat refuse, food, book-bindings (unforgivable-the vermin!), and other insects. They live in sewers, cellars, bakeries, groceries, rubbish tips, office buildings, restaurants, waste ground, hotels, derelict buildings, houses of parliament, flour mills, libraries, and homes. Fussy they're not, adaptable they most certainly are. At night, swarms of them slip out through cracks in the walls and floors to hunt for food, generously spreading germs on everything they touch, some of them extremely dangerous. Other species of cockroach, like Bear Grylls, prefer life outdoors (though like Grylls, they can put up with a hotel if they have to). These outdoor cockroaches can be found under leaves and stones or the bark of rotting trees.

The most common kinds of cockroaches found in houses in America are the Croton bug or German cockroach, the American cockroach, the brown-banded cockroach, and the Oriental or black beetle.

The Croton bug is smaller than the other kinds, but it is the most destructive and fast breeding. It derives its name from been first found in large quantities in the Croton waterworks system of New York City. The Croton bug is pale yellow-brown with two stripes on the front part of the body. The other kinds of cockroaches vary in colour from light to dark wood-brown.

Cockroaches can be discouraged from homes by keeping rooms clean and dry. Cockroaches grow and reproduce best where there is damp and dirt. They can be exterminated by using roach powders that contain sodium fluoride, borax, sodium fluoride, or pyrethrum. Roach powder needs to be dusted around water pipes sinks and other outlets. The cockroach ingests the poison when it grooms itself. It scrapes the foreign particles and dirt from its body with its legs and then draws its legs and feelers through its mouth.

Cockroaches can be trapped easily in large wide-mouthed jars. Food scraps should be placed in the jar and a paper funnel fitted to the top.

Cockroaches make up the cockroach family, Blattidae. For example The German cockroach is genus Blattella, species B. Germanica.

The nervous system of the cockroach is decentralised, with some functions distributed in the ventral ganglia. Even though it is decentralised, the insect's nervous system is similar to that of a vertebrate in its structure and mechanism of function. Thus, a decapitated cockroach can still walk. A cockroach can survive total decapitation for up to several weeks before eventually succumbing to eventuation dehydration or starvation. They are without doubt, among the toughest insects on the planet. Some species can remain active for up to three months without food, and a month without water. They can survive on limited resources, such as the glue on the

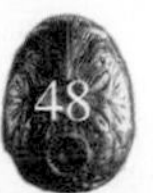

backs on labels. Some species can survive without air for up to forty minutes. Others can lower their heartbeat or survive being submerged in water.

A popular belief about cockroaches is that if a full-scale nuclear conflicts were to break out, they would inherit the earth (Who knows? They might evolve to make a better job of it that us) . There is some truth in this belief. The lethal dose of ration for a cockroach is six to fourteen times that of a human being. This is due to the difference in cell cycle. When a cell divides, it is at its most vulnerable to radiation. A cockroach's cells divide only once, when it moults, which is once a week for a juvenile cockroach. Not all cockroaches would moult at the same time, so some would be unscathed by radiation.

Who knows? Best be careful the next time you try to step on a cockroach, it may have a relative big enough to step on you!

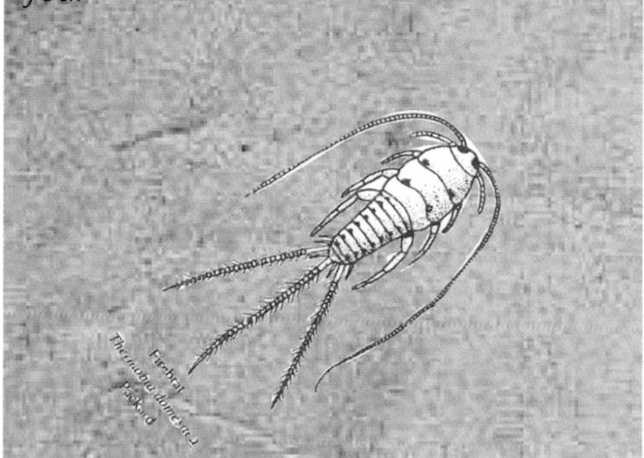

Mimic Analysis

"Mimic left a very large scar on my chest...on my existential chest, and I learned the hard way that the English language films had to be slightly less experimental."
GUILLERMO DEL TORO

"Little by Little I've been gaining freedom, I've been experimenting more and more, but it was difficult for a while after Mimic."
GUILLERMO DEL TORO

Mimic was personally the most unhappy experience of Guillermo's creative career. His darkest cinematic period. The proverbial long dark tequila of the soul. Interfered with by the studio, it's fair to say that *Mimic* was very nearly the violated monument to a career that was almost stalled before it began, like one of the foetuses floating in 'limbo water' in *The Devil's Backbone*. Factor in the huge amount of willpower, hard work and effort to get Cronos made (which, while it was creatively satisfying and a great achievement, it took years of Guillermo's life, and he put himself in debt for it as we've seen in the preceding chapters.) Let that sink in for a moment, there very nearly were no *Hellboy* movies, no *Pan's Labyrinth* , he would not have been able to present *The Orphanage*, and all the other projects he would become famous for post-*Mimic*. So in a negative way, we cannot underestimate the importance of *Mimic*. If not for his career-saving films, *The Devil's Backbone* (which renewed his creativity, and displayed the natural progression of the huge depth of *Cronos*), and *Blade II* (which revived his sheer love of the fun of making movies), it is extremely unlikely you would be reading these words.

Until one day, when perhaps Guillermo will get to do a director's cut of *Mimic*, we will never know the full extent that his original creative vision was hindered. But on careful investigation and research, certain revelations to come to light.

In the original concept, the Judas Breed were engineered to be irresistible to the common cockroach, who, on mating with the Judases, took away a hormone that caused their metabolism to go into overdrive, literally starving to death in a matter of hours, no matter how much they ate (a concept that would inspire the feeding cycle of the Reapers in *Blade II*).

The concept of the Judas Breed was originally to be built up more slowly, giving them more the feel of an urban myth (and reality can often hide unseen behind a myth). While jogging near Fifth Avenue, Peter sees a homeless person drawing a warning to his fellow homeless people on a manhole cover, a drawing of a sinister man in an overcoat (referred to by Leonard as Long John in the released version of *Mimic*, also known as *The Overcoat Man* or *The Stickman*).

Susan's desire to have a baby was originally a crucial part of the concept of *Mimic*, desperately and fruitless trying everything she can to get pregnant. At one stage she thinks she's succeeded, but later, upon taking a test is heart-broken to find it' negative (a scene which does survive in the version of *Mimic* the studio released).

Originally, what appears to be a chapel in the cellar of the building the CDC cordoned off was intended to be a sweatshop where clothes baring the label PROUDLY MADE IN THE USA were manufactured by immigrant Chinese slave labour. It was similar in sentiment to the point Guillermo makes in *Cronos* about richer countries exploiting poorer countries almost vampirically. Originally, two police officers investigating the fallen paint cans that both preceded and marked the passing of the preacher, investigated the mess and found a group of badly treated, infected workers in the cellar. There was to have been a religious element in the sweatshop with hypocritical religious slogans every where like 'No liquor, No drugs, No Profanity'.

Many of the immigrants were clearly infected, two out of five having internal haemorrhaging. Peter originally quarantined them with antibiotics. This was also to have been a new variant of Strickler's Disease. Peter and Josh discover the sweatshop was a place of real urban horror. Two shifts, people rotating from bed to work, one toilet. It was run by Triad, Chinese Mafia, using slave labour from Yuan. The preacher the Mimic chased to his death the Reverend Harry Wong, was their front.

Then Peter and Josh see an Asian cop, Yang, talking to a Chinese woman on a stretcher, who is 'hollow-eyed, near-death. Her hand weakly hangs on to the cop as if for dear life.'

Peter tells Yang to tell her she's going to be alright, that they'll take care of her. He does so, but she's crying from fear. Yang shakes his head and says. "She's delirious. Keeps saying the 'Dark Angels' are coming for her. She says they took some of her people away." People ask who these 'Dark Angels' are. Yang replies. "Probably a gang. Chinese people, man, They come up with some wacky stuff."

As her stretcher is rolled into a waiting vehicle, on the wall nearby is the strange drawing of the Stick Man or Long John, or the Overcoat Man, that Peter saw while Jogging earlier.

All the Chinese characters, the preacher, Yang, and the infected woman appear in the end credits of the version of Mimic released in the cinema, so it's fair to assume

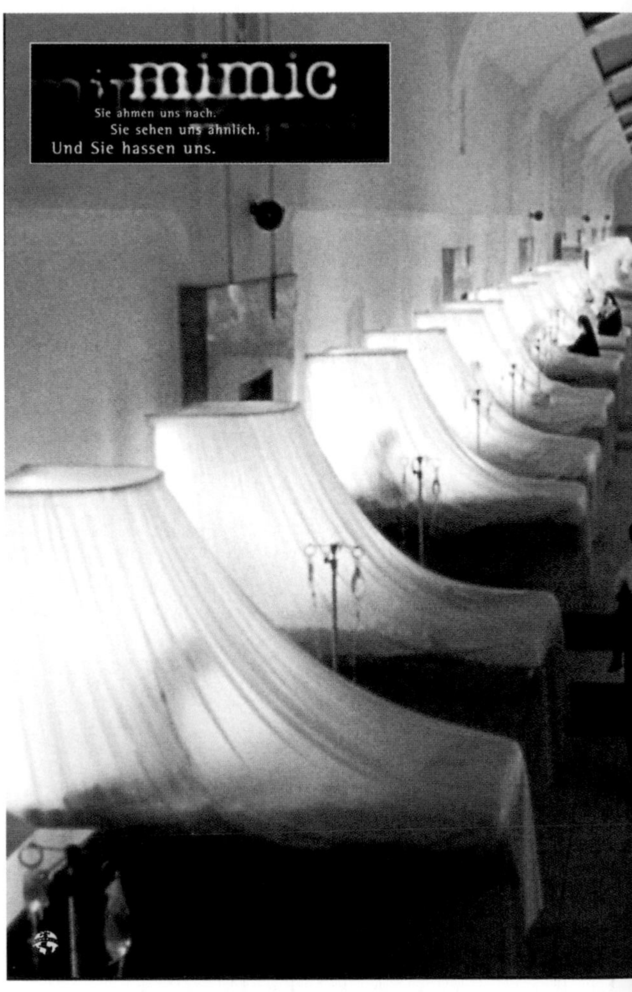

Strickler's Disease – in quarant

the scenes were filmed but were removed. Once we know this, Manny's comment to his grandson makes perfect sense. "Chuy, listen to me. They have Jesus on the cross, but that is not a holy place." We can only imagine how crushing it must be to put your heart into a film and then have it ripped out. Just before these lines were spoken, Manny tells Chuy. "A friend is the one you can trust. When you are

with a friend, no matter where in the world, you are a home. In this city, a friend is a hard thing to find." True on many levels, that of big cities, and of the duplicitous nature of the Mimics themselves, and sometimes that of working with a studio that doesn't share your vision.

Later Josh tells Peter that they found 33 workers in the sweatshop but there were 35 listed in Reverend Wong's roster, which makes Peter think about what the Chinese woman said.

Then there was to have been a scene where Peter and Susan, logically in the light of what she's discovered, take a cab to see the two boys who found the insect. Which explains what they were doing in the scene in the released version of *Mimic*, where Peter is shown where they found the insect and picks the padlock to the locker room. In the released film, this scene sits in isolation and makes little narrative sense. Susan also tells the boys. "We're here to deal." Which is a nice pay off to the Ricky's earlier line to Susan.

The original description of the *Mimic* that watches Susan and Peter in that locker room is almost poetic. 'Terrifying in its doll-like simplicity. In the darkness, its features seem indiscernible, inert, almost frozen in a perfectly symmetrical pattern."

Chuy was originally to have been shown to be able to perfectly mimic people's walks as well as sounds, giving a symmetry of mimicry from our world with that of the insects.

Susan and Peter's childlessness is given poignant voice when she says sadly of the insects. "Ironic, don't you think? These guys can hatch hundreds of offspring in a single clutch of eggs, right? And here we are..."

In the original script, it's clear that the disease the Chinese sweatshop workers have is a new form of Strickler's carried by the Judases. (Originally it was intended Susan's assistant would get the disease from a bite from the specimen the boys bring her.)

Originally the crucifix in the chapel/ sweatshop was meant to be upright, but in the finished version of the film, it's toppled and decapitated. I think inadvertently it symbolises the martyred state of Guillermo by the time the studio had finished with him.

Originally, and logically, the Mole People, the homeless people who live in the tunnels played a much more important part in *Mimic*. 'Three homeless people-emaciated, toothless, sleeping intertwined for warmth. In the dim light, they almost seem like a single organism."

The description of the insect Jeremy finds at the sewage filtration plant was fantastic and shows what Guillermo's original vision was, had he been allowed to realise it. It also shows the love of paintings and artists, that we see to great effect in his work (The inspiration of Goya on the Pale Man in *Pan's Labyrinth*, for instance). 'What lies on the stretcher before than looks more like a demon from a Brueghel painting. A three foot insect. It's mephitic, pink-white body is rotten, falling apart. The head's intact, with strange, large jaws thrown wide open. The chitin on one is half gone.' It also brings back fond memories the creatures in Roy Ward Baker's fine Hammer film version of Nigel Kneale's *Quatermass and the Pit*.

Originally the tunnel where the Mole People lived was described thus, in a scene before the one where Leonard explains about the Mole People to Peter and Josh. '...an abandoned encampment, made of cardboard wall, electrical wiring, elaborate debris...The walls are completely taken by layer after layer of hand-carved initials and messages. Everything from 'Kilroy was here' to elaborate quotations from the bible.

Originally when Leonard says, 'Down here's the land of talk." he went further. "They mark that area with a sign or drawing, and its as good as closed. We had one fella...for years said he was Bela Lugosi. Got him on Geraldo."

Originally Susan and Peter had spoken on the phone. The reason she goes to the subway platform is to meet Peter when he returns and share her findings with him. In the released version, she just turns up.

Again the poetry of the original script is lost in the released version of *Mimic*, in the scene where Manny reports Chuy missing. 'On Manny's dining room table, a heap of unpolished shoes has accumulated. The radio is playing a sad, elegiac Tango." That is a beautiful piece of writing. It shows Guillermo's love for his characters, that Manny has neglected his miserable livelihood, and how much work he has to do to support them both, the tragedy and loneliness of his plight, (truly a stranger in a strange land), and a grandparents love for their grandchild, a strong autobiographic theme for Guillermo in his *Cronos* debut. It's also interesting to note that, many years later, a pile of shoes would surface with even more sinister connotations, in the Pale Man's banqueting hall in *Pan's Labyrinth*.

Again, when Susan finds herself in the rapidly empty subway. 'Susan pushes through the turnstile, enters the long corridors of gleaming tile, s somewhat de-humanizing atmosphere, straight out of a George Tooker painting. Very Creepy.'

It's worth sharing the original description of the Overcoat Man-'The man's face tips back, raising the complex, glittering insect head...The thing charges, it's 'coat' opening to reveal six leathery wings, fully extended. The wingspan blocks the whole tunnel, they vibrate rapidly. Susan tries to run, but the creature hereafter known simply as 'The Mimic'-leaps on her chest.'

The Old Armoury station it was originally explained was built in the 1940s, but abandoned when they ran out of money. 'It's like Grand Central's dead little brother. Tiled mosaic walls, columns, monumental arches. Spaces for shops. A group of abandoned turn-of-the-century subway cars on parallel tracks.'

Little touches like Susan's weakness for sweets saving her life when she's captured by the Mimic were removed.

The place the unfortunate Josh meets his death was originally connected with the chapel/sweatshop fronted by the Chinese preacher. (In the released version of *Mimic*, scenes, geography and even motivation are often very confused). Originally the sewing machine he tries to use to pull himself away from the attacking Mimic belonged to the sweatshop. In the released film, you have no idea why a sewing machine should suddenly appear as part of the plot.

A scene where Manny opens a cabinet and takes the razor we see later does not appear in the finished film.

Another magical scene, one that really shows Guillermo's intentions to make a more fantastic film, that didn't make it occurred after Peter and Leonard have fallen. 'A ring of flares burns in the darkness like an island. Peter lights another one, revealing a space buried in layers of dust and time. Cracked mannequin faces stare out from an unopened tailor shop. A flower parlour decorated with cob webs. A yellowed newspaper on the floor, its headlines reading: GERMAN TROOPS DRIVEN BACK ACROSS RHINE. (A similar headline from the same period would later appear in *Pan's Labyrinth*).

Originally Manny was to use lit shoe

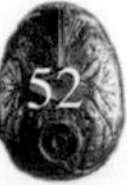

polish to get the creature off Leonard's leg. 'Is how we make lose the ticks back home.' It's only a small scene, but in films like *Pan's Labyrinth*, such similar small scenes reveal so much about the characters.

The scene in the subway rail car, where Susan reveals the creature's mimicry of the human face, also revealed her anguish at her inability to conceive and her guilt at what, in a sense, she and Peter have conceived, the Mimics. 'Susan closed the multiple mouth parts into a self-contained bud shape, then pushed back the 'face' mandibles. "This has evolved to mimic the most dangerous predator it's ever had..." She holds it in her hand, like Yorick's skull. The Mimic's head obscenely mimics her own. She inserts it into the shoulder cavity. She stands back. "...us." The thing now looks like The Overcoat Man. She continues. 'Mantids can mimic. We gave the Judas that code...' Manny quotes. ...and behold he will come that walks as a man, yet is not a man...'Susan comments bitterly. 'This, is our baby, Peter. Yours and mine. Aren't you proud?'

Shortly after, Susan was to have revealed the full scale of the threat the Mimics pose when she looked at 'subway map on the wall. Red, blue, and orange lines branching through the boroughs like veins. 'All these... they're like tunnels of an insect colony. Once these things hit a certain population density, they'll have to move out, form new colonies... We have to get help down here. Burn the tunnel...'

Also missing is the scene where Manny tells Susan of his concern for Chuy, which really further defines his relationship with his grandson, a few brief lines, and you feel you understand his pain.. "I didn't protect him, lady. He trusted me. And I didn't protect him...His father...I lost his father to the streets and now, Chuy...'

There was to have been a scene where the Mimics devour part of the mimic Leonard killed. Susan, in a tribute to Captain Rhodes in George A Romero's classic *Day of the Dead*, tell them to 'Choke on it...'

Again there was an evocative description of the switch room. 'The space is even more dusty than the rest of the station. Spider webs strung over old machinery. White Doric pillars support the ceiling like skeletal bones. 1940s style lamps are built into their sides.'

Susan introduces the Judas Breed in Mimic

Another scene that was a great favourite of Guillermo's that was cut, was the Mimic's mass-mating ritual, which sounds like Hieronymus Bosch meets Rob Bottin!

It's also made clear in the original script that the reason the creatures haven't killed Chuy is because he can mimic them, thus continuing the theme of mimicry in the film.

Originally, when Manny found Chuy, he discovered 'An albino mimic. Another leap for evolution. Its form is different from the other Mimics. Sleeker, more supple, almost beautiful. And while its movements are still not completely human, there is a kind of unearthly grace to them that at the very least entrances us. The thing raises itself to

its full height, dwarfing the boy. It stands over him like a king over his court fool. Chu giggles happily. It's all a game to him. The albino clicks in response-a long, leisurely sound, as if trying to communicate with the boy. Chu pulls his spoons out and begins to play them, making a perfect imitation of the sound. Manny starts to tremble as the creature gazes upon him with huge, expressionless 'eyes'. The albino clicks his jaws, moving in toward Manny. Chuy plays his spoons in perfect imitation. Manny stands under an archway in a swirl of dust. He raises his arms, like a prophet. He lets go of his razor and kneels. "God has closed his eyes. This, he cannot see..." His vacant eyes, fill with tears, he prays quietly, a strange serenity invades him. The Albino's jaws open and charge...'

As the electricity comes on in the abandoned subway, the original intention was to have 'the lamps on the columns burst into flames from the power surge. Fire illuminates the station like a Greek temple.'

Originally the albino Mimic was to lead the attack on the railcar, and Leonard's death was meant to be much more heroic, electrocuting himself to destroy the attacking Mimics.

There was to have been a funny scene where Susan has to climb out of a tight space, and she comments. 'I'm really glad I'm not pregnant.'

The original ending of *Mimic* was intended to be far darker than the impossibly neat one the released version of *Mimic* has, after all their creation could well seal the fate of the human race. When they've both escaped Peter tells Susan. "It'll be fine...They're still down there. We'll seal the whole system, go in with whatever it takes..." But Peter's voice evidences a lack of conviction now, he's trying to convince Susan and himself of something he doesn't fully believe. "it'll be fine...We nailed them before, we'll do it again..." He hurries to meet the MTA cops.' Then Susan sees 'commuters move to and fro, moving up and down and in and out of the illuminated areas of the station. In the crush of onlookers is one deadpan face-a Mimic, hugging the shadows, waiting for its moment.' Then she sees two more, she's horrified. "They've come up." Then 'the train announcer declares "The 11:16 local to Plough Keepsie, boarding now, Track 32 the 7.20 Connecticut local, making connections to South Norwalk."

The last shot of *Mimic* was to have been an overhead view of the main terminal 'from here the people are dots, their importance no greater than a colony of ants.'

It's reminiscent of the Pod People dispersing themselves and more pods to other towns in the dark 1978 remake of *Invasion Of The Body Snatchers*, and the logical ending, not a Hollywood ending, these creatures have been engineered to survive, and employ the most useful traits of cockroaches, mantids and termites. Their existence is to

As above, so below

survive, breed and evolve. Guillermo also likes some loose ends in his films, and as all too often happens in real life, there is not always a happy ending.

Another clue to the disappointment of *Mimic* is that the films production featured second and third assistant directors (including Rick Bota and Robert Rodriguez), this in a film by a director who wants to direct every scene himself tells you something went very wrong.

Finally, the disinterest of the studio can be seen in the lacklustre treatment *Mimic* has received in DVD, not only are there no director's cut or audio-commentary, or any special features, but Guillermo's name is absent from the front cover of the DVD! Surely, even from a commercial pint of view, it would make sense to at least state 'from the director of *Pan's Labyrinth* and *Hellboy*, like all the other DVD's of Guillermo's work. Even the English sub-title track is littered with inaccuracies, truly no one cared. Hopefully one day justice will be done and Guillermo will get to supervise a directors cut of *Mimic*.

There is a positive side to this (hard though it might be to see at first). Guillermo has never again suffered such an ordeal. He came back with *Blade II* and *The Devil's Backbone*, with his love of film making and creativity intact. He has shown tenacity all his life, and no better example here, truly, 'what does not kill us, makes us stronger.'

Mimic does have some good points, performances are generally decent. The set design by Carol Spier is terrific. The film is beautifully shot. It features a fine soundtrack, and in parts it is lovingly reminiscent of 1954's creature classic *Them* (which features an amazing climax in the Los Angeles storm drains with the US Army fighting giant mutated ants. A film that would be an influence on such films as James Cameron's *Aliens* (1986). Them is a truly tense and atmospheric film, one that makes great use of light and shadow, and well worth checking out.) Plus some scenes in *Mimic* really do invoke a sense of wonder and nail-biting suspense.

He learned what to avoid in the future, a baptism of fire that forged a stronger person and director, and for this in a world where people so easily give up, I admire him. I do not like to think of the fantastic films we would have missed otherwise. He also found collaborators he would work with on happier films in the future, like Carol Spier and Norman Reedus, who plays Scud in *Blade*. He would also get to do some fine suspenseful work in the happier production of *Hellboy*.

Like the Mimics themselves, Guillermo managed to survive, and much good work lay ahead. And one day we may see the true *Mimic*!

Guillermo did some insect wrangling on Mimic (he'd previously done some on Cronos)

"...If you don't dose them with a little bit of CO2, they immediately hide from you."

"On Mimic, I paid about $120,000 for effects, which the studio later paid back because the shots I'd wanted stayed in."

Rob Bottin

Rob Bottin is a cult American special effects artist, who did some sterling creature work on *Mimic*. His special effects work is totally memorable. In fact, Rob is The Man. In particular his work on *The Thing* is unforgettable and an outstanding. His love of physical effect work has meant his work hasn't dated, and he shares this love for physical effects with Guillermo. The Los Angels born Bottin for his first break aged 14 when he submitted some work to Rick Baker, who hired him to work on various films.

His big break was an on-screen man to werewolf transformation in *The Howling* (another film that made a huge impression on its release). He also worked on the classic *Piranha* (1978) Rob was introduced to director John Carpenter by Carpenter's cinematographer Dean Cundey. (Cundey was cinematographer on such outstanding films as *Escape From New York* (1981) (personally, my all-time favourite film). Cundey also did sterling work on the fantastic *Big Trouble in Little China*). Bottin did special effects for *The Fog*. *The Fog* (1980) is one of Carpenter's finest films, a dark Lovecraftian tale of vengeful ghosts, leper messiah's returning one hundred years after their betrayers sent them to a water grave, featuring Carpenter favourite Jaime Lee Curtis (and interestingly, in a film that was inspired by *The Birds*, Curtis' real life mother Janet Leigh, appears in *The Fog*).

In fact, *The Fog* is packed full of references to other works, and coupled with a typically driving Carpenter synth-score (in itself very inspiration, check out the Carpenter inspired work of the fine group Zombi for proof), and a very talented cast and crew, it's a modern classic. It marked Bottin's acting debut. He played Captain Blake (A.K.A Wormface), a part that always sticks in the mind of people viewing *The Fog*.

He would collaborate successfully again with Carpenter on his remake of Howard Hawks' *The Thing From Another World* (1951). His creature-work in Carpenter's *The Thing* (1982), defy description, they truly are Lovecraftian in the best sense of the word, with a hint of Gustav Doré thrown in for good measure.

Panned on its release, *The Thing* is now considered to be a modern classic, which is as it should be! Rob worked on *The Thing* for a year and five months straight, making himself so ill, Carpenter had him sent to hospital to recuperate on completion of production. Rob would go on to produce much fine work in the future. On *Robo-Cop* (1987), *Total Recall* (1990) and *Fight Club* (1999). He designed the amazing 'lounge lizard' make-up effects on Terry Gilliam's marvellous adaption of the late and much missed Dr. Hunter S. Thompson's *Fear and Loathing in Las Vegas*. Putting the incredible imagination of Ralph Steadman on screen is no easy task, and Rob deserved an Oscar for his efforts. For my money, one of the greatest films Rob has been involved with was Stephen Sommer's incredibly entertaining *Deep Rising* (1998), starring the gorgeous Famke Janssen, with the addition of Rob's incredible monster, this film truly is a modern Beauty and the Beast!

Rob Bottin & his creations from The Thing

Chapter Three
The Devil's Backbone

Carlos responds to a call from beyond the grave

"What is a ghost?" asks the narrator. "A tragedy condemned to repeat itself time and again."

A bomb drops from a plane, to descend to the orphanage courtyard below (yet it doesn't explode, it is not the explosion but the warning of the explosion to come). A boy lies bleeding on the ground as the narration continues. "An instant of pain, perhaps. Something dead which still seems to be alive. An emotion suspended in time like a blurred photograph."

As the credits role we see deformed foetuses, trapped like insects in amber themselves, right down to the colour scheme (a deliberate choice of Guillermo's for as we shall see, everyone in this tale is like an 'insect trapped in amber'.)

It is 1939, and the bitter and bloody Spanish Civil War draws to a close with Franco's forces gaining the upper hand.

Against this backdrop, a young boy named Carlos (Fernando Tielve) is brought by his guardian to a remote orphanage. He thinks he will only be there a short while until his father (a 'red', fighting against Franco) returns for him. Sadly, though he does not know it, his father is already dead.

Embedded in the courtyard of the orphanage is the now defused bomb, a German bomb dropped by the Nazi's Condor Legion (who inflicted so much carnage on the civilians of Guernica) as part of their aid to Franco's fascists, part of testing the blitzkrieg tactics they would soon employ in Poland). The bomb is festooned with ribbons tied to it by the children, as though in their innocence they think the horror of war can be neutralised by such a gesture. "They came, they defused it...and they left it there. Nobody can move it." (This event is inspired by a favourite book of Guillermo's, *The Castle Of Otranto* by Horace Walpole, the book that kick started the genre of Gothic Fiction). Carlos gives it an experimental tap to make sure, as kids do.

They are watched by Carmen (Marisa Peredes), the orphanage's administrator and Dr Casares (Federico Luppi, who had previously appeared in Cronos, in a fine performance as Jesus Gris), her assistant. Carmen adjusts her artificial leg and wearily notes she has yet another mouth to feed. The war takes limbs and creates orphans, it is a beast that devours happiness and spews out misery.

Carlos spots what appears to be the ghost of a boy his own age. He goes to investigate but is distracted by two orphans. One makes the introductions. "I'm Galzez, he's Owl. He doesn't speak but looks a lot."

Dr Casares tries to persuade Carmen to take Carlos on, telling her he is the son of a comrade killed in battle, "a leftist, a brave man." Carmen doesn't agree, she knows, like so many women whose husbands have died in war, that she's the brave one. While men tend to the business of killing, life will always be the responsibility of the women, would a man so blithely take life if he could understand its true value like a woman does? Living is always much harder than dying. She knows what the Nationalist will do when they get the orphanage. "Ricardo was a man of books, of ideas. He decided to die and leave me here

to defend his ideals. The Nationalists will arrive any day and what will they find? Reds looking after the children of Reds." She also wants Casares to take the gold kept in her safe for her late husband's cause. "At least you can buy guns. I can't even buy bread with it." Dr Casares leaves the 'choice' to Carmen. Only a man could say. "The boy goes hungry here or gets killed out there.' To a woman that is no choice.

Outside Carlos shows Galzez and Owl his collection of comics and toys, until Jaime (Inigo Garces), an older and stronger orphan, helps himself to a comic. Carlos starts to fight with him, but is distracted at the sight of his guardian driving out of the orphanage's gates without him. The sight of Carlos crying, his few belonging scattered around him is heart-rending. The day a child realises he is alone in the world, he begins to cease to be a child. This doesn't stop Jaime taunting him and mocking his grief.

Dr Cesares treats him with great sympathy. He picks up a fallen copy of the *Count of Monte Cristo* (a favourite book of del Toro's since childhood, he has written a script entitled *Montecristo*, which was in development with Francis Ford Coppola at one point, it was to have been a western version where the Count has a clockwork hand), and cleverly distracts him from his grief. "Has Edmund Dantes broke out of prison yet? Has he met Abbot Faria? Do they manage to escape?" Carlos doesn't know yet. "Why don't you read on and tell me?" He asks Dr Casares if Carmen is his girlfriend. Dr Casares ducks the question answering that she's the Principle (Which is true in a way, she's the principle around which his life revolves, like a planet around the sun. In this orphanage, she is the Sun Queen around which everything revolves. It's her strength that keeps it together). Carlos doesn't want to stay, he wants to be with his father, but Casares tells him he's staying with them 'just for a while.'

Later, Carmen takes Carlos around the orphanage. She tells him his soap has to last all year. The dormitory seems as immense as the loneliness he feels inside. Carmen assigns him to bed number 12. He asks why there are so many empty beds. She replies. "Some boys run away, but I wouldn't advise it. It's a day's walk to town. The nights are cold and the days..." Giving him the key to his locker (keys are an important part of *The Devil's Backbone*), she tells him it isn't a prison. But it is, it may not have bars, but when you have nowhere else to go, the awful truth is, you are in prison. (Everyone in *The Devil's Backbone* is in a prison. Carmen is imprisoned by her artificial leg. Dr Casares is imprisoned by his impotency. Jacinto is imprisoned by his own bitterness and self-hatred). Jamie's friends note Carlos has been given the bed of someone called Santi. Jaime doesn't want to hear Santi's name spoken.

In the kitchen, Jacinto, the caretaker, entertains two shady looking friends, Marcello and The Pig. The cook, Conchita (Irene Visedo)

Sergio Leone days...

is his fiancé, she tells them that when she and Jacinto marry, they want to buy a farm. Outside, as Jacinto sees his friends off, he tells them he will try and find the 'Red's gold' tonight. Cochita doesn't like them. Jacinto reveals his past as an orphan. "When I was a kid, I'd stand here in the middle of the yard and I'd look up at the sky. I dreamed of getting out of here. I prayed to become rich so I could buy this dump and tear it down." He doesn't want anyone to know he spent fifteen years in the orphanage. He hates himself far more than he hates the orphanage. True hate always comes from within, and it shapes the world in its own image.

That night, in his bed, Carlos is distracted by eerie noises. He sees Santi's name scratched on the wall. There is a shadow moving beyond the curtain that surrounds his bed. But drawing back the curtain, there is nothing there. Like all kids, he looks under the bed

...Mario Bava nights

Finally, a pitcher of water (essential in such a dry dusty place) spills, waking the rest of the orphans. They think Carlos spilt it and he is put in the position of having to go to the kitchen to get more water. Someone asks, "what about the 'one who sighs'?" But no one answers. Carlos turns the tables by pressurising Jaime into coming with him. (We've all been here, when we were kids we hated having to get up in the middle of the night, when all the things we're afraid of seem much more real). Outside in the courtyard, they walk towards the bomb which throws a huge shadow by moonlight. Jaime doesn't believe the bomb is safe. "Put your ear against it, you'll hear ticking. That's its heart. It's still alive and it knows we're here."

Inside the kitchen they start drawing the water. A huge butcher's scissors falls and Jacinto goes to investigate. Seeing nobody, he draws back some tiles revealing the hidden safe. Jacinto is called away.

Carlos descends a spiral staircase, where he sees the ghost , who tells him cryptically that 'many of you will die'. He runs away from the spectre, but some of the orphans smash the jug of water with slingshots and Jacinto catches him.

Dr Casares is listening to a gramophone record and reciting from a book. Dr Casares is a creature of the intellect rather than of the flesh. "Out, out, yearning of mine. Let not respect bind you. It flatters pity not to be able to hide. Let your lips bear witness to the blaze in your heart. No one will believe the fire if the smoke sends no signals. He who cares for his wellbeing keeps not his feelings silent. My grief is greater than I. And that being so it will be easier for it to defeat me, than for I to command it." It has defeated him, his spiritual love for Carmen is as impotent as his physical love, unable to say those three most important words to her, an unhappy prisoner of fear. He touches the wall behind which lies the object of his love, Carmen, her artificial leg on the locker beside her bed. The wall between them a symbol of his impotent desire for her. "Consideration does not suffice to prevent the cry. He is a brave prisoner who does not break down his gaol." Behind the wall, Carmen cast aside her bed clothes and we see the stump of her leg. She undoes the straps of her artificial leg. It is like some hellish medieval contraption, almost like a puppet leg (and it reflects Guillermo's love for strange devices).

The next day, Carlos does not divulge his reason for being out of his bed after hours, nor does he name Jaime, though Dr. Casares

is smart enough to figure it out for himself, an act which earns him grudging respect in Jaime's eyes.

As part of their punishment, the boys have to raise a crucifix in the courtyard (this is because the war is nearly over, in an attempt to placate Franco's forces when they come.) They struggle with the heavy weight. "For a dead guy he sure weighs a lot." It is symbolic of the weight that has crushed the representatives of the legally elected government of Spain in the War. Dr Casares looks on regretfully.

"Christ in the yard and John the Baptist in here. Are things that bad?" Carmen can only answer helplessly. "If the new Spain is Catholic and apostolic... Ayala said so. Catalonia is about to fall then Madrid will fall and then..." Dr Casares interrupts her. "There's talk of a ghost. Have you heard?" "Yes, sometimes I think that we are the ghosts." Casares looks out at the boys laughing over a clockwork frog. Carmen tells Casares to go back to Argentina while he still can. But he still foolishly believes that England and France might intervene. He must know that England and France have placed an arms embargo to stop the Republicans receiving aid in their fight with Franco. She tells him that it's just wishful thinking, that he's like her late husband. He denies this and their fingers meet, the nearest they have every come to expressing their unspoken love (their love too is trapped in amber).

Carlos is staring into the pool of water in the basement of the building. "Are you the 'one who sighs'? Do you live down there?" He is interrupted by Jaime and his gang, they throw him to the floor but he fights back, throwing a stone at Jaime, who topples into the water. Carlos dives in after him and rescues him. Jacinto comes across the scene and picks up the knife. "Who's is this?" Carlos says it is his, and Jacinto viciously cuts Carlos's cheek. "If anything happens to you, I get the blame. Say a word about this and I'll cut you in half." He stares at the pool of water, as though his mind is elsewhere.

Later, Dr. Casares cleans Carlos's cut. "Our Carlos has been here five minutes and he's in trouble already?" Carlos asks him if he believes in ghosts. Casares replies. "I'm a man of science. But Spain is full of superstition. Europe is sick with fear now, and fear sickens the soul and that in turn makes us see things." He indicates a foetus in a jar, it has a prominent deformity of the spine. This scene also has elements of the alchemist's workshop seen in *Cronos*, and is equally full of symbolism and meaning.

Casares himself hopes for an alchemical transformation as we shall see, drinking the 'limbo water' from the jar in the hope of transforming his impotency. "They call this 'the Devil's Backbone'. They say a lot of things. That this happens to children who shouldn't have been born -'Nobody's Children' . But that's a lie. Poverty and disease, that's all it is . The liquid they're in is called 'limbo water'. In the old days it was made with various spices...cloves, rum. So this is very, very old rum," He opens the jar and inserts a ladle into the liquid (which greatly resembles the water in the pool). "I sell it in town and the money keeps the school going." Carlos is astounded, asking. "Do they drink it?" "They say it helps cure blindness, kidney ailments, and also, apparently, impotence." Casares cradles the glass he's drawn at this. "Rubbish.

The Devil' Backbone' real monster – the huma monster

But you know, after sixty, men will pay anything just to..." Raises his finger erect, the same finger he linked with Carmen. "...you know. So if you're going to believe in ghosts and all that rubbish, you should have a sip of this to heal your wound." This is an adult way of ignoring what Carlos has to say and proving it's just superstition. (A strong theme in Guillermo's work is adults not listening to children). Carlos refuses and leaves. Once Carlos is gone, Casares wistfully drinks the 'limbo water'. He (and Carmen) are both as imprisoned as Santi, imprisoned by their own inability to express their love for each other, imprisoned in their own loneliness. Casares in particular, wrongly believes love is worthless unless it can be expressed physically.

That night in the dormitory, Jaime offers Carlos some of his treasured items to keep the stolen comic book, to which he refuses. When Jaime grows up, he wants to draw comics, "with more fights, more treasures, and big ships with lots of cannons (an echo of the young Guillermo's love of comics). A sigh is heard, and a ghost is mentioned. Jaime acts as though he doesn't believe in the ghost, almost guiltily, as if he knows more than he says.

The sigh is that of Carmen having sex with Jacinto. Youth and age. Ending and beginning. Alpha and omega. Carmen says it's the last time. But he's scornful. 'Same old story'. Carmen needs the physical expression of love, though frustratingly for her, love doesn't come into it. Jacinto uses this opportunity to take what he hopes will be the correct keys to the safe. (they are not, an act which will have tragic consequences) She tells him not to make noise. He asks her if she's afraid of Casares hearing. But she tells him she's not afraid, she ashamed. Jacinto's envious eyes miss little. As he attaches her artificial leg (what Guillermo calls ' the amputated Cinderella moment'), he comments. "The old man looks at you with love. He did that even when your husband was alive." She gazes on the primitive prosthetic wearily. "I don't like to think of this leg. Somedays I can't bear it, but I need it to stay on my feet. She is not just referring to her false limb. She can't resist Jacinto, and sadly, in the next room, Casares is all too aware of this.

In their dormitory, the boys discuss the war. "...the earth's so dry here and air's so hot that the dead get stuck halfway to heaven." Carlos learns more of 'the one who sighs. A boy named Santi (Junio Valverde) disappeared the night the bomb fell. Since then, no one has dared to take Jaime on. Santi slept in what is now Carlos's bed, number 12. The teachers believe the bomb scared Santi and he ran away. Some of orphans believe a cutthroat got him and sold his blood to rich people to cure their tuberculosis. What they are sure of is the ghost appeared after the bomb

The following day Dr Casares is taking bottles of 'limbo water' to town to sell. Jaime has a huge crush on Conchita and give her one of his treasures, a cigar ring. In a rather sweet scene she kisses him and tells him it's beautiful. One of those little gestures that mean so much. It has been a long time since anyone has shown any act of kindness to Jaime, and it's the small acts of kindness that make life worth living, that prevent the heart hardening to cold stone.

In class, Carmen shows the boys a scene of ancient man hunting woolly mammoths. "Can anybody tell me what these elegant gentlemen are hunting?" Owl ventures that it might be a pig. Carlos correctly identifies it as a mammoth. Carmen explains (and this will have great significance at the climax of *The Devil's Backbone*). "In those days, men had to act in groups. No one could give up. Imagine the death of a mammoth. It must have been terrible." Jamie draws a mammoth in his sketchbook.

That night, Carlos sneaks a look at Jaime's sketchbook. He finds a picture of the ghost, and knows Jaime must know more of Santi's death than he has let on.

In town, Casares has sold the 'limbo water'. Before he can leave there is a commotion. There is about to be an execution. "International Brigade. Two Spaniards, six Canadians, one Chinaman."

In a heart-rending moment, he sees Franco's troops are about to execute Carlos's guardian, Ayala. Ayala catches Casares's eye until the officer in charge of the firing squad barks. "You, look at your damn feet." Facing a wall, the International Brigade are murdered one by one by a single pistol shot. Casares can barely reign his feelings in. "Someone you knew, Doctor?" He shakes his head unconvincingly. He knows the war he's tried to avoid is breathing down his neck now. It's just a matter of time

Back at the orphanage Carlos sneaks out to the courtyard. He approaches the black accusing cenotaph that is the bomb and asks it a favour. "Bomb, if you're alive, tell me where Santi is." In response, there is a harsh grating metallic sound, a ribbon on the bomb flies off, as though in the breeze, towards a doorway, where he sees the ghost. Carlos asks. "Santi, talk to me. I don't want anyone to die." "Many of you will die." Santi approaches, his ethereal cracked visage haunting, moving and terrifying. He is like a cracked porcelain doll, ghostly blood flowing from his cracked eggshell thin skull. All the king's horses and all the king's men won't be able to put Santi back together again. Terrified, Carlos runs. Santi follows, the red mist around his head like a crimson halo. Terrified, Carlos locks himself into a closet. The eye of Santi, as yellowed as the 'limbo water' gazes through the keyhole(This is Guillermo's favourite shot in the entire film, again the theme of keys). In the morning, when the cupboard door is opened, Carlos screams and runs out.

At breakfast, Casares tells Carmen what he witnessed, unaware that Jacinto is eavesdropping. He explains that Ayala was taken prisoner, and may have talked. They plan to go to Marseille, with the boys, using the gold, which belongs to the cause the boys were orphaned for." This is like a red rag to a bull for Jacinto, he has built his whole future around the gold, it is for him alone, not to save the lives of the children. Ironically, this is the nearest Casares comes to expressing his true feelings for Carmen, a cautionary tale for all of us who procrastinate through fear, thinking there will always be a tomorrow. The refuge of the coward is always in 'another day'. "I always thought there'd be an afterwards. There is no afterwards...if anything happened to you."

After breakfast, Jacinto confronts Carmen as she makes preparations to bring her boys to safety. "You can go, but the gold stays here." Carmen's disgust for him is palpable. "Is that all you care about? The gold? I hid you here so you wouldn't die outside with no one to mourn you. You know what, of all the orphans you were always the saddest. The lost one. A prince without a kingdom." He grabs the hand she holds her keys in telling her to shut up, but she won't, the harsh truth cannot be silenced. "The only one who was really alone." Casares intervenes, pointing a shotgun at Jacinto. "Get out of here or I'll kill you." Jacinto laughs at him. "Look who's come to save you. The old sage. Will this weapon work?" A cruel reference to Casares's impotency, and like all the most hurtful jibes, it has a kernel of truth, it has to have a core of truth to hurt. Casares cannot shoot him. Jacinto then proceeds to say exactly what he does with Carmen, with no regard to the feelings of those listening, including his own fiancé. Carmen hits him hard in the face with her hand full of keys, and Jacinto, bleeding and crying, more alone than ever.

As the boys pile into the truck, Casares asks Conchita to bring some cans of fuel for the journey. She spots a trail of fuel leading from the truck.

Carmen bravely tried to raise the boys spirits. "It'll be a long journey. The older boys will have to look after the little ones. If any of you are scared, you can sit with me."

Conchita discovers Jacinto has taken all the fuel and is about to use it to blow the safe. Conchita gives the warning as Jacinto ignites the fuel. Alma and Carmen desperately, heroically, hopelessly try to put out the flames and are caught killed in the initial explosion. Then there is a second explosion as the truck ignites.

A fiery hell has come to the orphanage but not from the monsters outside, but from the monster they nurtured within. There was no sign on the outside, but within, Jacinto's soul is as twisted and malformed as any of the misfortunate creatures floating eternally in Casares's jars.

His eardrums ruptured by the explosion, bleeding from his wounds, Casares staggers to his feet. If only he'd been able to pull the trigger. If only...it is the story of his life. Conchita has survived, but many of the boys are dead, others are wounded. Where is his beloved Carmen? He finds her bleeding and broken in the ruins, her artificial leg has come loose. Looking at Casares with dying eyes, she says. "I'm very cold." He tells her she'll be alright but the chunk of glass embedded in her says otherwise. Casares sends Carlos for his medical bag. He takes it, watched by the foetus floating in its limbo water. A silent witness to the bloody legacy of a twisted man's greed.

Conchita knows she's the only one who can go for help. "They won't have heard the explosion in town. And it was just one of many. We can't expect any help. If I walk all night, I'll get to town by noon tomorrow."

Casares tries to tell the dying Carmen his true feelings for her in the only way he knows how. "I can't hear you. This time let me do the talking. I've leaned a new poem.... Stay by my side as my light grows dim. As my blood slows down and my nerves shatter with stabbing pain. As my heart grows weak and the wheels of my being turn slowly .Stay by my side as my fragile body is wracked by pain, which verges on truth and manic time continues scattering dust and furious life burst out in flames. Stay by my side as I fade. So you can point to the end of my struggle, and the twilight of eternal days at the low, dark edge of life." (Alfred lord Tennyson's 'In Memorium, a heart-rending scene, but made more so by the sad fact that even at the end, Casares cannot simply say-"I love you.")

There were flames...and the Queen died.

Conchita sets off on her long journey. As Dr Casares leaves Carmen's body, he is wracked with guilt and regret. "That son of a bitch! I should have killed him while I had the chance. But he'll be back, and I'll be here waiting for him." But Casares too is dying.

The surviving boys are camped inside the shatter building. Jamie asks Carlos. "Could you kill somebody? I could. What you said about Santi is true. He's dead. But I didn't kill him." "I thought..." "I was with him. I saw everything. It started in the pit. I dared him to come down with me to gather slugs." Santi found Jacinto trying to open the safe. He brutally interrogated Santi, trying to find out who was with him, in the process Santi struck his head off a pillar. Jaime witnessed the whole horrible event. Bravely Santi did not give him away. Jacinto tied and weighed Santi and threw him into the pool to hide his cowardly crime. Blood and bubbles a silent witness to Santi's death.

Once Jacinto left, Jaime ran from the scene of the crime, just as the bomb fell. A metal marker descending from the heaven, a silent metatron to the atrocity just occurred.

Jaime's heart burns with the desire for vengeance. "I was always afraid of Jacinto, very afraid. But not anymore. The next time I see him, I know I am going to kill him."

In the desert, Conchita is met by the returning Jacinto. This time he has his two brutish companions, Marcello and The Pig, with him. He tells Conchita to apologise to him. She refuses. "You're an animal" She would rather die bravely than submit to him. He stabs her. Her death has a great courage and nobility. If you're going to die, it should be with such dignity.

Later at the orphanage, the survivors hear a car. They are hopeful that Conchita has returned with help. The boys help Casares to

his feet. He tells Jaime to play a record on his gramophone. "Turn the horn towards the windows."

But it is Jacinto that has returned, the criminal returning to the scene of his crime. Casares makes what is his dying declaration, a last will and testament. "All my life I have always stopped short, left things unfinished. I'm not going to leave you alone. I promise you. I will never leave this place."

Carlos talks to Santi, who tells Carlos to bring Jacinto to him.

Jacinto has entered the orphanage, and taking possession of the gun, sets the boys to digging through the rubble where the safe was. He gives Jaime the ring he gave to Conchita, so Jaime will know what has happened to the brave and unfortunate woman.

This only spurs Jaime on more. Once he and the surviving boys are locked up and alone, he tells them that Jacinto killed Santi and that he will do the same to them. He knows that only by becoming a unit will their greater numbers overwhelm the stronger men. Inspired by the mammoth hunt Carmen showed them, they fashion spears from lengths of wood and broken glass. Galvez climbs through a window, twisting his ankle badly as he drops to the ground.

"He said I'd be alright, and that we should be brave."

Some of the photos in the safe are of Jacinto as a child, Carmen had kept them there for safekeeping. In these photos we see the seeds of the monster Jacinto would allow himself to become. He tells his disinterested companions his story. "My father, he was from Calanda. He was an accountant. My mother was from Toledo. And that's me. It's blurred, 'cause I moved." He sees that Carmen has written on the back of the photo, as though she knew what the young Jacinto would grow into. "How lonely, the prince without a kingdom...the man without warmth. Jacinto, 1925, in Malagna." Here we have a glimmering of no sympathy but some understanding of Jacinto. What's uncanny is that judging by her inscription on the photo, Carmen had some premonition of the seed inside Jacinto that would blossom into such a poisoned vine. Yet, she still took him in and nurtured him, which speaks volumes for her kind heart and hopeful nature. Nature or nurture, the eternal dilemma. Sometimes love does conquer all, but Jacinto's case, his own nature won, and everyone else lost as a result.

Reading this brings him back to the present with a vengeance. He knows the gold must be in the orphanage. "We'll find it, and

The hunter is about to become the hunted

Jacinto and his friends have discovered the safe is devoid of gold, with only papers and photographs within.

The now-dead Dr. Casares, a halo of lies heralding his arrival (Again Guillermo's love of insects, and also reminiscent of other avatars of the other world in his films, like the Pollen in *Pan's Labyrinth*), keeps his word from beyond the grave and helps Galvez.

tomorrow we'll burn everything." "And the boys?" "They've got no parents. They've got no one. Who'll miss them? We're at war. A drop in the ocean." He spits contemptuously to emphasize his point, not seeing the irony, no one would miss him either. His companions don't care what he does, but they fear the approaching war, and want to leave the following day.(Looters would be shot, unless they were the ones sanctioned by Franco.)

Jacinto cranks up the gramophone, shotgun in hand he explores the ruined orphanage. He comes across Carmen's artificial limb, her shoe still attached. He discovers a hidden compartment inside the limb full of gold ingots. His friends drive off and leave him but he doesn't care. All the gold is now his. He spots the boys watching and chases them. They lead him into the depths of the building, near the pool. They have led him into a clever trap, the hunter is now the hunted, the predator has become the prey. He boys stab him with their homemade spears, they will slay their mammoth and it will be terrible. They drive him into the pool, where weighed down with the stolen gold (weighed down like the bad wolf in the children's story) he quickly sinks to the depths. Where Santi waits. Before Jacinto can divest himself of the gold, Santi squeezes the last of the air from his lungs.

In the same manner as Santi's death, only blood and bubbles mark Jacinto's passing.

The boys leave the pool. They return the rifle to Dr Casares, and they leave. Casares is now the silent sentinel of the orphanage. He watches them leave in a shot reminiscent of the final frames of John Ford's *The Searchers*. Casares is destined to haunt the shattered orphanage as much as Santi. He narrates. "What is a ghost? A tragedy condemned to repeat itself time and again? A moment of pain perhaps. Something dead which still seems to be alive. An emotion suspended in time. Like a blurred photograph. Like an insect trapped in amber. A ghost. That's what I am."

Thus, we have come full circle, with *The Devil's Backbone* ending in virtually the same fashion as it began.

THE CASTLE OF OTRANTO by HORACE WALPOLE

"...what a sight for a father's eyes,-he beheld his child dashed to pieces, and almost buried under an enormous helmet, one hundred times more large than any casque ever made for human being.!"

Guillermo del Toro, when writing *The Devil's Backbone*, was greatly inspired by *The Castle of Otranto*, first published in 1764 by Horace Walpole. From this book, Guillermo takes the device of a huge inanimate object in the courtyard as a portent of a crime past and a doom yet to come. It has in common many other elements too, the presence of the supernatural, the prince without a kingdom, and hidden treasure.

The Castle of Otranto by Horace Walpole is widely considered to be the first gothic novel, kick starting a literary genre which would truly flower in the nineteenth century and remains popular and influential to this day. The full title of the book on its first publication was the rather more long-winded 'The Castle of Otranto, A Gothic Story. Translated by William Marshall, Gent. From the Original Italian of Onuphrio Muralto, Canon of the Church of St. Nicholas at Otranto.

The first edition claimed to be a translation based on a manuscript printed at Naples in 1529 and recently rediscovered in the library of "an ancient Catholic family in the north of England." It was further claimed that this manuscript derived from an older story that dated all the way back to the Crusades. The Italian manuscript and also the alleged author 'Onuphrio Muralto', were Walpole's fictional creations, and 'William Marshall' was his pseudonym.

In the second and subsequent editions, Walpole acknowledges authorship of his work. He wrote: "The favourable manner in which this little piece has been received by the public, calls upon the author to explain the grounds on which he composed it:..as an attempt to blend the two kinds of romance. The ancient and the modern. In the former all was imagination

and improbability: in the latter, nature is as always intended to be, and sometimes has been, copied with success..." There was some debate at the time about the function of literature, that is, whether or not works of fiction should be representative of life, or more purely imaginative."

Interestingly (and revealing of human nature), the initial edition was well reviewed, the said reviewers believing the novel to be medieval fiction. Once Walpole admitted authorship, however, many critics dismissed it as far-fetched romanticism. Then, as now, labels are all important!

The Castle of Otranto tells the tale of Manfred, Lord of the said castle. The tale begins on the wedding day of his unhealthy son Conrad to the princess Isabella. Just prior to the wedding Conrad is killed by a huge helmet that falls on him from above.

This inexplicable occurrence, it seems to Manfred, ties in with an ancient prophecy, "that the castle and lordship of Otranto should pass from the present family, whenever the real owner should be grown too large to inhabit it."

Scared that Conrad's death marks the end of his family line, Manfred believes he will avoid the prophesised doom by marrying Isabella himself and divorcing his present wife Hippolita, whom he believes failed to bear him a suitable heir.

Manfred's attempts at this marriage are disrupted by a series of supernatural events involving the appearance of numerous oversized artefacts and body parts, and the arrival of the true prince, Theodore of Falconara.

Brisk, and entertaining, in the marriage of the historical and real with the supernatural and unreal, we see the influence this book has on the youthful Guillermo's work to come. The book is a delightful romp, well written and entertaining, and worth a read.

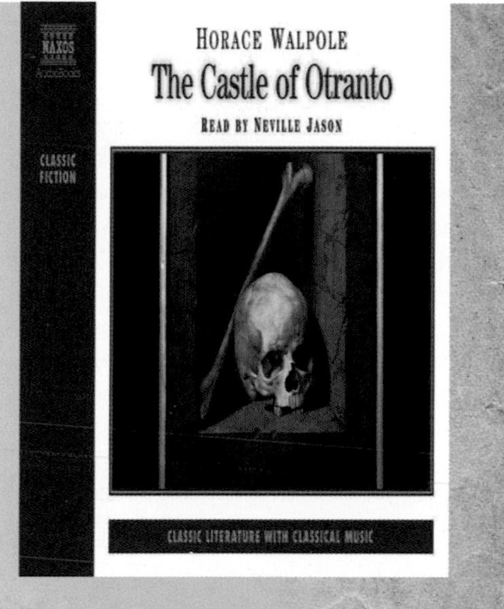

The Cathedral of Otranto

The Devil's Backbone - Analysis

The Devil's Backbone is the film that gave Guillermo back the chance to exercise his creativity after his bad experiences on *Mimic*. It is a microcosmos of the Spanish Civil War interpreted through the influences of Gothic Fiction. Guillermo sees Carlos (Fernando Tielve) as the force of innocence in *The Devil's Backbone*. Tielve originally auditioned for a part as an extra but del Toro knew he had found his lead. Both Tielve and his co-star Inigo Garces (who played Jaime) had cameos as guerrilla soldiers in *Pan's Labyrinth*, which Guillermo sees as a sister film to *The Devil's Backbone*. *The Devil's Backbone* has the male energy, while *Pan's Labyrinth* has the female energy. Del Toro favourite Fedrico Luppi (Dr. Casares) narrates at the end and beginning of the film, proving opening and closure to this very gothic tale. It's worth noting that the names of protagonists are spelled with the letter 'c', and those of the antagonists begin with the letter 'j', all part of the story's repetitions.

About to learn one of life's harsh lessons

Guillermo del Toro's original script did not have all the elements of the finished film. After treading a script by Antoni Trashorras and David Munoz, he decided to combine his script with theirs. It was originally intended to produce the film in Mexico and it was to be set during the Mexican Revolution. The funding to do this was insufficient and when Pedro Almodóvar came in as producer the production was moved to Spain and the setting to that of the Spanish Civil War.

The Devil's Backbone is deeply inspired by the works of gothic fiction. Guillermo believes a ghost is something waiting to happen. "Always, so that's what the film is about...things waiting to happen." The orphanage serves the same function as the haunted house in a gothic romance.

Eduardo Noriega (Jacinto) has his own ideas on what a ghost is. "I think that it's somebody or to be more precise 'something', a feeling, an emotion, that for some reason has been trapped, and doesn't want to go when it has to. When I read the script my first impression was of a story about an orphanage having been trapped. It was physically trapped by the Civil War, as were the characters who had also stayed at this orphanage and had been trapped emotionally by it. I had the feeling it's a sad story of ambitious people who had wished for something and that, for different reasons hadn't succeeded."

Marisa Paredes (Carmen) believes, "a ghost is an obsession. A ghost is something you can give flesh to, from the moment your brain is able to see it."

Federicco Luppi (Casares) thinks

ghosts are "the conscience, a bit mute but eloquent. And they are there to remind us..."

Guillermo describes *The Devil's Backbone* as "a ghost story set in Spain during the Thirties. It's not got much to do with the Civil War, 'cause the war is just the background of the story although it's always present in the activities of the characters. It's a story which is a micro-universe of the war, shot in a building, which is haunted, where a crime was committed and where a ghost asks for revenge." There are all classic elements of the Gothic Novel, a literary genre that still exerts great influences even in the 21st century. One of the most important revelations in *The Devil's Backbone* is this, the ghosts are friendly, its the humans we have to look out for. The humans are the real monsters. After all, compare the amount of people you know in real life that have been harmed by a ghost, to the amount that have been harmed by another human being.

Antonio Trashorras gives his insight into how *The Devil's Backbone* came into being. "Guillermo and I have known each other for years now. We're united by common interests, which are mainly horror literature, science fiction cinema, comics. We share a bit of the same universe and this film is somehow the fortuitous result of the mix. On one hand, the mix of what I and David [Munoz] had written in a script called 'The Bomb' and on the other, another script that Guillermo del Toro had written in Mexico, with many things in common with ours, that was called *The Devil's Backbone*." This is why Guillermo believes in retrospect it was for the best that he set aside his work on *The Devil's Backbone* script to work on *Cronos* instead.

Eduardo Noriega gives an insight into the mind of his character. "Jacinto is a very ambitious person...but life hasn't helped. He had a very tough childhood and most importantly, he suffers from a total lack of affection and tenderness. It's crucial for me, when I'm preparing for a character, to usually do, amongst other things, an outline of my character, to prepare a vision of its evolution." Guillermo notes that 'the character was originally conceived stronger, more brutal, like a beast. Eduardo added a higher intelligence and a much darker pathology. The beauty of the character is from the outside he has to be as perfect as possible but inside he had to be a moral ruin."

Noreiga further expands. "Guillermo and I knew for a fact we had to give him a human touch. We had to find his sensitivity or his weaknesses. He has this armour. He has a well-built character for the outside world. But there are some concrete moments where we witness his pain or what he feels." This is true, we detest Jacinto's actions, but we can see where they come from, he will do anything to satisfy his misplaced craving to belong at any cost, to burn out the shame he feels at his lonely youth. I also see him as being possessed by the orphanage, he was there an inmate, now he works there as an adult, a prisoner of economic circumstance and the war that approaches. He is as much a ghost as Santi, cursed to haunt a place he loathes. He is in as much of all limbo as the foetuses that float eternally in Dr Casares' jars. He hates himself far more than anyone will lever hate him.

Carmen has a great passion for life but is held back by her amputation. Guillermo says of her. "Marisa, her characters are full of life, they are very strong. I was keen to see the beauty of a wild animal with a broken leg. To watch this grand woman who is grounded by a metal leg." Marisa Paredes says Guillermo "wrote probably the most complete biography of a character that I ever got to read. The perfume she would wear, the books she would read and of course he gave me the history of Carmen...up to the moment when the film begins."

Fedricco Luppi describes his character. "I've always done characters that are a bit rough, terrible...Here was a type of individual hiding behind his veil of unreturned love. More than an unreturned love, it's a hidden love, that he's able to express in a manly fashion, always loving in the shade, reciting and learning poems. He's an incurable romantic which in a way generates a very lively attitude. There is a scene where they are in the village when some prisoners are going to get shot, during the war, where tremendous fear and terror radiates. He almost can't control himself. In a way, it marks the turning point for the character from here onwards. He promises to himself that he'll never abandon the boys." As we see, he doesn't break his word, he fails at everything else, but this promise he will not break, and as a result his sad spirit will join Santi's for eternity.

Guillermo wanted to avoid patronising the children in the film and avoiding the clichéd way children are usually shot in film, part of his personal search for the truth. He was inspired by a series of comic book stories, "'Paracuellos', Jimenez's little stories. When writing one of the first versions of the script, we carefully read Paracuellos," The casting of the children was done with this in mind.

Guillermo had strong ideas for the ghost. "What happens is with the phantom. I can do certain images that I can't do with others. This film has for example certain images which I found to be very poetic. They can only exist in art cinema or in fantasy cinema which basically allows for the rules to be broken."

Marisa observes something that will become even more apparent in future films. "He's capable of creating an absolutely magical and wonderful world, he's a very bright guy. He has in fact, a very personal touch. He mixes terror, almost science fiction, with very special attention to characters." This is nothing new to Guillermo veteran Luppi. "He trusts a lot and I found that interesting. He's not worried about giving exactly what the public wants, but neither does he want to disappoint them."

Guillermo understands the significance of *The Devil's Backbone* in his own body of work. "For me it's my first film. I think it's the first time I feel this happy upon finishing a film." But thankfully not the last time.

To understand the significance of *The Devil's Backbone*, we have to bear in mind it's place in the del Toro canon, it follows *Mimic*, a film where Guillermo did not have the proper degree of control, so *The Devil's Backbone* came to him like a miracle, and was a chance to regain his love for the fantastic. It is the foundation for the films that would follow. Guillermo was to construct *The Devil's Backbone* with a rhyming structure , elements within the film mirror each other. It opens as it closes with a similar narration. The foetus in the jar echoes the water in the pool. The good characters names start with 'C', those of the bad characters begin with 'J'. Jacinto is a possible future for Jaime, his dark mirror image. This repetition is a very deliberately constructed part of the structure of *The Devil's Backbone*, and the deeper we dig, the more of it we unearth.

But the mirroring of elements does not confine itself merely to *The Devil's Backbone*. *The Devil's Backbone* and *Pan's Labyrinth* are constructed to rhyme with each other. Guillermo says, "the opening and closing narration. The arrival of a kid at a building that is going to hold a magical event. The explanation of the dark side of the building. Moving the gothic tradition into an insane place."

Guillermo was inspired by a gothic novel called *The Castle of Otranto* by Horace Walpole. "The terrible secret from the past haunting the hero. The hidden treasure....Beyond everyday life lurks a

A kiss before betrayal

terrible secret, a terrible existence.'

But, *The Devil's Backbone* is also a highly, even bravely personal film for Guillermo. He sees it as a rite of passage movie, and he drew from his own experiences at Jesuit school, which he describes "as close as I can imagine to going to prison. One day, given the right elements, I would be killed." One can easily see that Guillermo is coming to terms with his own childhood fears and nightmares in *The Devil's Backbone*. Our demons cannot be exorcised unless they are made flesh. Dark matter manifests itself as monsters.

The bomb – the reminder of the unavenged crime

A good example of Guillermo's Mexican culture in his filmmaking, is rather than having endless reams of exposition, he would rather tell the story through action, show rather than tell. He knows it is guilt that drives Jaime to be a bully, it is not cut and dry as it might be in western film. Jacinto too, hates himself above all others, he is in enormous pain, as so many people are inside, poisoning them, unable to express it. His behaviour stems from trying to release the horrible feeling within, wheras someone else might have harnessed these feelings for good, with him it is for evil.

The young Guillermo, like so many other children, if they were listened to, saw monsters in his bedroom. "The loneliest time was at night. Night is where creatures emerge from inside you. Goya said-'the sleep of reason produces monsters'. War is the absolute lack of reason and produces monsters." The long corridors in the film are also autobiographical, a childhood memory of Guillermo's grandmother's house.

He sees the gothic building as a character too. The gothic building represents spiritual architecture, its pillars pointing to heaven. In *The Castle of Otranto*, one of the inspirations for *The Devil's Backbone*, the well is the centre of the building's subconscious, it's id, a function fulfilled by the amniotic pool in *The Devil's Backbone*. Guillermo also sees the pool as a symbol the audience can bring their own interpretation too, not like in Hollywood when meaning, if there is any, is often carved in stone.

Guillermo sees the kitchen in the orphanage as having fairy tale elements that will be so prevalent in *Pan's Labyrinth* 'an ogre's kitchen' complete with oversized butcher's knives. The bomb too is a character, serving as both reminder and warning, a device taken from *The Castle of Otranto*. "The iron mother, watching over the kids symbolises war, past crime...impending doom.'

The books Guillermo loved as a child all play their part, *The Monk* by Mathew G. Lewis. *Wuthering Heights*, The works of Dickens, who revealed that childhood is not benign. A view Guillermo unfortunately shares, stating that he has spent his adulthood recuperating from his childhood where he was deeply unhappy.

When Santi initially says 'many of you will die', it may be perceived as a threat, but as the story unfolded, we realise it is a warning. Santi is being concerned. The idea of the ghost as enemy is defused. The monsters are friendly. It is the humans who are truly dangerous. This is the opposite to the childish point of view of so many Hollywood films, rather it is the child's point of view. The one that rarely gets listened to. This is more like real life, and just like in real life, not every

Mysterious Warning by Eliza Parsons (1796). These were once thought to be figment of Austen's imagination but research by the likes of Montague Summers proved they were real.

Another influential Gothic novel was Matthew Gregory Lewis's *The Monk* (1796). While it contains elements, it shocked many readers, with its wicked (and doomed) title character, ghastly ghostly nuns and vile Inquisitors (can there be any other kind?). It was to be an influence upon Anne Radcliffe's final novel, *The Italian* (1797) which features the Inquisition.

The Romantic poets like Coleridge (with *The Rime of the Ancient Mariner*, inspiration for the Iron Maiden song of the same title), and Keats (with *La Belle Dame sans Mercy*), contributed to the Gothic. But it was the poetry, writing, life, and love-life), of Lord Bryon (memorably described by his spurned lover, Lady Caroline Lamb (who was presumably qualified to know!) as being 'mad, bad, and dangerous to know'.

Byron was a great inspiration for the Gothic, giving it the archetypal Byronic hero (Byron's exploits in Greece, prove that he was no coward, a fighter as well as lover, prepared to walk it like he wrote it). Byron features, disguised by the pseudonym 'Lord Ruthven' in Lady Caroline's Gothic novel, *Glenarvon* (1819). Byron also hosted the famous macabre story writing competition that included himself, Mary Shelly, John Polidori and Percy Bysshe Shelley, at the Villa Diodati on the Lake Geneva shoreline in Switzerland in the summer of 1816.

This notorious session (portrayed in Ken Russell's fine film *Gothic* (1986)), produced Polidori's *The Vampyre* (1819) and Mary Shelley's *Frankenstein* (1818). *The Vampyre* features the Lord Byron-inspired 'Lord Ruthven', and would go on to be incredibly influential, when we take into account it's influence on Bram Stoker's *Dracula*, the extent of it's influence on both the Gothic and popular culture is truly amazing.

Byron was inspired to suggest the competition by some ghost stories he was reading aloud to his friends. The influence of laudanum and Black Drop (a medicinal compound dispensed by Polidori that contained opium) also had an influence. Mary Shelly was influenced by many things in the creation of *Frankenstein*, including the Prometheus myth, and more sadly, the loss of her baby.

Moreover, Mary had visited an area with many gothic castles, one in particular caught her fertile imagination. That was Castle Frankenstein. Its name means 'Castle of the Franks. The castle also had a legend. A necromancer and alchemist called Johann Konrad Dippel was born in the castle in 1673, and signed himself 'Frankensteiner'. There was a belief in scientific circles that the electricity could be the key to restoring life to dead tissue, 'vitalism' as this process was sometimes called. Mary had herself visited a show called Phantasmagoria', a wild display of various electrical effects which left a vivid impression. Alchemy plays a part in her creation of the character of Victor Frankenstein, he is familiar with the works of Paraselsus and Albertus Magnus, from there he moves on to more scientific methods, he is the modern Prometheus after all. Automata were a popular curiosity in Mary's time, so no doubt, a lady like her, so interested in the latest developments was aware of them.

Her description of Frankenstein's creation is worth repeating, not only is it a masterful piece of writing, but it shows how often filmmakers have gotten Mary's creation wrong.

"His limbs were in proportion, and I had selected his features as beautiful. Beautiful-Great God! His yellow skin scarcely covered the work of muscles and arteries beneath; his hair was of a lustrous black, and flowing; his teeth of a pearly whiteness; but these luxuriances only formed a more horrid contrast with his watery eyes, that seemed almost of the same colour as the dun white sockets in which they were set..."

It is not the appearance of Frankenstein's creation that makes him a monster (human monsters all too often are considered 'beautiful' whatever that overused word really means), rather it is what lies beneath, what can be seen through it's eyes, the windows to the soul' Mary was

also inspired by her visit to Mont Blanc, but *Frankenstein* is more than the sum of it's author's experiences, of the books she read, of the things she had observed.

Frankenstein is a book that works on a multitude of levels, not least of which was fear. at the speed the world was changing, and the fear of science overriding religion, and the fear of man's nature, the question it asks could well be, "what makes a man a man?". It has occupied thinkers and philosophers , in universities and public houses, for centuries, and we are no nearer an answer now than Mary was that fateful night she put pen to paper. Mary did what all good artists do, she poured her essence, her life, her experiences into her story, and through some bibliographic alchemy created a work that still continues to be read and inspire to this very day. That is the key to good writing, put your heart into your work.

Also worth mentioning as a late example of the traditional Gothic novel is *Melmoth the Wanderer* (1820) by Irish writer Charles Robert Maturin.

In the Victorian era, the Gothic novel continued to mutate and survive, itself vampirically absorbing the influences of the world it existed in (but not necessarily of). One example of this was the 'Penny Dreadfuls' such as *Varney the Vampire*.

In America, Edgar Allan Poe's *The Fall of the House of Usher* (1839), is a fine example of this, Poe's work was later further popularised by a series of films starring Vincent Price. Ambrose Bierce produced some fine stories like *The Incident at Owl's Creek*, his satirical *Devil's Dictionary* is also well worth a look (a more recent edition includes some fine illustrations by Ralph Steadman, famous for both his satirical cartoons and his imaginative illustrations for the works of the much-missed Hunter S. Thompson).

Bierce himself was very much the Byronic hero. He had twelve siblings, all of whose first names started with the letter 'a' (perhaps his father wanted his children to be first on every list and role call. Bierce fought in the American Civil War, rescuing a battled wounded comrade, while later in the war being wounded himself after a career of great distinction. After a life full of many adventures and misadventures, Bierce found himself in Mexico during the Revolution. He joined up with Pancho Villa as an observer (this was a man in his 70s, that we should have his energy and lust for life at that age!). He subsequently disappeared. This is still a great mystery, which is as it should be. We can be sure, however, that the great man did not want to die in ill-health in bed (the Vikings feared this too). His letters home were very up-tempo and give the impression he didn't expect to come home. He wrote: "To be a Gringo in Mexico-ah, that is euthanasia."

In England Emily Bronte's *Wuthering Heights* (1847) transported the Gothic tale to the Yorkshire Moors, complete with spectral apparitions and the Byronic Heathcliffe. Her sister Charlotte's *Jane Eyre*(1847) also mines a similar vein. Both books, I feel, represent the terrible domestic prison so many unfortunate women found themselves trapped in.

Irish writer Sheridan le Fanu's *Uncle Silas* (1864) is influenced by both Radcliffe's *Udolpho* and Walpole's *Otranto*. Even more significantly, his short story collection *In a Glass Darkly* (1872) included the highly influential vampire story *Carmilla*, which in turn was an influence on Bram Stoker.

Le Fanu. Maturin, and Stoker make up a sub-genre known as Irish Gothic inspired by the Irish landscape (which would be a strong influence on William Hope Hodgson's *House On The Borderland*), colonial oppression, Celtic myths, and the fine tradition of Irish ghost stories. Le Fanu in particular was inspired by (and peacefully campaigned against)the Colonial Government's indifference to the terrible Irish famine of 1845-47, commonly known as The Great Famine, in which 750,000 Irish people (British citizens) died, with at least an equal number having to emigrate in the hope of surviving. The population of Ireland declined from 8 to 6.5 million, but that statistic cannot hope to give an indication of the level of suffering and misery, it left a huge scar on the Irish psyche and is still vividly remembered to this day.

Charles Dickens was influenced by the Gothic novels he had read in his youth. He incorporated the darkness and

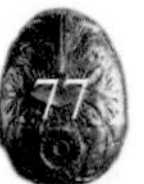

atmosphere of the Gothic novel into his own books, especially in his final unfinished novel *The Mystery of Edwin Drood* (1870). (Interestingly, in January of 1914, a mock trial was held in London for the murder of Edwin Drood. This light-hearted farce was constructed by many members of the literary establishment and the foreman of the jury was none other than George Bernard Shaw).

The 2005 *Doctor Who* episode *The Unquiet Dead* featured Simon Callow as Charles Dickens in the period during the writing of Edwin Drood (Callow puts in a fine performance as Oliver Haddo, a professor possessed by the spirit of Aleister Crowley in Julian Doyle and Bruce Dickinson's entertaining romp *The Chemical Wedding* (2008). Bruce is the lead singer of British heavy metal legends Iron Maiden. Julian has directed videos for Iron Maiden, and has worked extensively with Terry Jones (on his excellent thought-provoking *Medieval Lives*) and also with Terry Gilliam. Most interesting of all in the light of the influence of the Spanish Civil War on two of Guillermo's films, Julian's late father Bob was the last surviving Irish member of the International Brigades that fought against Franco in the Spanish Civil War, I can heartily recommend Bob's autobiography *Brigadista*, not only as an insight into that war, but also as an insight into the Ireland and Britain of the time that we don't learn about at school, inspirational tales of courage not being high on the priority list of the school curriculum. It is also a very uplifting read. Bob's courage in the small everyday wars people usually ignore is most impressive, His rescuing of unfortunate immigrants from harm in the London of the 1950s for instance.

It's also interesting to note this wasn't the first international brigade with a Spanish connection. A group of Irish volunteers, the San Patricios fought for Mexico against America in the Mexican war of the 1840s. They were executed by the Americans following the war's end). Edwin Drood gave a name to a fictional band in *Jonathan Creek*. But most significantly it provided the inspiration for Dan Simmons's novel *Drood* (2009), which has been optioned by Guillermo to direct. It's a perfect project marrying his love of the Gothic with his fascination for Charles Dickens. *Drood* covers the events of the last five years of Dickens's life and the writing of and inspirations for his final novel. The tale is told from the point of view of Dickens's friend and fellow author, Wilkie Collins.

The Victorian era was ripe for the Gothic. It was an extremely morbid and unsettling time. Queen Victorian herself wore the black of mourning for her husband until her own death. Technology and the industrial revolution moved forward in leaps and bound, making a few wealthy while the majority of people lived lives of hard labour and low mortality. Women were little more than the property of their husband, possessing no vote and few rights. (It makes me laugh when people refer to 'the good old days', what were the bad ones like then?). England expanded her colonial domination of the large areas of the world, bringing great wealth to a few and untold misery to millions. All potent fuel to fire a writer's imagination. This led to a revival of the Gothic which produced some of literature's best known works, such as Robert Louis Stevenson's *Strange Case of Dr Jekyll and Mr Hyde* (1886), Oscar Wilde's *The Picture of Dorian Gary* (1891), Henry James' *Turn of the Screw* (1898), and the tales of Arthur Machen. The work of Arthur Conan Doyle also has something of a Gothic atmosphere.

Bram Stoker's *Dracula* is so influential, so adapted, and even parodied at this stage that people often forget about the source book itself. Stoker was inspired both by Irish stories he heard from his grandmother as a child, and European history and mythology (the legendary Vlad the Impaler figures large, as does the legacy of Elisabeth Bathory, herself quite an influence, on cinema, literature and music, with even a highly influential band naming itself after her). Stoker was married to the beautiful Florence Balcombe (who once had Oscar Wilde as a suitor). Stoker was

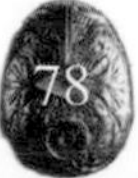

the famous actor Henry Irving's personal manager, and may have based some aspects of *Dracula*'s character on him.

Stoker produced several novels including the hallucinogenic *Lair of the White Worm* (made into a mad romp of a film starring the lovely Amanda Donohue in an unforgettable performance, and directed by Ken Russell in 1988). Stoker may have also been a member of the Hermetic Order of the Golden Dawn, which at various stages featured everyone from Irish poet W.B Yeats to English occultist, poet, writer and mountain climber Aleister Crowley.

In the late 19th and early 20th century, several writers would follow the Gothic tradition, Including notably M.R James, Hugh Walpole, Algernon Blackwood, and William Hope Hodgson. Mention must also be made of the work of Daphne du Maurier, especially in such works as *Jamaica Inn* (1936). I must make special mention of William Hope Hodgson, in particular his magnum opus *The House on the Borderland*. Hodgson was a fascinating character, who ran away to sea at the age of 13. Bullied by the older sailors at sea, he became a body builder to protect himself and was heralded as one of Britain's most powerful men. He won the Royal Humane Society medal for heroism after he saved the life of a fellow sailor who had fallen overboard into shark-infested waters. In 1902, he appeared on stage to apply the restraints to Harry Houdini.

Suffering from financial problems, and inspired by HG Wells, Poe, Jules Verne and Arthur Conan Doyle, he turned to writing to see if he could improve matters. His short satirical story *Date 1965: Modern Warfare* suggested future wars should be carried out by caged combatants. He wrote several stories cited by Guillermo as an influence that featured a character called Carnacki, such as *The Gateway of the Monster*.

It is his 1909 novel *House on the Borderland* that he is most remembered for (it would make a fine film!). It's dark brooding otherworldly atmosphere is heavily inspired by the time spent by Hodgson in Ireland, in particular the area of dark otherworldly beauty known as the Burren in County Clare, a limestone desert, full of ancient Celtic monuments and unusual plants. It has to be seen to be believed. Hodgson's tale also invokes the Celtic belief in an otherworld so apparent in *Pan's Labyrinth* (there is a big connection between Ireland and Spain in the Celtic period). I will say no more of *The House on the Borderland* save that I recommend it highly. Hodgson was a brave man, and volunteered to fight for Britain in World War One, and was tragically killed by an artillery shell at Ypres in April of 1918.

The influence of the Gothic is still going strong today. Witness the many entertaining films that Hammer Films produced in their late fifties to sixties heyday, Dracula, Frankenstein, Sherlock Holmes, the Werewolf, and many more were interpreted by Hammer (many by Guillermo influence Terence Fisher). Hammer's films such as the classic *Plague of the Zombies* (1966), *Rasputin the Mad Monk* (again 1966), and *The Reptile* (you guessed it-1966. Must have been something in the water that year!) are steeped in Gothic atmosphere, these dark fairy tales are modern classics and are well worth seeking out.

The Gothic genre has also given its name to an entire genre of music, and it would be fair to say, in this dark period of the 21st century, the Gothic is more relevant than ever, as both an escapism and an interpretation.

Other well-known Gothic novels include *The Mysteries of Udolpho* (1794) by Ann Radcliffe, *The Monk* (1796) by Matthew G. Lewis, *Frankenstein* (1818) by Mary Wollstonecraft Shelley, and *Melmouth the Wanderer* (1820) by the Irish novelist Charles Maturin. In Northanger Abbey (1818), Jane Austen satirised Gothic novels and their vivid impression on readers. The Gothic novel also influenced such American writers as Nathaniel Hawthorne and Edgar Allan Poe.

Chapter Four
Blade II

PARIZCKA BLOOD BANK. PRAGUE. CZECH REPUBLIC.

A man with a prominent scar bisecting his chin enters a blood bank. It's not the most sanitary place to give blood, cats roam freely everywhere, the crackle of flies being electrocuted fills the air like dark music. He waits beside a man with a jar, who tells him excitedly. "They pay cash here and there's no limit to how many times you give...they even buy it in the jar." (We are in the same 'vampire as junkie' vein as Cronos here).

A stern woman approaches the scarred man. "Jared Nomak? We're ready for you." Nomak (Luke Goss) follows the woman deep into the bowels of the dank building. There is a vampire glyph on the wall, this is obviously a blood bank in the deeper sense of the word. This is a dark underworld, a twilight place where the normal rules of society do not apply. She hits him with what appears like a standard barrage of questions, but it has the oppressive atmosphere of a prisoner being taken for execution, what she naively believes to be a sheep to the slaughter.

"In the past twelve months have you gotten a tattoo, or undergone any ear, skin or body piercings?" "No." "Where did you get that scar on chin?" "Childhood accident." "You say you don't have any immediate next of kin, is that right?" "Not that I'm in contact with." "Nobody to call in case of an emergency?" "No one." "No family?" "I told you, no. Are you telling me I can't be a donor?" "It depends. We came up with some unusual results on your blood test." "What? How unusual?" She punches a code into a computer terminal. "Let me explain. Your blood has a very rare phenotype, one we haven't encountered before." Doors bolt shut behind him, he's like a trapped animal. They sit Nomak on a sinister chair. A technician tells him. "This is a good news-bad news scenario, Jared. Good news for us for us..." He pulls on a glove whose fingers terminate into evil needles connected with tubes for draining blood. "...bad news for you."

Nomak appears to be crying as the technician activates a pump to collect his blood. Suddenly he starts laughing, his face distorting. He leaps out of the chair with a feral roar, and bites the woman in a explosion of blood. A guard puts three shots into Nomak's back to no effect. Nomak kills the guard and grabs the doctor. Looking up at a close circuit TV camera, like a performer on stage, Nomak astonishingly announces, with massive contempt. "Vampires. I hate vampires." Something comes out of his mouth, like a swarm of tentacles, and the screen goes blank. We're only minutes into the film and already Guillermo has set us up for what we expect from the first *Blade* and turned everything on its head. If Nomak isn't a vampire...what is he? From the first scene Guillermo has announced that this is *Blade* in his own unique style.

As the credits role, Blade (Wesley Snipes) narrates his own back story, quickly running over the events that transpired in Stephen Norrington's fine *Blade*. "Forget what you think you know, vampires exist. My name is Blade. I was born half human, half vampire. They call me The Daywalker. I have all their strengths, none of their weaknesses, except for 'the thirst'. 20 years ago I met a man that changed that. Whistler (Kris Kristofferson, Whistler's first name is Abraham in honour of Bram Stoker's vampire hunter Van Helsing). He taught ne how to hold the thirst at bay. Taught me the rules. Gave me the weapons to hunt with, silver, garlic, sunlight. Two years ago he was attacked. They took him and turned him into the thing I hate most. I should have finished him off. Now I'm hunting him. And nothing will stand in my way."

Blade has now reached Prague in his hunt for Whistler, he cuts down a group of vampires with silver bullets, they disintegrate in firestorm of cinders and sparks (this is the disintegration you see in Terrance Fisher's *Dracula* films taken to a higher technological level). Two vampires make it to their motorbikes and try to escape. One of them, wearing a feather boa, is Rush (Santiago Segura -star of Alex de la Inglesia's fine *Day of the Beast/El Día de la Bestia*-1995). Blade garrottes one of the vampires, taking control of his bike, and captures Rush, who pleads ignorance of Whistler's location. Blade tells him laconically. "Take me to him and I'll consider you a loose end." Applying the wheel of the bike to Rush's head improves the vampires memory, "He shot himself. Then he turned. We just kept him alive."

Rush brings Blade to where Whistler is been held (Not obvious in the finished film, but this is the Tasty Moo Cow company, a front for vampires to transport blood. In *Hellboy II*, the front for the Troll Market is the Happy Cow meat packing plant). Whistler's guards while their boredom by playing cards and snorting cocaine laced with blood (yet more imagery of vampires as junkies). They hear someone at the door. "It's me, Rush, let me in." Blade shoots a guard through the door and using Rush as a shield, burst in. The guards shoot Rush. "It's not silver but it hurts like hell." As Blade cuts a swathe through the guards, he promises Rush, 'catch you later.".

He finds Whistler in suspended animation in a tank of blood. Blade announces grimly. "Old man, look at what they've done to you." Whistler is now a vampire. Blade opens the tank and Whistler falls out, suspended in cruciform pose by a series of tubes. Blade draws his katana sword to slay Whistler, but his old friend opens his eyes and he cannot kill him. "Let's go home."

Back at Blade's headquarters, we see that he has a new weaponsmith, Scud (Norman Reedus, who previously played a part in Mimic), who tells Blade. "I got a bad feeling about this, B. Listen to his breathing. He's already dying. He's in pain. Why don't you put him out of his misery?" Blade is determined to give Whistler the same chance he gave Blade 20 years ago. "They had him on stasis in a halfway house. I'm giving him an accelerated retro-viral detox, like a heroin addict. Make him go cold turkey in one night." He tells Scud to get out, this is between mentor and pupil. "If there's anything left of you in there, Whistler, listen up. In the morning those blinds are going to open, whether you're cured or not." Blade remember the last words the infected Whistler spoke to him two years before. "Listen, Blade, you're going to have to finish me off." "No." "Give me that damn gun...now walk away."

At Dawn, Blade opens the blinds as promised, Whistler is human again, he asks Blade. "How'd you find me? I started out in Moscow, then Romania. They kept moving you around." "How long was I gone?" "Too long." "They tortured me almost to death. And then they let me heal in a vat of blood so they could get at it again."

Whistler doesn't hit it off with Scud, while they argue, a pair vampires, one male, one female, trigger the motion sensors that guard Blade's headquarters, and then destroying the security cameras with magnesium flares. The vampires, dressed in all-over ninja outfits to protect them from daylight, they knock out Whistler, and Scud surrenders.

Blade throws on heavy guard light. The vampires' night-sights adjust to compensate (a nice design straight from the pages of Guillermo's famous notebooks). There is a dramatic swordfight between Blade and the vampires, culminating in Blade and the female vampire having each other at sword point. The male vampire tells the female vampire. "Put your sword away." Then he tells Blade. "Your people shot first. We are here to deliver a message. We represent the ruling body of the Vampire Nation. They're offering a truce. They want to meet with you." He gives Blade a cylinder, who gets Scud to turn the lights off, telling him to take off his mask. The male vampire introduces himself and his companion. "My name is Asad (Danny John-Jules). This is Nyssa (Leonor Valera)." It's obvious there's an immediate connection between Blade and Nyssa. Asad tells Blade intriguingly. "You have been our most feared enemy. But now there's something else loose on the streets. Something worse than you."

On the helicopter journey to the vampires' lair, Nyssa is amused. Scud asks her what's so funny, she replies. "They tell stories about Blade as the Bogeyman. Frankly I'm disappointed...he agreed to come along so easily." Scud gets Blade to reveal what is under his coat, enough semtex to level a city block. Scud asks Nyssa if she's still disappointed, she's now clearly impressed.

At the vampires fortress they observe that it's heavily guarded by the vampire's well armed human familiars, the spots from their weapons' laser sights dancing over the new arrivals.

Nyssa uses the cylinder Asad presented to Blade to open the huge door to an inner chamber (actually an ancient temple the vampire fortress is built around). "The true power of the Vampire Nation lies here. Blade introduced to an incredibly ancient vampire, Overlord Eli Damaskinos (Thomas Kretschmann) (At one point Damaskinos had long flowing locks, this idea was sensibly dropped). He tells Blade. "Welcome Daywalker. It has been said, 'be proud of your enemy' and enjoy his big success', in that regard, I should thank you." "For what?" Damaskinos's aide, Karel Kounen (Karel Roden), answers him. "For eliminating Deacon Frost..."

Blade sees the vampire brand on Kounen's hand. "You're human." "Barely, I'm a lawyer' (an additional bit of witty dialogue from Guillermo). Damaskinos describes vampirism as a virus that creates new parasitic organs in the human body." Kounen explains. "Unfortunately, viruses evolve too. We've encountered a new one. We dubbed it the Reaper Strain, and like any good pathogen, it appears to have found a carrier." He puts on a disc of Nomak in action at the blood bank.

"There, Jared Nomak." Damaskinos continues." Born a vampire, but an anomaly like you. Unlike the rest of us, however, he feeds on not just humans, but vampires as well." "Looks like he was doing me a favour." Nyssa puts it differently. "You're missing the point. Their vampire victims don't die, they turn. They become carriers." Assad adds. "You've got to understand. These things are like crack addicts. They need to feed daily. Nomak's been up for 72 hours. By our estimates, there are already a dozen Reapers. There'll be hundreds before the week is out. Thousands within a matter of months. Do the math." Blade is astonished. "Wait. Let me get this right. You want me to hunt them...for you?" Damaskinos puts it bluntly. "When they are finished with us, who do you think they'll turn on next? Your precious humans. Not one of them will be left."

Koenen tells Blade they've been training a small tactical unit called the Blood Pack, they want Blade to lead them, even though Nyssa reveals they've been training to hunt Blade.

Back at his headquarters, Blade explains to Whistler that he's decided to play along for now. "They'll take us in deeper than we've ever been. Get a chance to see how their world really ticks." Whistler isn't impressed, and Scud voices his concerns about Whistler to Blade. "Nobody goes cold turkey from the thirst in just one night."

As night falls over Prague, Nomak watches a girl buy drugs, when she leaves he motions the dealer into an alleyway. "Looking to get hooked up?" "Maybe, what do you have?" "No problem. Horse, Hawaiian ice, whatever you need." "Whatever I need. I like that. What if I need you?" Nomak attacks the dealer, joined by the other Reapers.

In his headquarters, Blade injects himself with the serum for the thirst. The compassion is clear, both Nomak and Blade are slaves in their own way.

Assad introduces Blade to the Blood Pack. There is a huge vampire with facial tattoos ironically called Lighthammer, and his flame-haired girlfriend Verlaine (Marit Velle Kile), a long-haired Irish vampire amusingly called Priest (Tony Curran). An oriental vampire called Snowman (Donnie Yen, also a fight choreographer on Blade II), the chainmail wearing Chupa (Matt Schulze), and Reinhardt (Ron Perlman). Reinhardt asks Blade nastily, "can you blush?" He replies. "Oh, I get it. I see now. You've been training for two years to take me out, and now, here I am, Ohh, so exciting, isn't it?"

Blade starts taunting Reinhardt, who's nowhere near as fast as Blade, and puts an explosive device on the vampire's head. "Silver nitrate, rigged to go off if anybody tampers with it. I'll have the detonator with me...if you so much as look at me wrong." Blade has established he's in charge. "From now on, we work as a unit." Nyssa is impressed, Blade tells her. "You want to catch the hunter? You start with the prey. We'll target all the night places where vampires congregate. Blood banks, safe houses, the bigger, the better. So what's first?" "The House of Pain."

Later, outside of what looks like a derelict building, Blade asks Nyssa. "Where's the entrance? I don't see any signs, no vampire glyphs." "No, because of you, we've had to rethink our habits, tighten our security." She hands him infra-red binoculars and then he can see the glyph. The fact that she's willing to reveal this shows some feelings towards him are developing and making her careless, because Blade will surely use this information in the future.

Whistler is distributing Blade's special vampire killing weapons to the Blood Pack. ".38, .45 and 9mm calibre. All with foil capsules at the tip, filled with silver nitrate and garlic extract. This hyper-velocity stake gun spits out a silver stake at 6,000 feet per second. Since you suckers don't like sunlight, we've modified the gun's entry light with a UV filter. Pop it open- instant UV light."

Scud shows Blade a new concealed weapon. "It's got a pneumatic syringe delivery system. The vials are filled with an anti-coagulant called EDTA. One punch with this, you'll blow your target up like a balloon. The cartridge ejects. Automatic reload." "Nice."

Blade (Wesley Snipes), cooler than Van Helsing in Blade II

Whistler wants to come with them, but they won't let him. Blade tells him to set up a loo-out post on a nearby roof. "Cover our backs." "So the Blood Pack's calling the shots now?" Reinhardt threatens. "Better curb that dog of yours or we'll do it for you." In answer Blade reminds him of the explosive.

Like a modern-day Wild Bunch, Blade and the Blood Pack enter the House of Pain. In Whistler's gunsights, only Blade appears warm. Nyssa warns Blade. "You're about to enter our world. You will see things. Feeding. Remember why you're here." "I haven't forgotten." Priest asks what are they looking for, Reinhardt tells him, "anything that looks suspicious." Everything in the House of Pain looks suspicious, as Blade wryly comments, "you got to be kidding me."

The Vampires are feeding and indulging in *Hellraiser*-style body modifications. There's an amusing moment where Blade spots Rush, as he puts cameras in place so Scud can monitor the action. Blade tells Scud. "The whole place is a safe house. The windows are painted black, one access door, 200, 300 suckheads here." Priest suggests killing all the revellers, 'just to make sure." (In a deleted scene, he also expresses a wish to make 'Reaper tartare'). Reinhardt is tempted to kill Blade. "God, it would be so easy." But Blade already has the laser sight of his gun on Reinhardt.

Beneath the floor of the nightclub, in the sewers, Nomak and the Reapers wait. Nomak knows Blade is there. Outside a group of Reapers target Scud, while the rest covertly enter the House of pain to feed. Nyssa is seized

by Nomak. Blade comes upon them. Nomak tried to make a deal with Blade. "Daywalker. What am I to you? Is the enemy of my enemy my friend...or my enemy?" Nyssa uses the distraction to escape and Blade shoots Nomak at point blank range in the head.

Meanwhile, there are Reapers on the dance floor...and they want to kill a lot more than the groove. Priest is attacked.

Incredibly, Nomak has survived a point-blank headshot. Blade realises daylight is his only ally here. Lighthammer also battles a Reaper in the nightclubs foul kitchen.

The Blood Pack kill vampires left and right as they fire on the Reapers. Silver has no effect on this new breed, but the same cannot be said for the vampire bystanders, who are collateral damage to their own kind.

Snowman pins a Reaper with his sword, it just scuttles away from the blade like a huge spider. (Blade II's 'The Thing'-moment).

Priest puts up a good fight but he's bitten, the creatures mouth opening like an insect's to reveal it's feeding apparatus (the original idea, again, is straight out of Guillermo's notebook) while Reinhardt crucifies a Reaper with the silver stake gun.

Lighthammer's Reaper is on the floor, and he's not impressed. "You ugly little beast." It leaps up, clamping its nails into his back like a vice, its huge mouth opening to bite. Bellows like sacs appear in the Reapers back as he begins to draw out Lighthammer's blood. He manages to fight off the Reaper. Verlaine comes to his assistance. He denies the creature bit him.

Scud uses UV light to destroy the Reapers. He goes on the radio to the Blade and the Blood Pack. "Listen to me, if you're under attack, use your UV lights." Reinhardt experiments with UV light on his captured Reaper, and sure enough the creature spectacularly explodes.

As daylight dawns, the Blood Pack must withdraw, leaving Blade alone to confront Nomak on a walkway. Nomak again tries to make a deal with Blade. "You want me so bad, Blade? Here I am. Why kill me? You and I, have the same enemy. We want the same thing." Blade isn't interested in talk. They fight, Blade injects Nomak with Scud's new weapon. Nomak's face bubbles and distorts, then he laughs. He's survived and launches himself at Blade, plunging them both over the edge of the walkway. On the ground, he and Blade fight, until the rising sun drives Nomak back to his underground lair. Leaving Blade alone in the devastated nightclub.

Later Blade asks Nyssa why she didn't tell him the Reapers were immune to silver and garlic. "I didn't know. "If you did, would you have told me?" "I think you know the truth when you hear it." "Then why didn't he kill you?" But before he can pursue this line of enquiry, they're interrupted by Priest's screams as he changes into a Reaper, he begs Chupa to kill him, but it's too late. Reinhardt lops off the top of Priest's skull (a nice homage to Romero's classic *Day of the Dead*), but to little effect. Blade shoots holes in the ceiling, thus destroying Priest by sunlight.

Whistler mocks the performance of the Blood Pack. They want to know why Whistler deserted his post. By way of answer, he takes them to a trapped Reaper he discovered while they were fighting in the House of Pain. "Saw it moving in the alley and followed it down, Found it here just liker this. I think they came through here. It was trying to crawl back in the culvert, caught his arm. Been gnawing at it like a coyote." Like all Guillermo's monsters, there is something sad about the fast-expiring creature, it didn't ask to be what it is. Blade descends into the culvert. He can hear (but not fear), the Reapers.

At Damaskinos's fortress, Kounen tells him. "They've made contact with the reapers." "Any casualties?" "One so far." "It was not Nyssa, I trust." "No. This is a dangerous game you're playing, Damaskinos, Blade is too volatile. You're not going to be able to keep manipulating him." "You worry too much. I've been informed by our friend on the inside that events are unfolding as scripted." "You've already lost one of your own. How many more are you willing to sacrifice?" "Everyone." "Even your own daughter." "yes, even her." Damaskinos descends, in the manner of the legendary Elizabeth Bathory into the pool of blood that keeps him alive. (It certainly doesn't keep him young looking. This scene was designed by Mark Mignola, marking the start of his professional association with Guillermo.

A rather good line was cut here, when Kounen asks Damaskinos is prepared to sacrifice his daughter Nyssa, Damaskino's indicated one of Guillermo's beloved jars and said 'A jar over there contains what was once my human heart, only a fool would appeal to it now).

Blade realises the Reaper Whistler found had been one of the guards at the blood bank. He realises what's killing him. "Time, His metabolism is burning too fast. They need fresh blood every couple of hours or they'll start feeding on themselves. Nomak's different, he's the carrier. It all started with him, it'll end with him."

Nyssa autopsies the creature. Scud reluctantly opens its retractable insectile jaws, its barbed tongue flexes. Nyssa comments. "Only the tongue caries the virus. It is injected through these barbs. It has bifurcated masseter muscles. Overdeveloped, allowing for a much stronger bite. The jaw structure remains the same but there's no mandible bone...Its fangs inject a neurotoxin...paralyses their victim while they feed." Scud can see only one way of destroying the Reapers. "Garlic don't work. Silver, that don't work. We got to go with the sunlight right." Nyssa understandably isn't keen. "That's deadly to us too, so let's see what else we can find."

She makes an incision on the Reaper's chest. "These things are as different from us as we are from you." She removes its ribcage. "The heart is encased in bone. Only the side is vulnerable." She realises the creature still has some vestigial life remaining, and cutting her finger, and letting the blood drip into it's chest cavity, the creature's organs start to respond, even though it's brain is dead, the body still tries to feed. Blade announces. "We got six hours before sunrise. Be ready by then." Asad asks. "What happens at sunrise?" "We hunt." "In broad daylight?" "Sunlight's the only edge we've got. They'll be more vulnerable then." "And so will we." "Lets be real about one thing. I don't expect everybody to make it back tomorrow. Remember to protect yourselves... at all times." (This is what Guillermo refers to as *Blade*'s Lee Marvin/*Dirty Dozen* moment. Guillermo has also bemoaned the fact that studios shy away from casting Lee Marvin types these days).

Outside, Scud is looking for phosphor rods, to see if he can make UV flash-grenades.

Nyssa asks Blade why he hates vampires so much. He tells her. "It's fate. It's in my blood." "It's in mine too. I'm a pure blood. I was born a vampire. You know the thirst better than any of us shooting that serum of yours. The only difference between us, is that I made peace with what I am a long time ago." She leaves Blade with food for thought, she knows when he kills vampires, he is trying to kill the part of himself he hates.

Whistler and Scud are attempting to make the UV grenades. Scud tells Whistler that Blade looks on him as a father-figure, and how he and Blade met up, when Blade saved him from vampires. The UV grenades work. "Alright. Papa's got a brand new bag."

As Blade and the Blood Pack tool up, Chupa asks how they are going to find the Reapers. Nyssa explains that they are going to use pheromones from the Reapers adrenal glands to attract them. Blade tell them to use their firearms to drive the Reapers to the UV bomb pack Scud has rigged up. Whistler notices Blade making sure Nyssa knows to take cover. Whistler doesn't like the growing affection between the two, telling Blade. "Looks to me like you're getting confused as to which side of the line you're standing on." "Those are real hollow words coming from a man who just spent two years running with the enemy." "What the hell is that supposed to mean?" "You know, Whistler, there's an old country and western saying, 'keep your friends close but keep your enemies closer'."

As the sun rises, Blade and the Blood Pack enter the sewers and split up. As soon as Blade is out of sight, Rheinhardt and Chupa attack Whistler, who activates the pheromone spray. Lighthammer turns into a Reaper and kills Snowman. Courageously, Verlaine sacrifices herself to kill Lighthammer. Chupa is killed, allowing Whistler to escape. Blade goes back for Nyssa, in time to witness

Asad's death. Blade sprinkles the rest of the pheromones on himself, detonating a UV grenade as a diversion, leads the surviving Reapers into a trap. He detonates the UV bomb pack, wiping out all the Reapers, save for Nomak, who gives Whistler a ring, telling him. "You will survive this only to tell Blade about this ring. About the truth." And he whispers something in his ear.

The original vampire hunter meets the new breed. Nomak reveals the truth to Whistler

Blade has gone back for the wounded Nyssa, giving her his blood to save her. He's watched by Nomak. Suddenly, Blade and Whistler are captured by a team led by Karl Kounen.

Blade wakes up to find that, along with Whistler and Scud, he's been held prisoner in the vampire's lair. Whistler tells Blade. "Someone's been keeping tabs on us from the inside...They've been lying to us from day one. The Reaper strain didn't evolve. It was designed. Nomak told me I saw him back in the sewers. He let me live." Damskinos interjects sarcastically. "Did he? How generous of him. I brought you here to see the fruits of our labour. For years I've struggled to rid our kind of any hereditary weaknesses."

He opens a tank containing jars of foetuses (Guillermo must have a factory to supply all the fake foetuses in his films). "And so, recombining DNA was simply the next logical step. Nomak was the first. A failure. But in time, there will be a new pure race, begotten from my own flesh, immune to silver, soon even to sunlight." Whistler interrupts him by throwing the ring that Nomak gave him back in the sewers. "I got a question for you, you lying son of a bitch. You want to explain how Nomak got a hold of this ring." Nyssa picks it up and the truth about her father dawns on her. Damaskinos replies arrogantly as he leaves. "I would have thought that was obvious at this point. I gave it to him, of course. A gift from father to son."

Rheinhardt is delighted, and electrocutes Blade, and clubs Whistler (never has a character of such advanced years endured so much punishment in a film, at one point Guillermo was going to print 'I punched Whistler' t-shirts for the cast). "The wolf has lain with the sheep long enough." In reply, Blade tries to detonate the bomb on Rheinhardt's head, but nothing happens. Scud laughs. "I'm sorry, man, B, you're wasting your time...The bomb's a dud. It was never supposed to explode. It was just supposed to make you feel in control." Rheinhardt smirks, takes of the bomb and tosses it to Scud. "Thought you had me on a short leash."

Scud shows a vampire glyph inside his lip. "I'm one of Damaskinos's familiars. They needed my help to bring you here to control Nomak. Whistler was bait. He's your only real weakness...Pretty soon they're all going to be daywalkers, man. When that happens, I'd rather be a pet than cattle." But Blade reveals he's been on to Scud since he turned, and the bomb Scud's holding isn't a dud. He detonates it, blowing Scud up (What Guillermo calls a Terry Gilliam explosion). Whistler comments sarcastically. "I was just starting to like him." Blade is electrocuted again, while Whistler is dragged away.

Blade is brought by Kounen to an operating theatre, complete with an operating table with lethal spikes. Evil, even by lawyer standards, Kounen gleefully tells Blade as he's strapped to the table and impaled by the spikes. "We're going to harvest your blood, every drop of it. Then bone, marrow, organs, everything. We'll find the missing key to creating daywalkers. Now, this might hurt a bit." (Another crucifixion moment, this time designed by Mike Mignola).

Rheinhardt is tormenting Whistler with Blade's sword. "I wonder how many vampires he's killed with this thing?" "Not nearly enough." "Just makes sending you to the next world all the sweeter." "Been there, done that." Rheinhardt doesn't realise that Whistler has picked the locks to his cuffs, while Nomak, having followed them, is outside the building, awaiting his chance to get in. (Something not in the original script, but added by Guillermo, to make the story flow better.)

Nyssa confronts her father. "What else should I find out? I trusted you, with my men, with my will, with my life. You sent us out there. You sent me to die. Our enemy saved my life twice, and you have used us, your own children." Damskinos grabs her by the throat. "Make no mistake, Nyssa, those blood ties mean nothing to me when measured against the ascendancy of our race. Who do you think God really favours in the web? The spider or the fly?" (Another of Guillermo's additional lines, make no mistake Damiskinos is the spider, everyone else is just a fly to him, even his daughter).

Blade tells Kounen that Nomak wants revenge on the people who created. Kounen isn't bothered. "Fortunately for us, he doesn't know this location." But now he does, and tears his way through the guards. Whislter uses the distraction to knock out Rheinhardt and escape from him. Whistler kills Kounen and frees Blade, but the Daywalker is weak and needs blood to recover. Whistler drags him to his feet. "Come on, kid. Don't you even think about dying on me. You didn't give up on me, I won't give up on you.

Reinhardt ambushes Blade and Whistler in Damskino's laboratory, but Blade makes it to the reviving pool of blood. Emerging (this was inspired by Martin Sheen in *Apocalypse Now*), revived, he kills the attacking guards (who very politely attack him one at time, so he can defeat them, rather than rushing him and overwhelming him). Reinhardt comments. "You want anything done right, you got to do it yourself." Blade asks Reinhardt. "Can you blush?" As he bisects him with his blade. As they leave, Whistler destroys the laboratory.

Nyssa traps Damaskinos in the building so he can meet his fate at Nomak's hands. "Isn't it sad that you die not by the hand of your enemy, but by that of your own children." Damaskinos tries to talk his way out of death, telling Nomak. "All that has befallen you, it was a terrible tragedy. An unforgivable mistake, but you've returned to me. We will find a cure. Take your rightful place by my side. You are, after all, a prince. Together we will conquer it all." "If what you say is true, why does your voice tremble so?" Nomak bites his father, telling him. "I've spared you my fate. You will die. Out of this wound, your blood, you life, will flow." (Again, these additional lines are Guillermo's, their Shakespearean moment, as is the notion that Damaskinos is so old, his blood is no longer red. Luke Goss would play another character (Prince Nuada) in *Hellboy II*, who kills his own father).

Nyssa throws her ring on her father's dying body. "Finish it off, my brother. Let's close the circle." Nomak bites her just as Blade enters the room. The two battle royally, with Blade eventually stabbing Nomak in the heart. "It's strange. It hurts. It hurts no more." And Nomak pushes the Blade in the rest of the way, dying in a fiery disintegration. (Inspired by the one in Terence Fisher's *Dracula* (1958).

Tragically, Nomak's death arrives too late to save Nyssa, she tells Blade. "It won't be long. I can already feel it burning inside of me. I want to die while I'm still a vampire. I want to see the sun."

Tenderly, Blade carries Nyssa in his arms to the room. She sees the beauty of the rising sun for the first time, even as those same rays bring about her death. She embraces Blade and serenely, peaceful,

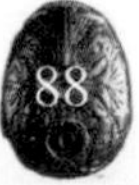

disintegrates in his arms, like a beautiful ghost of the shadows, dissolving like an ethereal wraith in the first rays of the rising sun.

Later, in London, Blade catches up with Rush. "You didn't think I forgot about you." And kills him. It's back to business as usual for the Daywalker.

Blade II was released on March 22, 2002, despite this being traditionally a bad time to release a sequel, but incredibly, Guillermo Del Toro's *Blade II* went on to make an impressive $80 million in the United States, and $150 million world wide. In its first week, *Blade II* earned $32, 528,016 from 2,707 theatres. *Blade II* also went straight in at number one in the United Kingdom and Singapore. There was an incredible alternative idea for *Blade II*, which David Goyer pitched as *Mad Max* with vampires, with the vampires triggering a blood tide that vampirises the Earth, and reduces human beings to being cattle for the now dominant vampire race. Some day perhaps...

Terence Fisher

"...a greater influence on Cronos was Terence Fisher. I really liked Hammer's colour palette, an aesthetic that was very Gothic but very modern too, a strange mixture. Fisher, I think, was a guy whose framing was impeccable. Few people give him the credit he deserves, not only as an artist but as a craftsman, s storyteller. The precision with which he placed the camera, camera movements, the lenses he used, the clarity of the image. He had a grasp of visual design which was equally powerful as the black and white movies made by Universal. So both James Whale and Fisher are, to me, the two great fathers of classic horror cinema."

GUILLERMO DEL TORO

"The Hammer film shot, the Christopher Lee disintegration...We referenced the Hammer Films of Dracula, Terence Fisher's Dracula(1958), where you see the corpse collapse very slowly, they were my favourite shots in the Dracula movies. I wanted to do the high tech version of it."

GUILLERMO DEL TORO ON NOMAK'S DEATH SCENE IN BLADE II.

"I never made horror films. They're fairy tales for adults."

TERENCE FISHER, AS QUOTED IN THE LONDON DAILY TELEGRAPH, NOVEMBER 27, 1976.

Terence Fisher (23 February 1904-18 June 1980) is in my opinion, one of the most under-rated and influential directors of the 20th century. With a considered measured style, he brought Gothic horror to cinema goers in glorious technicolour, resurrecting a moribund genre in much the same way as Dracula himself was resurrected in Fisher's superb Hammer films. He has been a strong influence on the films of Guillermo Del Toro.

Dismissed or castigated by the critics at the time he was directing, only in recent years have Fisher's films being recognised as the fine examples of cinematic art that they are and their director finally considered an auteur. Fisher's films are a potent blend of myth, repressed sexuality and fairy tales. Three traits his films have in common with Guillermo's. He didn't like the term 'horror' applied to his work.

There are certainly religious themes. Fisher's typical hero defeats the powers of darkness with his faith in good and in reason. This provides a contrast to other characters who veer from the extreme of being superstitious and dull or scientifically precise and detached., and the hero is one who defeats the powers of evil by a faith in reason and good (the evil characters are either superstitious or coldly rational).

His films were graphic by the standards of the time and highly visually accomplished. It is no exaggeration to say that he changed the direction of horror. He was a master storyteller, particularly when his films were set in a period I like to think of as Victorian Gothic (where even the Transylvanians have precise English accents, and good usually triumphs over evil).

Though I have to say, even non Victorian Gothic films directed by Fisher like

Island of Terror (1966) have their charms (It was only the second horror film I ever saw and I was very influenced by the fact that it is set in my native Ireland). He was like a painter, using every part of the frame to his advantage. One of Fisher's directorial traits is that characters should reveal themselves by deeds as well as words, a trait Guillermo shares with him. Fisher kept a tight control over his films costs, making the maximum use of a precise economic style, every image on the screen serving the story, not its director's ego. He kept his films within budget, and it would be fair to say that much of his style evolved from this. Fisher is spoken of as a kind, gentle, modest man, which sadly goes a long way to explaining the lack of kudos, respect, opportunities and material rewards that Fisher received in his lifetime. The modest and kind go unnoticed while the aggressive often take all the rewards.

Terence Fisher was born, Feb 23, 1904, in Maida Vale, England. He was an only child and his father died when he was only four years old. Nowadays we might be tempted to assign all kinds of directorial traits to Fisher from his father's death, but that would be pure speculation in his case, I suspect the man did what so many had to in those days and just got on with it. Fisher joined the Merchant Navy at 16. On leaving the Merchant Navy, he began to work in the film industry in 1933, first as a clapper boy, then as an assistant editor.

Encouraged by Morag, his devoted wife, he joined the Rank Organisation's Training Programme for film directors. He learned a lot of his precise style and meticulous framing by working as an editor on such films as *The Wicked Lady* (1945) before making his directorial debut in 1947 with *Colonel Bogey*. Fisher did not have the benefits many of today's director's have, either financially or creatively. He was a journeyman who worked for a fixed salary and often had to take films that didn't emotionally engage him.

The Curse of Frankenstein (1957) was beginning of the Hammer Films we all know and love, and this was where Fisher really started making his mark. With years of learning his craft the hard way, Fisher was incredibly visually accomplished. With this film and those that followed, Fisher changed the face of horror forever! It's as simple as that. Fisher is that important. He was the master storyteller, to this day, the majority of his post-*Curse of Frankenstein* films are both a delight to watch and a master class in how it should be done. His highly influential *Brides of Dracula*, despite not featuring Lee as Dracula, is like looking at a gorgeous series of painting presented as a drama.

This was beginning of Fisher's successful collaborations with Peter Cushing and Christopher Lee, who were the Karloff and Lugosi of their day, together the three revived horror in glorious grand guignol colour, rescuing it from the decline it had fallen into. Nothing would ever be the same again. giving the horror genre a much needed infusion of blood.

Beautifully photographed by Jack Asher from an accomplished Jimmy Sangster script, and embellished with a rousing James Bernard score and Jack Asher's camera work. This is as it should be! It also be mentioned that production designer Bernard Robinson's sets gave Hammer's Gothic films their distinct look. *The Curse of Frankenstein* enjoys the distinction of being the first Gothic film in colour, though it was almost in black and white.

Now Guillermo Del Toro puts a huge amount of thought into the colour palettes of his films too, and he is inspired by Fisher in this, where he sets the tone with colour, choreography, framing and structure (Peter Sasdy is clearly inspired by Fisher's example on the fine *Taste The Blood Of Dracula* (1970)). It would be fair to say that the fabulous colour palette on *The Curse of Frankenstein* is partly due to Hammer's simply wanting to exploit the medium of colour films to the highest degree.

Cushing's Baron is no cackling madman, he is extremely intelligent and self-confident, what sets him apart from his

fellow men is his total single-mindedness in achieving his goals. Christopher Lee brings great pathos to his role as the Creature (much as Ron Perlman does as *Hellboy* for instance). Lee is far too underrated as an actor, to give a performance of this quality under such make-up is a laudable feat. The make-up on this film deliberately had to avoid the Universe look, which gives the film a distinct identity.

Fisher's number one priority was to delight his audience (something many filmmakers seem to have forgotten). We have to realise the hugeness of what Fisher was undertaking. He was walking in the footsteps of James Whale (*Frankenstein*, 1931) and Tod Browning (*Dracula* 1931, and *The Mummy* 1932). He really was walking in the footsteps of giants, and more than managed to leave his own impressions.

Fisher's heroes are always in control of themselves, men of action, a nice example for today's world, where 'men' fall to pieces at the first setback. His experience as an editor stood him in good stead, like Guillermo would after him, he edited on camera. He would begin with a realistic base and then bring the supernatural into the story, often setting up his films in the first few minutes, the beginning of *Cronos*, the alchemist prologue is a fine example of his influence on Guillermo in this manner (and an impressive opening sequence for a debut film, it's also a way of saying, 'I don't make films by committee the modern way, I follow the old masters in this').

Fisher's *The Hound of the Baskervilles* (1959) is, in my opinion, the finest cinematic adaption of a Sherlock Holmes story (on television that honour goes to the late lamented Jeremy Brett). It was also the first Sherlock Holmes mystery to be filmed in colour.

The film opens with a gloriously Gothic shot of sinister moors, its atmosphere further enhanced by James Bernard. A narrator tells us to 'know the legend of the Hound of the Baskervilles'. We see the wicked Hugo Baskerville ('a wild, profane and godless man) torturing an unfortunate man. This is a well of inspiration that Hammer would draw from again, most effectively on the marvellous *The Plague of the Zombie* (1966), which also starred Andre Morrell).

It shows the unbound cruelty of those whose money and position puts them outside the law (and how little things have changed). Having killed the poor man for his and his friends amusement, he decides to give the dead man's daughter to the tender 'mercies' of his drinking companions to pay a debt 'in kind with a plaything I was keeping for myself'. Discovering she has escaped he decides to let loose his dogs on her, 'I'll get her and may the hounds of Hell get me if I can't hunt her down'. Having killed the girl, Sir Hugo himself is killed by a hound of terrible appearance, giving rise to the legend of the Hound and a Baskerville curse.

In the Victorian era, Sherlock Holmes (Peter Cushing) and Doctor Watson are told this tale by the Baskerville's lawyer Dr Mortimer, concerned for the safety of the new heir to the Baskerville estate, Sir Henry Baskerville (Christopher Lee). He finishes his tale with a dramatic flourish: "Therefore, take heed and beware the moor in those dark hours when evil is exalted, else you will surely meet the Hound of Hell, the hound of the Baskervilles."

Peter Cushing's Holmes is very much the rational Fisher hero, telling the lawyer, "you might have done better to consult a priest than a detective.' But when Sir Henry (who has a weak heart) finds a tarantula in his boot (and another boot has mysteriously gone missing), Holmes knows that hound or no hound, Sir Henry is in very real danger. Fisher masterfully wrings the maximum suspense out of the scenes with the tarantula, constantly cutting to Lee's eyes, and back to the creature (Guillermo shares this use of the eyes to convey emotion and create suspense, particularly in *Pan's Labyrinth*). Cushing's Holmes establishes himself as a man of action by killing the spider. He agrees to take the case. "The powers of evil can take many forms...avoid the Moors when the powers of darkness are exalted." Holmes agrees to take the case. "My professional charges are on a fixed scale, I do not vary them, except then I remit them altogether", (though, he amusingly contradicts this rule when he accepts a 'most generous' cheque from Sir Henry at the film's conclusion).

When Sir Henry and Doctor Watson get to Baskerville, the strange happenings continue, making this a most gothic adaption of Arthur Conan Doyle's the *Hound of the Baskervilles* (complete with a fine turn from the distinguished John le Messier). Make no mistake, whatever form it takes, Holmes is fighting evil (real evil, not the psychobabble we pass wicked behaviour off as today). At one point he comments. "There is more evil around than I have ever encountered before." And another time he observes. "The powers of evil can take many forms." When he needs to recruit the help of a local religious man, he asks him. "Will it help you if I tell you I am fighting evil as surely as you do?" Holmes is at all times, the picture of rationality, on finding a bloodstained knife on some ancient altar on the moors, he comments. "Some revolting sacrificial rite has been performed here."

The element of the family curse is brought into the story in the shape of a Spanish girl Cecile (Marla Landi) who loves on a farm near the moors with her father Stapleton. Sir Henry falls instantly in love with her. Cecile tells Lee of her late mother. "She was born in Spain and there she would die." She hates the frugal life she lives but as she comments, "weeds are not killed by the frost...we still live."

The smitten Sir Henry asks her if she's lonely. Cecile truthfully replies, telling him something that is sadly still true today. "I am very lonely. When you are poor, no one wants to know you." The colours of the film are beautiful, we have to imagine the impact it had at the time, my parents have often told me of the vivid impression made by the colour palette of the Hammer films. Remember, if anyone could afford a television in those days, it was in black and white, the colours of a Hammer film were a revelation.

Holmes has been secretly on the moors investigating already. He goads Sir Henry into going alone to Cecile's house, telling him. "I hope you enjoy your rabbit pie." But this is a ruse, to draw the evil out in the open, for Holmes has realised that Cecile and her father are also descended from Hugo Baskerville and intend to use Sir Henry's weak heart to stake their claim to the family fortune. Cecile's hatred when she reveals the truth to Sir Henry is more scary than any hellhound, left alone bitterness can grow into something horrific, yet we must also have sympathy for this neglected lonely creature, indeed, weeds are not killed by the frost, but it freezes their sad hearts. She tells him her father and her are 'descended from those who died in poverty while you scum ruled the moors.'

In a thrilling finale, Cecile's father Stapleton meets his death at the hands of his own hound and Cecile drowns in the moor. A fabulous film and one that in a just world would be accorded classic status. Cushing is an absolutely splendid Holmes (and would deservedly go on to play the role a number of well regarded television performances. The 1968 BBC series included such staples of the Holmes cannon as *A Study in Scarlet*, *The Boscombe Valley Mystery*, *The Sign of Four*, *The Blue Carbuncle*.

In the 1980s, Cushing would again play Holmes in Tyburn's *The Masks of Death* (directed by the talented Roy Ward Baker who directed such classics as Hammer's *Quatermass and the Pit* (1967). Andre Morrell gave a fine intelligent performance as Doctor Watson (banishing memories of Nigel Bruce, and Lee is ever inch the dashing romantic hero. To say its worth watching would be elementary (sorry!).

Dracula Prince of Darkness (1965) marked the return of Christopher Lee to the title role. Curiously and effectively, Lee speaks no dialogue (the great man says the dialogue was too stupid to recite, why does no one ever use Bram Stoker's dialogue?). This does however give him a fine dramatic presence.

The film begins with a recap of the events of the first Dracula film (including the disintegration that made such an impression on Guillermo). Peter Cushing does not appear as Van Helsing, instead we have Father Sandor (a fine powerful performance from Andrew Keir) as Dracula's nemesis. Having prevented (with a warning shot from his rifle, though interestingly Sandor will not take a human life under any circumstances) a superstitious priest and a mob of peasants from staking a corpse from fear it might rise from the grave, Sandor quickly establishes that he is a man of faith who loathes ignorance while acknowledging evil does exist and fighting it. Every frame is beautifully composed by Fisher, for maximum story-telling effect. Having prevented an act of desecration, Sandor visits an inn where he meets four English travellers, the brothers Charles Francis Matthews) and Alan Kent (Charles Tingwell), and their wives, Diana Kent (Suzan Farmer), and Helen Kent, played by the beautiful Barbara Shelley who is quickly and cleverly established by Fisher as the most straight- laced member of the party."

Sandor tells them that his fellow monks have no idea he shoots the deer he brings home to them. "I'm sure they believe the venison I bring home drops dead by the divine will of God!" Helen is shocked, much to Sandor's gentle amusement. "I enjoy shocking people's susceptibilities." When they enquire if the locals in the inn are his flock, Sandor bellows, "I wouldn't tolerate them!"

When he discovers the route the party is taking, Sandor warns them to stay away from Dracula's castle. After the travellers tell Sandor there's no castle marked on the map, he tells them in solemn tones that would have done credit to a biblical prophet. "Because it is not marked on the map, does not mean it does not exist."

They set off on their journey but as darkness falls, he abandons them near Castle Dracula. A rider-less coach appears and takes them to the Castle (How more Goth can you get? The answer is none more Goth!).Seeking shelter, they enter the castle, where they find a table set with fresh food (it's straight out of a fairy tale, think of the Pale Man's banquet table in *Pan's Labyrinth*). A sinister shadow enters the room (this is cleverly set up by Fisher to echo a similar shot in his first *Dracula* film, the shadow, reaction and music there made us think we would see a hideous monster, instead we see the suave Christopher Lee.

In this case, he fools us again, for the shadow is of Klove, a servant of the Late Count Dracula). Klove begins to serve them broth, and informs them that his late Master Count Dracula left instructions that visitors. He tells them. "My master died without issue at least in the accepted sense of the term." Helen knows something is wrong, stating, "Everything about this place is evil...the worst part of it is, I'm the only one that can see it." When they drink a toast to Dracula, the seemingly simple device of music, the dimming lights, and having a breeze blow the candles is extremely effective.

Alan tries to reassure the worried Helen, "You'll forget about all this in the morning." She replies in sepulchral tones. "There'll be no morning for us." Her words prove prophetic, she is most vulnerable in Fisher's universe because of her superstition.

That very night, Alan goes to investigate a noise, and is struck down by Klove, who uses his blood to reanimate Count Dracula from his ashes (This is very reminiscent of the resurrection of Sammael in the Machen Library in *Hellboy*). Then, to ease Count Dracula back into the land of the living (so to speak), Klove lures Helen to Dracula who vampirises her the unfortunate woman, horrified by the sight of the vampire and her husband's dead body (Fisher uses the masterful device of Dracula's arm as a wipe here, note that we never see the actual bite).

Diana and Charles are attacked by Dracula and Helen. Helen is burnt by Diana's cross (a scene we see at the end of *Hellboy*, when Professor Broom's cross burns a similar brand into *Hellboy*, reminding him

he has a choice).

Continuing the theme of the crucifix, Charles fashions a makeshift cross from a broken sword, which repels Dracula and they manage to escape. They are discovered by Father Sandor, who reminds them, "I warned you not to go anywhere near the castle", before taking them to his monastery. There, they meet Ludwig, an unfortunate lunatic reminiscent of Renfield from Stoker's *Dracula*. Sandor explains something of the nature of Dracula and the vampires of the Carpathian mountains. "He is already dead, he is undead. He can be destroyed but not killed."

With Ludwig's aid, Dracula enters the monastery, while Helen is staked by the monks. Sandor explains. "This is a shell, when we destroy it, we destroy the evil." After Helen's staking, Fisher uses music and light to convey that her soul is at peace. Charles and Sandor pursue the Count back to his lair, where they manage to halt the Count's rampage (for the time being at least), by trapping him under ice (a scene racked with tension, Fisher sets the stage with a master's skill).

The sight of Dracula under the frozen waters of his own moat is one of the most memorable in cinema.

Fisher's *The Devil Rides Out* (1967), adapted from Dennis Wheatley classic novel is one of his finest films, with the theme of good verses evil very much to the fore. Here he shows he believes that embracing evil is a choice, just as embracing good is a choice, that the dark forces can only enter his character's lives if they allow them, or refuse to fight them. Amusingly, the film was released as *The Devil's Bride* in the U.S for fear that it might be mistaken for a Western if released under its original title.

Christopher Lee gives one of his best performances as the Duc de Richleau, while Charles Gray's Morcata is the embodiment of Satanism (Morcata was based on Aleister Crowley, whom Wheatley knew personally, which gives you an idea of the authenticity of his work). "*I* shall not be back but *something* will tonight. Something will come for Simon and the girl."

The opening montage of occult and alchemical symbols used by Fisher for the opening credits, tells you all you need to know, and sets the stage and creates the atmosphere briskly and without the need for a single word of explanations. Symbols are powerful, Fisher understood this, as does Guillermo. The script by Richard Matheson is superb. Hammer once planned to film a Matheson-scripted version of *I Am Legend*, one cinema's great 'what-ifs'. The Duc is courageous and straight-forward. "I'd rather see you dead than meddling in black magic."

The film is enhanced by a brilliant use of music and lightning, as for example, in the Duc's confrontation with the demon in Simon's telescope room. Fisher frequently cuts to his protagonist's eyes. This increases the tension in his expert hands, and also increases the human drama, reminding you these are people, with real fears and feelings. Wheatley himself (a friend and neighbour of Lee's, who brought this project to Hammer) was delighted with the film.

Wheatley's knowledge of the occult was vast, and he always took it seriously and warned against it. My mother introduced me to Wheatley's books, something I remain grateful for to this day, and certainly his work is well worth tracking down.

As my final example of Terence Fisher's legacy and influence, I have chosen *The Gorgon* (1964), starring the dream team of Barbara Shelley, Peter Cushing, and Christopher Lee, the cast also includes Patrick Troughton Again James Bernard's fine music enhances the atmosphere and John Gilling contributes a fine screenplay.

It would take an entire book to do justice to Terence Fisher's body of work, it is enough to salute not only the influence this fine director continues to have on directors like Guillermo, but also to watch his films for the sheer pleasure they continue to give, and that alone is the greatest legacy a storyteller can have.

The film begins with an ominous warning. "Overshadowing the village of

Vandorf stands the Castle Borski...From the turn of the century a monster from an ancient age of history came to live here...and the spectre of death hovered in waiting for her next victim." *Pan's Labyrinth* gives a similar importance to the cycle of the moon, as it is when the moon is full that Magera the Gorgon turns her next victim to stone. Barbara Shelley plays Carla Hoffman, the unfortunate woman possessed by the spirit of Magera.

Peter Cushing's Dr Namaroff is rather more amoral than the typical role Cushing plays for Fisher but he imbues the part with typical conviction. "It never ceases to amaze me that the most noble work of God, the human brain, is the most revolting to the human eye." After a local girl falls victim to Magera, her suicidal lover is blamed. His father, Professor Jules Heitz comes to Vandorf to prove his innocence. He is stone-walled by Dr Namaroff. "You're not suggesting there's any connection between a character from mythology and your father's death?"

Sadly he too falls victim to Magera, just managing to write a final message to his surviving son as his hands turn to stone. This is very similar to the scene in *Cronos* where Gris desperately tries to write a letter of explaining events to his wife while his hands become less and less responsive. His son Paul comes to investigate and will not be dissuaded. "In less than a week I've lost my father and brother. I'm not very concerned with what happens to me." Tragically Paul falls in love with Carla, who, not knowing her true nature, recites the legend of the Gorgon. "So hideous was the Gorgon that anyone who looked on her was petrified...the proper word is 'gorgonised' which literally means 'turn to stone...every myth known to man is not without an authentic basis."

Paul discovers the truth when he unearths his father's petrified body (In a scene very reminiscent of *The Plague of the Zombies*." Paul receives help from his father's friend, Prof. Karl Meister (Christopher Lee). The slight glimpse that Paul has had of the Gorgon has marked him. Meister comments. "You look as though you've been in your grave and dug your way out." Namaroff is gorgonised, and Paul sees enough to eventually kill him. Inspired by the myth of Perseus, Meister manages to kill Magera, by avoiding looking at her directly and decapitating her.

Sadly, it is the head of the unfortunate Carla that tumbles to the ground. All Meister can comfort the dying Paul with is by telling him. "She's free now, Paul. She's free." You can see the influence of this film in the ending of *Cronos* and *The Devil's Backbone*. *The Gorgon* is a doomed love story, a dark fairy tale, and while events are resolved, they are not happily resolved. It is a film full of dark, poetic majesty, and another fine example of Terence Fisher, one of horrors most influential and entertaining directors.

The Devil Rides Out & The Curse of Frankenstein – classics from the Terence Fisher canon

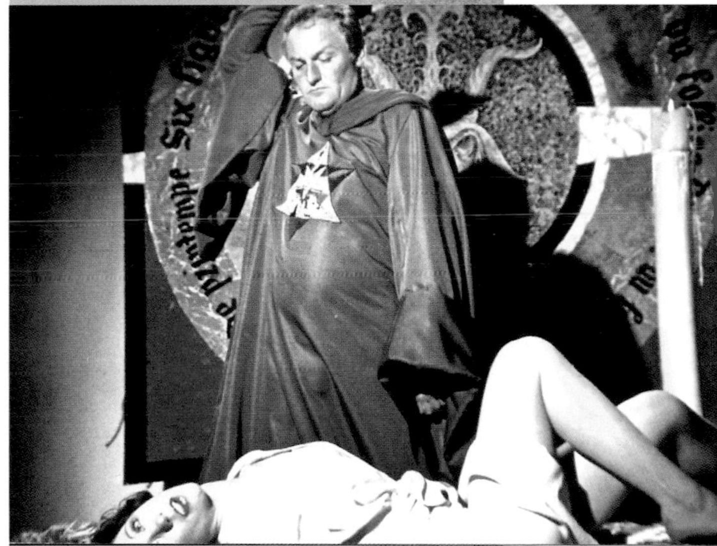

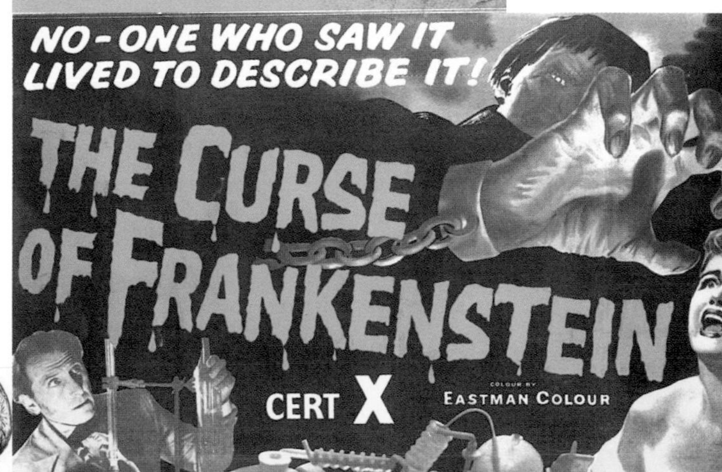

Blade II - Analysis

Made immediately after *The Devil's Backbone*, *Blade II* is just as important a film in Guillermo's cannon in its own right. While *The Devil's Backbone* restored Guillermo's faith in his own artistic and story-telling abilities after the unpleasant major studio experience he suffered making *Mimic*, *Blade II* proved that that Guillermo was not just an arthouse horror director. It showed he was quite capable of merging his unique vision to an existing franchise (*Blade II* is the most successful of the *Blade* films trilogy). It also marks the beginning of his creative collaboration with Mike Mignola, which would lead to the fine *Hellboy* films.

And indeed, *Blade II*, with its high energy anime-inspired visuals, dark gothic sets, a marked increase in horror from the previous entry, and the inspired creation of the Reapers, is a fine film in it's own right. It's variety in film-making that makes an auteur, not a steadfast bland following of the expected path.

Blade is not without its flaws, the majority of which can be laid at the doorstep of David Goyer. Some of his lines are howlingly clunky, and indeed the ones Guillermo was able to add to the film work much better. But it's the reintroduction of Whistler which is the most glaringly obvious flaw in *Blade II*. Whistler clearly killed himself in Stephen Norrington's excellent *Blade*.

The energy of the film just about lets him get away with shoe-horning Whistler back into the film. While on the first two Blade films, Goyer was saved by having two very talented directors carry the film, on the dire *Blade:Trinity*, Goyer himself directs (Guillermo was offered the film, but turned it down), producing a confusing, sorry b-movie (in the bad sense of the term) mess, which appears to be a dumping ground for all the ideas not used in the previous two films, reaching the nadir of introducing a Dracula that looks more like a wrestler than the Prince of Darkness-a sad coda for such a promising franchise, especially when you consider the achievements of the previous directors.

Aware that Norrington had raised the bar with the epic 'Blood Shower' nightclub fight at the start of the first film, Guillermo intended to do things differently on *Blade II*. So, he gave a signature del Toro scene, rather than a signature Norrington scene. "We wanted to graduate the movie so that we literally had the biggest and best fight of the movie towards the end. And we know that the first one had a great opening, the 'Blood Shower' was fantastic. We knew that if we opened with an action scene, we would have to top that, and risk never being able to achieve that again." Thus, the scene which introduces Nomak at the Blood Bank (which was twenty minutes further on in the original script), is a horror rather than an action scene. The 'I hate vampires' moment was something Guillermo had tried to include in three screenplays, he humorously calls Nomak's first seen victim, "the Jackson Pollock Bite...Red Number 5, hanging on the wall of a museum."

Originally, Guillermo wasn't too keen on directing *Blade II*. "They came to me the first time, it was tunnels and sewers and Reapers transforming...I did that movie. I don't want to do that again...The idea of the Blood Pack was more fun...*The Dirty Dozen* of vampires." Intriguingly, they were originally interested in Guillermo directing the first *Blade*, something he feels would have been "a catastrophe, going from *Cronos* to *Blade* would be like shock therapy. I think *Mimic* has more things in common with *Cronos* in terms of atmosphere and so forth. *Cronos* to *Mimic* was a leap, then *Mimic* to *Devil's Backbone* was like was like going back and finding my personality on certain things...then *Blade II* was just 100% pure fun...*Devil's Backbone* was a chance to grow as an artist, *Blade II* was a chance to grow as a craftsman...A fusion of what I do and what was required...I think *Blade II* is a very Catholic exercise in modesty in the sense that I was not there to make Guillermo del Toro's *Blade II*, I was there make *Blade II*-the kick-ass movie."

When Guillermo pitched his concept of *Blade* to Michael De Luca (who wrote a fine script for one of John Carpenter's most under-rated films, *In The Mouth Of Madness*) at New Line, one of the scenes he talked about was that of *Blade* talking over a

vampire's motorbike, a garrotting the vampire. "I demonstrated it and broke two chairs."

Guillermo had nothing but respect for Stephen Norrington's sterling work on the first *Blade* film, to the extent of watching every piece of film Norrington shot."... to make it the logical evolution to what Norringtonproposed. I wanted very hard to serve the franchise."

Lighthammer prepares to change sides

Guillermo sees an element of Sergio Leone's work in *Blade*. "Blade is a character who sees the world in black and white, a character with a very small dramatic arc, very small. You don't see Blade come out at the end of the movie [with] 'I shall embrace all forms of life.'

Santiago Segura, who plays Rush, is a friend of Guillermo's and a huge star in Spain, while Donnie Yen, who plays Snowman, is a huge Hong Kong action movie star.

Guillermo's dedication to *Blade II* was such that, on discovering New Line had auctioned off the props from the first film, that he bought some of those props on e-bay to use as references.

The animosity between Scud and Whistler Guillermo refers to as "a rivalry between the new wife and the old wife." (In a fore-shadowing of the *Hellboy* films to come, Scud is wearing a BPRD t-shirt as an in-joke).

The high tech of the first movie meets the old-world gothic Guillermo loves, really comes to the fore with Demaskinos's lair. The high-tech building is built around the ancient Roman temple the ancient vampire uses as his inner-sanctum. It's clear that Guillermo has a real understanding of the ancient monster (There is actually a proper term for the science of monsters: Teratology.)" It's the ancient arrogance that Demaskinos has accumulated over the centuries that proves his downfall. He is "a character so old and so used to winning that he really is cocky about how he plays the game with Blade, and eventually loses because he is very full of himself, full of hundreds of years of victories."

Of course, the film features Guillermo's beloved creatures (or parts of creatures) in jars. "...my favourite things in life, things in jars. I cannot avoid it. I have to have intestines or foetuses in jars."

Goyer's plot doesn't allow for quiet character moments. It's always on the move, driving the story forward. Guillermo sees its sense of pace as important. "It's very much like a comic book rhythm, and that I appreciate and admire...he has a very good sense of rhythm for this type of movie." *Blade II* was not supposed to bear a great resemblance to reality. "Very little, because the whole thing was so outlandish. I wanted a world where you literally could walk into a nightclub in full regalia, with weapons, with a uniform, with incredibly big swords, and no one would stop you....Working on this movie was a pleasure in the construction of that world because the palette of colours (daylight is blue, the nights are amber, to create a comic-book feeling), textures and shapes, allow me to have probably one of the most experimental, creative, and free movies visually. It's the one I've had the most fun inventing stuff, images and crazy moments."

The idea was to satisfy his own gothic sensibilities while still staying true to *Blade*. "The idea was to do *Blade II*, not *The Devil's Backbone II*, as such ,the way the camera moves, the way the camera work...the rhythm of the movie is something I was experimenting on and discovering a lot as we went along.... I talked to Goyer about making this the *Dirty Dozen* kind of movie, the interaction between *Blade* and Perlman is half the *Dirty Dozen*, half *They Call Me Trinity, My Name Is Trinity*. In Mexico, those Italian Terence Hill and Bud Spencer movies were so huge and I enjoyed the slapstick fighting so much...It has that kind of audience satisfaction...funny energy."

Kung Fu fighting Blade style

Guillermo returned the loyalty and commitment shown by Ron Perlman on *Cronos*, by fighting to have Perlman cast as Rhinehardt. "I am Ron Perlman's agent in the world. I keep trying to find him the best jobs I can. He [Rheinhardt] is the very first Nazi played by a very large Jewish man from LA in many years."

Guillermo felt that Goyer's lines suited the flow of the movie. "I love the simplicity of Goyer's lines. Seriously, I enjoy them, the comic book moment that he puts the flachette on Rheinhardt: 'Now you have an explosive device stuck to the back of your head. 'It's such a beautiful matter of fact statement. It establishes the relationship of command between the Blood Pack and Blade, and it was a great very dynamic way, that is, they are gonna hate each other for the rest of the movie and they will remain like that, rivals for the rest of the movie...These guys, even if they hate each other, when they are working as a team they try to be as efficient a group as possible."

Guillermo also found it a relief, after *Mimic*, to work with someone else's script. "That's what was liberating on *Blade II*, first of all to direct someone else's screenplay... that we had agreed not to try to make real, to try to make a comic book, it was great."

Guillermo plays credit to Goyer and Norrington's pioneering work on the first film. "The first one deals with all the mythos and all the front-load of who the character is. On the second one I was blessed to be working on the shoulders of all that work and just have fun. This is the main thing about this movie, I wanted it to be totally and absolutely fun, and Goyer's dialogue, and Goyer's energy, and the pacing allowed me to do that...We're just pulp. I love the idea of taking something pulp and elaboration it visually, with a lot of care."

Realism was not the aim, the idea was create a very alternative world to our own, where regular rules do not apply,

something Guillermo was very aware of. "They are unloading automatic high-powered guns in the middle of the street. I didn't want any of the real world in this thing...The yellow night, the amber night, all these things cooperate to make this more comic-book and more funny."

Guillermo had very specific ideas for the House Of Pain. "We wanted to introduce the feel of the place by the tools that you saw, and the amount of people, and the energy, and all the things that are taking place in there. The idea of the design of this club, you have a place where as a vampire you can come and play in the artificial sun...I wanted the House Of Pain to have a little more atmosphere. It's impossible to generate the suspense that you can generate with regular people in a situation of jeopardy....You generate suspense more with Scud than the Blood Pack or Blade, because essentially Scud is the audience. He is the only character in the movie that you can feel for. Because everyone else has superpowers or automatic guns. So no matter how much atmosphere you put into a scene where Blade walks into a creepy room, you're not afraid because he is Blade, so this is our precious moment of atmosphere."

Blade's feelings for Nyssa are understandable because as Guillermo sees it, "Nyssa is probably one of the most human vampire characters in the movie."

The action packed set pieces in the House of Pain illustrate Guillermo's growing strength as a storyteller here, dealing with multiple action scenes. "Both the editor and I thought it would be more efficient to keep them parallel...and they all reach the same points at the same time. I am the proudest of the movie in terms of craftsmanship, because as a director it tests a lot of what it is to rhythmically build a sequence, in the editing room it really pushes you to create these things."

Not for nothing do Blade and the Blood Pack bring to mind memories of *The Wild Bunch* as they approach the House of Pain.

"One of my favourite things in the movie was to do an exaggerated shoot out, like no shootout has ever been done. I wanted to out-Peckinpah Peckinpah in the amount of bullets and squibs...I wanted it to be literally ridiculous to the point where they were destroying the walls, they were killing other vampires, they were blowing up the floor to pieces...and the Reapers are unfazed...The level of violence in the attack of the Reapers towards Priest and Lighthammer, I wanted it to be very high to show like a rabid dogs kind of attack...Reapers are the crack-addict version of vampires. They don't want to hear your story...when is the last time anyone talked to a burger. No one talks to burgers, the Reapers don't talk to their victims....Less is more in atmospheric movies. In action/horror movies, more is more...I wanted to make a variation from the vampire with the pointed teeth, which is a thing we inherited from Lugosi's *Dracula*, really it has varied very little in the rest of vampirism history. In *Cronos* I created what I consider a very unique take on vampirism, from an intellectual point of view. I think that vampirism as a symbol is absolutely open to interpretation. Vampirism is an addiction, it can be interpreted as an erotic proclivity, can be interpreted as a religious analogy...you can make it political social...When you read about vampirism all over the world, you realise that every culture has interpreted the vampire in a certain way...Chinese vampires can turn into foxes...Mexican vampires look like Chihuahuas."

Guillermo understands the attraction of vampirism. "When you're young, you yearn to preserve that youth, and when you're old, you yearn for that youth you've lost...In *Cronos* it was more a little tale about Catholic guilt, addiction, religious catharsis and so forth, about a guy who feels he's alive only after he dies, and how worthy his life really was, and you only achieve immortality when you give up everything, a very Catholic view...I hope someday to do a movie about vampires who've been alive so long they don't really care about anything anymore. I really think that after 500 years you would get a little jaded."

Of course, in the light of those Catholic comments, Guillermo having Rheinhardt impale a Reaper is entirely intentional. "Again this is a little crucifixion moment which I cannot avoid."

The Reapers are a polar opposite of the romantic Gothic Byronic vampire, they are more like leeches, Guillermo's inspired idea was to have a creature whos mouth occupied half its face. The original Reaper designs were more shape-shifting, and were somewhat reminiscent of the creatures in *Mimic*.

"A leech is not worried about its features, you cannot see a handsome leech, they're all just there to do what they do, half their face would just be a pumping machine... I had the idea of having their mouths expand, a creature that keep its feeding apparatus hidden until its time to feed." The Reapers are a mix of actors in make-up, prosthetics and CGI. "Most people these days go too much with CGI effects and not enough with physical to sell them."

Something Guillermo has always tried to do is to use the CGI to complement the physical effects, not to overwhelm them.

To emphasise the difference between the Reapers and regular vampires, Guillermo wanted them to have a completely disintegration. "The explosion of the Reapers I wanted to do, again, very comic-book like. What I wanted was like anime and comic books, when a character explodes, sometimes you can see the skeleton, a mili-second before they fully explode, and you can see here the x-ray, what we call the x-ray moment and then they explode like nobody's business."

Guillermo is quick to explain that the horror of *Blade II* is very different to the horror of *The Devil's Backbone*. "I define horror as two different types of horror. One is playing hide and seek, which is atmospheric movies where you are dealing with the absent, someone is hiding, is he gonna be found? Are they gonna scare him when then find him? If you're searching for him, you open doors, and is he gonna jump out...That's one type of horror. The other one, which is this one, is tag, and you're it. With tag, more is more...I wanted from the start to make *Blade II* an absolute comic book movie...you should just sit back, eat your popcorn, and have fun...The main thing about a comic book movie is for it to be done intelligently by someone who really knows the genre as a literary genre, with the sophisticated, complex and difficult language that comic books have...For me, it is a form of art...There are comic books that stand right next to a Thomas Cole painting, the Mona Lisa, that are that great as human created pieces of expression . I approached that with enormous respect and discipline and tried to translate that to the screen. There are different types of comic book as there are different types of movie and I wanted this to be the comic books I read as a young guy...that have the kind of exaggerated language that Jack Kirby would have for example. I wanted to give the movie that kind of exaggerated language... We push certain sounds beyond the reality... The dialogue has a certain awkwardness that makes it uniquely comicbook."

Guillermo shows Priest's transformation to a Reaper as painful to say the least. "The aftermath of being bitten by a Reaper is not pleasant...It's not a kind of languid 'I'm going to lay here in my nightrobe until I turn into a vampire' kind of transformation... This is to say the least a very graphic moment and I wanted to have humour in that graphic moment because anime is like that. Anime combines the visceral with the funny." Some of the discarded Reaper designs were even more insectile and extreme.

Blade also follows Guillermo's theme of different realities beneath what we perceive to be reality. "Beneath the world beneath, there is another world yet, that they will have to explore in order to find the Reapers." As above, so below.

The scene where Damaskinos enters his blood bath is significant as being the first on-screen collaboration between Guillermo and *Hellboy*'s creator, who designed the scene. "The Mike Mignola moment. It was lit and designed to look like a *Hellboy* comic book, with all the statues in the background, the contrasted light, and this pool of blood, all very graphic and very comic-book like, in the style Mignola uses."

After *Cronos*, which had second and even third unit directors imposed on Guillermo, he was insistent that would not happen on *Blade II*. "This movie was a challenge in the sense that one of the first conditions I asked from the studio was that they allowed me to shoot this movie without any second-unit, like a little independent film. I like the idea that every single thing you see in the movie is done by me."

Autopsy scenes are a popular theme in Guillermo's films, with the Reaper autopsy being one of the most dramatic of all. "To me this is a beautiful, fascinating scene.... Because the amount of ingenuity that goes into creating these things is enormous. It is not like a gore film, like a cheap splatter film, and it looks real...If something is dead, then it should have been alive. It's a strange logic, kind of what I call retro-logic...The Reaper

Rheinhardt has a Sergio Leone moment

(autopsy) scene makes the Reapers feel real and feasible. It takes it to a different level of reality. We're beyond terminology and into biology, showing if you try to kill these things, they keep on moving. It reinforces the 'otherness' of the Reapers and it clarifies a lot of things including their only vulnerable point... the side of the heart, which is something you see the Harryhausen movies, and when you see many fantasy movies, they say 'you can only kill the Cyclops if you hit the space between his forehead and his left nostril.' It sounds insurmountable, but of course at the end of the movie, the hero is perfectly positioned between the forehead and the nostril to kill the monster as Blade does."

The unusual colour palette Guillermo favours in *Blade II* goes all the way back to his formative days of filmmaking. "I like the juxtaposition of yellow light and blue light, this is something that as a young filmmaker in Super 8 I started to experiment with and everyone kept telling me, 'it's wrong, you cannot combine those two things, professional cinematographers will have only one colour source light"...It takes it away from reality."

The UV grenades were also inspired by Guillermo's early work. "This is one of the weapons that we came up with that was loosely inspired by the Cronos Device, which a device that looks cute and does very little and then explodes into something brutal, and I wanted very much to have that feeling on the light grenades."

Blade II also improved Guillermo's editing skills. "The great thing about the process of editing as you shoot, is when you approach the set the next day, you have exactly in your mind what you need to finish the sequence. It gives you the discipline of being able to cut on the set, on paper...Whatever got in the way of the rhythm and flow...out it go."

Guillermo's notebook provided some inspiration for the design of the Blood Pack's uniforms."...each character personalises the uniform with a little touch here and there... The uniforms were very inspired by Japanese anime."

As on *The Devil's Backbone* and *Pan's Labyrinth*, Guillermo's love of books inspired the creation of the Reapers. "The idea with the Reapers was, one of my favourite books is *I Am Legend* by Richard Matheson. What I wanted for you to have the sense with the Reapers, is a constant flow of them. Blade has to fight a lot to keep them at bay...they just keep coming like lemmings." It's interesting to note that Guillermo was one of the choices to direct *I Am Legend*.

Guillermo speaks highly of working in Prague, saying the movie was made possible by the Czech Republic. "The craftsmanship they bring to sets is very old world, the precision and pride they bring to their craftsmanship in creating murals is just really amazing and shows in the movie...I think the House of Pain sequence with 400 extras was another example for me of what the Czech experience is...the most hard-working group of extras...I was expecting hell and I got heaven...I'm a really boring guy in daily life. I don't like nightlife that much and I enjoy daylight, what I wanted for the House of Pain is a place where people can go to drink a human without problems."

Carol Spier, who was production designer for *Mimic* (where she says comic-books provided inspiration there too) did a fine job on *Blade II*. The tunnel sets took 14 weeks to build and was longer than a football field. Blade's warehouse lair was shot in a disused Soviet missile factory. "We went into old corroded places that had been used to fabricate bombs during the Cold War, during the Russian occupation of Prague and we transformed them a little bit and made them more gothic."

Guillermo describes the style as goth-tech, inspired by the surroundings and a coffee-table book called *Dead Tech*. Guillermo wanted to blend the East European look with gothic, which often involved blending sets with existing structures. "A very modern sensibility with a very classic almost ancient world visual." While Damaskinos's lair was inspired by a book called Underground Rome...This movie invokes a fantastic underworld wheras the first one was much more urban."

Mike Mignola was a big influence on the look of *Blade*, particularly on what Guillermo calls the "James Bond on acid type of set. We had Mike Mignola design it or have conceptuals for it to give it a comic book feeling. There are some images in the movie that are completely Mike Mignola inspired, that seem right out of the *Hellboy* comic books."

Guillermo's interest in history inspired the aftermath of the detonation of the UV bomb. "I wanted to give a very twisted fairy tale. A Pompeii landscape. "I remember the Pompeii figures in a National Geographic documentary and I wanted to do this twisted fairy tale image of Blade standing among the burnt enemy."

Blade II restored Guillermo's faith in working with major studios again after his unpleasant experience on *Mimic*. "One of the reasons I enjoyed the movie is, we did the movie and we were left alone, and we were truly given a chance to experiment. This and *Devil's Backbone* are the two shooting experiences I have enjoyed the most."

Of course, Guillermo understands that on someone else's franchise, no matter how much experimentation takes place, certain rules have to be followed. "On the first *Blade*, the last act is James Bond and the same is true for this one. He's put in jeopardy by the villains torture devices, he bleed almost to death, then regenerates and kicks ass."

Blade II was also a chance for Guillermo to work again with two old friends. "One of the two casting things that I was really happy to get away with was Ron Perlman who had worked with me in *Cronos*, and Norman [Reedus], whom I gave his job on film in *Mimic*. I loved his delivery of the lines on *Mimic* and I insisted that he played Scud."

One of the most moving moments in *Blade II* is Nyssa's serene death, where, realising she is infected with the Reaper virus, and after what has occurred with her father's deceit and betrayal, she no longer wants to live. She wants to die an almost samurai death. She wants to see the sun that will kill her as a vampire, disintegrating like a ghost in Blade's arms (A scene that was ripped off in Stephen Sommers's *Van Helsing* (2004) even appearing at the same point in that movie, *Van Helsing* is a film that is shining example of the fact that having a huge budget, cast and special effects, but the absence of a good script, produces the most disappointing results).

This is one of the scenes that drew Guillermo to *Blade II*. "This is one of the things I was very attracted to in the movie when I read the screenplay. I loved the ending, him taking Nyssa out into the sun. The almost poetic image in the middle of a movie that was going to be like a rock concert of brutality. It's a bit against the grain which I like...I wanted the moment of her death to be different from the other vampires, in that she accepts the death. She does not explode into flames. She burns more slowly, and she essentially dies before burning. I find it very beautiful. The way a warrior accepts pain."

In conclusion, it can be seen that *Blade II* is an important film in Guillermo's body of work. Not only did it allow him to have fun filmmaking again, but it shown that he could work with a major studio again. In this respect *Blade II* is the second part of the post-*Mimic* healing process that began with *The Devil's Backbone*.

It also marks the beginning of his collaborations with Mike Mignola, and together Guillermo and Mike have gone on to create magical cinema together. *Blade II* also continued and built on Guillermo's previous collaboration with his friend Ron Perlman, and again the two friends have gone on to produce much good work together. You can see that no matter how big the budget and how high the stakes (sorry!), Guillermo works best when he's allowed (as he wasn't on *Mimic*) to produce films the way he did in Mexico, even back in his Super-8 days, with his friends, for the love of the film, a collaboration concerned with making the best possible film, where everyone isn't just doing a job, but giving 100% to something they love, and something they're all in together, not as unappreciated employees waiting for their pay cheque (and how many people reading this have suffered under working conditions that aren't co-operative).

The key to happiness in working life for employers and employees alike is to adopt Guillermo's method. Think how much happier our working lives would be, whatever field we work in, if everyone had worked hard, was appreciated and had fun. The proof of this method is on screen for all to see). Guillermo has a personal philosophy that says rather than avoiding pain and taking the easiest possible path, it is from suffering and heartache we grow (as people and as artists). His blossoming on *Mimic* and *Blade II* proves this. Orson Welles put it best. "You know from past experience that whenever you have been driven to the wall, or thought you were, you have extracted yourself in a way which you never would have dreamed possible had you not been put to the test. The trouble is that in your everyday life you don't go deep enough to tap the divine mind within you."

(*"No real Reapers were hurt during the making of this film!"*)

Chapter Five
Hellboy

"In the coldest regions of space, the monstrous entities Ogdru Jahad-the Seven Gods of Chaos-slumber in their crystal prison, waiting to reclaim Earth...and burn the heavens."

DES VERMIS MYSTERIIS (*PAGE 87)*

The man who will adopt Hellboy, and bring him up as his own son, Professor Trevor 'Broom' Bruttenholm (John Hurt), narrates. 'What is it that makes a man a man? Is it his origins? The way things start? Or is it something else? Something harder to describe. For me, it all began in 1944. Classified mission off the coast of Scotland. The Nazis were desperate, combining science and black magic, they intended to upset the balance of the war. I was 28, already a paranormal adviser to President Roosevelt. I could never have suspected that what would transpire that night would not only affect the course of history but change my life forever."

Oct 9 1944 Scotland

A platoon of US soldiers approach the ruins of an ancient derelict monastery, it's an impressive Romanesque ruin. They take position in a graveyard, watched over by a statue of the crucified Christ (A common element in much of Guillermo's work). The young Professor Broom (Kevin Trainer) offers a box of rosaries to the leader of the troops, Sgt Whitman (Angus MacInnes). "Your men, they'll need these." The gruff sergeant hands it back, asking. "You a Catholic?" "Yes, among other things. But that's hardly the point." "Well, you're gonna need one of these." Whitman chambers a round into an automatic and hands it to the horrified Broom. "I abhor the use of violence...I wouldn't want you to think me mad, Sergeant." "No, three days too late for that, 'professor'.

The sergeant walks away. Broom looks up at the statue of Christ. He alone knows the evil they will face (This is a very Terence Fisher inspired moment, both in framing and theme). The soaked Whitman is not enjoying his visit to the island, telling Broom." You're wasting our time. There's nothing on this island but sheep and rocks." "Ruins, not rocks. The ruins of Trondham Abbey, built on an intersection of ley lines, the boundaries between our world and others." "Hell, a week ago I never even heard the word 'parabnormal'. "Paranormal!" corrects Broom. The troops continue to advance on the Abbey ruins. Then Whitman sees that Broom isn't mad after all. The Abbey is swarming with Nazi troops and technicians, moving around the thick stone walls and archways, a dozen of them assembling a strange machine with huge metal rings, not unlike a gyroscope, setting up lights. Soon something wicked this way comes.

A banner with a swastika and occult symbol desecrates the abbey wall (This is all very Hammer horror by way of Terence Fisher set up, that of evil in a holy place, and also the gothic ruins, the atmosphere and the lighting). Broom comments to Whitman sarcastically. "They must be here for the sheep." It's nice to be proved right!

While the Nazis bustle around making arcane technological preparations, they are being observed by a sinister looking Nazi officer in black leather, monitoring the work, his features obscured by a mask." Whitman sees him through his binoculars. "The freak in the gas mask?" He hands the binoculars to Broom, who recognises the masked man. "Karl Ruprecht Kroenen, Hitler's top assassin and head of the Thule Occult Society. If he's here this is worse than I thought."

A machine cranks into life with a whirl of cogs and gears. Floodlights come on. Watching are Grigory (Karel Roden) and Ilsa (Bridget Hodson). Grigory hands Ilsa a small leather-bound book, with hand drawn notes and illustrations, telling her. "No matter what happens tonight. This book will guide you back to me." He presses the book into her hand, and she gazes on him devotedly. "I will not leave you." As an added bonus, he throws in a few perks with the book. "I grant you everlasting life, youth, and the power to serve me." He anoints her head. They are interrupted by General Von Krupt, indicating a pocket watch. "Ilsa, Grigory...it's time." He continues. "Five years of research and construction, Grigory. The Furhrer does not look kindly on failure." "There will be no failure, General. I promised

Herr Hitler a miracle...I'll deliver one."

Kroenen straps a huge Mecha-Glove onto Grigory's arm, power cables run from the glove, which is a mirror image of Hellboy's mighty fist. Grigory announces. "What I will do tonight can never be undone. I will open a portal and awaken the Ogdru-Jahad, the seven gods of Chaos. Our enemies will be destroyed. And from the ashes a new Eden will arise. Ragnorok!"

Electricity flashes between the Mecha-Glove and the machine as a portal to the Ogdu-Jahad opens. A floodlight is sucked into the void, it illuminates the monstrous Ogdu-Jahad, their gigantic bodies imprisoned in huge crystals, their huge eyes watch the floodlight impassively.

Broom knows there's no time to spare, the fate of the world literally hangs in the balance. "The portal is open. We have to stop them."

One of the Nazi technicians is alerted by Corporal Matlin (Jim Howick), the combat photographer, taking a photograph. Whitman doesn't mess around, he hurls a grenade. The blast throws a Nazi into the portal where its energy disintegrates him. A falling pillar from the ruined abbey flattens another, and the soldiers use the confusion to attack. In the pitched battle that follows, Professor Broom is wounded.

Kroenen puts up a savage fight, killing an American soldier with every shot he fires. When he runs out of ammunition, he extends a blade from beneath each arm of his great coat (something like the weapons Scud manufactures in *Blade II*) and cuts through his attackers with clockwork efficiency, the blades spinning like deadly rotors.

Bleeding, Professor Broom crawls towards a dying soldier, trying to reach his grenades. Kroenen spots Broom and prepares his lethal blades. Just as Broom reaches the grenades, Whitman shoots the assassin. The bullets have no more effect on Kroenen than insect bites but the distraction gives Broom the chance to throw a grenade beneath the spinning gyroscopic blades of the Nazi's occult machine. Kroenen tries to reach the explosive, the machines blades slicing the tips of his fingers. The explosion throws him against the

Hellboy – the Red Right Hand of Doom for monsters

walls of the abbey, then for good measure, he's speared by a fragment of debris from the explosion. Grigory is pulled into the vortex, losing his eyes in the process as it closes behind him.

Sergeant Whitman helps Professor Broom to his feet, telling him. "It's almost over." "No. It's not. The portal has been open for too long. Something may have come through. Have your men search the area thoroughly."

They see the spike that had impaled Kroenen, but the assassin isn't there. Corporal George Matlin, the platoon's combat photographer, comments. "He's gone." Broom doesn't think so. "For now." Matlin asks him. "When you said something came through, from where?" In answer, Broom looks at a 13th century carved religious fresco depicting heaven and hell. Broom is wearing a rosary wrapped around his arm. As Broom bandages his wounded leg, Matlin asks him. "Do you really, really, believe in Hell?" "There is a place, a dark place, where ancient evil slumbers, and wants to return. Grigory gave us a glance tonight." "Grigory, that's...that's Russian, right." "Grigory Yefimovich Rasputin. Occult advisor to the Romanovs. In 1916, at a dinner in his honour, he was poisoned, stabbed, clubbed, castrated and finally drowned and yet we saw him here tonight."

They hear a noise in the crypt beyond. The professor advises caution...hidden among the carvings or gargoyles and demons, is the infant creature who we will come to know as...Hellboy!

Startled, the frightened Matlin opens fire. "What the hell is that? An ape?" Broom replies. "No, it was red, bright red. Lower your light, you're scaring it." They are joined by the other surviving soldiers. They think Matlin has been shooting at a red ape. Then one of the soldiers notices 'it's got a big stone in its hand." Broom informs him that it is his hand. Matlin is impressed. "Look at the size of that whammer." The soldiers move to shoot it but the professor stops them. He feels an immediate kinship with this new arrival, in their own way they are both two lonely creatures looking for a friend. There aren't many paranormal advisers to the President, and there aren't many red demons with a stone hand. Broom opens a Baby Ruth Bar, and takes a bite to show the baby demon that it's safe, and offers it to the creature, who takes it. He offers it another, telling the soldiers to get him a blanket. He tells the new arrival. "Come on, its safe, jump down." He jumps down, Broom is surprised to discover. "It's a boy." He's echoed by Corporal Matlin. "It's just a baby boy."

The soldiers crowd around for a look, they are all touched. He might have come from hell, but he got a pretty positive reception from a group of men who've obviously seen the hell of war. Even, then he has something special about him. Broom is like a proud new father with his son. Corporal Matlin takes a photograph of them all together.

Professor Broom's narration resumes. "There we were. An unready father for an unwanted child. The boys gave him a name that very night. In retrospect perhaps not the most fortunate. But nevertheless a name we all came to use. We called him Hellboy."

A montage of occult symbols, newspaper headlines, comics, and TV reports, reveal that Hellboy has not only grown into an adult, he's also grown into an urban myth suspected of working with the FBI. "The government hides the truth." "FBI make deal with evil boy." "Does he live near you?" "Half-man, half-devil." "What is it you say this agency does?" "I kid you not, it hunts monsters."

BIRGAU PASS, MOLDAVIA, PRESENT DAY.

Three travellers trek across the frozen ground of a gigantic rock formation. The Sherpa guide announces. "What you seek is in there." The snow is cleared from a stone and a carving revealed. Grigory's leather-bound book is consulted. The symbol matches an illustration in the book.

The three travellers enter a vast cathedral-like chamber, the size of a massive stadium, full of carvings and statues. The cyclopean architecture dwarfs the travellers. An eerie light from above illuminates a spectacular labyrinth. The stone floor is covered in grooves radiating from a shallow stone basin. The book is once again consulted. The Sherpa guide (Pavel Cajzl) announces. "This is a sacred place...give me my gold. We shouldn't be here." In response, a gold ingot with a swastika carved on it is dropped on the frozen floor. As the Sherpa goes to retrieve his blood money, he receives a very familiar blade through the chest. As he stains the frozen stone red with his blood, which quickly begins to flow into the carved grooves, tracing a glyph (shades of *Blade II*) the other two travellers reveal themselves.

It's Ilsa and Kroenen. Clearly Rasputin's promise holds through, Ilsa hasn't aged a day, and the assassin looks much the same too (though he has the advantage of a mask to hide any wrinkles). The blood fills the stone basin, from which arises Grigory Yefimovich Rasputin! (In the manner of Wesley Snipes in Blade II, which was itself a homage to Martin Sheen's character in *Apocalypse Now*) Ilsa is delighted. "Master!" But shocked too. "Your eyes! What did they do to your eyes?"

LEXINGTON ONCOLOGY CENTRE, NEW YORK

Two doctors are examining x-rays. Doctor Jenkins (Tara Hugo) asks the male doctor(Ricard Haas). "Have you told him yet?" "No." "You should." They are referring to Professor Broom, now aged, but still possessed of great dignity, still wearing the rosary from the night he found Hellboy wrapped around his wrist. They give him the bad news, it's the worst news. "Malignant sarcoma. In the lungs..." Broom shuffles a unique-looking pack of tarot cards (clearly one designed by Guillermo). He asks. "Approximately...how long?" "Maybe six weeks. I can arrange for hospitalisation and pain management. Make the time more bearable." "No. I'd rather be at home. I have some arrangements to make...for my son." Broom pulls the 'Death' card from the tarot pack as the Doctor tells him, "you can always get a second opinion." Ruefully, Broom replies. "That won't be necessary."

Broom walks to a BPRD car, driven by Agent Lime (Brian Caspe). It's clearly Halloween, kids are running around in masks, there are carved pumpkinheads. He glances at a TV in a shop window, a familiar face to Broom is being introduced by the announcer. "Tom Manning is head of Special Operations at the FBI. He joins Pat the presenter in the studio tonight to go over the latest Hellboy sighting."

In the studio, Manning is shown a blurry picture of Hellboy. "That's the tail and these are the horns." Manning is very experienced at handling Hellboy sightings, you could say he's a natural born liar. He says. "I have a question, why is it in these pictures...the pictures of aliens, UFOs, the Yeti, Hellboy. Why is it they're always out of focus?" He laughs but Pat isn't giving up so easily. "Why don't you tell me about the Bureau of Paranormal Research and Defence?"

Watching on TV, Broom is amused, Manning takes this question coolly as well, the picture of sincerity as he lies. "I want to tell you, I want to tell the American public one thing. Now, this Bureau...for...um" Pat prompts him. "Paranormal Research and Defence." "There...is...no...such...thing."

BUREAU FOR PARANORMAL RESEARCH AND DEFENCE, NEWARK, NJ.

A man on a scooter arrives at the gates of what is the BPRD headquarters but masquerades as 'Squeaky Clean Waste Management Services". He punches a code into a keypad at the gate. A voice asks him. "What is it?" "John Myers (Rupert Evans). FBI. Transfer from Quantico." A retinal eye scanner emerges, and scans his identity. This confirmed, he is allowed through the gates and into the headquarters itself. He enters a vast hallway. He's standing dead centre on the BPRD logo, a hand holding a sword. The desk that faces him bears the legend: IN ABSENTIA LUCI, TENBERAE VINCIUNT. Myers introduces himself to the agent at the desk, who tells him bluntly, "you're late, that's what you are, five minutes." He tells him he's going to "Area 51 (a nice in-joke, Area 51 being the supposed site where the American government hides UFOs), Watch your hands and elbows."

Myers is standing on a lift which descends deep into the complex beneath him. Passing thorough an ornate door, he enters a beautiful library. Several books are left open.

A voice asks him to "turn the pages please, if you don't mind." Myers is spooked to find the voice coming from a humanoid creature, Abe Sapien (Doug Jones) floating in a tank of water. "These, you're reading these?" A voice behind him confirms this. "Four books at once, every day, as long as I'm there to turn the pages. My name's Professor Trevor Broom."

Myers is about to introduce himself, but the psychic creature in the tank does it for him. "John T Myers. Kansas City 76. T stands for Thadeus, mother's older brother. Scare on your chin happened when you were ten. You're still wondering if it's every going to fade away." Myers is stunned. "How did it...?" Broom corrects him. "He. Not 'it'! Abraham Sapien. Discovered alive in a secret chamber of St Trinian's Foundling Hospital, Washington. His name was taken from this little inscription stuck to the side of his tank. Broom indicates a small piece of antique paper" "Icthyo Sapiens. April 14, 1865." "The day that Abraham Lincoln died. Hence Abe Sapien."

Broom uncovers some rotten eggs which he sends into Abe's tank. "Rotten eggs. A delicacy. Abe loves them." Myers looks like he's going to gag from the smell. He asks Broom. "How does he know so much about me?" "Abe possesses a unique frontal lobe. Unique, that's a word you'll hear frequently around here." "Sir, where am I exactly?" "As you entered the lobby, there was an inscription: 'In absentia luci, tenebrae vinciunt', 'In the absence of light, darkness prevails.' There are things that go bump in the night, Agent Myers, make no mistake about that... we are ones who bump back."

Broom enters a key into a door and he and Myers enter a long corridor lined by glass cases containing occult artefacts, it's a walking museum tour of the BPRD's history. A mummified hand, a clay golem, a pagan altar, and some fairies, similar to the ones from *Pan's Labyrinth*. As they walk, Broom fills in Myers on the history of the BPRD. "1937. Hitler joins the 'Thule Society'. A group of German aristocrats obsessed with the occult...1938, acquired the Spear of Longinus, which pierced the side of Christ. He who holds it becomes invincible." They pause briefly in front of the actual Spear of Longinus in a glass case. Broom continues. "Hitler's power increases ten-fold....1943, President Roosevelt decides to fight back. The Bureau of Paranormal Research and Defence is born....1958, the Occult Wars finally come to an end with the death of Adolf Hitler." Myers corrects him. "1945, you mean...Hitler died in '45." Broom laughs. "Did he now." He introduces Myers to Agent Clay (Corey Johnson). "Oh, Myers, this is Agent Clay, take his lead. He'll make the introductions." Broom hands Myers two Baby Ruth bars. Myers looks worried and asks Broom. "You're not coming?" "I hand picked you from a roster of over seventy academy graduates, make me proud."

Clay explains to Myers. "They're not speaking. Mr Broom had him grounded." "Grounded. Who's grounded?" Clay opens a very strong-looking steel door. "Okay, you saw the fish-guy, right?" "Oh yeah. I mean that was weird." "Yeah, right." Clay pulls the door open. "Well, come on in, meet the rest of the family." Inside there are cats everywhere (the sign of a good guy! Who doesn't love cats?), TVs playing cartoons, it's a colossal bachelor pad. Clay briefs Myers. "He gets fed six times a day. He's got a thing for cats. You'll be his nanny, his keeper, his best friend. He never goes out unsupervised." Myers is still none the wiser. "Who?"

By way of answer, Clay hands Myers a comic book entitled *Hellboy the Uncanny*." A deep voice announces. "I hate those comic books. They never get the eyes right." Myers sees the huge red figure pumping iron. Hellboy (Ron Perlman). He's astonished. "Hellboy! He's real." Clay confirms this, it's all routine to him. "Yeah, sixty years old by our count. But he doesn't age like we do. Think reverse dog years. He's barely out of his twenties." Hellboy has noticed something new about Clay's hair. "What's with the hair, Clay? Finally got the implants?" Clay blushes. "It'll fill in." Hellboy has noticed Myers. "Who's your squirt?" "Agent Myers is your new liaison." "I don't want him. What, you get tired of me, Clay?" Clay indicates that Myers should give Hellboy the candy, but Hellboy ignores the new agent. "Father's back?" Clay nods." Hellboy asks like a chastened child. "He still angry?" "Well, you did break out." "Ah, I wanted to see her.

Nobodys business." "It is. You got yourself on TV again." Hellboy speaks to Myers for the first time. "'Myers'. You got a first name, 'Myers'." Clay quietly warns Myers not to stare at Hellboy's horns, he files them to fit in. Myers manages to stammer out his first name. Despite Clay's warning, he cannot take his eyes off the stumps of Hellboy's horns. Hell boy asks him. "What are you looking at, John." "Nothing...nothing..." Myers is rescued from his embarrassment by a Code Red Alert. Hellboy is delighted. "Hey, it's playing our song. C'mon, John, lets go fight some monsters."

Later, they approach the source of the alert in their covert transport disguised as a garbage truck, The Machen Library in Manhattan, a fabulously imposing building (It's named the Machen Library in homage to ghost writer Arthur Machen). A Halloween banner advertises an exhibition entitled Magick: The Ancient Power. Outside, are police, reporters, emergency crews. A TV reporter is doing her report on camera. "We're here at the Machen Library where just two hours ago an alarm was triggered. The N.Y.P.D has yet to issue a statement. We've got SWAT teams, paramedics, you name it, and now here comes a garbage truck." She's astonished by its arrival. "A large garbage truck."

Inside the truck. Hellboy comments to Abe, as he looks out at the crowd. "Look at those ugly suckers, Blue. Just a sheet of glass between them and us." "Story of my life." "Outside. I could be outside." "You mean outside with her." "Don't get psychic with me, [illegible]" "Nothing psychic about it, you're easy." "How am I ever gonna get a girl? I drive around in a garbage truck." "Liz left us, Red, take the hint." Hellboy picks up his huge gun, The Samaritan (So named because it puts the monsters it shoots out of their misery). "We don't take hints."

Clay is waiting with other BPRD agents, agent Quarry (Stephen Fisher), Stone (Garth Cooper) and Moss (James Babson), who have sealed off the area. Agent Lime is covering the roof. All the agents are activating their locators. "Seal the doors, Red and Blue are coming in....1900 Hours. An alarm was tripped, and a large entity, a type 5 reported, very aggressive, six guards dead." Hellboy is surprised. "I thought we'd checked this place. Fakes and reproductions." Unknown to Hellboy, Professor Broom is already there, he says. "Not everything is faked." Hellboy tries (and fails) to hide his cigar from his father. As Hellboy opens a large arms locker, Broom explains. "The entity is still in there. Video surveillance shows a 16th century statue was destroyed. St Dionysius the Aeropagite." Hellboy has heard of it. "Wards off demons." His father concurs. "The statue however was hollow." Hellboy asks. "A reliquary?" Broom explains. "A prison. The Vatican considered its occupant dangerous enough to include on the List of Avignon. Of which, by the way, we hold a copy." Hellboy indicates a special clip of bullets. "Perfect job for these babies. Made 'em myself, holy water, clove leaf, silver shavings, white oak, the works."

Abe hold his hand to the door, and quickly pulls it way, as though his mind has come into contact with something horrible. "Behind this door, a dark entity, evil ancient and hungry." Hellboy quips. "Oh well, let me go and say hi."

Hellboy enters the exhibition hall like a gunfighter in a spaghetti western. The hall is full of the same banners as the one on the outside of the building. He picks up a slimy boot and [illegible] Abe. "Better hit the books, Brother Blue. This place is trashed. We definitely need more info on [illegible]." Myers asks Abe with surprise (He doesn't realise that Hellboy is defined by his own loneliness, his own uniqueness, his job defines him). "No one goes with [illegible]." He likes it that way. The whole lonely hero thing." Abe starts go through his mobile library of ancient grimoires and bestiaries .

In the trashed exhibition hall, Hellboy spots the type [illegible] entity. "Hey! 'Stinky'. Kitchen's closed. What you having? Six library guards raw plus belts and boots...you're gonna need some heavy fibre to move that out." Abe radios Hellboy, he's found the creature's identity. "This entity's name is Sammael, the Desolate One, son of Nergal..."

In the exhibition hall, Sammael (Brian Steele) jumps down to confront Hellboy, who tells it. "Listen, Sammy. I'm not a very good shot. But the Samaritan here uses really big bullets. So, what do you say, we work this out nice and peaceful?" But Sammael doesn't want to give peace a chance. Hellboy follows it, letting loose with the Samaritan's awesome firepower. Bringing it down ,Hellboy is triumphant. "That's it for you, Sammy." Abe radios Hellboy. "Red, you need to hear the rest of the information." "Nah, he's taken care of." "No, listen to this. Sammael the Desolate One, Lord of the Shadows, Son of Nergal, Hound of Resurrection..." "See, I don't like the sound of that." "What, Hound of Resurrection? Harbinger of Pestilence? Seed of Destruction?" "Cut to the end, how do I kill it?" "It doesn't say."

Sammael revives and Hellboy loses his gun. The creature uses him as a punchbag and fires him out of the building (in a nice homage to Ash in *Army of Darkness*). When Hellboy lands, Grigory is waiting. "Child, all grown up, I see." Hellboy recognises Grigory from long ago. "That voice..." "It was the first lullaby, you ever heard, my son. I ushered you into this world. I alone know your true calling." "Name this!" Hellboy pulls his gun, but Rasputin vanishes. Sammael attacks again, a tentacular tongue crushing Hellboy's gun hand, until a hail of bullets from puts it down. Hellboy resents his assistance. "What do you think you're doing?" "Helping you." "No one helps me. My job!" Hellboy gives Myers a tracking bullet to load. Now they can track the seeming indestructible creature as it runs into to the city with the agents in pursuit. Amusing, Myers tries to cover up what's happening to passers-by. "Crazy costumes, trick or treat!"

Sammael makes it to a motorway, which holds up Hellboy. Myers is hit, and it looks the next car will finish him, until Hellboy holds up his huge hand. "Red means stop!" He punches the car with his hand, saving Myers. Leaving Myers, he follows the fluorescent green trail from Sammael. "Sammy, you got a leak." Sammael has made it into the underground (favourite Guillermo territory). The creature tears into a tube train that hits Hellboy. While Sammael manages to escape , the train driver (a nice cameo from Santiago Segura, Rush from *Blade II*) beats Hellboy with a fire extinguisher as he clings on desperately, telling him. "Hey, I'm on your side." "Yeah, sure." Humans! It's what you look like that matters to them. Hellboy goes under the train, which scrapes the stumps of his horns making them glow red hot. He's then jumped by Sammael (who's like the *Predator* as envisaged by H.P. Lovecraft). Using his red right hand, Hellboy channels the electricity from the live rail into Sammael, cooking him (Interestingly, originally the transport cop in *Mimic* was supposed to die heroically this way, taking the Mimics with him). Hell boy cracks. "I'm fireproof. You're not." Hellboy calls Myers. "I've just fried Stinky. Tell father. I'll be home. But he shouldn't wait up." Myers wants to go with him, but Hellboy turns off his tracer and leaves. He doesn't see the spirit arise from Sammael and split into two.

ABANDONED SUBWAY AREA, LOCKER ROOM

Kroenen is listening to an ancient gramophone. Ilsa is shaving Grigory's head (This scene works on two levels, it shows her devotion to Rasputin, after all, she has waited 60 years for his return and her feelings are stronger if anything, and secondly, it is a quote of a shot of Luis Bunuel in *Un Chien Andalou*).. She hands him two artificial eyes which he inserts into his empty sockets. He reaches for the two spirits that arose from the Sammael that Hellboy destroyed. "Sammael has fulfilled his destiny. Die in peace...and be reborn again and again." He closes his fist around the spirits. Ilsa says. "Only seven more days to the eclipse." Grigory knows this only too well. "The child will be there and so will we all...won't we?" The spirits he held in his hand are gone, and when Kroenen moves back, there are now two Sammaels.

BELLAMIE PSYCHIATRIC HOSPITAL. MINIMUM SECURITY UNIT.

Hellboy has stolen some beer, and enters the gothic looking hospital to see Liz Sherman (Selma Blair). He spotted by a patient. "There's a big red man down there." But the patient is not believed, and besides, who'd notice Hellboy at Halloween. "Santa's not due for another month!"

Hellboy stands like a statue watching Liz in the garden of the hospital (the trees are covered by plastic to protect them from frost, they look reminiscent of the plastic covered statues of archangels in Dieter de la Guardia's apartment in *Cronos*). Liz knows Hellboy is there. He tells her. "I brought beer." She sees the injury Sammael gave Hellboy. "Oh, Red., your arm. You'd better get that looked at." "I wanted to see you."

Back at the Machen Library, Manning is once again displeased with Hellboy, telling Professor Broom. "Every time the media get a look at him, they come running to me. I'm running out of lies, Trevor." "Thought you liked been on television." "I do. So, how many escapes this year alone, five?" "Tom, he's our guest, not a prisoner." "Well, your guest happens to be 6-foot-5, bright red, has a tail and is government funded." "I know where to find him. I'll get him back."

Abe picks up a knife with a ragnarok symbol on the hilt, a dragon and swastika. Manning spots him. "Hey, Fishstick, don't touch anything." "I need to touch it to see." "To see what." "Past, future, whatever this object holds." "Is he serious?" "Don't worry about fingerprints, never had any...Professor, they were here." Manning is sceptical. "Who was here? Nixon, Houdini, Jimmy Hoffa, who?"

The Professor knows better and takes Abe very seriously. "Show me, Abe, show me what happened here." Abe places Professor Broom's hand on his hand that holds the knife. Time flows backwards, Abe and the Professor are in the museum before Sammael's release. A guard is doing his rounds. Kroenen is there, examining the case of the statue of St Dionysius the Aeropagite. Ilsa smashes the glass case with a hammer, and Kroenen's blades slice the statue open, allowing Ilsa to remove a cylinder from within. The guards have spotted her, and she sends Kroenen to deal with them. He uses his blades to deflect two of the guard's bullets back to them. The rest of their shots just bounce off his ornate clockwork breastplate. Like an automaton, he cuts a swath through the remaining guards.

This done, Grigory joins them, tell Ilsa to "ready the welcome, my love." Ilsa pours a substance from the cylinder, which Grigory explains is "salt, gathered from the tears of a thousand angels. Restraining the essence of Sammael The Hellhound. The Seed of Destruction." The Russian mystic breaths a green mist onto the salt. "This I can promise, Sammael, for each one of you that falls, two shall arise." Sammael begins to form from the swirling salts (it is very Ray Harryhausen-inspired, and very inventive too, with the creature manifesting first in skeletal form, then flesh growing on its bones. It's also reminiscent of the resurrection of Dracula in Terence Fisher's *Dracula Prince of Darkness*, as the Dracula's skeleton and subsequently his body, reform from his ashes).

Professor Broom is stunned by the vision he's shared with Abe, he feels faint. When Abe goes to assist him, he accidentally discovers his friend is dying. "You are very sick." Professor Broom tells him. "I don't want Hellboy to know. Sixty years ago they tried to destroy the world and they're back. In my lifetime they're back to finish the job."

Meanwhile, Hellboy is trying to persuade Liz. "I miss you at the Bureau. Abe's crazier every day. Father's still mad at me...Come back, Liz. Come back." "No, H.B. Not this time. I don't like it here, but I haven't had an episode in months." A ball of flame hovers over her hand. "You know what? I'm learning to control it. I'm learning where it comes from. For the first time in my life I'm not afraid. Looks like your ride's here." Hellboy comments. "Nanny squad!"

Myers volunteers. "Sir, can I go first?" Clay is sceptical. "He barely knows him." Broom has faith in Myers though. "Then he should make it his business to change that."

Liz tells Hellboy the news he least wants to hear. "Listen, H.B. I've got a chance out here. So if you really care about me....you won't come back." He's crushed (a wonderfully subtle and moving performance from Ron Perlman. He has more emotion in his eyes or a single gesture than most actors manage in an entire film). He tries to let on that he's not heartbroken as she walks away. "Yeah, I gotta go too...lots to do."

Myers exchanges a brief glance with Liz as he approaches Hellboy, who, despite

Kroenen – Human evil incarnate

the pain he's in, cracks. "What took you so long?" "Come on, time to go home. Tape you up." "What are you? A boy scout?" "Nope, I never was." "Well, you could have fooled me." Hellboy collapses. Myers helps him. "you've lost a lot of blood." Hellboy she's his father. "This is nothing. You know he'll kill me, don't you..." The irony of Hellboy been unafraid of monsters but sacred of his aged father is not lost.

Back at the Bureau, Abe attends to Hellboy. "You were burned by some organic acid." "I'm lucky that way." Broom is concerned about Hellboy's future, telling him. "I worry about you." "Me?" "Well, I won't be around forever, you know." Abe has removed an egg from Hellboy's wound. "How long was it latched onto you?" "About five seconds." "Touched you five seconds... laid three eggs." "Didn't even buy me a drink." "The stinger detaches itself from the tongue and injects the eggs. They're very sensitive to heat and light. They need a humid dark environment...to breed." Myers asks Hellboy. "Did you ever loose track of him?" "Well, lets see, there was that moment when I had a train on top of my head." Broom makes a quick decision. "We can't risk it. Tomorrow you'll go back to the tracks with a group of agents. Search out the whole place from top to bottom. Find those eggs and destroy them."

Later, Myers checks out Liz's file. "Elizabeth Sherman." He's developing a crush on her, despite learning of her pyrokinetic power.

At the Bellamie Psychiatric Hospital, Grigory is watching the sleeping Liz. "My master is calling your name, my girl. You must return to the child. So once again. Dream of fire." He kisses her forehead. There is a red glow and she dreams of being back at school. She's been bullied by a gang of kids who chase her, call her a freak and hurl stones at her. In her dream, she's angry and hurt, she's wreathed in flames and she destroys her tormentors. In the hospital, she burns her room, a firestorm sweeps through the hospital.

At the Bureau, Myers brings Hellboy's food into him. Hellboy asks Broom. "How many buildings does she have to burn

down. She belongs here." "That's not what she feels. She may never feel it. Her choice." Myers asks. "Professor...that girl you're talking about." Hellboy warns him. "Think twice." Myers ploughs on regardless. "I read her file, she blames herself for that explosion in Pittsburgh. I think I can help. I could talk to her. I can bring her back." Hellboy asks him sarcastically. "What was it that landed you this job pushing pancakes. Huh? What was it? Punctuality? The way you part your hair? What is your area of expertise?"

Myers tell Broom later. "He doesn't want me with him. I know that much." "You're doing fine." "No, I'm not. He respects Clay...I'm not your guy." "I am dying, Agent Myers. Like any father, I worry about him. In medieval stories, there is often a young knight who is inexperienced but pure of heart." "I'm not pure of heart." Abe interjects. "Yes, you are." Broom continues. "Rasputin is back for him. What I ask of you is to have the courage to stand by him when I'm gone. He was born a demon, can't change that, but you will help him, in essence, become a man."

At the devastated Bellamie Hospital, Myers gets out of a cab. Liz is being kept in isolation, but it's nothing compared to the isolation she feels in herself.

A doctor tells him. "She was making great progress and now this, we'll be closed for months. And it put a big dent in our thorazine supply. She's been like this since it happened. Are you sure you want to go in?" He does. "Miss Sherman. I'm Agent Myers, F.B.I. Can I call you Liz? It's a beautiful name?" "60% of all women in the world are named 'Liz'." "Well, it's impressive by my standards. My name is John. John T. Myers. Dr Broom asked me to invite you back to the Bureau. No special precautions. No security escorts. Just you and me in a taxi like regular folks." "That doesn't sound like him. "Well, Miss Sherman, he's asking you back, but it's entirely your choice." "Choice, huh? That's cute. I've quit the Bureau thirteen times. I always go back. Where else would I go?"

ABANDONED SUBWAY AREA

Hellboy, Abe, and agents Clay, Moss and Quarry, are searching the abandoned cellar of the Benjamin Institute, a turn of the century orphanage, closed since they moved the sewers in 1951. Clay tells them. "You said those eggs need it dark and humid. Well they hit the Jackpot. The subway lines, they all converge right around here. Right below us is the old Vandevere Reservoir, it was abandoned in the mid-30s." Abe can sense a pulse. "Most of the eggs are in a cistern behind a brick wall." Clay announces they need to go back and request a special type 2 permit. But Hellboy bypasses the red tape by punching his way through.

Kroenen stops working on his clockwork hand (whose workings resemble that of the Cronos Device) as he hears Hellboy's fist pounding on brick, his lidless eyes bulging. He's like a black widow whose web has been disturbed. He places two pieces of ancient parchment in an envelope that he pockets. Then he prepares for battle.

Having broken through the wall, Hellboy lifts up a manhole cover swarming with cockroaches (*Mimic*'s Revenge!) on the other side. Abe comments sarcastically as he drops glow rods into the huge tank of water below . "We lead a charmed life." Inside the tank, unseen by the B.P.R.D agents, is a swimming Sammael. Hellboy hands Abe an ancient piece of finger in a jar. "This should cover your tail fin. Reliquary. Straight from the Vatican. Bone from St Dionysius...looks like a pinky." Remind me why I keep doing this." "Rotten eggs and the safety of mankind." Abe enters the reservoir and starts to recover the eggs, placing them in a flask.

Sammael darts past.

Clay is

fretting about his hair implant. "This doesn't really look like doll's hair. Be honest, Red, what do you think?" "I'm thinking of doing it myself." Hellboy asks Agents Quarry and Moss by radio, if they've found anything, but they've had no luck. Hellboy throws a glow stick down a tunnel and spots Kroenen. He chases him into the damp labyrinth of disused tunnels. Clay follows but loses them both.

Abe finds a huge cluster of eggs, as he reaches for it, he loses the Reliquary. He can't retrieve it and he's no longer protected. The creature attacks Abe, wounding him and trapping him in an alcove.

Quarry and Moss get a signal from Abe, when they look at the reservoir's entrance, they see two Sammaels. Like much of the B.P.R.D's equipment, the flamethrowers are highly complicated to start and Sammael gets the first agent before he can fire, then chases the other. Trapped by a speeding subway train, Sammael catches him.

Hellboy has entered Kroenen's lair. It's a dark alchemist's den, full of strange devices, cogs and clockwork body parts. He finds a medieval woodcut of Sammael. Overhead waits the real thing. Hellboy look up. "Didn't I kill you already?" Sammael attacks, hurling them both down a vast lift shaft to crash into a station below. Sammael smashes Hellboy into a wall, tiles flying everywhere. A nearby phone rings. Hellboy pulls the phone off the wall and uses it on Sammael like a 21st century version of a morningstar. "It's for you...you shouldn't hurt people!" Sammael repairs the damage to its body and wings at Hellboy. "You missed!" Sammael didn't, he's destroyed the supporting column beside Hellboy, causing the office above to collapse on top of him. "Hey, Chunk-face, you can do better than that. Big monster like you." It can, it hurls Hellboy onto the next level.

Ivan gives Hellboy, Agent Lime and Manning the grand tour of the Moscow catacombs

Just as Sammael is about to attack again, he saves a box of kittens. As Sammael's tongue snakes out towards him, Hellboy grabs it. Holding the kittens in one hand, Hellboy swings Sammael by the tongue, through an observation window. Sammael tries to drag Hellboy after it (the sight of the kittens looking on is hysterical, ignorance truly is bliss). Just as he's about to plunge after Sammael, a speeding train decapitates the creature. Hellboy returns the box of kittens to their grateful owner. Hellboy pats a kitten on the head. "My job!" (Again we see Hellboy is defined by what he does not who he is.)

As before, Sammael's spirit escapes and divides. At the same moment, as if on cue, the eggs begin to hatch as the wounded Abe leaves the reservoir. The water begins to bubble, desperately Abe activates his tracer signal. Hellboy radios Clay. "I'm getting a signal from Abe, I'm on my way back."

Clay has his own problem, he's located Kroenen, who winds up his clockwork mechanism. Clay shoots. Bullets bounce off the ornate chest plate. Where they enter the costume, sand flows out (an idea taken from Hammer's fine *The Mummy's Shroud* 1967), and Kroenen stabs him. As Hellboy approaches, Kroenen lies down, turns a lever on his chest plate, spasms and lies still.

Meanwhile, Liz is travelling back to the bureau with Myers by taxi as promised. It's clear some kind of attraction is forming between them.

Back at the Bureau, Abe is in intensive care. Manning isn't pleased, he tells Hellboy. "He'll make it. Not everyone was so lucky. We had two agents die today. Clay probably won't survive the night." "Not now, Manning, please." "My problem with you, you're reckless. Those men expected you to lead them as a team. Where were you?" "I knew those men better than you did." "That makes it alright, then." No, it doesn't make it right. But I stopped that thing, didn't I?" "Yes, you did. That's what you do. That's why we need you. You have an insight. You know monsters." Hellboy picks up on the implication, that not only does Myers hold him responsible, but the reason Hellboy can catch monsters is that he himself is a monster. "What're you trying to say?" "This whole thing is a farce. Because in the end...after you've killed, after you've captured every freak out there...there's still one left...You!" "Hey, Manning. I wish I could be more gracious, but..." Hellboy picks up a huge cylinder.

Meanwhile Professor Broom is welcoming Liz back. She tells him. "It's only for the weekend, Professor Broom. Then I shall be on my way." "Oh, you should have a look around. We made some changes around here." The cylinder Hellboy picked up flies through a nearby window. The shaken Manning tells Broom. "I want that thing locked up, starting now." Liz comments ruefully. "Nothing's changed. Home sweet home." Hellboy is thrilled to see Liz, even going so far as to praise Myers for the first time. "You did it, buddy, you did it." Hellboy doesn't see how disappointed everyone is with him.

Myers goes to see Liz, asking what's the story behind the rubber bands on her wrist. She tells him. "It's something I learned in therapy. I'm depressed, one rubber band. I'm impatient...two rubber bands." "Maybe I should get you a fresh pack." "Yeah, maybe two."

Hellboy is trying to write a letter to Liz (a scene which echoes the scene in *Cronos* where Jesús Gris tries to compose a letter to his wife, which in itself echoes a scene in Terence Fisher's *The Gorgon*). Hellboy hasn't realised that Myers has a crush on Liz, and asks his new liaison for help. "You're a talker. What's a good word, a good solid word for 'need'. "Well, 'need' is a good solid word." Hellboy isn't impressed. "Too needy." "Well, start in, you got nachos coming."

Speak of the Devil (to pardon a *Hellboy* related pun!), and in she comes, in the shapely form of Liz. She's astonished at how many cats Hellboy has since she was last here. "Oh, my God, look at them all. Who had babies?" "Liz, there's something I need for you to hear, and it's..." She interrupts him. "Will it take long? Because I'm actually going out." Hellboy is astonished. She confirms that she's going out. "Yeah, for a cup of coffee, but go ahead, read." Hellboy's suspicions are aroused. "Are you going alone?" "No, Myers is taking me." Again, speak of the Devil, Myers comes in, telling Hellboy. "Hey, your chilli's getting cold." Hellboy glares at him. "Not hungry!" Liz asks Hellboy. "Is there something you'd like me to hear?" He lies. "It's just a list. It's not finished." "Okay. Well then, later." Myers asks Hellboy if there's anything else he needs. Hellboy is not fond of Myers at this moment. "Well, good night." Hellboy crushes a can, probably wishing it was Myers' neck. "Goodbye!"

Professor Broom is performing an autopsy on Kroenen, dictating his findings into a recorder. "Subject: Karl Ruprecht Kroenen. Born in Munich, 1897." Broom pulls back the sheet from Kroenen's body to reveal a grey arm covered with stitches and scars. "Suffered from a masochistic compulsion... commonly known as surgical addiction. Both eyelids surgically removed..." Kroenen's body is a roadmap of surgical scars. "...along with his upper and lower lips." He puts his hand on an ornate dial on Kroenen's chest. "The blood in his veins dried up decades ago. "Broom pulls the dial, revealing an intricate clockwork mechanism. "Only dust remains." Broom puts down the ticking mechanism. "What horrible will could keep such a creature as this alive?" He takes the envelope Kroenen earlier placed in his clothing, and reads the scraps of paper within.

An agent hears a pounding from Hellboy's quarters, and opens the door to investigate. He finds Hellboy has punched

a hole in the wall large enough to enter an adjoining lift shaft and escape into the world outside. "Damn it, Red. Not again."

In the outside world, Liz is outside a coffee shop, taking photographs as autumn leaves fall. She doesn't spot Hellboy watching her from a nearby rooftop. Myers is talking to her about Hellboy. "I admire him. He's a force of nature..." Hellboy mutters to himself. "What are you two talking about? What is so fascinating, so important?" He doesn't realise he himself is the subject.

Myers continues to Liz. "No. He's determined. Unstoppable." She replies. "Some people would call that cocky." Myers is actually being very loyal to Hellboy despite his feelings for Liz." "He's just strong." "Yeah, that he is." Then Myers comes up with what has to be one of the simplest and truest pieces of wisdom ever. "My uncle, he used to say we like people for their qualities...but love them for their defects. He loves you, you know." Of course she knows, women always know. She nods confirmation and Myers asks her how she feels about Hellboy. She replies. "I don't know. I grew up with him. But now every time I see him, I get confused. There's hardly a day that goes by that he's not in my mind. Even now...I feel like he's here."

Indeed he is. He watches Myers bring her coffee scornfully. "No cream and sugar, moron. She takes it black." Hellboy is very jealous. "She took his picture. Damn!" Hellboy, makes a very noir-esque leap (and angry) leap for another building and ends up hanging off the edge of it, as Myers and Liz talk below. He's spotted by a kid as he climbs to safety. "You're Hellboy!" "I'm on a mission." The kid is thrilled." Below Liz is asking Myers. "Tell me something about you. Where do you come from?" "I lived with my uncle most of my life. Then I went to Quantico, went to the top of my class. I'm nothing..."

At the Bureau, an agent informs Broom of Hellboy's breakout and asks if they should send out some scouts. Broom is despairing of his son ever growing up. "Enough, enough, enough. He'll never change. A child. Always a child."

In his quarters, Professor Broom places the fragments of parchment he took from Kroenen into a machine in order to understand its significance. His quarters feature a beautiful statue of an angel wielding a sword (an inspiration for the B.P.R.D logo), as well as fabulous ancient books and artefacts. He reads the parchment. "Sebastian Palckba, number 16...Moscow. Who wants us in Moscow?" As he speaks, in the autopsy room, Kroenen suddenly arises, a self-winding clockwork perpetual motion killing machine. He recovers his hand and reattaches it, its intricate clockwork mechanisms clearly visible. He re-inserts the key that Professor Broom removed from his chest, and literally winds himself up. His weapons and uniforms restored, he's now ready for action. His 'death' was simply an effective ruse to gain access to the Bureau's secret headquarters.

On the rooftop, the kid has bought milk and cookies to Hellboy. "My mom baked them." Hellboy's thoughts are elsewhere, he now sees the world through the green coloured haze of jealousy. "She's laughing... she's sitting on a park bench, and she's laughing." Hellboy takes a cookie. "That's it. I'm done." The kid comments. "They don't look like spies." "Are you kidding me? Look at this guy. Those shady little eyes, that phony grin." "hey, he's yawning. He's bored." "Yeah, the old yawning trick. Watch his arm." Sure enough, Myers attempts to put his arm around Liz. Hellboy starts to pick up stones. "First he wants my job, then he wants my girl." As Myers tells Liz. "We all have a side to hide." Hellboy hits Myers on the back of the head with a well aimed stone. The kid's suitably impressed. "Nice shot!"

In his quarters, Broom is looking through a book with a picture of Rasputin. He reads. "Sebastian Plackba, number 16. It's Rasputin's mausoleum." Kroenen is descending the spiral stairs to Broom's quarters, like a macabre automaton made to amuse some medieval despot. Broom spots him. "I see the puppet. But where is the puppeteer?" Grigory is there too and announces. "Very good, Professor Broom." "It was you. The scraps of paper...Liz's sudden relapse and return." "Bread crumbs on the trail. Like in a fable. They both distract him...and guide him exactly where I need him." "Moscow." "His destiny.

The real beauty and the beast

And the last clue...will be left by the late Professor Broom. You raised the child. Nurtured him. So in return...I will permit you a brief, brief glimpse of the future."

Grigory places his hand on Broom's head (the same hand that healed the Tsar's son and helped topple an empire). Broom sees a vision of a wasted landscape, flames reflected on a pair of glasses, a tattered newspaper headline screams APOCALYPSE. He sees a devastated New York, its skyscrapers are shattered. The only light comes from burning buildings, for there is no sun to be seen. The huge tentacles of the Ogdru Jahad rake the earth below. Watching over this Hell on Earth is Hellboy. His horns fully grown, wearing royal regalia, a halo of fire crowing his head.

Grigory tells Broom. "He will open the portal and bring about the end of the world." The vision ends and Grigory delights in telling Broom. "If only you had him destroyed 60 years ago, none of this would have come to pass. But how could you have known? Your God chooses to remain silent. Mine lives within me. Every time I died and crossed over, a little more of the master..." Something moves under the skin of Grigory's hand."...came back with me. He disclosed to me the child's true name. Would you like to know it?"

Broom faces his end with great courage, he knows what is truly in Hellboy's heart, its nurture not nature. Broom tells Grigory. "I know what to call him. Nothing you can do or say...can change that. I call him...son." In the background, Vera Lynn sings, 'We'll meet again." An echo of the world Hellboy came into, and a future promise for the one his father his father is about to enter.

Broom places the rosary he wore the night became father to Hellboy on the page of book opened with Rasputin's picture. "I'm ready." Rasputin places his hand on Broom's hand over the rosary and tells him. "It'll be quick." Kroenen places a gloved hand on Broom's shoulder, and kills him with mechanical emotionless efficiency, while the stone angel watches sadly, a silent witness to the passing of a brave man.

As his father dies, the jealous Hellboy is on a rooftop receiving wise council from the kid. "Just go there and tell her how you feel. My mom says that..." "It's not that easy, okay? Plus, you're 9. You're not old enough to be giving me advice." Then, cars arrive with Bureau agents to collect Myers and Liz. He hears Liz cry "no, not him", and he knows something is terribly wrong.

Hellboy returns to his dead father, for sixty years his guiding light, the man who saved him, and brought him up, that brought him through the storms of life. Gently this huge unworldly creature holds his father in his arms, frail and lifeless now, but Hellboy remembers the stormy night he came into this world and how his father held him then. In his sorrow, he is more human than human.

Later, Professor Broom's body is taken on its final journey. Overhead, Hellboy watches heartbroken, unable to go to his own father's funeral. Has anyone ever been more alone than Hellboy is at this moment.

never seen him like this, never. Should I stay? With him, I mean?" Abe is playing with a Rubik's Cube in his tank. "Listen, I'm not much of a problem solver. Three decades, I've only completed two sides. But I do know this much. If there's trouble...all us freaks have is each other. And I'm stuck here. So, take care of the big monkey for me, will you?" And they touch hands through the glass of Abe's tank. Abe's point to Liz is well made, contrary to appearances she is like Hellboy and Abe, once again, it's what's inside that counts in the end. Inside, beauty is the beast.

TOPOCKBA MILITARY BASE, MOSCOW

A limousine is escorted into the base by an armed guard. With the high ranking Russian General Lapikov are Grigory and Ilsa. They enter a huge warehouse, full of weapons, artefacts and items of historical value. The General tells Grigory and Ilsa. "I have accumulated many objects of great interest...preserving our heritage. Many like me believe Mother Russia to be very close to a historical rebirth." Soldiers cut off the seal on a huge crate. As they do Grigory comments. "Rebirth? I like that." The crate is opened to reveal a huge rock covered with carved glyphs, it radiates unearthly power. General Lapikov explains its origins. "Twenty tons of stone. This fell from the sky into Tunguska Forest."

Usually it's a monkey on the back, not a zombie

Tears are always lost in the rain. In his hands Hellboy holds his father's rosary from the night he found his son.

This is as much a Catholic moment in Hellboy as any of the imagery in, say, Cronos. Hellboy's father's death is a major guilt trip for Hellboy. He feels he could have saved Professor Broom (Though, even assuming he could have done so, Death was breathing on the unfortunate man's shoulders anyway). Thus, guilt is the fuel that feeds his furnace of rage, something Grigory knew all too well.

Later, Liz tells the recuperating Abe. "He hasn't spoken to anybody in three days, not a word. He won't eat. He won't sleep. I've

Rasputin recognises it very well. "June 30th 1908. The Romanovs took possession of it immediately. I've wanted it for ages." General Lapikov tells him. "You're aware of course, there's no way you'll get it out of Russian territory." Ilsa opens a case full of Russian gold. "He is aware. Our guests are coming in."

Back at the Bureau, Manning briefs his agents. "Volokolamsk Fields, 50 miles from Moscow, that's where we're going. Sebastian Plackba, number 16. That's the only clue we have. We've collected and destroyed thousands of eggs, but we have no trace of this Sammael or this Rasputin. We leave as soon as we get clearance and equipment. Hellboy's coming. I'm not pleased about that, but I will be in charge this time. We either wrap this or I'm closing this freakshow for good."

Myers watches Liz go to visit the heartbroken Hellboy. She finds him in his father's quarters, looking at the book his father left open at Rasputin's picture. She tells him. "I'll come to Moscow if you're still going." "I am. But I have something to say. I understand what you don't like about me. I do. What I am makes you feel a little out of place out there." "Red, I don't..." "Listen. I'm not like Myers. He makes you feel like you belong, which is good really." He indicates his horns, he wants to belong, wishes he fitted in (in their hearts, everybody does). "I wish I could do something about this...I can't. I can promise you two things: One, I'll always look this good. And two, I'll never give up on you. Ever." "I like that."

RUSIAN AIRSPACE

A B.P.R.D transport flies in Hellboy's team. Hellboy explains what they'll be facing, showing the team an ancient image of Sammael. "This engraving here represents Sammy. Text reads: 'One falls, two shall arise, Sammael.' We'll have to nail them all at once, and the eggs." Manning is trying to assert his authority. "And when we do, no mumbo-jumbo." He puts a belt of explosives on the table. "Double-core Vulcan-65 grenades. We've installed a handy little timer. You set it, you walk away. Cable pulls the safety pins. Kaboom! Easy to clean. Easy to use."

VOLOKOLAMSK FIELDS, MOSCOW

The B.P.R.D teams drives in trucks through a snowstorm. Liz radios Hellboy, who is concealed inside a crate labelled 'Live Cargo', reading a map. "Sparky to Big Red. Do you read me? Come in?" Hellboy is amused. "'Sparky?' Who came up with that? Myers?" "Yeah. We're leaving the main road, so hang on!" Hellboy is rattled by pot-holed surface of the road. "This had better be the place or I'll puke." Suddenly the truck stops, the side of the crate is removed, and Liz tells Hellboy to come and see 'Sebastian Placka, number 16', a huge cemetery, a vast Russian necropolis, the falling snow giving it a fairy tale quality. As the Agents walk through the frozen graveyard, Manning announces. "Forget it. We're never gonna find Rasputin's mausoleum. It's practically a city. And it stinks. And it's muddy. I think what we have to do here is we have to make a grid, and we go in by quadrants.

Maybe satellite photography." Hellboy pats Manning on the shoulder. "Let me ask for directions." Hellboy activates an arcane device. "Come on, baby, find me a talker." The device leads him to an ancient crypt. Hellboy dives in. He lifts the lid off the coffin below, revealing a mummified corpse. Hellboy uses a special medallion and utters an incantation, 'animam edere, animus corpus' and the corpse splutters into life (This scene is another homage to Dracula's resurrection in Terence Fisher's *Dracula: Prince of Darkness*, this time when the resurrected Dracula's (played by Christopher Lee) regenerated hand grips the stone side of his tomb). It isn't pleased at being awoken. "What do you want?"

Manning is complaining. "This is ridiculous. I run this show, not him. This guy's nothing but trouble. Ten minutes, we're out of here." Liz has had enough of Manning's moaning."Will you shut up and let him do his thing?" Myers spots the returning Hellboy, with the corpse strapped to his back. It announces 'sixty feet further comrades. Hellboy adds. "And three rows in." Manning is astounded. "What the hell is that on his back?" Hellboy introduces his reluctant guide. "This here is

Ivan Klimentovich. Say 'hi', Ivan." Ivan doesn't particularly like Hellboy (It was probably a lot warmer in his coffin). "Go that way, Red Monkey!" (Ivan's appearance is inspired by bog mummies, the mummies of Guanajuato, and the mummified Capudin monks of Italy).

Hellboy leads the agents into a gigantic mausoleum, a virtual cathedral of the dead. "Ivan says there's a whole network of tunnels down there. Goes on for miles." Reaching a huge chamber, Hellboy reassures everyone. "We'll be alright as long as we don't separate." As if to make a liar out of him, huge spiked iron gates spring up, splitting the agents into two groups. Now separated, Hellboy radios Liz. "Hey, Sparky. Tell everyone to turn their locator belts on. Anybody sees anything..." "I'll say..." "Marco." "Polo." Myers is doubtful, he asks Hellboy. "Are you sure about this?" "On a scale of one to ten: two. Don't worry, Boy Scout, she'll take care of you. She's a tough one."

Hellboy leads Manning and Agent Lime further into the tunnels. Manning isn't happy, telling Hellboy to "ask your buddy how far this thing goes." As if in answer, a railing Hellboy was leaning on falls into a seemingly bottomless abyss. Hellboy asks his reluctant passenger: "How you doing up there, Ivan?" The undead Russian isn't enjoying his tour of the labyrinth. "If I had legs I'd kick your ass?" Hellboy has a request for Agent Lime. "Would you mind holding this guy for a while? He is so negative."

An ornate steel door slams shut behind them. Gigantic mechanisms begin to move into life, terrifying Manning. "What the hell is that?" Hellboy begins to move. "Something big...Lime, come with me." Manning counters his order. "No. Stay put. Stop. You listen to me. We're gonna go back. You can take that door apart." Hellboy doesn't see any sense in doing that. "Whatever it is, it's coming for us. Now, we gotta move forward."

Manning orders Lime to stay put, telling Hellboy he's not afraid of them (though clearly he is). "I'm in charge, we go back." But the labyrinth has other ideas. A huge hammer smashes through the bridge they're standing on, sending the unfortunate Lime and Ivan toppling to the bottom of the abyss. Ivan comments ruefully as he falls. "I was better off dead." It's fair to say that Manning's countering of Hellboy's order to Lime cost the agent his life (and Ivan's un-death).

A metal door begins to shut at the other end of the bridge, and Hellboy decides the time for negotiations are over. He hurls Manning beneath the closing door, and runs to escape the swinging hammer, which is rapidly reducing the bridge to rubble. Hellboy barely makes it under the door (there's a nice Indiana Jones moment with his tail).

There's a little moment between Hellboy and Manning where they bond a little, though that might be down to their predicament. Then, they hear music, of a very familiar era. Hellboy draws the Samaritan. At the end of a chamber, Kroenen is chilling out, as only a 100 plus year old undead assassin could, listening to his gramophone. Manning cuts himself off a spike, alerting the creature. Entering Kroenen's chamber, Hellboy lifts the stylus off the record, but there's no sign of the assassin. Manning only has a tiny cut. "Hey, really went deep."

Then Kroenen attacks him, intending to give him a more serious one. Manning is terrified. "What's wrong with you?" Hellboy blocks Kroenen with his fist, and gets his nose cut for his trouble. Then, he loses it, hammering the assassin, with blow after blow to his masked head. "You killed my father. Your ass is mine." Kroenen is punched across the room, only to start a ghastly mechanical laugh, like a gramophone winding down. Hellboy is puzzled. "What are you laughing at, you Nazi son of a..." In answer, the floor collapses beneath Hellboy and Manning. Beneath lies a pit full of spikes festooned with ancient skeletons.

Manning and Hellboy are hanging on for dear life. Manning manages to climb out, while Kroenen tries to cut the rope Hellboy swings by. Manning starts throwing cogs at Kroenen's head to distract him. Hellboy uses the opportunity to loop the rope he's swinging by around Kroenen's neck, throwing the assassin into the pit, impaling him on the spikes, sand running out of his body where he's being punctured.

For good measure, Hellboy drops a huge cog on him. "That's all for you, pinhead." Manning drops a tiny one after it for good measure. Hellboy goes to light ups a cigar, but Manning stops him. "What are you doing? You never light a cigar that way. You use a wooden match. Preserves the flavour. You see?" Hellboy is impressed with the results. "Thank you." "Thank you." He goes forward to see if he can connect with Liz's team, leaving Manning behind.

Elsewhere, Liz's team are exploring a tunnel. Myers asks Liz. "So he thinks you and I...That's why he's mad at me. But it's not true, right?" In an adjoining tunnel, Hellboy can hear them. Liz asks Myers what he's talking about. He explains. "Well, that, you know, you feel that way about me." She's amazed. "you want to know that here? Now?" "Yeah." "Red, white, whatever. Guys are all the same."

Manning radios Hellboy. "Have you found them yet?" "I got them right below me. It's a matter of minutes." "Okay, good. Could you hurry up? Because it's a little spooky in here."

Liz, Agent Stone, and Myers have entered a chamber containing several Sammaels guarding a cluster of eggs. A steel door rolls shut behind them. Agent Stone activates his grenade pack, telling Myers to do the same. Liz radios Hellboy. "Get your big red butt over here." Hellboy starts punching through the ceiling. "I'm coming for you, kid."

The Sammaels kills Agent Stone, and Hellboy crashes in. The eggs start to hatch as Hellboy battles the Sammaels.

Hellboy puts up a terrific fight but even he can only withstand such massive odds for so long. Liz knows this and tells Myers to hit her, a deliberate ploy to make her angry and activate her power as a firestarter. This is an important moment for Liz. It's the moment she realises she truly loves Hellboy. Abandoning control goes hand-in-hand with true love. Reluctantly he does so. Flames begin to dance around her hand, she warns Myers. "You should be running." She incinerates the creatures and the eggs. Myers is knocked unconscious by the blast.

As Myers regains conscious, he hears Ilsa's voice. "They are all here. All of them." Grigory is pleased. "Just the way it was promised." Ilsa notices Myers is awake, she has his grenade pack. "This one's awake...Thank you for this." She destroys the timer for the detonator of the grenade pack. Myers sees that Hellboy has been manacled to a massive wooden yoke.

They are in a large church-like space, complete with statues holding swords (the look is inspired by a film called *The Scarlet Empress*). Liz is on the altar. Grigory is reading from the Bible. "'And I looked...and beheld an angel. And in his right hand the key to the bottomless pit.' These were words I heard as a peasant boy in Tobolsk. And now, the door." Grigory indicates the stone from the Tunguska explosion,. "Sent by the Ogdru Jahad...so that they might at long last enter our world." Ilsa tells Hellboy. "You are the key, the right hand of doom. Your stone hand, what did you think it was made for? Open the locks." Myers is aghast. "Don't do it, Red. Don't do it." Ilsa knocks him out, as the open dome above reveals the moon, an eclipse is about to begin (the significance of the moon will be seen again in *Pan's Labyrinth*). "Silence." She tells

Sammael – the Seed of Destruction

Hellboy. "Imagine it. An Eden for you and her." Hellboy refuses. Grigory asks. "In exchange for her soul then? Open the door." Hellboy still refuses. Grigory has a way to force Hellboy. "As you wish." He draws Liz's spirit from her body and tells the distraught Hellboy. "Her soul awaits on the other side. If you want her back, open the door and claim her." Hellboy struggles against his yoke to reach Grigory, who tells him. "Your true name is inscribed around the locks that hold you. You cannot break them, no matter how strong you are." Ilsa interrupts. "The eclipse has begun."

In the sky above, darkness begins to eat the moon. "You true name...say it." Grigory takes Hellboy's father's rosary from him and tosses it away. "Become the key." Reluctantly Hellboy agrees. "For her." Then Grigory tells Rasputin his true name. "Anung un Rama. Repeat it." Hellboy does and his manacles fall away, his horns re-grow and the glyphs on his stone arm glow. A halo of fire crowns his head. (Here we really see that the glyphs on Hellboys arm are as Celtic as anything in *Pan's Labyrinth*).

He inserts his stone hand into the stone, turning the lock within. The stone cracks and a beam of crimson light erupts, shooting upwards into the sky, the beam blazing to the moon. On the other side, the Ogdru Jahad move in to claim the earth, their crystal prison cracking and crumbling, allowing the huge Lovecraftian monsters their freedom.

Myers has managed to free one hand from its manacle, he reached for the fallen rosary. Grigory tell Hellboy to open the final lock. Myers shouts to him. "Remember who you are", and tosses the rosary to him. Hellboy catches it reflexively and the crucifix burns its impression into his hand (A very Terence Fisher inspired shot). Ilsa tries to stop Myers but he knocks her out. Grigory desparately wants Hellboy to open the final lock, will nature defeat nurture? Grigory snarls. "Believe me, I have lived long enough to know, not a tear will be shed for this world."

Myers has freed himself, he knows the fate of world depends on his convincing Hellboy, he indicates the rosary. "You have a choice. Your father gave you that." Grigory is frantic. "No, you don't. Open it. Do it." Hellboy looks at the brand the cross burnt on his hand and snaps off his horns. His halo of fire fades and the stone stops sending its beam of fire to the heavens. The Ogdru Jahad fade back to their own plane and the moon returns to normal.

Grigory is astonished. "What have you done?" Hellboy stabs Grigory with one of his horns. "I chose." As Hellboy goes to Liz, the dying Grigory tells him. "You will never fulfil your destiny. You will never understand the power inside you." As Hellboy cradles Liz, he replies. "I'll just have to find a way to live with that." Grigory's dying, has revealed his true unworldly nature, he really has brought a part of his god back from the other side. Grigory uncovers his abdomen, long fleshy pseudopods squirm in the wound, like living intestines. "Child, look what you've done. You've killed me...an insignificant man. But you have brought forth a god." A baby version of one of Ogdru Jahad burst forth from Grigory, it is Behemoth, Guardian of Thresholds, Destroyer of Worlds.

Carrying Liz and followed my Myers, Hellboy leaves the dying man who ushered him into our world, and is shortly about to leave it. Ilsa tells the dying Grigory. "Hell will hold no surprises for us." Behemoth is growing larger by the minute and the thing that should not be brings a huge tentacle down on Ilsa and Grigory.

Myers tells Hellboy. "I took a grenade belt. The damn things broken." Hellboy knows he can't let Behemoth live, telling Myers. "Keep her safe, will you? Whatever happens, don't leave her alone." "I won't." "You're okay, Myers. Stick around." Myers throws Hellboy the grenade belt. "Hey, Red, just pull the cable." Hellboy cracks. "I didn't get you anything." "Are you gonna be okay alone?" "How big can it be?"

In answer to Hellboy an enormous tentacle snakes around the corner and grabs him, pulling him back to the chapel. By now Behemoth is a frightening size. Hellboy, like a medieval demon knight, pulls a sword from the hands of a statue of an angel. (This too, is a classic fairy tale element). Hellboy severs tentacles to get near enough to deliver the grenade belt. As he pulls the cable, the creature swallows Hellboy and the explosives, there is a huge explosion, the blast hurling Hellboy out of Behemoth and across the church. Landing in a shower of parts of the now dead Behemoth, Hellboy comments. "Gonna be sore in the morning."

Returning to Liz and Myers, the B.P.R.D agent informs him. "She's got no pulse. She's not breathing." Hellboy whispers to Liz. "I was so foolish..." The rest of what he says is audible only to her, but it works and she revives. They embrace, and Liz asks. "Red, in the dark, I heard your voice. What did you say?" "I said, 'hey, you on the other side, let her go. Because for...for her I'll cross over. And then you'll be sorry." They kiss as Liz's flames engulf them both (They're the perfect couple, after all, where else will she find a boyfriend who's fireproof?).

This is, to me, the most romantic scene, and it looks like an illustration from an ancient book, with the snow-white heroine and her red demon hero. Myers, while disappointed at not winning Liz, remembers Professor Broom's words. "'What makes a man a man?' A friend of mine once wondered. Is it his origins? The way he comes to life? I don't think so. It's the choices he makes. Not how he starts things but how he decides to end them."

CODA

Hellboy the movie ends with the sight of Manning still where Hellboy has left him. For some reason, no one is in any hurry to rescue him...

Top pic: The *eyes* have it. Rasputin's return
Middle: Abe Sapien - from underwater to undercover
Bottom: Kroenen - A Clockwork Zombie

Pics this page: the underwater sequence from Dario Argento's Inferno

Inferno

"The film of Argento's which I like best is of course Inferno. I think Argento is a very powerful instinctive director, and so Inferno combines Argento with Mario Bava's underwater sequence. Which is, if you see Hellboy, in the scene with Abe Sapien underwater. I was seeing Inferno..."

Guillermo Del Toro

Tungusku

"I used the Tunguska forest explosion at the turn of the century, to say that it was created by this incredible chunk of cosmic stone landing on Earth. Sort of a really heavy delivery by cosmic Fedex. The elderly gods say: 'you want a portal? Let me send you a portal. BOOM! We destroyed the entirety of Tunguska Forest."
GUILLERMO DEL TORO

The Tunguska Explosion occurred near the Lower Stony Tunguska River in Siberia, Russia on June 30, 1908. The cause of the explosion is still hotly debated today. The most likely cause by the airburst of a large comet or meteorite fragment at a height of approximately six miles above the surface of the Earth, the object is thought to have been tens of metres across.

Estimates of the energy yield of the airburst vary from 5 to 30 megatons, with 10-15 megatons being the most likely range. To put this in perspective, this is approximately equivalent to the US Castle Bravo thermonuclear explosion detonated in February of 1954, which was a thousand times more explosive that the bomb detonated over Hiroshima. The airburst from the Tunguska Explosion toppled approximate eight million trees over 830 square miles. It is believed the earthquake from the blast would have measured 5.0 on the Richter Scale, had it been in use at the time.

The Tunguska event is still very relevant today, if an explosion like it took place today, near or on a large city, the effects do not bear thinking about. Tunguska is often mentioned in debates on asteroid deflection.

The Tunguska Explosion sounds like something from the pen of H.G. Wells, yet it is very real. At 7:17 local time, the Tungus natives and Russian settlers in the hills to the northwest of Lake Baikal saw a column of bluish light, almost as bright as the sun move across the sky. Ten minutes later, there was a flash and a sound likened to that of artillery fire. Those closest to the explosion said the sound moved from east to north. The noise came complete with a shockwave that knocked people to the ground and shattered glass hundreds of miles away. The majority of the witnesses did not see the explosion, only the sounds and tremors, which registered on seismic stations in Russia. The Tunguska Explosion produced fluctuations in atmospheric pressure significant enough to be noticed.

In the weeks following the explosion, the night skies over places like London were so bright that it was possible to read a newspaper. This phenomenon was caused by particles of dust suspended in the stratosphere. In the US, the Mount Wilson Observatory and the famous Smithsonian Astrophysical observatory, recorded a decrease in atmospheric transparency that had a duration of several months. This was also caused by the suspended dust particles.

Due to the isolated area the explosion occurred over, the event received very little investigation. In the face of Russia's disastrous involvement in the First World War, the Russian Revolution, and the Russian Civil War that followed, Tunguska was not considered of any great importance in a time of such terror and suffering.

It wasn't until 1921, that the first expedition reached the scene of the Tunguska Explosion. It was led by Russian mineralogist Leonid Kulik as part of a survey being carried out by the Soviet Academy of Sciences. He assumed, judging by local reports, that the explosion had been caused by a large meteorite impact. The Soviet government decided to finance an expedition to the Tunguska region, in the hope that meteoric iron could be extracted to aid Soviet industry (which tells you a lot about post wars, post-revolution Russia. Even assuming there had been meteoric iron, how could it have been transported back from such an isolated, remote and inhospitable site in sufficient quantities to make economic sense?)

When the expedition found the site in 1927, they were astonished to discover

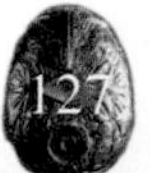

there was no crater. Instead there was an area of scorched trees approximately 30 miles across. A few trees at ground zero were still standing.

Expeditions that returned to the area in the 1950s and 1960s discovered microscopic and magnetised spheres in the soil that contained high proportions of nickel relative to iron, which is also found in meteorites. The concentration of the spheres was also found to be consistent with the distribution of debris from a meteoric object. Also, the peat bogs in the area show an abnormally high proportion of iridium, similar to the layer found in the K-T boundary.

Some of the more far-fetched theories as to the cause of the Tunguska Explosion included, black holes, antimatter, a crashing UFO and an experiment by Nikola Tesla (so Guillermo's idea of the Ogdru Jahad sending a portal to Earth is in good company).

It could have been an asteroid, but the absence of a crater seems to mitigate against this. A comet or a meteorite being composed of ice and dust, could completely vaporised on impact with the atmosphere of the Earth, which could also explain the bright lights seen in the sky after the impact.

Whatever the cause, over a hundred years later, the Tunguska Explosion is still providing fuel for the imagination of thinkers and dreamers everywhere. It's very pulp-inspired to mix fact and fiction. And it could happen again...

Hellboy - Analysis

Hellboy was originally to have been introduced, in our time, by now the now elderly Corporal Whitman, the combat photographer with the team of soldiers that accompany Professor Broom in his mission to prevent the Nazis bringing the Ogdru Jahad to Earth.

That Hellboy would appeal to Guillermo was never in any doubt. The key to Hellboy is this, he looks like a monster, but thinks like a man. The last thing he wants to be is the Beast of the Apocalypse, Guillermo sees him as a regular guy, who just wants to belong. "Something that combined the super-hero action genre with a much more human approach, and at the same time we had the trappings of a great gothic fantasy, full of monsters, full of adventures...I was instantly in love with it....One of the keys to the comic is to understand that even though Hellboy is 6'5", bright red, has horns and a tail...he's a regular Joe. He's a blue-collar hard-working guy. His job just happens to be a monster hunter."

That *Hellboy* the movie is born of Hellboy the comic is as natural to Guillermo's work as being influenced by Gothic novels or the Spanish Civil War. "In my life, comic books have been a huge influence for me. I was a collector of comic books even before I learned to read. I was just content and happy in seeing the images or looking at the cartoons. And as I learned to read, I learned to read with both horror-movie magazines and comic books. And all my life, comics have remained as important an art form in my mind as film, theatre, painting, anything. And the authors, if I had to single out the single most important authors of comic books fro me, they would be Will Eisner, Bernie Wrightson, Richard Corbin and Mike Mignola.

Mike Mignola, in my later years, already as a young adult, fascinated me with his use of light and shadow, with his amazing bold line work, but also the way he gave birth to my favourite superhero in my adult years, which is Hellboy...I really thought it was, visually, so rich and powerful. And I wanted to try and translate some of the characters

and the images to film."

Guillermo was also influenced by influenced by Mexican comics. "There was also a strange comic book in Mexico. There were several Mexican comic books that were a big influence on me...*Fantomas* was one which was based on the serial character created in France. But also, there was a comic book called *Duda* in Mexico in the late 60s. It was sort-of a Charles Fort type of speculative science/occult fiction. I think that was my first exposure to one of the recurring themes in Mike Mignola's cosmology which is the link between the Nazis and the occult, this has been speculated quite a bit in fiction and in film. The first and better known exponent of this is obviously the Indian Jones movies....*Raiders of the Lost Ark*. But it has been speculated even before in pulp fiction and in serials and certainly in the *Doc Savage*, *The Shadow*, and *The Spider* type of pulp novels, the Nazis and the occult walked hand-in-hand. And there is fact to support some of these things."

Guillermo and Mignola, in *Hellboy* have linked Nazi occult interests with the creations of H.P. Lovecraft, something that Guillermo researched intensively. "When I was writing the screenplay, I was investigating some of these...in the time when Hitler was growing up, as a young man, Vienna was one of the cities in Europe with the most activity around spiritualism and the occult. Back then, also, many of occultists works were trying to tie their theories with some form of pseudoscientific fact. And, as a matter of fact, Hitler joins, as expressed in the movie by Professor Broom, a society called the Thule Occult society, the Thule Society was founded on the legend of Ultima Thule, where the secret knowledge...of a lost civilisation was guarded by highly intelligent extraterrestrial beings floating somewhere in outer space that could be contacted through magic mystical rituals and incantations."

"So you can see that the Thule Society had a very Lovecraftian belief. In the movie, we use all this technology like the balls and the gyroscope and the magnetic fields, which were extremely cutting edge back then to sort of replicate the effect of the eclipse and the right hand of doom of *Hellboy* at the end. But all the scientific things that are there, some of which look very much like Dr. Frankenstein's laboratory equipment are based on existing technology in the early '40s."

Guillermo originally intended the gyroscopic machine you see the Nazis use at the beginning of *Hellboy* to be very different. "Originally, in the screenplay, this was a series of rails, that arranged themselves into pentagrams and hexagrams...But we went more for the magic and works of Rasputin and the sort of scientific effect being replicated by the machine."

Guillermo set up the ritual in *Hellboy* the movie to be very different to that in the original comic. "It set up the mythology of the *Hellboy* into a different place than in the comic.

In the comic, there are two rituals going on at once. One being monitored by the good guys and the other ritual being performed by Rasputin and the Nazis in another place...For reasons not explained ever in the comic-book mythology, Hellboy is born into the place that the allies are monitoring even though the ritual is talking place in another location. And I decided that it would be a good idea to join both in a single geographical place and make the first exposure of Broom to Rasputin and Ilsa and Kroenen, sort of a big origin story."

So we see that Hellboy will get many of his positive traits from the man that will adopt him, the man that he will call father, Professor Broom. But it's also interesting to note, he takes a lot of traits from the Sergeant (there's more than a touch of Sergeant Rock to Hellboy, and I don't just mean his hand). Kroenen is introduced, and set up to become the kind of semi-indestructible, clockwork cyborg zombie we see him become later, to survive the destruction of his spine and hand.

Rasputin is also introduced, someone who will play an important part in Hellboy's future, it's almost a dress rehearsal for the final showdown in Russia at the end of the film, where the chess pieces are introduced for an end game with the future of Earth as prize for the victor. "Everything that makes Hellboy Hellboy is expressed in this sequence: His love for candy, him using his stone hand whenever he wants to get away with something and the fact that the link between him and Broom is one of compassion and love...Immediately Broom trusts him and takes care of him in this sequence. And from now on, the movie becomes the story of two fathers with a single son. He has one father in Broom and another father in Rasputin."

One of the things that makes Hellboy's introduction convincing is that Guillermo finds the facts that surround it to be convincing.

"Hitler wanted to possess the holy relics...important artefacts of all the cultures of the world. *Hellboy* would have been sort of a normal day for the occult troops of Nazi Germany, because if you think about how the Nazi troops raided several European cities looking for the Holy Grail or the Spear of Longinus...and there were entire teams dedicated to the search for Atlantis...When I fused the two locations into one, I decided on Scotland, which is a land deeply rooted in magic lore and myth. And in doing so, I did a little research and found out that, yes, Scotland was actually a very usual passage for Nazi submarines into the Atlantic and that anything that you come up with, if you look hard enough, you'll find facts to support...In

the case of *Hellboy*, also what was quite an interesting coincidence is that some of the theories that supported the Thule Society's knowledge or the occultist's movements in Vienna were based on things, like Madame Blavatsky, that talked about mystical origins for the human race...but also about us inheriting knowledge and power from creatures in outer space...not exactly the Ogdru Jahad, but quite, quite similar."

The use of labyrinths in Guillermo's films did not begin with *Pan's Labyrinth*, it's also an important aspect of *Hellboy*. There is the labyrinth of the opening sequence, of the ice cave, and the final labyrinth underneath the Moscow cemetery. In this case it represents the difficulties Hellboy will have in choosing the right path. This ties in well with narration at the start and end of the movie that says a man is made a man by the choices he makes not by his circumstances or place of birth, in other words we could remake our own world in our own true inner image had we but the courage to do so, which would make the world a better place for ourselves and others.

Guillermo deliberately designed the title sequence to have the form of a labyrinth, "because I felt that a labyrinth very well represented everything about the movie, about choices and taking different turns and choosing different destinies. You know, a labyrinth, it is said, is not a place to be lost but a place to find yourself. And that is one of the mystical principles of a labyrinth or one of the ideas, is that you can find your path in a labyrinth towards the right place to be. And many labyrinths were created as mosaic work and tile work in the churches, Gothic churches, and walking the labyrinth while meditating and thinking or praying, was a form of finding your own truth, your own self, and I thought the movie had enough images that were similar to labyrinths and bifurcating corridors and so forth."

The influence of the old pulp novels is a strong influence on Hellboy, stories from *Doc Savage* and *The Shadow*, were a big influence on both Guillermo and Hellboy creator Mike Mignola. For instance, Hellboy's constantly ripped shirt is inspired by *Doc Savage: The Man of Bronze*. "Even in the titles of his *Hellboy* adventures-'Seed of Destruction', 'Wake the Devil'. Compare them to some Doc Savage titles, like 'Death Had Yellow Eyes', or 'The Talking Devil', or 'Devil's of the Deep'. These were novels that also integrated, in some of the cases, occult elements or supernatural elements with high adventure, action and pseudoscience." But Mignola hasn't placed restrictions on what Guillermo can do with his character, trusting him with his creation. "He hasn't sanctified the mythology of *Hellboy*. He is one of the great creators in that he remains flexible."

An important part of Guillermo's story telling technique is that of 'show, not tell', if at all possible. In real life, words are often hollow, a person can make any statement, but that does not make it true, wheras actions speak volumes, actions literally do speak louder than words. Professor Broom does not tell Hellboy that he loves him, he proves it by his actions, when he learns he is going to die, the only thinks of his son's future, like any good father would, to the extent that he rejects a painless death to give him time to make preparation (and ironically, as a result, because in Guillermo's world, actions always have consequences, he meets his death at the hands of an old enemy, one he met for the first time on the night of Hellboy's birth into our world. He has made the ultimate sacrifice out of love for his son, a sacrifice which allows Hellboy to become a man, to be reborn by his father's sacrificial death).

It's also very significant that a man who truly knows that the occult is real gets his second opinion from a tarot card. Guillermo sees Broom's choice of Myers is similarly informed, by Arthurian legends. "He is pure of heart. He is the young fresh knight of the Round Table, that will always have his heart in the right place and take right decisions."

Guillermo is of course inspired by religious imagery. The same Catholic-inspired iconography that features so strongly in *Cronos* for example, can be seen when Myers enters the B.P.R.D headquarters, in the shape of "the statue in the background of Myers, which is an angel fighting a demon. This is a very characteristic statue found in many churches, especially in Mexico. This is a very popular statue representing good triumphing over evil. And when I was trying to give sense to the logo of the B.P.R.D...it's a very combative logo of a hand holding a sword, and we started rooting it in Catholic mythology. I felt the best way was to represent an archangel fighting a demon as what Broom considers the B.P.R.D's sort of Arthurian/Camelot-like function...The dark needs the white to keep the balance. What is great is, in the movie, they meet in the middle. Hellboy is a monster that hunts monsters."

If the fates had decreed otherwise, we would have seen Guillermo's *Hellboy* movie much earlier (we have to remember how hard it was in those days for Guillermo to get his projects off the ground, something hard to believe now when he has so many choices), something that rankles Guillermo.

"One thing that particularly infuriates me is that this movie could have been made in 1998. By 1998, we had basically, unchanged, the screenplay of the movie ready to come out. We would have come out way before *X-Men*, way before *Matrix*, way before *Spider-Man*. But back then, before all these movies were successful....the term 'comic-book movie' was almost an insult to the studios. And we had a very tough time getting the movie set in a place that understood the premise, that understood that all these outlandish colours and all these outlandish things, demons being brought to Earth by mechanical Nazis, and all these things, were in reality, ways of speaking about simple human truths like freedom of choice, the purity of a love story between two beings that come from different backgrounds...And by the time the movie came out, some people were catching the movie in 2004, and thinking it was an afterthought of, say, *X-Men*."

It was also a very hard film to market, something Guillermo readily acknowledges. "I must confess that I admire the marketing team, for just taking the movie and pitching it to an audience, when, to me, it was a really hard movie to pitch. The word 'hell' alone, in movie created all sorts of funny circumstances...starting with some theatres that would not carry the movie because of the 'hell' in the title, so some theatres in the South that advertised the movie as 'Hello, Boy', because they were not happy with putting *Hellboy* next to *The Passion* at the time. Especially on Easter, some theatres mysteriously dropped the movie when it was still making money. And some toy chains refused to carry the toys...because of the word 'hell' on the boxes. And I find this is something that I actually wanted to explore... on the sequel to the movie, the extreme reaction in the 21st century in world that has grown sophisticated for the bad. Where we can accept all sorts of, I would say not sophistication, but really complex things in a Jerry Springer Show for the bad, but we are unable to go past a fun title like *Hellboy*. It's not Hellspawn. It's not Hellbeing. It's not The Hell Entity. It's *Hellboy*. It's self-defusing to me. I think that Mike is true to his influences... in that I refused at many points to have the movie be called something else."

Another difficulty in getting the green light (which seems absurd now we can see the finished result), but one that shows Guillermo's loyalty to both his friends and his inner vision, was his insistence that only one man could play Hellboy. "We migrated studios for many years because most of the studios didn't like the title page much less the screen play. And there were other reasons, including the fact that both Mike and I, like Rick Baker and his team, we all felt that *Hellboy* was Ron Perlman. And the fact that, for us, Ron Perlman has always been a star...and was a star in this movie....I met Ron when I was preparing *Cronos* and, ever back then, I was already in awe of this guy."

"I wrote him a letter, asking him to be in my movie, a movie that had a very small budget to pay an actor like him. I think we paid about 5% of the budget to him. And it was a big effort to get him. I wrote him a letter telling him that anyone who could do *Quest for Fire* and the hunchback in *Name of the Rose* and then do Vincent in the TV series *Beauty and the Beast* was an actor with the range and capacity for compassion in deformity and in weirdness and that I wanted to work with him. We met, and, like all my great friendships, the friendship was sealed over food. I have gotten this fat because I

have many friends and there have been many meals shared with them. Ron and I went to an Indian restaurant and I knew he was the actor to work for me because I said, 'Do you mind if I start with desert?' And he joined me in having two deserts before we ordered the meal."

"Also, to his credit, he asked me some questions about the character in *Cronos* that were really intriguing. They just were absolutely the right thing to ask about the character. He asked me, if the character worked in that factory, if you saw *Cronos*, 'what do they make in that factory?' And I said to him, 'it's been so long that no one remembers. The factory has been going for so many decades, they just make things, but no one remembers what they make.' And he accepted such a surreal Mexican explanation, and a bond and friendship was born."

"Also, Ron has something that most people don't value. To me, Ron Perlman is the Lon Chaney of the 21st century. He's an actor that not only knows how to wear makeup and how to make the makeup become alive. He is an actor that can be subtle in make-up. He can do nuance in makeup. Some great actors never get used to makeup, some great actors are really good with it, Laurence Olivier being one. It is a gift. It's not something you are trained for. It's not something you can explain to somebody else as a performer. It's simply a gift, and Ron has that in spades."

"Also, he has one of the most beautiful voices but he is capable of using it in a very colloquial way. He gave Hellboy that 'been there, done that' sort of quality. I wrote every piece of dialogue for Hellboy thinking of Ron. I knew his strengths, what he was good at, one of those things being a very dry, extremely dry, almost sandpaper dry humour, and I gave him a lot of that type of humour. Sort of one-liners that came from the situation. Not one liners that were cute or would be hip. . He doesn't say 'I'll be back', or things that are just theatre...He just seems to be a dry commentator on the situation. In other words, he has an ordinary point of view about extraordinary circumstances and missions. He has, like all of us, that desire to do the most work with the least effort. He has that underachiever quality that makes him adorable to me."

A massive influence on *Hellboy*, that is very important to mention, is that of Jack Kirby. Guillermo describes him as being "of enormous stature. He created hundreds of superheroes and characters that are now icons in comic books...He created or co-created *X-Men*, *Fantastic Four*, *Hulk*, *Captain America*, *Sergeant Fury*, *Silver Surfer*, *Captain Victory*, *The New Gods*, *Mighty Thor*. Most of the pantheon in the Marvel Library was created by Jack Kirby or allegedly co-created with Stan Lee. And his imagination had sort of a hard-boiled, tough-guy edge, and at the same time, a fancy absolutely incredible power to dream worlds and universes and mythologies...rivals Lovecraft or Lord Dunsany or Jules Verne or Edgar Rice Burroughs, any of these writers."

"I genuinely think that Jack Kirby is as important a cultural influence as any of the more recognised pulp writers or people like Burroughs in fantasy. I think Kirby was very neglected in later years, and finally I think he's achieving some of the notoriety and the fame that he deserves. Within the work, Jack Kirby creates a full-blown theology, you may say, in books like New Gods, that is absolutely flabbergasting." Kirby had a background in animation, that gave him a terrific sense of motion. "Mignola shares with him not only this fascination with movement but a movement that is executed by figures, by characters that look straight out of a Russian realism painting."

H. P. Lovecraft, and related literature, is another big influence on *Hellboy* and Guillermo himself. "Lovecraft, without trying, without having a method, fully gives birth to the Cthulu mythos, to the point that a lot of people search for the *Necronomicon*, thinking it's a true book in the Lovecraftian mythos. They really believe it

Abe Sapien

is a guy who is fascinated by the science and the fact. But he melds them, he shapes them to his own mythology, to his own desires... And reading for example in Lovecraft's *Mountains of Madness*, you find incredible, big passages dedicated to science and facts of Antarctica, before he dispenses with that and starts dwelling into blind albino, 7-foot-tall penguins (you don't pick up them, they pick up you, and kill you!) and gigantic cities built by ungodly creatures. And I think that Mignola has some of this."

"I'm sorry, Red, but that trenchcoat is so last year".

was written by Lovecraft. There is another writer that I admire, that relishes in creating volumes of knowledge, fake books. That's Jorge Luis Borges. And like Lovecraft, Borges likes to give the date of publication, the place of publication and the type of volume it was when the volume doesn't exist, and that I adore."

"And I think that Kirby and Lovecraft have these mythologies that are powerful because they are not necessarily polished to perfection, and this leads me to a point that I value in writing comic-book or genre movies. I think that a lot of people approach screenplay writing, in the post-1980s as an exercise in logic...especially having being exposed to many a recruited audience screening, with the post-screening dissection, where people make questions of the logic....and I despise this!"

"I think that mythologies sometimes just are because they are. You know, the fact that Mercury has wings on his feet, you don't have to explain the genetic process by which he got them. Or you don't have to explain why the Cthulu creatures have tentacles. I think there is just a burst of creation that Kirby and Lovecraft have, that is purely gut feeling and how their mythologies are shaped...that's pure artistic creation. Lovecraft like Mignola, like Kirby, like many great writers, like Melville,

Indeed he does, and one of the reasons *Hellboy* the movie works so well, is that both creators have so many shared literary interests, in this they are like brothers. "We share, Mike and I a fascination, for example, for a book that we cherish, called *Passport to the Supernatural* by Bernhardt Hurwood, I read his book on Poe and all his books about werewolves and witches and warlocks and vampires, and Passport to the Supernatural was my favourite and one of Mike's favourites, because he enunciates myth as a fact, and this is as great as many of the occult texts, were mythological texts that Mike and I admire...In a lot of American genre product, mythologies are crafted with an eye towards logic, and that, to me is a big mistake!"

Guillermo recognises *Hellboy* as also being one of the latest of a particular and special type of investigator. "The influence of a particular brand of detectives that is born at the end of the 19th century and they are occult detectives. We know that the 19th century saw the birth of the modern detective novel in the English language, arguably it started

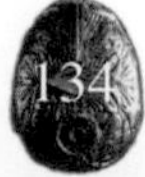

with *Murders in the Rue Morgue*. But, at the end of that century, in a pre-Sherlockian era, there were new types of detectives coming up. If you start tracing them down all the way to, for example, Joseph Sheridan Le Fanu, a fantastic ghost story writer from Ireland, you can find in the elements in his stories some detective-esque traits."

"But I think that it is really much later that they come to fruition, in the pulp years of *Weird Tales*, where by the way, Lovecraft and Robert E. Howard published some stories, comes sort of a golden age of ghost hunters, and some of the great characters were *John Silence* by Algernon Blackwood, *Carnacki the Ghost Hunter* by William Hope Hodgson, Jules de Grandin, who was a scrawny jockey-sized detective that was again, one of Mike and I's favourite characters, and these are all precursors to things that are incredibly popular right now. But I think if you go back and study these adventures in pulp, some of them do something that Mike adopts for the B.P.R.D in *Hellboy*. They use technology to supplement black magic and their knowledge of the dark arts. This whole thing about melding the dark arts and the magic with prosaic technology is in the comic book and the movie."

"For example, Hellboy has a very practical arsenal of weapons. He has all sorts of bullets, he has a sledgehammer, sawed-off shotgun...And then when he explains the content, for example, of his bullets, they have holy water, silver shavings. So he's using the knowledge of the occult manuals that Abe browses in the movie, but he's putting them to use in a high-tech way. And this was already evidenced in the electromagnetic gyroscopic portal that the Nazis had in the opening...one of the elements of the *Hellboy* universe that I wanted to preserve." But Guillermo brought many of his own ideas to *Hellboy*.

"In the book...the gun Hellboy has is given to him by the Torch of Liberty and it has no name. I love the idea of giving it a name, the Samaritan, because it puts the monsters out of their misery. And I love the idea of creating these hollow bullets that would break upon impact and dispense a secondary load. All these magical things, those were things that were created for the movie to express the B.P.R.D's sort of techno magic. The best weapon is still the low-tech fact that Hellboy is 7 feet tall, muscle-bound and has a really heavy object as a gun."

A marvellous thing about *Hellboy* and one of the reasons you instinctively know it's different to many of the cookie cutter comic book movies out there, is that it's origins lie deep in the strata of true pulp fiction (which covers a wide variety of genres, bound together by the quality(or lack of) the paper they used, but often associated in people's minds with the fantastic. My grandfather would read Western pulps sent home to Ireland from emigrants in America). Guillermo is quick to recognise the importance of the pulps.

"I wanted to point to the fact of these occult detectives. For about almost thirty years these occult detectives were the

Hellboy lays down the law to Sammael

most popular feature in the magazine Weird Tales, and actually the very reason why the magazine was considered popular...and many of the stories of Lovecraft or Howard or many of them, would not have seen the light of day, had it not been for these occult detectives."

"But it's fascinating about the good stories of these characters that they have an everyday setting. Some of them, like Jules de Grandin, have their stories set in New Jersey, which I love, that all of a sudden there are these soul-sucking monsters in a basement of a house in New Jersey. That is an impossibly modern take on the classic ghost or magical or dark story. And I think that Mike Mignola, and obviously me, were very influenced by this approach...I think the fact that you can use prosaic settings."

"The worse version of the story, the one I hate most, is where the detective explains it all to be a fraud. The sort of equivalent to: 'And I would have gotten away with it, had you pesky kids not showed up.' It's a really low-grade Sherlock Holmes-ian type of resolution through logic. But a low-rent version of the Holmes logic, which is sometimes really fascinating. and a true classic. But in the best ones like *Carnacki the Ghost Hunter* by William Hope Hodgson, one adventure takes place in a cellar, where a gigantic black mouth exists in the entire wall of a cellar and this huge mouth whistles an eerie tune. I mean, that is just so absolutely insane, that it has to have influenced Mike Mignola, who remains one of the great creators of insane imagery in my lifetime. And Mike is, if anything, just an unstoppable machine."

Guillermo realises a core element of *Hellboy* is using fire to fight fire, a thief to catch a thief, a monster to catch monsters, and this too goes back to detective fiction. "One of the things that Hellboy shares with detective fiction, if one goes back as far as the August Dupin stories that Edgar Allan Poe wrote. I remember in *The Purloined Letter*, Dupin enunciates that he has studied his archenemy's habits, very symbolically a guy called just D, much like his last name. And he say that he is gonna vanquish D by utilising the exact tactics that D has used to commit the crime. This enunciates an absolute dictum of the detective stories, which his, in order to catch a thief, one must think exactly as a thief. And in the case of *Hellboy*, in order to catch the monsters, one must think exactly as the monsters."

I feel that John Hurt as Professor Broom gives great gravity to the role. Both he and Hellboy are unique, and very alone, and when they find each other, they help make each other's world made sense. *Hellboy* the movie asks 'what makes a man a man?', which is a very good question. I would say, that the ideals held up in the film that make Hellboy a man, honour, loyalty, kindness and courage (traits sadly lacking in the 21st century world, which places ephemeral values like greed and cosmetic superficial appearance above genuine lasting value).

Hellboy is a man because he believes he is, not because of what he sees in the mirror, and that takes true courage, we all suffer from living up or down to other's expectations rather than our own, that's why we feel helpless, frightened and angry. The 21st century is so far being defined by those emotions.

I also feel that an even more personal aspect of Professor Broom's relationship with Hellboy is not just what makes Hellboy (the son) a man, but makes Professor Broom a father. In life I've observed that many times a biological father may make a bad father, and vice-versa. That Broom sacrifices a painless death to try and ensure Hellboy's future speaks volumes. Guillermo's own take on Broom is that he 'has a very essential loneliness that he reflects on the kid. Broom is an oddball, and he's out of place in the world. And when he sees this kid with innocent eyes, big innocent eyes, all wet like a puppy, he just projects onto him all the loneliness, and sort of odd existence he himself leads. He makes Hellboy understand that even the most incredible odd creature in life has a purpose."

It's interesting to note that one of the reasons that *Hellboy* is as personal a film to Guillermo as *Hellboy*, is that it too derives much from Guillermo's experiences growing up in Mexico. A prime example of this are the rubber bands that Liz wears around her wrist to control her temper and prevent her from exploding into flame. "This is something I learned when I was working as a voluntary in an insane asylum in my hometown of Guadalajara. It was a long story but I picked up a guy that had had an accident on the street. And it turns out that he was mentally deficient. I took him to the hospital, and they sent him to a mental asylum. And when I went to visit the poor man to see how he was the next day, he had escaped. And I went to the director of the asylum and said: 'Why is it so easy for the patients to escape?' And she said: 'Well, we are short of hands. If you care that much, why don't you join the staff. And I proceeded to join the staff."

"This mental institution was strategically placed behind a 19th century cemetery, and next door to the morgue. So during the period I was in that institution, which was a brief few weeks, I was exposed to some of the most beautiful funeral monuments where I used to have my lunch and write a little, in cemetery called Belén, a cemetery I visited for many, many years after that. And at the same time exposed to the most horrible things on my way to my car in the parking lot, through the morgue. But one of the things that I picked up during that stage, that they gave some of the patients since they couldn't give them the exact assistance they needed, they gave them little tricks to keep themselves at bay, and one of them was that, to use the rubber bands to help themselves, to remind themselves that they were about to lose their temper."

Another huge influence on *Hellboy* are the marvellous films featuring the beautiful animation of Ray Harryhausen. "Mike and I started talking about *Hellboy* as a Ray Harryhausen movie, because if one is to believe that in the horror genre there is a sub-genre that is called the 'monster movie', and in which, in that movie, the sole purpose of the movie is to showcase the monsters as much as possible...A contrarian impulse to that well-known law that what is not seen is more scary. Monster movies are supposed to be fun. And no monster movie was more fun than a movie with animation by Ray Harryhausen."

" Ray Harryhausen had such a strong personality that his movies are known as movies created by him, even though he didn't write or direct the movie...he came up with the ideas but didn't personally write the screenplay. And those movies influenced Mignola and I, and we wanted the battles of the monsters to very Harryhausen-esque... And we went for that type of dynamics. Some of the battles happen in full frame, like the battle of Hellboy versus the seven Sammaels in the cave at the end. That is totally the way a Harryhausen fight would have been staged with very little camera movement or no camera movement and in wide-shot."

"I met Harryhausen, along with Mike Mignola, a couple of years before doing the movie. And we actually propositioned to Harryhausen that he would come in and teach the animators a little bit of what made his technique so unique, and he didn't want to do it. He felt that movies nowadays are very violent...and he declined. But I had the chance to see him afterwards a couple of times including the privilege of having dinner at his house in London...I heard a couple of things that helped me plan things on *Hellboy*. He said he had been influenced very much in his set design and in his conception of monster layers by Gustave Doré, and that he loved the classical sense of proportion than Doré had in designing monsters. And we kept than in mind very much through the process of designing the sets for *Hellboy* and the creatures."

"Obviously, some are more outlandish than Doré would have imagined. There were not many tentacles in his engravings! But also, Harryhausen enunciated a beautiful thing. He said, 'Most people animate monsters acting like monsters, being mean and destructive... Monsters should be thought of as animals.'... he said, 'You should always imagine the monster in repose. Don't imagine the monster doing the bad things, imagine the monster as you would see a lion if you wandered into their patch of land in Africa."

Guillermo took the inspiration for Sammael's eyes from an old Western film by Carl Foreman, called *MacKenna's Gold*. "And at the beginning of the film there's a really beautiful close-up shot of a vulture blinking. And you can really see this membrane, just sweeping over the bird's eye, that became the reference for Sammael's eye."

I see a lot of Guillermo in the character of Myers, he's the character seeing Hellboy and everything that comes with him in a fresh light. Guillermo sees Myers almost as the audience's eyes. "The movie is its own creature. The movie is not the comic, but it's a great sort of jazz riff on what the comic is. Usually, these type of movies are done through the eyes of a guy that is new to the organisation. And therefore you have a high quota of exposition moments seen through eyes that are very fresh...I wanted this character to start being a monkeywrench in some of the cogwheels of the story. He becomes a third man in the relationship between Hellboy and Liz."

If one was to categorise say, *Blade II* as a big Hollywood movie, and *The Devil's Backbone* as a small personal movie, *Hellboy* is cross between both. Guillermo sees it as crucial in his canon of work. "*Hellboy* is a very dear movie, because before it, by accident, if not by design, the movies I did fell neatly into two categories. You'd have things like *Cronos* or (The) *Devil's Backbone* that were like very personal, small, sort of art-house horror movies...and things like *Mimic*, *Blade* being the big spectacle Hollywood genre-action movie...And to me, *Hellboy* is both. *Hellboy* is not only a movie that contains very personal moments for me."

" And I see it as a close reflection on the way I see life and love and a sense of choice one has when just going through life, but also its a big fun romp, it's a combination of those two. And to me, *Hellboy* was almost the beginning of a new life, where I could hopefully do big movies that were, at the same time, very quirky and very personal. And I think I was blessed by having Mike Mignola entrust me with his character to make this movie that way. It's as much a Mike Mignola creation as it is a Guillermo del Toro movie done with the care and love that the small movies have , and the spectacle and, hopefully, the scope of the other big movies."

Like all good movies, *Hellboy* has many layers, not least of which is the comment that Liz and Hellboy's relationship has on racism. Guillermo sees *Hellboy* as having metaphors in its monsters. "*Hellboy* was a movie that was hard to get off the ground, precisely because we wanted to keep all the quirkiness it had. Just the very fact that the guy was red, and that the red guy got the girl at the end...that was very freaky for most of the Hollywood studios...There is a country that bought the movie for international release, that had a most extreme reaction to the red guy getting the girl."

"And I found that really funny. It's sort of surreal racism...not unlike another Hollywood project in which I pitched to the studio that the hero of the movie should be African-American, and a wife that was white. And their reaction could have made proud a sheriff in a small town in the 1950s...The monster to me, is the last, ultimate minority. People's reactions towards monsters are perfect reflections of other little hang-ups that people have, be it racial or social or sexual. And that's the power of horror movies in reality."

At the heart of *Hellboy* are two love stories, the romantic love story between Liz and Hellboy, and the fraternal love between Broom and his adopted son. It's worth noting that the Hellboy and Liz romance is not handled in the typical way, in a sense beauty becomes the beast. Guillermo hasn't chosen to handle the romance in the typical way. "The easy version of this tale is that of *Beauty and the Beast*, which even in the most beautiful of tellings, demands that the beast gets turned back into a prince, in order for the love story to work. And I wanted very much not to do that. I wanted the beauty to turn into a beast at the end, to fully assume her deadly gifts of fire, and when she accepts herself for what she is, a monster, then she can love the monster. And I found that to be a very liberating premise."

The scene where Hellboy follows Liz and Myers is taken from an earlier screenplay Guillermo was developing called Meat Market: A Love Story. "And it had basically this scene, because the character was a Hellboy before Hellboy. It was a deformed brute that worked in a meat market and that was in love with the daughter of the meat market. And a wrote the scene with a character named Ernie following them, following her on a date, with the head of security at the meat market. And he followed them patiently...exactly what Hellboy does, and he actually threw a rock at him. I never finished the screenplay. I wrote only 40 pages. But I loved that it was fully a *Beauty and the Beast* type of love story. And when it came time to flesh that out...I always do one thing when I'm writing. I go back to my notebooks, which I carry with me everywhere and I reread all the pages of the notes I have. And if I find an element that I feel fits the movie, I use it. I take it out. It's almost like a shopping catalogue of ideas and moments, those note books."

One of the most distinctive aspects of Guillermo's movies is there use of clockworks and automata, something that on *Hellboy* comes from Guillermo rather than Mike Mignola. Kroenen is prime example of this. In *Hellboy* the movie, he's amped up massively from the comic-book becoming a Clockwork Gothic Terminator (Now that's a great title for a movie, contact Noir Publishing with contracts, film studios!). But Guillermo's fascination with clockwork goes back a lot further than his film making days.

"I have always been that way. When I was a kid there was a little encyclopaedia for kids, that had eight volumes that was probably the most influential series of books in my entire life. They told me that the movie director was the guide that made movies. I was making Super-8 films since I was 8, but I didn't know that you could actually have a profession called a 'movie director' Another volume talked to me about great stories in literature, and another one talked about crazy inventions. And that was my first exposure to the concept of an automaton. An automaton was basically a figure that replicated human movement and human function through low-tech, through gears and air valves and little things that are now seen as low tech."

"And I was so intrigued by the possibility of doing such a sophisticated function, in a robotic creature that was primitive, that I started investigating more and more about automatons. I actually own a little automaton at home. It's not terribly sophisticated but I am still very taken by the fact that it's a clockwork traditional little automaton. And Kroenen is sort of the low-tech cyborg...created only with existing technology."

Guillermo's films do not rely on exposition to tell the story, rather they work on the principle that , wherever possible, show rather than tell. This is a welcome antithesis of the typical Hollywood movie, reliant for example on the hero constantly explaining things to some vapid sidekick for the benefit of the audience. It's also a more European way of telling stories, and I feel, a touch of almost silent movie making."

I'm constantly struck by how silent story telling like Charlie Chaplin or Mr Bean, works at all levels, it transcends barriers like language, which is surely cinematic alchemy in motion, and something we need to see more of.

Guillermo believes that some people, when writing screenplays "...are very tempted to have the character articulate what happens. Much to the dismay of people that like that type of screenplay, I don't do it like that. So, some people have to live with the fact I think characters are defined by what they do and how they interact with each other, not by monologues in a coffee shop where they confess to each other how their life is." Thus, as Hellboy watches his father's funeral, in the rain, unable to attend because he's a 'monster', it speaks to us at a level beyond words, but in the heart. "...Hellboy to me, is defined as a changed lonely man in an image of him watching the funeral from afar, in the rain, and not being able to participate, because he's a monster."

"And from that moment on, there's a nuance change in Hellboy. He's more efficient. No one, from now on, will just hear him be glib or joke. He has a different gravity from now on."

The character of Rasputin in the *Hellboy* movie is rather different to one created by Mike Mignola. Guillermo sees this as necessitated by the medium of film. "Actually I think the character in the comics is superior to the Rasputin we did here, because the character in the comics as drawn by Mike

Mignola has an ascetic sort of spiritual air that is impossible for an actor to convey because a Mignola character is basically immobile. He's almost like a totem pole of spirituality and darkness that we couldn't do."

The giant Russian cemetery (which was shot in a vast cemetery in Prague, which gives it a terrific authentic Hammer Horror vibe, albeit on a huge scale), harkens back to two of Guillermo's childhood fascinations, cemeteries and tunnels (I myself remember as a child being fascinated with exploring an old tunnel system near where I lived). Guillermo has amazing stories about the tunnels he explored in his youth.

"The subterranean architecture under that, is an extension of that juvenile fascination with the morbid and the dark... When I was a kid I also explored a lot of secret passages. Guadalajara, my home town, was one of the cities where the Cristero Wars took place. Most people outside of Mexico have never heard of the Cristero Wars...after the Mexican Revolution, when the government was furiously anti-clerical, basically Catholic religion was outlawed in Mexico. It was a very dark, very secret little period of Mexican history. And during these 'Christian Wars', many a passage was carved underneath the city to go from churches to the sewers, and from the sewers to the houses of rich people, that, are mostly the most devout Sunday churchgoers in Mexico. And these passages were used to travel with a priest for Communion safely, without being seen by the authorities."

"My grandmother was actually a courier when she was a child. She actually told me one of the scariest stories ever. She was wondering through empty houses that had been bombed or dynamited by the authorities during this war. She was going through the ruins, and she actually saw a white ghost, the ghost of a woman that floated towards her with extended arms. And it was such an impact, hearing that story and hearing about the tunnels that when I became a very young teenager, a group of friends and I started exploring the sewers of the city to find these secret passages. And I'm happy to report that we actually traversed most of the city though these sewers, almost like Polish resistance heroes."

"We went in, and we travelled miles and miles. We encountered many things in there that have since made it into my movies. No giant cockroaches that look like humans but many wonderful things. We even encountered some sewer workers that told us a few stories."

"They told us the story of the time where underneath the main market on Guadalajara, they were opening the sewers, and they found an 8-foot rat in a heavy state of decomposition. The newspapers came in and took photos of the rat, and they appeared in the newspapers when I was a kid and it was a big scandal...Some zoologists from Mexico City were flown down to Guadalajara only to declare that the remains of the giant rat were those of a poor old circus lion. Many of those tales we shared over lunch in the sewers... I must also say that we did find one of those passages, that led into a big, crumbled area, and to many of us, believing that we were very close to probably a hidden treasure...This experience in the sewers, and the fact that some of the most outlandish, fantastic architecture I

Awaiting their Pan's Labyrinth debut...?

Kroenen cuts the opposition down to size in Hellboy

have seen was underground influenced me and the movies I made in a very unsubtle way."

"When I was jumping on board to do *Blade II* and I read it took place in the sewers, in the subterranean chambers. 'Okay, time to go there again." And I tried to make them different from movie to movie, visually. The *Mimic* shapes were all round, very round, almost like complete circles. Wheras the *Blade* sewers were more ovid and organic. With *Hellboy* we made an effort not to do anything that looked like a sewer, you have abandoned subway areas."

Guillermo's childhood adventures didn't stop with sewers and tunnels. "...As a kid, my friends and I, we used to get into old, abandoned houses, sometimes with permission, sometimes without permission, and used a very crude metal detector to look for buried treasures, since another tale that my grandmother told me was that she lived in a haunted house and that when they left it, some people dug in the patio and found four pots of gold that had been kept there since Revolutionary times."

The final confrontation with Rasputin allowed Guillermo to bring together many elements of the story. "You have Hellboy with the right hand of doom; and an archangel, a dark angel, holding with his right hand, a key, the key to the other side. You have, behind Rasputin, a cosmological clock, tracking the progress of the eclipse. The story behind all this, which is absolutely outlandish, is that Rasputin started building these catacombs back in the tsarist years. He started construction of this particular place because it was prophesised that the stone would arrive and that Hellboy would have to come to Russia to open the portal."

In the final analysis, *Hellboy* is the first of Guillermo's films to meld his small personal vision with a large scale Hollywood movie. Its importance cannot be underestimated. In the future Guillermo knew that he could have his cake and eat it too, by making the films he loves on whatever scale they require. It is in truth a 21st century fairy tale. In his own words. "That's what I hoped the movie could achieve at the end, a fairy tale...a fable told to myself when I was 11 or 12 years old."

Rasputin

"I felt that if Rasputin had seen a vision when he was young then it would make sense that he would be told to infiltrate the Royal Family in order to get the stone...,if Rasputin had that, then...if he had the access to the royal family, then the stone will be prophesised. It would arrive and he would try as hard as he could to get it. When he couldn't get it, he would be told: 'Let yourself be killed, to bring forth the change of the Royal Family, change Europe, and you will be resurrected in time to have another chance, another go at opening the portal. And that was the logic behind it."

GUILLERMO DEL TORO ON RASPUTIN IN HELLBOY II

The real-life Rasputin, in his own way, is just as amazing in his own right as the Rasputin of *Hellboy*, indeed, 'Russia's greatest love machine' was mad, bad and dangerous to know. Rasputin means 'dissolute' and the fact that Grigori was proud of that tells you much about him. He believed that 'sin was the first step to holiness.' His eventual assassin Prince Yussopov believed Rasputin had hypnotic powers, certainly his piercing eyes have a very unique quality. In other ways he was like a rock star (speaking of which Rasputin was an influence on Mastodon's incredible *Crack* The *Skye* album, check out the incredible Rasputin-influenced sleeve artwork by Paul A. Romano for proof) before there were any, he certainly believed in the motto: 'Have a good time all the time."

Grigori Yefimovich Rasputin (1816-1916), was a Siberian peasant, who became a mystic, gained the reputation of both a saint and a sinner. He exerted great and ultimately harmful influences on Nicholas II, the last Russian Tsar and his wife the Tsarita Alexandra, through his apparent ability to heal their sickly son, the Tsarevich Alexis.

Rasputin would contribute to the downfall of the Russian Empire, and indeed in his notoriety, is often more well known than the Tsar and Tsarita who gave him their patronage. Certainly he gave fuel to the fires of the enemies of the Romanov dynasty, which would fall in 1917.

Rasputin was called the Mad Monk (the title of the fine Hammer film of the same name in which Christopher Lee gives one of his best performances in the title role). Lee rightly believes the role of Rasputin to be one of his finest in a long and impressive career. Lee actually met two of Rasputin's assassins, Prince Yusupoff and the Grand Duke Dmitri Pavolvich, as a child. Lee wrote in his autobiography *Tall, Dark, and Gruesome*: "...It was such a good part based on an extraordinary historical phenomenon, but because of the eerie sense of contact with it through my childhood meeting with his assassins... Rasputin was a legendary enigma, a real actor's part, one of the best I ever had. From a mass of conflicting evidence, I tried to convey inspired wisdom and grotesque appetites. And I had a long-drawn out, exquisite death to get my teeth into. We couldn't actually do the death we wanted to, because Prince Yusupoff, that same man that I'd met as a child when my mother woke me to see Rasputin's enemy, would never permit it."

"Surely it is unique in an actor's life to have met Rasputin's assassins as a boy, to have played the part on screen in 1965, and to have met Rasputin's daughter Maria in 1976 (who said I had his "expression'). Finally, in 1997, I visited the Yusupoff place on the Moika canal in St Petersburg, and went down to the actual basement room where the murder took place."

Rasputin was also sometimes referred to a 'strannik' (a religious pilgrim) or a 'starets' (an elder), a title for monk confessor, by people who believed he possessed powers of faith healing and prophecy. Dostoyevsky wrote of the starets in The Brothers Karamasov. "The starets is he who takes your soul and will and makes them his. When you select your starets, you surrender your will. You give it to him in utter submission, in full renunciation."

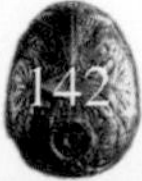

Opinion of Rasputin was divided sharply in Russia, as it still is today. Some people saw him as a wise prophet, a leader of men, many others (not without reasons), saw him as a libertine, a debauched fraud, a chancer out for everything he could get.

It's difficult to say with an certainty what Rasputin truly was, so much has been written about him, that he has become a legend, as much a myth as a man (or Mad Monk.)

Rasputin was born a peasant (though not necessarily a humble one) in western Siberia, in the small village of Pokrovskoye. He is known to have had a brother Dimitri and a sister Maria. Maria, who it is believed was epileptic, drowned in a river, and in a further bout of misfortune, Dimitri fell into a pond. Rasputin dived in to save him. They were both rescued by a passerby, but Dimitri died of pneumonia. Rasputin would go on to name two of his own children after his siblings. Considering how Rasputin was to meet his end, this is an eerie tale indeed.

Grigori's father, Efin Rasputin, raised horses. Apparently, in an early example of psychic ability, Rasputin was able to discover the identity of a man who had stolen one of the horses.

Age 18, Grigori would spend 3 months in the Verkhoturye Monastery, perhaps as a penance for thieving. His experiences in the monastery, coupled with a vision of the Mother of God, gave his life a direction as a wandering mystic. It is also said by some that he came into contact with banned Christian sect the Khlysty (flagellants). Though if he did really come into contact with them, it is not generally believed he ever joined their sect. But mud has a way of sticking and many would come to believe this (and a great many other things). In later years, when Rasputin had come into the orbit of the Tsar and Tsarita, such rumours reached the Tsar's ears via lurid newspaper reports . The Tsar investigated the tale, but actually fired his minister of the interior for allowing such rumours to be printed in the first place.

After leaving the monastery, Rasputin visited a holy man called Makariy, who would have a great influence on Rasputin, who modelled himself after him. Rasputin married a woman named Praskovia Fyodorovna Dubrovina in 1889, and they had three children, Maria, Varvara, and Dimitri.

In 1901, he went travelling as a stranik (pilgrim), and visited Jerusalem and Greece. In 1903, Rasputin came to St Petersburg. Here he was to gain a reputation as a starets with powers of healing and prophecy.

Rasputin was travelling through Siberia when he heard stories of Tsarivich Alexis's haemophilia. This disease was rampant amongst European royalty descended from the English Queen Victoria, who was Alexi's great-grandmother. Alexis, whilst holidaying with his family, fell from a horse, and was bruised, but his condition caused him to suffer days of internal bleeding.

Desperately worried, the Tsarita called on her best friend, Anna Vyrubova, to secure Rasputin's help, due to his reputation of being able to heal through prayer. He was indeed able to give Alexi some aid and relief, even though his doctors believed the boy would die. The sceptical claim he was able to do so by hypnosis. While those who believe Rasputin was genuine say he was able to alleviate Alexis's suffering from a distance, through prayer.

Rasputin also gave a lot of commonsense advice for the boy, such as plenty of rest, and this may well have helped. Certainly this was a time when medical intervention was as likely to kill as cure, so this minimal level of interference could have done some good. Bleeding in hemophiliacs can be aggravated or sometimes spontaneously induced by stress. Emotions can affect the blood flow, so if Rasputin could simply calm and reassure the child, it would have helped, calm and a feeling of well-being can help decrease bleeding.

Certainly, the Tsar and Tsarita believed in Rasputin, whenever Alexis got an injury that caused internal or external

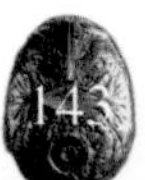

bleeding, his mother would call for Rasputin's assistance and the boy recovered. This gave Rasputin unprecedented access to the Royal Family, and great influence, anyone wishing to have an audience with them would have to go through him, something he took full advantage of. Rasputin, even if we allow for stories circulated by his and the Royal Family's enemies, was wilder than any present day rock star.

We can only imagine the level of resentment toward him, after all, a Siberian peasant has become one of the most influential men in Russia. Rasputin was on a great level of familiarity with the Royal Family. They in turn were fascinated by him. He would tell them old Russian stories, including those of the evil witch Baba Yaga. He called the Tsar and Tsarita, Batiushka and Matushka, the 'Father' and 'Mother' of the Russian peasants. Nicholas found great peace after conversing with Rasputin, while his wife went a great deal further.

She believed that Rasputin was personal emissary from God to her, the Tsar, and indeed Mother Russia herself. Such was her guilt over her son's condition, she felt God was somehow punishing her, so she felt that in Rasputin she had found someone who could intercede with God for her. A mother of a haemophiliac child is tormented by worry, and whatever we may think of her husband as a monarch, he understood and shared her worries.

Another factor that led to Rasputin becoming so important to Alexandra was her loneliness. Loneliness always makes people vulnerable, and when you are the Tsarita of Russian this is amplified a thousand-fold. She was far away from her childhood friends in Germany, and distrusted the manipulative 'friendships' that plagued her court.

She was not good with large groups of people, preferring one -on-one conversations. What she wanted was a sincere friendship that came from the heart, someone with which she could share her innermost fears with. Nothing is more depressing than to have to deal with a situation that never improves no matter how much effort is poured into it.

One way of dealing with this situation is excessive kindness to others. Alexandra certainly had a kind heart, she looked after a sick girl called Sonia Orbeliani for years, visiting her every day and tending to her at night. But it was not until she met Anna Vyrubova, that she found a friend she could trust, the Tsarita having made her acquaintance on one of her many hospital visits, and it was through Anna that the Tsarita met Rasputin. Anna had met Rasputin when he first arrived in St. Petersburg, and she was convinced he could help Alexandra. When Alexandra wished to communicated with Rasputin, Anna was the link between the two. In his first communication with the Tsarita Rasputin assured Alexandra that her son would not die. "God has seen your tears and heard your payers. Do not grieve. The little one will not die. Do not allow the doctors to bother him too much." What mother would not believe in a man who could promise her that? She felt that she had been delivered from Hell to Heaven such was her relief. She was not to know that he would help bring death to those who thought him their salvation.

Rasputin, for better or worse, caught the imagination of the mannered society he now moved in. They were not used to a man who would eat soup with his hand. He said that salvation was not possible unless one has been redeemed from sin. Thus, he believed that true redemption can only be achieving on committing sin.

Rasputin definitely made the already vulnerable Royal Family even more vulnerable, particularly with the outbreak of World War One against Germany. He was accused of having an unpatriotic influence on the Tsar and especially the Tsarita. With the Tsarita's German descent, she was especially vulnerable and was accused of being a German spy. Rasputin's increasing level of meddling in ministerial appointments and political decisions made the hate-mongering towards the

Royal Family even worse. When Rasputin volunteered his services by going to the front to bless the soldiers fighting there early in the war, the Grand Duke Nicholas, the Commander-in-Chief promised to execute Rasputin should he actually visit the front. The Grand Duke said. "Yes, do come. I'll hang you."

As even matters weren't bad enough for the Royal Family, Rasputin had a revelation that the Russian army would not achieve victory unless the Tsar himself took command. It's a clear indication of Rasputin's ever-growing influence, that the ill-prepared Nicholas did indeed take personal command of the Russian army, with catastrophic results for both himself and Russia.

While Tsar Nicholas was at the front, Rasputin's influence on the Tsarita Alexandra grew even greater (Russia was thick with rumours that the two were lovers, though it should be noted that these rumours were spread by enemies of the Royal Family. It's also an indication of how out of touch or arrogant the Royal Family was, that they didn't realise what was happening and take appropriate action before it was too late).

The Tsar and Tsarita, Alexandra in particular, refused to believe anything negative of Rasputin, no matter who it came from. The Tsarita had so long prayed for help, that nothing would persuade her than that Rasputin was the salvation she had hoped for her son. That is so often the way, people that want to believe something badly enough, will ignore any evidence to the contrary, no matter how convincing. The Tsarita's friend Anna Vyrubova supported her in this, believing Rasputin was a saint.

Rasputin quickly became the Tsarita's main adviser and confident. He persuaded her to sack government officials and to fill some government offices with his own handpicked candidates, which further eroded the Royal Family's ever-decreasing authority. The people were starving. Because of World War One, the incompetence of the government, and feudalism, Russia's economy was going downhill rapidly. Many Russian's blamed Rasputin and the Tsar and Tsarita. Vladimir Purishkevitch said in the Duma: "The Tsar's ministers have been turned into marionettes, marionettes whose threads have taken firmly in hand by Rasputin and the Empress Alexandra Fyodororna-the evil genius of Russia and the Tsarita...who has remained a German on the Russian throne and alien to the country and its people."

Felix Yussupov was in attendance for the speech and afterwards contracted Purishkevich, who quickly agreed to participate in the murder of Rasputin. Rasputin's influence over the Royal Family was a hammer used to beat him and the Romanovs by journalists and politicians who wanted to attack the integrity of the dynasty. They wanted to force the Tsar to give up his absolute political power, and to separate the Russian Orthodox church from the State. Rasputin made things progressively worse, and gave the Romanovs plenty of fuel to feed the flames of anti-Tsarist propaganda. He had public disputes with clergy members, he boasted about his ability to influence the royal couple, and by his very publically debauched lifestyle. Truly, Rasputin believed the path to God was by sinning, and thus, when he sinned, it was under the aegis of seeking salvation, he must have thought he couldn't lose either way.

Nobles in influential positions in Russian society, such as the Royal Court or the Duma, wanted Rasputin removed from royal influence...by ay means necessary.

Around this time Rasputin wrote an eerily prophetic letter, in it he stated that if he was to meet his death at the hands of nobles, that it would be end of the Romanov Dynasty, and that brothers would kill brothers, he also stated that the Romanovs would be killed by the Russian people within two years of Rasputin's death...

On 16 December, 1916, a cabal of noblemen, led by Prince Felix Yussopov, and the Grand Duke Dimitri Pavlovich (one of the few Romanovs to survive the Red

terror) put their plan into action. They lured Rasputin to Yussopov's Mokia Palace, for a party in his honour. Rasputin was led to believe that Yussopov's wife would be there, Rasputin was keen to see her, so that was an added attraction They gave him cakes and Madeira wine laced with a massive dose of cyanide. Rasputin was supposedly unaffected, two and a half hours later, although he had taken a dose large enough to kill five men.

The Grand Duke Dimitri suggested they give up and go home, their nerves were on edge buy another member of the cabal. Purishkevich, kept calm, and decided they must finish what they had begun,

Yussopov agreed, he was worried that Rasputin would survive until the morning, leaving the conspirators no time to conceal the body. So, Yussopov returned to finish Rasputin off. He found the starets calling for more wine. Telling him to look at a crucifix and say a prayer, Yussopov shot Rasputin in the back with his revolver. Rasputin fell, and the conspirators left. Yussopov later described Rasputin as having the eyes a viper, full of diabolical hatred. Yussopov had left without a coat, and returned for one, and then decided to check the body.

Then, Rasputin opened his eyes, and attacked Prince Yusopov, trying to throttle him. The other conspirators shot Rasputin three times. Incredibly, the Mad Monk still lived. Them they beat Rasputin into submission and wrapped him in a blue curtain and then threw him into an icy river. Ironically Rasputin met his end by water as had his brother and sister before him.

Rasputin's autopsy reported the presence of water in his lungs, which shows he didn't die until he was immersed, and his arms were found in an upright position, as though he had tried to claw his way out from under the ice...

But the conspirators did not save the empire. Revolution broke out within three months. As Rasputin prophesised in his letter, the Romanov Dynasty was to all intents and purposes finished, with the Tsar and Tsarita, and their children being brutally executed. Following the Revolution, Russian was plunged into a bitter Civil War, as the White Russians tried to hold back the Red Russians. Many people do not realise that following the Russian Revolution, Allied Forces invaded Russia.

There were a number of reasons for this, fear of a Russo-German alliance, fears of Bolshevism spreading, and that the Bolsheviks would make good their threat not to pay back the huge amounts of money Russia had loaned from foreign powers. The allies consisted of a multi-national force, which included Japan, France, the US (The "American North Russian Expeditionary Force"), China, Serbia, Romania, Canada, the UK, Poland and Italy.

The Allies fought until 1920 when a combination of reasons including war weariness led to their withdrawal. The Civil War continued until three years later when the White Army was finally defeated. By the time the Civil War ended, combat, disease, starvation, and retaliation and revenge, had cost the lives of over 20 million Russians. The last Tsar and Tsarita were dead...and Rasputin had achieved an immortality in death, few cannot have heard of him, or his reputation, which very much refuses to die.

Automatons

"Clockwork and automatons obsess me. I always dreamt as a kid of owning and creating a life-size human automaton. Other kids were thinking about playing football or being astronauts and I was just obsessed by gears and mechanics."

GUILLERMO DEL TORO

"There were great monks who were great alchemists. There was one I like in particular called Aurillac, who constructed a metal head, made of Bronze, which answered certain questions asked of it. That influenced Cronos, the idea of the mechanical apparatus."

GUILLERMO DEL TORO

The word Automaton is taken from the Greek root word automatos, which means 'acting of one's own will'. It is more commonly associated with non-electric moving machines, particularly those that have been created to resemble human or animal actions, such as the jacks on old public striking clocks. There are many fabulous legends such as those of Hephaestus, God of mechanical art, who was reputed to have made two female statues of pure gold which assisted him and accompanied him wherever he went. He was also credited with creating Talos, a giant made from brass which guarded Crete against invaders. Talos's sole vulnerable point was his ankle (as seen to great effect in *Jason and The Argonauts* 1963).

There were also inventors creating many working devices such as the famous Heron of Alexandria (c.10-70AD) who designed many early machines. Heron was a great engineers and inventor. He built the first recorded steam-powered device, the aeolipile (which predates the Industrial Revolution by several centuries), and a windwheel, and a fire engine. He also constructed the world's first vending machine. He created a number of automata (often used to amaze at temples), including statues that poured wine (a talented model-maker named Richard Windley has reconstructed many of Heron's devices for History Channel's *Ancient Discoveries* series, and they truly are amazing to see in action. It's like a myth coming to life. Particularly his reconstructions of Heron's Fountain and Heron's Archer, an archer shooting the dragon guarding the Golden Apples of Herperides).

But automata as we know them today really started to come into being in the 15th century when Leonardo da Vinci designed many ingenious machines. These include a self-propelled cart, in the absence of an internal combustion engine, he designed his machine to be powered by its operator using springs. He also designed a self-propelled cart for a theatrical staging of Orpheus.

There seemed to be no limits to Leonardo's imagination. He designed river dredgers, swing bridges, mechanical saws, paddle boats, fortresses, bombards and catapults. His Codex Alanticus, a collection of Leonardo's designs complied together after his death contains a design for a barrage cannon which even today looks like it came out of some alterative reality. His armoured car however, really grabs hold of the imagination. This to all intents and purposes was a tank, it was designed with a tortoise shell like cover, and its circular shape allowed for a series of cannon to be mounted around its circumference. Certain problems would have prevented its practical application, in the absence of an internal combustion engine, the tank would have to depend on the muscle power of its operators turning central cranks to move it. It would have been difficult to manoeuvre on a muddy battle field.

However, as with many of Leonardo's designs, it was far ahead of it's time. Certainly such a machine would have been terrifying in battle, and it offered a 360 degree arc of fire, and a fair degree of protection for its operators. He also came up with a spectacular design for a scythed chariot (In Renaissance Italy, and Europe as a whole, wars were common place, and

any designer or creator seeking patronage would also have to work in this field).

Leonardo produced two designs for this chariot, now preserved in Turin. He also came up with various designs for multi-barrelled machine guns, which again were ingenious (perhaps too ingenious, Leonardo may have been to far ahead with these designs to interest possible patrons), but the long and complicated reloading required may have rendered them impractical in the heat of battle. Leonardo was fascinated by flight, and with his knowledge of anatomy, he created several designs inspired by the actual wings of birds.

Leonardo created a lion automata in honour of King Louis XII. It advanced toward the King , stopped, opened its chest with a claw and pointed to the fleur-de-lis coat of France. Most fascinating of all, in 1495 he designed a humanoid automaton. It resembled a medieval knight clad in German-Italian armour. It was designed to imitate several human motions, including moving its neck and arms and sitting up (It resembled the knights that would much later feature in *Bedknobs and Broomsticks* (1971)). It fairly sparks the imagination to think of creations like that being designed centuries ago.

The Dominican Friar, Albertus Magnus, tutor to Thomas Aquinas, built an animated clockwork doll either an innocent version or one built with demonic intervention. Whatever version is true, Thomas Aquinas destroyed it

The Smithstonian Institution has in its collection a clockwork monk about 15 inches high, possibly dating as early as 1560. The monk is driven by a key-wound spring and walks the path of a square, striking his chest with his right arm, while raising and lowering a small wooden cross and rosary in his left hand, turning and nodding his head, rolling his eyes and mouthing silent prayers. From time to time, he brings the cross to his lips and kisses it. It is believed that the monk was manufactured by Juanelo Turiano, mechanician to the Holy Roman Emperor Charles V.

The Renaissance witnessed a revival of interest in automata. Heron's ideas became popular again. May clockwork automata were built in the 16th century, especially by the goldsmiths of the Free Imperial Cities of Central Europe, some to be found in cabinets of curiosities, others in garden grottos. Descartes wrote that the bodies of animals are nothing more than complex machines that could be replaced with cogs and pistons.

In 17th century France was where many of these ideas that would go on to inspire the Industrial Revolution. In 1649, the young Louis XIV, had designed by Camus, a miniature clockwork coach, with all the people and capable of movement, while in 1688, General de Gennes constructed, a peacock that ate. The world's first successfully built biomechanical automaton is considered to be The Flute Player, invented by the French engineer Jacques de Vaucanson in 1737. He also created the Duck, an artificial duck made of gilded copper, which drank quacked, ate, and splashed about in water, and appeared to digest its food like a living duck.

18th century automaton creators include the prolific Frenchman Pierre Jacquet-Droz and his contemporary Henri Maillardet. Pierre, with the help of his son Henri-Louis created three of the most famous automata of all time. The first to be created-known as 'The Scribe' (1769)- was a representation of a small child seated on a stool. In his right hand he held a goose quill pen, which he dipped into an ink well and wrote Les automates Jaquet Droz á neuchatel or Jacquet Droz mon Inventeur, his glass eyes following the creation of each letter, it could also write Je pense donc Je suis, which certainly gave observers pause for thought (It was still a long way off *The Terminator* and Skynet though).

The second creation was 'The Draughtsman' (1774), another representation of a child who drew a picture in pencil of Lois XV or a cartoon of a dog called 'Mon Toutou', while holding down the paper with his right hand and blowing away the excess lead powder with breath

created by a bellows within his chest.

The third creation was larger and christened 'The Musician', which was a representation of a teenage girl in a brocade dress who played a selection of Henri-Louis's composition on a pipe organ in the shape of a wooden harpsichord. Unlike less complex automata, she actually did touch the keys in order to produce the notes, and at the end of each performance would give her audience a pleased glance. While Maillardet, a Swiss mechanician, created an automaton capable of drawing four pictures and writing three poems. Maillaerdet's Automaton can now be seen at the Franklin Institute Science Museum in Philadelphia. Belgian born John Joseph Merlin created the mechanism of the Silver Swan automaton, now at Bowes Museum.

The famous magician Jean Eugene Robert-Houdin (1805-1871) was known for creating automata for his stage shows. In India, there was the famous Tipoo's Tiger (which is encountered by Bernard Cornwell's Sharpe character).

The period 1860 to 1910 is known as The Golden Age of Automata. During this period, many small family based companies of Automata makers work successfully in Paris. From their workshops they exported thousands of clockwork automata and mechanical singing birds around the world. It is these French automata that are collected to today. The main French makers were Roullet of Decaps, lambert, Phalibois, Renou and Bontems. The fine film *Sleuth* (written by Anthony Shaffer, based on his own play, and starring Laurence Olivier and Michael Caine) features a number of fascinating automata.

Whatever period these automata date from, they continue to perform their original function, which is to delight the eye and inspire the imagination.

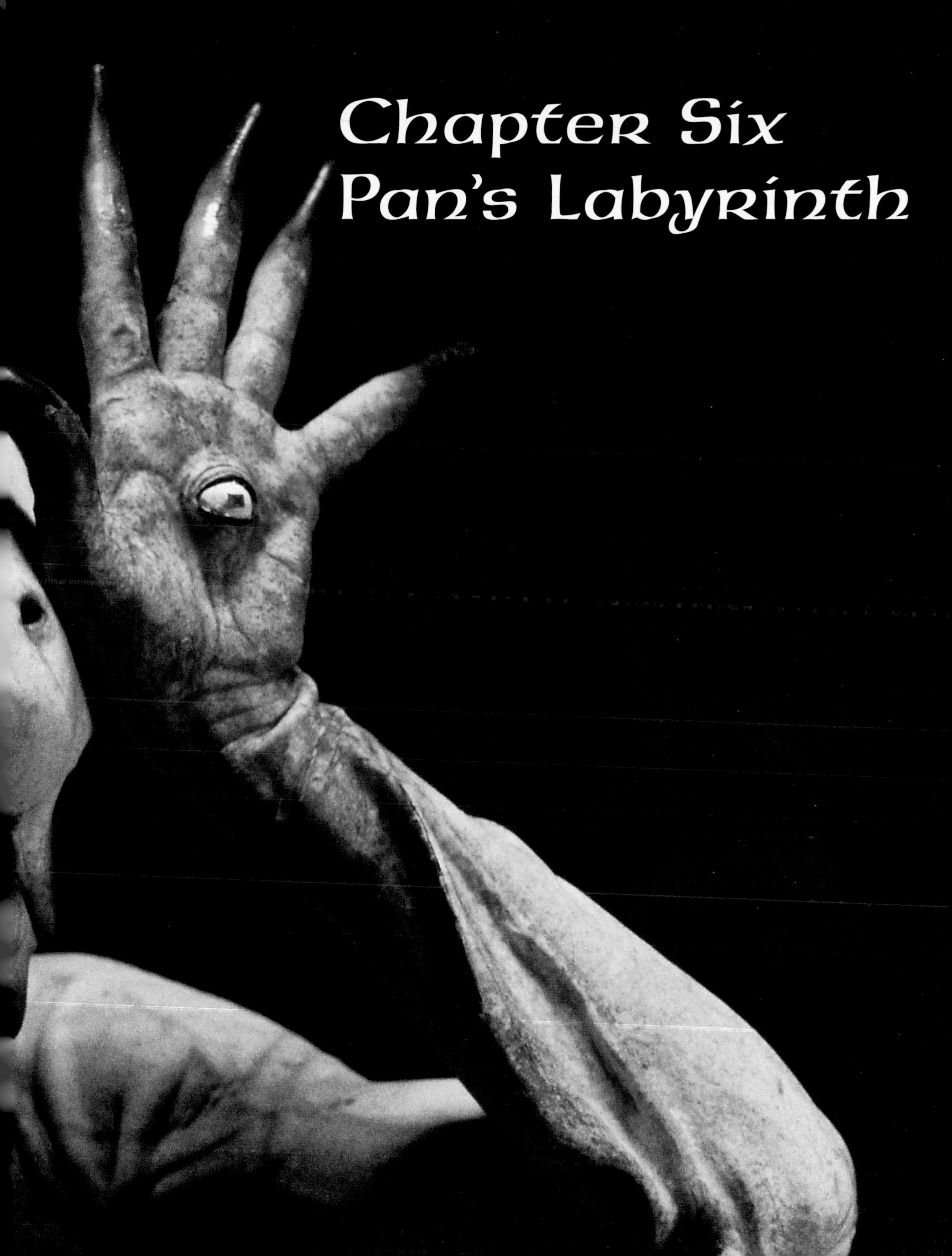

Chapter Six
Pan's Labyrinth

Previous picture spread: The intimidating Pale Man

PAN'S LABRINYTH/'EL LABERINTO DEL FAUNO'

"Spain. 1944"

"The Civil War is over. Hidden in the mountains, armed men are still fighting the new Fascist regime. Military posts are established to exterminate the Resistance."

Pan's Labyrinth opens in a circular fashion, as circular as the many Celtic spirals we shall see in the film itself. A child lies on the ground, apparently dying.

A narrator tells us. "A long time ago, in the Underground Realms, where there are no lies or pain, there lived a princess who dreamt of the human world. She dreamt of blues skies, soft breezes and sunshine. One day, eluding her keepers, the princess escaped. Once outside, the bright sun blinded her and erased her memory. She forgot who she was and where she came from. Her body suffered cold, sickness and pain. And eventually she died. However, her father, the king, always knew that the Princess would return, perhaps in another body..."

We see a ruined church and a shattered building, the wasted land of Spain following the war with Franco's fascists. A military convoy drives past, as the narration continues. "...in another place, at another time. And he would wait for her, until he drew his last breath, until the world stopped turning."

Inside one of the black cars that form the military convoy, a young girl named Ofelia (Ivana Bacquero) is reading a book. The pregnant woman, the girl's mother Carmen (Ariadna Gil) sitting beside her comments. "I don't understand why you had to bring so many books, Ofelia. We're going to the country, the outdoors." She takes the book, and in the patronising fashion all people use about things they have no empathy with, says. "Fairy tales! You're a bit old to be filling your head with such nonsense..." A sudden spasm of nausea from the child she is carrying hits, her. She holds a handkerchief to her mouth. "Ask him to stop the car, please Ofelia. Your brother is acting up."

By the very fact that the convoy halts, it's obvious this pregnant woman is regarded as important by the fascist soldiers. A soldier calls for water for the Captain's wife.

Ofelia wonders off into the sunlit forest, Pollen dances magically in the air. But only her eyes are open to the wonderment of such an everyday event. Everyone else's eyes are closed, particularly to the beauty around them. She finds a carved piece of stone, which belongs to a carved monolith nearby, it's empty socket staring at her imploringly, almost choked with ivy. The days when this carved faun was worshipped have long been swept away by many centuries of human cruelty. Ofelia puts back the missing eye, as if in response, a strange otherworldly insect flies out of the carving's mouth (This is symbolic, by replacing the eye, Ofelia's own eyes are opened to the magic world, and the magic begins with the appearance of the insect).

Ofelia is enchanted, but is brought back to 'reality' by her mother. "Ofelia, come here!" Ofelia tries to share her experience with her mother. "I saw a fairy." But her mother's ears are closed to such things. All she's concerned with is Ofelia's appearance for when she meets her new stepfather, the Captain of the fascist outpost at a commandeered mill the convoy is taking them to. "Just look at your shoes! Let's go. When we get to the mill, come out to greet the Captain. I want you to call him Father. You have no idea how good he's been to us. It's a word, Ofelia...just a word." In this, she is as blind as she is to the magic Ofelia sees in the world. 'Father' is not a word, it's a duty, that requires love, empathy, and hard work. There are many such 'Fathers' such as the Captain in the world, but few real fathers, a father is a title hard earned, not a word easily assumed.

As the convoy sets off, the insect follows.

At the mill, Captain Vidal (Sergio López), a stern, cruel-looking man, as precise as the clock he looks at impatiently. "15 minutes late." He comments as the convoy arrives. He greets his wife. "Carman..." He touches her belly, it's the son Carmen carries that's important to him , not his wife.."...welcome." He has

a doctor standing by with a wheelchair. She doesn't want it. Even if it's just subconsciously, she knows it is a part of his desire to control everything at all costs. She tells him. "That's not necessary. I can walk perfectly well." He's insistent. "Doctor Ferreiro prefers that you don't exert yourself." "No." "Come. Do it for me." She complies and tells Ofelia. She puts out her hand to him timidly. He grabs it roughly with his gloved hand, hurting her. "It's the other hand, Ofelia." He orders a woman called Mercedes (Maribel Verdu), still beautiful but the pain of years of war etched on her face, to bring their luggage.

Ofelia spots the insect that has followed her, and dropping her book, tries to catch it. It leads to a carved gateway, with a faun's face carved on it. The kindly Mercedes catches up with Ofelia. "It's a labyrinth. Just a pile of old rocks that have always been here. Even before the mill. Better not go in there. You may get lost." Mercedes has retrieved Ofelia's fallen books. "Have you read them all?" A soldier interrupts. "Mercedes. The Captain is calling." Mercedes tells Ofelia. "Your father needs me." Ofelia corrects her. "He's not my father. The captain is not my father. My father was a tailor. He died in the war. The captain is not my father." Mercedes puts her arm around Ofelia kindly. "You've made that clear enough" Shall we go?" "Have you seen my mother? Isn't she beautiful?" "Yes." "She's sick with baby. Did you notice?" They are watched by the insect perched atop the carving of the faun that guards the entrance to the labyrinth.

In his headquarters inside the mill, the Captain is scrutinising a map intently. "The guerrillas are sticking in the woods because it's hard to track them up there. Those bastards know the terrain better than any of us. We'll block all access to the woods. Food, medicine, we store it all, right here. We need to force them down, make them come to us. We'll set up three new command posts. Here, here and here." He turns to Mercedes, invisible to him until this moment. "Mercedes, ask Dr. Ferreiro to come down."

Ofelia's eyes are opened to the Otherworld

The Doctor (Álex Angulo) is attending to Ofelia's mother, producing a bottle from his bag. "This will help you sleep through the night. Just two drops before bed. Two drops only." She takes his prescription. "Very good. All of it. Good. Don't hesitate to call me if you need anything. Day or night. You or your nurse." After the doctor leaves she tells Ofelia to close the door and turn off the lights.

Mercedes tells Dr. Ferreiro. "You have to come up and see him. The wound is getting worse. His leg isn't any better." She hands him a parcel. "This is all I could get. I'm sorry. Captain Vidal is waiting for you in his office." (Interestingly, there is a carved head of the faun on the banister).

Ofelia has witnessed their conversation. Her mother calls her, and asks her if she's afraid, being in this old creaking building. She says she is a little scared. Her mother tells her. "Nights here are different from city nights. There, you hear cars, the tramway. Here the houses are old. They creak, as if they were speaking. Tomorrow I'm going to give you a surprise." "A book?" "No. Something much better." This shows the

growing gulf between mother and daughter, Ofelia can think of no better surprise than a book, an escape from her unpleasant reality, while her mother doesn't even consider a book.

Ofelia doesn't like her cruel stepfather, and in the honest manner of children, simply asks her mother. "Why did you have to get married?" Her mother gives her an honest answer too, but it's that she got married for the worst possible reason, one that happens all too often, and causes misery that can last for generations. "I was alone too long." Not realising until it's too late that there are much worse things than being alone, if love doesn't come into the picture, it will all end in tears.

Her words have hurt Ofelia (who was just as alone as she was, but because of being able to escape into her books, never felt alone, a crucial difference. She also knows she was with her mother and cannot see why her mother would feel alone with her for company.), who tells her indignantly. "I was with you. You weren't alone. You were never alone." "When you're older, you'll understand. It hasn't been easy for me either." The unborn child begins kicking again. "Your brother's at it again. Tell him one of your stories. I'm sure he'll calm down." Ofelia lays her head tenderly on her mother's swollen belly and begins to tell a story, one of her own creation, unlike her mother, Ofelia is not blind to the worlds within, waiting to be born.

"My brother, my brother...Many years ago in a sad, faraway land, there was an enormous mountain made of rough, black stone. At sunset, on top of that mountain, a magic rose blossomed every night , that made whoever plucked it immortal. But no one dared to go near it because its thorns were full of poison. Men talked amongst them selves about their fear of death, and pain, but never about the promise of eternal life. And everyday, the rose wilted, unable to bequeath that gift to anyone, forgotten and lost at the top of that cold, dark mountain, forever alone, until the end of time." Ofelia is also subconsciously making the point that her mother was never as alone as the rose, the story also makes the point that it's only when we lose our fear, whether it be of death or anything else, that we truly live, that we truly fulfil our own potential. That is the only true immortality.

Dr Ferrieiro makes his report to the time-obsessed Captain, and tells him Carmen is very weak. The Captain tells him. "She'll have as much rest as she needs. I'll sleep down here. And my son?" A soldier has come in to make his report, the Captain ignores him and repeats his question. Dr. Ferrieiro tells him there's no reason to be alarmed but that his professional opinion is the Captain's wife should not have travelled at such a late stage of pregnancy. The Captain dismisses his opinion, saying a son should be born where his father is. He is even more dismissive when the doctor asks how he can be so sure the baby is male. There are no doubts in the Captain's world.

The soldier finally gets make his report. "At 8 o'clock, we detected movement in the north-western sector. Gunfire. Sergeant Bayona searched the area and captured a suspect. The other one's his son, here from the town."

The two unfortunate men are under armed guard outside. The son tells the Captain. "Captain, my father is an honest man." "Let me be the judge of that. Take off your hat in front of me." He does so. A soldier shows a gun to the Captain. "We found this weapon on him. It's been fired." The son protests. "My father was hunting rabbits, Captain." The Captain doesn't want to hear, he is lord of life and death over this father and son. "Again-keep quite." He takes a pamphlet from the father's bag and reads it. "'No God, no country, no master'? Just like that-how do you like that?" A soldier comments. "Red propaganda, Captain." The son protests. "It's not propaganda, sir." The father explains. "It's an old almanac, captain. We're just farmers." "Go on." "I went up into the woods, Captain, to hunt for rabbits. For my daughters. They're sick." "Rabbits?"

The Captain is cynical, he takes a bottle out of the father's bag. The son protests. "Captain, if my father says so, he was hunting rabbits." Without warning the Captain brutally beats the son in the face with the bottle, mortally wounding him. The

father cannot believe this monster has done this atrocity. "Murderers. Son of a bitch." In reply, with no more compunction than if he was swatting a fly, he fatally shoots the father, putting another shot in the head of the son. Going through the bag, the murdering fascist bastard does find rabbits. They were telling the truth all along. He just brutally murdered two innocent men for nothing. He has utterly no remorse, like all his ilk, wherever in the world, whatever period of history, now or then. He's more put out at being disturbed by his men telling them. "Maybe you'll learn to search these assholes properly before you come bothering me.

Meanwhile, the insect has gotten into Ofelia's room. She calls for her mother, but the doctor's medication has knocked Carmen out. Ofelia greets the insect. "Hello. Did you follow me here? Are you a fairy? Look" She opens one of her books and shows the creature an illustration of a fairy (reminiscent of one of those in Oscar Wilde's stories). Amazingly the insect morphs its shape to mimic the illustration. This is the start of Ofelia letting the magic world into our world, and reshaping reality accordingly. The creature indicates Ofelia should follow it. "You want me to go with you? Outside? Where?" She follows the creature to the labyrinth.

Once within, she descends a set of steps that lead to a chamber with a carved monolith and a strange cloven-hoofed creature, a very ancient looking faun (Doug Jones) , covered with moss, his hair white, eyes covered by cataracts. This faun has been here for a very long time indeed. He's delighted to see Ofelia. "It's you! You've returned. Don't be frightened." The Faun opens a box releasing two more fairies. With the natural curiosity of a child overcoming fear, Ofelia introduces herself. "My name is Ofelia. Who are you?" "Me. I've had so many names...Old names that only the wind and the trees can pronounce. I am the mountain, the woods and the earth. I am a faun." He bows humbly and says. "Your most humble servant, Your Highness." Ofelia tries to correct him, "No, I'm..." He not having any of that, he is in no doubt who Ofelia really is, the princess from the story the narrator told.

"You're Princess Moanna, daughter of the King of the Underworld." "My father was a tailor." "You are not born of man. It was the moon that bore you. Look on your left shoulder and you will find a mark that proves it. Your real father had us open portals all over the world to allow your return. This is the last of them. But we have to make sure that your essence is intact, that you have not become a mortal. You must complete three tasks before the moon is full"

The Faun produces an ornate ancient-looking book. "This is the Book of Crossroads. Open it when you are alone and it will show you your future, show you what has to be done." The Faun fades back into the shadows, when Ofelia looks at the book it is blank. "But there's nothing here." This is a good metaphor. All our futures are unwritten. Until we use the power of our will and imagination to shape them. Now the moon is significant as a feminine force, and reflects Ofelia fulfilling her destiny.

The moon, in mythology, was not considered to be static like the sun, rather it was constantly changing shape, feminine in its cycles. It is a metaphor for transformation, for revealing potential. The moon does not generate light, yet it reflects light, you could see it as a mirror for the sun. The moon watches over the earth at night, and there are many people that believe in has a significant effect on human behaviour.

The following morning, the Captain grooms himself for the day's duties. He is a compulsive obsessive as well as a murdering monster. Unbelievably devoid of any empathy towards the two innocent men he murdered in cold blood, he tells Mercedes to prepare their rabbits for dinner. With great self-control, she tells him the rabbits are too young. But he has an answer to everything. "Well, maybe they'll do for a stew." But he's on a roll of nit-picking, this time with his coffee. "This coffee was burnt. Taste it yourself. You should keep an eye on it." "As you wish, sir." In the kitchen, Mercedes hands the rabbits to the cook and tells her of the Captain's latest complaint. An old woman working in the kitchen is not impressed. "He's nothing but a fussy dandy." The Captain is having the local mayor and his

wife, the local priest and some other local 'dignitaries' (at least the ones that were on the fascist side when the civil war ended). So, Mercedes and the serving women have to find additional food in a time of food shortages. These poor women are virtually slaves for the side that won the war.

Ofelia's mother shows her a dress. "Ofelia, your father is giving a diner party tonight. Look what I've made for you. Do you like it? What wouldn't I have given to have a dress as fine as this when I was your age! And look at the shoes. Do you like them?" Ofelia has little interest, answering unconvincingly. "Yes, they're very...pretty."

Ofelia retrieves the Book of Crossroads from its hiding place behind the radiator in the bathroom. Suddenly, in the morning sunlight, the pages come alive with images and words. Ofelia finds a mark in the shape of a crescent moon, just as the Faun said she would, at the moment her mother tells her through the bathroom door that she'll look like a princess. The irony is that she's just discovered she really is a princess! (This is similar in construction and theme to the scene in *Cronos*, where Jesús Gris uses the Cronos Device in his bathroom, while outside the door his wife also talks about a dress. Once again, Guillermo has masterfully juxtaposed the fantastic with a mundane mirror image in everyday 'reality').

In the kitchen, having finished peeling vegetables, Mercedes rolls the knife she's just used into her clothing, telling the other women to "make sure those chickens are cleaned properly." Ofelia comes into the kitchen in kitchen with her new dress to the delight of the women working there. Mercedes asks Ofelia if she wants milk with honey, and takes the girl with her to the cow so she can milk it, not many refrigerators in post-civil war Spain! Ofelia asks Mercedes if she believes in fairies. Mercedes relies. "No. But when I was a little girl, I did. I believed in a lot of things. I don't believe any more." (This can be interpreted in two ways, both equally valid. Mercedes is referring to her disillusionment with life due to the horrors of the war, such as the shock tactics of Franco's brutal 'Army of Africa', who committed terrible atrocities to break the will of the people he wished to defeat, particularly against women.

Mercedes supported the elected government and found herself on the losing side to the fascists. The things she's seen have haunted her and killed her love for life. We can easily imagine her before. She is still beautiful, but in the way of an old photograph, with all its vitality faded by life. It can also be interpreted as the way that our 'rational' world destroys imagination, ironically in it's 'rationality' condemning people to cold, lonely hopeless lives, truly we are a self-defeating people, not content with destroying each other brutally and the world and all it contains, we also destroy the dreams and potential within ourselves, surely a sign of some innate self-loathing and low self-esteem at the heart of the human condition.).

In the honest way that children do, Ofelia tells her. "Last night a fairy visited me." "Really?" "And it wasn't alone, there were lots of them, and a faun, too." "A faun?" "He was very old, very tall, and smelled like earth." The mention of a faun has awakened a memory in Mercedes' head. "My mother warned me to be wary of fauns."

The Captain comes for Mercedes. Soldiers are unloading the contents of trucks into the mill's huge storeroom. Flour, salt, oil, chicken soup, olives, bacon, all the food in the area." The Captain shows Mercedes a packet proudly. "This-this is real tobacco. And the ration cards. I need you to check the inventory." "Very well." Mercedes is more interested in the medical supplies badly needed by the rebels (so-called by the fascists, who actually were the real rebels against an elected government). The Captain brings her back to reality, impatiently demanding the key to the storeroom. "Is this the only copy?" She replies. "The only one." "From now on, I'll carry it."

One of the Captain's men calls his attention to distant smoke. The Captain realises it's the rebels and brings a squad of his men to attack them.

In direct contrast to the evil intent of the Captain, Ofelia walks into the wood, reading from her book. "Once upon a time, when the woods were young, they were home to creatures who were full of magic and wonder. They protected one another, and slept in the shade of a colossal fig tree that grew on a hill, near a mill. But now, the tree is dying. Its branches are dry, its truck old and twisted. A monstrous toad has settled in its roots and won't let the tree thrive. You must put the three magic stones in the toad's mouth and retrieve the golden key from inside his belly. Only then will the fig tree flourish again."

How unlike the present time, when instead of magic, the forest is full of the 'reality' of hate and fear. There is a clear analogy here. The fig tree is Spain, the huge toad is Franco and his fascist supporters, who have grown fat at the expense of the entire country, to the extent of vampiricly draining it dry. The three magic stones are freedom, truth, and justice, poison to any totalitarian system. Once they are introduced in the body of the old corrupt system, and destroy it, such concepts being toxic to the fascist system, then the entire country can thrive, not just a corrupt elitist minority.

Three is also an important number in fairy tales. There are three stones for instance, and Ofelia has to complete three tasks. (Fairy Tales are full of threes, there are three Billy Goats Gruff for example, and Three Little Pigs).

Ofelia enters the dying tree through a crack in its side. It's like birth in reverse, apt in a film that is all about rebirth. Once within, she crawls through a dark muddy passage. A virtual return to the womb. Ofelia's dress is a very deliberate reference to Alice in Wonderland, here, like Alice she is about to enter a magical world via a tunnel. Yet, the Alice in Wonderland reference goes two ways, when she leaves the dress outside the tree on a branch, she is leaving behind the adult concerns represented by the dress and concentrating on her own concerns and those of her interior world and the magical world.

The Captain and his men have found the source of the fire. The Captain declares. "They were here less than twenty minutes ago. They left in a hurry. A dozen men, at most." One of his men finds a lottery ticket, he finds a medicine bottle . "Antibiotics...They're here." He shouts to the watching rebels. "Hey, you left this behind. And your lottery ticket. Why don't you come back for it? Who knows? This could be your lucky day." Then the soldiers ride off, watched by the rebels.

Inside the tree, Ofelia has located the toad. "Hello. I'm Princess Moanna, and I'm not afraid of you. Aren't you ashamed living down here, eating all these bugs and growing fat while the tree dies?" In reply, the toad's huge tongue snakes out. Ofelia picks up the stones she dropped, then tricks the toad into taking them with an insect. Regurgitating its stomach (in the manner of a shark that has swallowed a hook), the creature deflates like the witch in *The Wizard of Oz*, and Ofelia is able to retrieve the key. By the time she has made her way out of the tree, night has fallen, and the dress her mother gave her, that she hung on a branch of the tree to keep clean has been blown into the mud. As the icing on her particular cake of misery, a torrential rain begins to fall.

The Captain consults his watch as his guests arrive. Carmen, Ofelia's mother does not know where her daughter is.

At the dinner table, the Captain introduces his guests to Carmen. At the dinner table he shows off his plan. "From now on, one ration card per family. Take a look at them." The doctor isn't impressed. "Captain, I'm not sure it'll be enough."

The local priest pauses in stuffing his face to announce, in the pious 'do what I say, not what I do' manner of people who have everything preaching about or to people who have nothing. "If people are careful, it should be plenty." The Captain as always is absolute. "We can't allow anyone to send food to the guerrillas in the mountains. They're losing ground and one of them is wounded."

This sends off warning signals in Doctor Ferrieiro's mind. "Excuse me, Captain, how can you be so sure?" He shows everyone the medicine bottle he took from the rebel's campsite. "We almost got them today. We found this...Antibiotics." The priest (Eusebio Lázaro) announces piously. "God has already saved their souls. What happens to their bodies hardly matters to him."

This is the kind of rhetoric the

priests would use to prisoners in Franco's concentration camps, while supporting a brutal and illegal fascist regime. The unctuous mayor announces. "We'll help you in any way we can, Captain. We know you're not here by choice." The Captain corrects him. "You're wrong about that. I choose to be here because I want my son to be born in a new, clean Spain. Because these people hold the mistaken belief that we're all equal. But there's a big difference: the war is over and we won. And if we need to kill every one of these vermin to settle it, then we'll kill them all, and that's that. We're all here by choice." And the Captain's guests toast the ogre who rules them with the power of life or death. "By choice."

Mercedes gives the kitchen staff instructions to make coffee, and tells them she's going outside for more wood. Once outside she makes a signal, but stops when she sees Ofelia return from the woods.

At the dinner table, a hatchet-faced woman, ceases pecking at her dinner like a greedy crow and asks Carmen how she met the Captain. Carmen explains. "Ofelia's father used to make the captain's uniforms and after he died, I went to work at the shop. A little more than a year ago, the Captain and I met again." The woman comments. "Curious isn't it, finding each other again." The Captain interjects. "Please forgive my wife, she hasn't been exposed to the world. She thinks these silly stories are interesting to others." The Captain undermines Carmen completely, humiliating her in front of strangers, and something more, it's very convenient how the obstacle to the Captain marrying Carmen died. There lingers a possibility that he may have had something to do with it. Mercedes comes in to say Ofelia has returned and Carmen leaves with her.

"When Hellboy met Pan"- Mike Mignola's incredible rendering of the Faun

An officer says to the Captain. "Have I told you I was acquainted with you father, Captain?" "No. I had no idea." "In Morocco, I knew him only briefly, but he left a great impression. An excellent soldier. The men in his battalion said that when General Vidal died on the battlefield, he smashed his watch so that his son would know the exact hour and minute of his death. So he would know how a brave man dies." The Captain dismisses this story out of hand. "Nonsense. He didn't own a watch." It is unlikely that a captain wouldn't own a watch. Is it that the Captain doesn't believe in myths? Or that he has no imagination? More likely he simply doesn't want to be overshadowed by his more heroic father.

Carman tells her daughter. "What you've done hurts me. When you've finished your bath, you'll go to bed without supper. Sometimes I think you'll never learn to behave. You've disappointed me, Ofelia, and your father too." You mean the Captain?" "Him more than me." When her mother leads, Ofelia smiles, delighted at both upsetting the Captain and making the point that he isn't her father. The fairy returns, and she tells it. "I've got the key. Take me to the labyrinth."

The fairy does so. Once there, she shows the Faun the key. She is very much Dorothy in the land of Oz. He indicates the huge carved monolith at the centre of the labyrinth, which features a carving of a faun, a girl and a baby. He says. "That's me, and the girl is you." "And the baby?" But the Faun doesn't answer her question instead he praises her success. "So, you retrieved the key. I'm glad." The fairy flies around them. The Faun tells Ofelia, as if to further change the subject away from her question. "She believed in you from the very beginning. She's so glad you succeeded. Keep the key. You'll be needing it soon. And this too." He gives Ofelia a piece of chalk. "Two tasks remain and the moon is almost full. Be patient. We'll soon stroll through he seven circular gardens of your palace." "How do I know what you say is true?" "Why would a poor little faun like me lie to you?" But answering a question with a question is a classic way of avoiding giving an answer.

The following day the Captain opens the storehouse, it's guarded at gunpoint, degrading for the hungry people waiting for their rations. A soldier tells them to have their cards ready, while another soldier repeats the fascist, almost quasi-religious, mantra. "This is our daily bread in Franco's Spain, kept safe in this mill. The Reds lie, because in a united Spain, there's not a single home without fire or bread."

Ofelia looks at the Book of Crossroads. "Come on, show me what happens now." The books pages fill with the image of fallopian tubes, like a warning signal in blood. At that moment, her mother screams, she's haemorrhaging heavily."

After attending to Carmen, Doctor Ferreiro tells the Captain. "Your wife needs uninterrupted rest. She'll have to be sedated most of the time. The girl should sleep somewhere else. I'll stay here until the birth." "Make her well. I don't care what it costs or what you need. Make her well."

So, Ofelia can no longer stay in her mother's room. Mercedes takes her to her lonely new quarters in the attic. Out of her innate kindness, she tries to comfort Ofelia. "Don't worry. Your mother will get better soon, you'll see. Having a baby is complicated." In the honest way of children, Ofelia amusingly replies. "Then I'll never have one." Ofelia tells Mercedes she knows what she's been up to secretly. "You're helping the men in the woods, aren't you?" Mercedes is scared that Ofelia will betray her to her stepfather. "Have you told anyone?" "No, I haven't. I don't want anything bad to happen to you." "Nor I to you."

What Ofelia desperately needs in her loneliness is kindness and human comfort, she asks Mercedes. "Do you know a lullaby?" "Only one, but I don't remember the words." "I don't care. I still want to hear it." So Mercedes hums the lullaby, none the less sad and beautiful for being a melody without lyrics. They mirror each other in their loneliness and friendship. They represent the past and future of the ordinary Spanish woman touched by the war. Mercedes too was once full of dreams like Ofelia, she too believed in fairies. But real-life monsters like the Captain put a finish to such dreams, and Mercedes knows sadly that the same monsters are turning their attention to Mercedes and everything she holds dear. Innocence is always endangered by evil, something the life-worn Mercedes knows only too well.

That night, Mercedes retrieves some items hidden beneath a flagstone in the kitchen. She's startled by the appearance of her friend and ally Doctor Ferreiro. "Are you ready?" "Yes." "Then let's go." As they trudge through the forest the Doctor says. "This is sheer madness. When that man finds out about us, he'll kill us all. Have you thought about that?" "Are you so afraid of him, Doctor?" "It's not fear, at least not for myself." She shushes him, there are armed men in the forest. But it's okay, they're their own people, the rebels. She embraces one of them. "Pedro, Pedro, my brother."

Back in Ofelia's new quarters, the somewhat younger-looking Faun visits her. "You didn't carry out the task." "No, my mother is sick." The Faun brushes her explanation away. "That's no excuse for negligence." He

produces a foetal-looking vegetable, similar to the ones the women were preparing in the kitchen, explaining to her. "Look, this is a mandrake root. A plant that dreamt of being human. Put it under your mother's bed in a bowl of fresh milk. Each morning, give it two drops of blood. Now, we have no time to waste. The full moon will be upon us. Take my pets to guide you through. You're going to a very dangerous place, so be careful. The thing that slumbers there, it's not human. You will see a sumptuous feast..." He hands her an hourglass. "...but don't eat or drink anything. Absolutely nothing. Your life depends on it."

Pedro leads the Doctor and Mercedes to the caves the rebels use as a base, she tells him. "I've brought some orujo, tobacco, cheese. Mail for Trigo and Piloto."

The Doctor goes to examine a rebel with a wounded leg. "Let's see how that leg is doing, Frenchie." Frenchie grimaces. "How do you think its doing?" "Lets see."

One of the rebels reads a paper. "British and C-C-Canadian troops, disembarked on a small beach in the North of F-F-F..." Another rebel takes the paper from him. "France, stuttering idiot. France." He reads. "More than 150,000 soldiers give us hope... under the command of General Dwight D. Eisenhower..." The Rebels believed the Allies would return the help they gave the allies in hindering the Fascist's assistance of the Nazis, as they would soon discover, they would repay their courage by abandoning them to Franco's mercies...and he had no mercy.

Frenchie asks the Doctor. "Is it really bad?" The Doctor, sadly, can only give him bad news. "Look, Frenchie, there's no way to save it." So he'll have to amputate in terrible conditions with no anaesthetic save some liquor. He tries to reassure Frenchie. "I'll try to make as few cuts as possible." Just as he's about to make the first incision, Frenchie stops him, wanting a moment to come to terms with what he's about to lose, realising that it's as good as a death sentence, a crippled rebel won't last long. Then he gives the nod for the Doctor to begin.

Ofelia opens her book and words and pictures fill it's previously blank pages. She reads. "Use the chalk to trace a door anywhere in your room." She starts to do so. "Once the door's open, start the hourglass. Let the fairies guide you. Don't eat or drink anything during your stay, and come back before the last grain of sand falls." She opens the door she has made, and enters a huge vaulted chamber beyond. At the end of the chamber is a beautifully set table, piled high with a magical array of tempting foods (Shades of Hansel and Gretel). At the head of the table is a man with no eyes, white skin over where the sockets should be. Two eyes lie on a plate in front of him. He is the Pale Man (This room mirrors the room the Captain gave his banquet in, the layout is a mirror image, and there is a monster at the head of both tables).

Disturbing paintings of the Pale Man (again played by the very talented Doug Jones, the Laurence Olivier of acting under prosthetic make-up) killing children shout out mute warnings. As does a pile of children's shoes in the corner, ancient and dusty (mirroring the pile of shoes in Manny's apartment in *Mimic*, but even worse, they mirror the piles of shoes belonging to those murdered by the Nazis at that very moment in Germany. The result of the allies burying in their heads in the sand when Fascism began to rise in Spain and Germany, until it was too late).

Ofelia releases the fairies, who fly to three cupboard doors set in the wall (again the rule of three), and indicate that she should use the key she retrieved from the toad to open a particular one. At the last moment she changes her mind, and puts the key into the lock of the cupboard door beside it. At the end of the corridor the sands of time are running fast.

Reaching into the cupboard, Ofelia retrieves a knife. Having followed her own judgement and made the right decision, she now proceeds to make a wrong one. Despite the Faun's warning, and the desperate gestures of the fairies, she takes a little food from the table. As she does so the Pale Man's hands start to move and a horrible unearthly sounds emits from its mouth. It takes the eyes from the plate and inserts them into the stigmata on its hands. Holding them up to its eyes, the Pale Man looks. It gets up and

kills two of the brave fairies that try to protect the terrified Ofelia (This is a direct quote of one of Guillermo's favourite painters, Goya, taken from his famous painting Saturn Devouring His Son. It is also a quote from George A Romero's classic *Day of the Dead* (1985),

The Faun stays sharp

Everett Burrell who worked on these effects also worked on Romero's film, and Guillermo wanted the bites to be similar). The sands are running out and she's trapped in the corridor. Quick-witted, she manages to draw a new door just in the nick of time and escapes the creature, who howls his rage at being thwarted from the other side.

The rebels escort Mercedes and the Doctor back through the forest. Pedro (Roger Casamajor) tells Mercedes. "We'll soon have reinforcements from Jaca. Fifty men or more. Then we'll go head to head with Vidal. The Doctor isn't impressed. "And then what? You kill him, they'll send another just like him. And another...You're screwed, no guns, no safe shelter....You need food, medicine. You should take care of Mercedes. If you really loved her, you'd cross the border with her. This is a lost cause." "I'm staying here, doctor. There's no choice." Though Pedro does tell Mercedes she has to leave. She hands Pedro the key the storeroom. "Here's the key, but you can't go down there now. It's exactly what he expects." "Leave it to me."

Despite her kindness and courage, Mercedes disparages herself to her brother. "I'm a coward." He knows nothing could be further from the truth. "No, you're not." "Yes, I am. A coward for living next to that son of a bitch, doing his laundry, feeding him...What if the doctor's right and we can't win?" "At least we'll make things harder for that bastard."

At that moment, the said bastard is shaving, going through his compulsive morning grooming routine, as his clock clicks ever louder (it's worth noting, that in the film, when we see the Captain polish his shoes, that we remember this too is a reference to fairy tales like *Tom Thumb*, where shoes are significant). He slashes at his own reflection in the shaving mirror. A symbolic slash at himself, for here is a man who hates himself more than everyone else (a trait shared with Jacinto in *The Devil's Backbone*). Mirrors are an important element in fairy tales. Think of the magic mirror in *Snow White*.

Ofelia carries out the Faun's instructions with the mandrake root. The mandrake comes alive upon entering the warm milk, resembling for all the world, a foetus, a mirror image of the one Carmen is carrying with such difficulty and pain. Ofelia goes beneath her mother's bed to carry out the rest of the faun's instructions with the mandrake. While she's under the bed, the Doctor and Captain Vidal enter the room. The Doctor takes Carmen's temperature and the mandrake's magic has already begun work, as he announces with surprise. "Her temperature is down. I don't know how but it is." The Captain asks. "But she still has a fever?" "Yes, but it's a good sign. Her body is responding." Then the Captain really shows how little he cares for Carmen, all he wants is a son to bear his name, his pathetic self-serving desire for

immortality through another, the only true path to immortality is when one loses one's fear of death, giving it no power, and putting others first. A rare thing in our world, where governments, institutions, advertisers, and even people in their own relationships rule by fear. Fear is sadly often the ruling human emotion today, not love.

Vidal tells the Doctor. "Listen to me. If you have to choose, save the baby. That boy will bear my name and my father's name. Save him." Vidal is interrupted by the sound of explosions outside, and the two men leave, giving Ofelia the opportunity to get out from under the bed. She addresses the unborn baby in the most heartrendingly sincere fashion. "Bother...little brother. If you can hear me, things out here aren't too good. But soon you'll have to come out. You've made Mamma very sick. I want to ask you one favour for when you come out, just one: don't hurt her. You'll meet her, she's very pretty, even though sometimes she's sad for many days at a time. You'll see, when she smiles, you'll love her. Listen, if you do what I say, I'll make you a promise. I'll take you to my kingdom, and I'll make you a prince, I promise you, a prince."

Vidal comes on the scene of the cause of the explosions. The rebels have derailed a train. The train driver tells him. "I sounded the whistle, but they wouldn't move. I tried to stop, but it was too late. The fireman and I jumped out just in time, but look at the mess they made." The Captain asks. "What did they steal from the freight cars?" The fireman tells him. "They didn't open a single one." Vidal spits. "What the hell are you talking about?" "This whole mess, they didn't open any of the cars. They didn't take anything." "Nothing? Are you sure?" "God only knows what they wanted, other than to waste our time." That's exactly what the rebels wanted, the penny drops for the Captain as an explosion sounds from their distant headquarters.

The rebels have attacked the Fascist base, raiding the storeroom, a truck explodes (in the manner of a similar truck explosion in *The Devil's Backbone*). As the Captain arrives, a soldier reports to him. "They came out of nowhere, Captain. They have grenades, they went up the hill."

The Captain realises the lock of the storeroom hasn't been forced. The Captain is then informed a small rebel unit has been surrounded on the hill. The Captain leads the attack. He talks bravely, telling one of his officers. "Go ahead, Serrano, don't be afraid, this is the only decent way to die." But he looks like a man blustering to hide his own fear and is careful to make sure he doesn't die himself. When the rebels are defeated, he finds a wounded soldier, but one that can't talk and so is no use for interrogation under torture by the Fascists. The Captain torments the wounded man by pointing his gun at him, the unfortunate man pushes the pistol away, until the Captain shoots him through the hand, killing him. The Fascists execute the wounded rebels until they find one who's shot in the leg, suitable for interrogation.

Mercedes hears they've captured a rebel, she's scared for the rebel, and that she or the Doctor might be found out, but she's most scared they've captured her beloved brother, Pedro. The Captain won't let her into the storeroom, but before the door closes, she sees it's not Pedro, it's the rebel with a stammer. Mercedes brings up some food for Carmen. She cannot understand how Ofelia's mother has gotten so much better but she's glad.

Inside the storeroom, the Captain is about to conduct the interrogation. When offered a cigarette by the Captain, the rebel defiantly tells him to "go to h-h—h-hell." The Captain sneers to one of his officers, Garces (Manolo Solo). "Damn, Garces. We catch one, and he turns out to be a stutterer. We'll be here all night." Garces says simply. "As long as he talks." The Captain agrees. "Garces is right. You'd do better to tell us everything. But to make sure it happens. I brought along a few tools." The Captain wields a lethal-looking hammer, he's done this before, many times, this is a bloody ballet he's rehearsed often. "Just things you pick up along the way. At first I won't be able to trust you, but after I use this, you'll own up to a few things. When we get to these..." He shows the prisoner a pliers. "...we'll have developed a...how can I put this? A closer bond, much like brothers. You'll see." He shows the terrified prisoner a knife, and throwing in an extra piece of sadism inspired by the poor man's speech defect.

"And when we get to this one, I'll believe anything you tell me...I'll make you a deal. If you can count to three with out st-t-tuttering, you can go. Don't look at him, look at me. Above me, there's no one...Garces." "Yes, Captain? If I say this asshole can leave, would anybody contradict me?" "No one, Captain, he can leave." Captain Vidal is really having 'fun' now. He announces happily. "There you have it. Count to three!" With a titanic effort, the prisoner gets 'one' out, then 'two'. The Captain mocks him, dangling the poisoned carrot of false hope in front of him. "Good! One more and you're free." But he can't get the 'three' out, and the Captain strikes him viciously with the hammer. This scene really defines Vidal's need for total control through total brutality.

That night, the younger looking Faun comes to Ofelia in her bedroom. "Your mother is much better, Your Highness. Surely you must be relieved?" "Yes, thank you. But things haven't turned out so well." "No?" "I had an accident." She hands him the box that had contained the fairies. The Faun enquires. "An accident?" The surviving fairy leaps out of the box and whispers into the Faun's ear. The Faun is furious. "You broke the rules!" "It was only two grapes. I thought no one would notice." The Faun is aghast. "We've made a mistake." "A mistake?" "You failed. You can never return." "It was an accident!" "You cannot return...The moon will be full in three days. Your spirit shall forever remain among the humans. You shall age like them, you shall die like them and all memory of you shall fade in time. And we'll vanish along with it. You will never see us again."

The Faun and the surviving fairy leave Ofelia with all her hopes as shattered as those of the Captain's prisoner's fingers. Who has not been in her position, if they were truly honest, alone, scared, with seemingly no hope of things improving? We can all relate to Ofelia's predicament in our own unique way.

Outside in the rain, the Captain washes the rebel's blood off his fingers, though in truth, he could wash until the stars in the sky burn out, innocent blood can never be washed away. The Doctor approaches, a soldier holding an umbrella over his head. The Captain tells the Doctor in a breezy, off-hand fashion, as though torture is no big deal. "Good day, Doctor. Sorry to wake you so early, but I think we need your help."

Within the storeroom, it's clear the rebel, this soldier of misfortune, has been terribly tortured, his face is swollen, his hand a useless, shattered claw. The Doctor is disgusted, this is his personal breaking point, his stiff-upper lip limit. All this he can bear to witness no longer. He demands of the Captain. "My God, what have you done to him?" "Not much. But things are getting better." He notices a bottle in the Doctors bag, and an alarm of recognition begins to go off in his head, and he takes the bottle. "I like having you handy, Doctor. It has its advantages." The Captain leaves to confirm his suspicions. The rebel tells the doctor that he talked, not much but he talked, and he begs the Doctor to kill him.

In his quarters, the Captain compares the bottle he took from the Doctor's bag with the one he found in the remains of the rebels' camp. They are the same.

In the meantime, bravely the Doctor gives a mercy killing to the rebel, giving him an injection. "It will take away the pain. It's almost over."

The Captain is furious. He orders one of his men to, "watch Dr. Ferreiro. I'll be right there." Ofelia is under the bed, feeding the mandrake as per the Faun's instructions, to save her mother. She notices the mandrake doesn't seem to be moving anymore, and asks it if it's sick. She brutally pulled out from under the bed by her stepfather.

Outside the officer ordered by Vidal tells the guard on the storehouse to 'call him." "Who?" "Who else, you imbecile? Ferreiro""

The Captain retrieves the mandrake. "What the hell is this?" He goes to crush the mandrake, his answer to anything that doesn't fit his tunnel vision view of the world. Ofelia begs him to stop, she alone knows that's what has been keeping her mother well. Carmen awakes and tells Vidal to leave her alone. Despite her health, despite the fact that he is terrifying her innocent daughter, he barks like the ogre in human form he truly is, brandishing the mandrake. "Look at this! Look at what she was hiding under your bed! What do you think of this?" Carmen asks her daughter. "Ofelia, what is this thing doing under the bed?" Ofelia truthfully tells her. "It's a magic root the Faun gave me." But of course, they don't believe her.

The Captain rants at his pregnant wife, and of course the Fascists were notorious for their hatred of reading, intelligence, free-thinking and imagination, and like all cowards and bullies, it has to be someone else's fault, never his. To the extent of blaming a bed-ridden pregnant woman, carrying his child no less, even for his wife his cruelty and spite are clearly visible. "This is all because of that junk you let her read. Look at what you've done." Carmen tries to cool the Captain's vile rage. "Please, leave us alone. I'll talk to her, darling." He sneers. "Fine. As you wish." He leaves to take care of the Doctor.

Ofelia desperately tries to explain to her mother. "He told me you would get better. And you did." Even this unarguable fact, that of her miraculously improved health, does not sway Carmen. "Ofelia, you have to listen to your father. You have to stop all this." "No. I want to leave this place." "Please, take me away from here. Let's just go, please." "Things are not that simple. You're getting older. Soon you'll see that life isn't like your fairy tales. The world is a cruel place. And you'll learn that, even if it hurts." Carmen hurls the mandrake onto the fire to emphasise her point. "Ofelia, magic does not exist. Not for you, me, or anyone."

Thus, as is a core truth in life, Carmen creates a reality that reflects her own beliefs. She has destroyed the magic of the mandrake, which burns and screams in a disturbingly human fashion, as it does so, her own baby spasms,

In the storehouse, the Captain has discovered what the Doctor has done, the rebel has died peacefully from the Doctor's injection. The Captain is bewildered, to him, his way is the only way, freedom of thought terrifies him. He asks the Doctor. "Why did you do it?" "It was the only thing I could do." "No. You could have obeyed me." "I could, but I didn't." "It would have been better for you. You know it. I don't understand. Why didn't you obey me?"

With his answer, which in this time of great cowardice, is an example to us all. The more brave people we have in the world the better, we have already got enough people who will do anything they're told to, no matter how wicked. "To obey-just like that, for the sake of obeying, without questioning, that's something only people like you can do, Captain." Captain Vidal shoots the brave Doctor as he walks away with great dignity. His death has the quality of a noble, dying animal. He takes off his glasses, wipes the rain from them, as though he wants to see where he is going, and dies.

The Captain is told of his wife's predicament and calls for the troop paramedic. As they wait outside Carmen's room, both Ofelia and Vidal are dark mirror images of each other. Ofelia is concerned both for her mother and unborn brother, Vidal cares nothing for Carmen save as a vessel for his son, his supposed immortality in this world, he cannot even find it in his black heart to hold her hand, or give her a hug, when she most needs it.

It's a terribly painful birth, and sadly, while Ofelia's brother survives her mother does not. The price of her loneliness was death, and leaving her daughter alone in the world at the mercy of the true monster that is Captain Vidal. So many people condemn themselves to a life of hell because they believe there can be nothing worse, here, as always, we see it can be much worse.

At the burial of Carmen, the same priest who attended the Captain's banquet, spouts the same hollow hypocrisy he did at that feast of fools. Words are meaningless with out intention and deed to pack them up. "Because the paths to the Lord are inscrutable. Because the essence of his forgiveness lies in his word and in His mystery. Because although God sends us the message, it is our task to decipher it. Because when we open our arms, the earth takes in only a hollow and senseless shell. Far away no is the soul in its eternal glory. Because it is in pain we find the meaning of life and the state of grace that we lose when we

are born. Because God in His infinite wisdom, puts the solution in our hands. And because it is only in His physical absence that the place he occupies in our souls is reaffirmed."

Such words are cold comfort to a newly orphaned and lonely child crying unseen tears beside her mother's grave. Now she is more alone than she ever has been, she looks at her mother's empty wheelchair, a piece of silent symbolism that speaks volumes of the emptiness in her own heart, far more so than any graveside speech ever will.

As Mercedes puts his newly arrived son to bed, the Captain (who doesn't display the least sign of grief for his late wife), says. "You knew Doctor Ferreiro pretty well, didn't you, Mercedes?" "We all knew him, sir. Everyone around here." "The stutterer spoke of an informer. Here...at the mill. Can you imagine? Right under my nose, Mercedes, please..." He indicates for her to sit down, and continues his probing line of speech. "....What must you think of me? You must think that I'm a monster."

He offers her a drink. "It doesn't matter what someone like me thinks, sir." He hands her the drink, telling her. "I want you to go to the storehouse and bring me some liquor, please." As she goes, he asks her if she isn't forgetting something. "Sir?" "the key...I do have the only copy, don't I?" Now she knows he suspects her, he has an eye for details. He continues. "You know, there's an odd detail that's been bothering me. Maybe it's not important, but the day they broke into the storeroom with all those grenades and explosives, the lock wasn't forced. As I said, it's probably not important." As Mercedes goes to take the key, he grabs her hand in same rough manner he grabbed Ofelia's and warns. "Be very careful."

After leaving the Captain's quarters, Mercedes removes various items from her hiding place, and then goes to Ofelia's room. She tells Ofelia she's leaving. Ofelia wants to come with her. Initially, Mercedes refuses, but eventually relents, knowing in her heart, how alone Ofelia is, and so monstrous the Captain, that she feels bringing her with her to the rebels is safer. But making their way through the woods, they are intercepted by the Captain and his men. He knew Mercedes was helping the rebels , it was just a matter of drawing her out.

Back at the mill, the Captain asks Ofelia. "How long have you known about her?" Then he slaps her, his own stepdaughter. "How long have you been laughing at me?" He orders his men. "Watch her. And if anyone tries to get in...shoot her first." Vidal goes through Mercedes' bag, taking letters to the rebels and other items, and says sarcastically. "Dried meat, tobacco. If you had asked for it, I would have given it to you, Mercedes."

He tells Garces he wants the names of those who wrote the letters in front of him tomorrow, and that he can leave him to interrogate Mercedes alone. Garces asks him if he's sure. Vidal sees Mercedes as no threat. "For God's sake, she's just a woman."

When Garces leaves, the defiant Mercedes tells him. "That's what you've always thought. That's why I was able to get away with it. I was invisible to you." Vidal sneers, as he prepares the same routine he uses to terrorise all his prisoners, bad enough to torture a bound and wounded man, but to torture a woman is even worse again, is their no cruelty Vidal will not stoop to? "You've found my weakness: Pride. But it's your weak points we're interested in." He displays the hammer as before and goes into his routine, sadly well oiled with blood at this stage. "It's very simple, you will talk and I have to know that everything you say is the truth."

He doesn't see Mercedes remove the knife from her dress. He continues, enjoying the sense of brutal power and the sound of his own voice. "We have a few things here strictly for that purpose. Nothing complicated." Mercedes cuts through the ropes that bind her. "Things we learn on the job. At first I'm not going to trust..." She slashes the cowardly Captain across the back with her knife." And as he turns, stabs him, slashing him as he falls to the ground. She sticks her bloody knife into his mouth. She tells him some home truths. "I'm not some old man! Not a wounded prisoner... Don't you dare touch the girl. You won't be the first pig I've gutted." And to emphasise her point, she slashes open his cheek.

Leaving the storeroom, with a

Ofelia prepares to carry out her first task

territory. Hit several times, Garces goes down and the other horses are panicked. Within seconds, the fascist soldiers are dead, dying, or fleeing for the sanctuary of their base. Mercedes is reunited with her brother.

supreme effort of self-control, she cleans the knife and returns it to her dress, and walks past the soldiers, who, while they are surprised the Captain has apparently freed her, they are more interested in checking if the numbers on the lottery ticket they found at the rebel campsite are the winning ones being announced on the radio. They are rudely jerked back to reality by the sight of their bloodied Captain staggering from the storeroom, ordering them to bring Mercedes back.

As Mercedes runs to the forest, she is chased by soldiers mounted on horseback who surround her (interestingly a scene very similar to this one, appears in a different context in Hammer's *Plague Of The Zombies*). Garces tries to get Mercedes to surrender. "It'll be better if you come with me without struggling. The Captain said that if you behave..." Mercedes is under no illusion as to what the Captain will do to take his revenge, whether she 'behaves' or not (You have to admire and be inspired by the courage of this lady, that we should all be as brave as her in our own lives). Garces smirks. "Don't be a fool, sweetheart. If anyone's going to kill you...I'd rather it be me."

Suddenly Vidal's lapdog buckles, he's been shot. In their bloodlust, and thinking they only had to contend with a single woman on foot, the fascists have strayed into the rebel's

Ofelia is still locked into her room. The surviving fairy flies onto her hand, the Faun has returned, now extremely youthful looking (the more Ofelia believes, the younger he gets). He says. "I've decided to give you one last chance." Gratefully, Ofelia runs into the Faun's arms. He asks her. "Do you promise to do what I say? Will you do everything I tell you, without question? This is your last chance. Then listen to me. Fetch your brother and bring him to the labyrinth, as quickly as you can, Your Highness." "My brother?" "We need him." "But..." "No more questions." "The door's locked." Handing her the magic chalk, he tells her. "In that case, create your own door."

Only two fascists have survived to make it back to their based. The cut Mercedes gave the Captain's face, gives him a mocking smirk, is this his true nature exposed, or is nature in fact mocking him? In a moment that defines his character greatly, Vidal as always must be in control and stitches up his own face using his shaving mirror to guide him. Meanwhile Ofelia has used the chalk to create a door way to his quarters and has come for the baby. He takes a shot of liquor to deaden the pain, though it actually causes more than it numbs as it soaks into his stitched cheek. He senses someone in the room with him and draws his pistol, but he finds no one. One of his men interrupts him, telling him. "Serrrano is back. He's wounded." The Captain leaves and Ofelia takes the opportunity to drug his drink.

The Captain goes to the wounded Serrano (César Vea) and demands. "Where's Garces?" Serrano shakes his head painfully. The Captain continues his questions. "How many were there?" "I don't know exactly, Captain. Fifty men, at least."

A soldier reports some more bad news to the Captain. "The rest of the men didn't make it Our watch posts are not responding." The Captain is getting worried now and asks. "How many men do we have left." "Twenty, maybe less, sir." The worm has finally turned, now the fascists are the minority. The hunters have become the hunted.

Ofelia tells her brother reassuringly. "We're leaving. Together. Don't be afraid. Nothing is going to happen to you."

The Captain gives his surviving men orders. "Put them on picket duty at the tree line. If the rest of the squad gets back. I want to see them. Radio for reinforcements now." Just as he's about to take his spiked drink, he picks up his precious watch, then drinks. As Ofelia leaves, there's an explosion outside, the rebels are attacking. The Captain orders her to leave him, but bravely she defies him and runs. He follows, but the drug he's unknowingly ingested is taking effect. He follows her into the battle, his men are being slaughtered, it's definitely not as easy as torturing prisoners, and the knife always hurts more at the business end of the handle.

Meanwhile, Mercedes has come for Ofelia, but realises she's already gone.

The Captain has followed Ofelia to the labyrinth. Its walls open up, taking her directly to the heart of the labyrinth, directly to the Faun, leaving the Captain to struggle to find her in the maze. The Faun tells Ofelia. "Quickly, your Majesty. Give him to me. The full moon is high in the sky, we can open the portal." Ofelia sees that the Faun has the knife she took from the Pale Man's banqueting chamber. "What is that in your hand?" The Faun explains. "The portal will only open if we offer the blood of an innocent. Just a drop of blood. A pinprick, that's all. It's the final task." But Ofelia will not do it, she knows it's wrong. "You promised to obey me. Give me the boy." "No. My brother stays with me." He tries to tempt her. "You would give up your sacred right for this brat you barely know." She's steadfast. "Yes, I would." "You would give up your throne for him? He, who has caused you such misery, such humiliation?" "Yes, I would."

The Captain has finally reached the centre of the labyrinth. He cannot see the Faun, his mind is closed. (This only proves he is hard-hearted, dull and has no imagination, you need a soul to see magic).

The Faun tells Ofelia. "As you wish, your highness." The Captain takes the baby, and cold-bloodedly, shoots Ofelia. The ultimate monstrous act from the worst monster of all...the human monster. Yet, even he has his part to play, as Ofelia bleeds onto the spirals carved on the ground (aptly, a Celtic motif that symbolises the circular nature of time, the illusion of death, and the return to the womb to be reborn. In Celtic lore, symbols have a deeper and more universal meaning than words. The spiral also symbolises power waiting to unfold and mighty creative force of increase and decrease that lies dormant within us. You can see the spiral in nature, in rings of trees, fingerprints, ears, and snail shells), it is her blood, her innocent blood, given bravely, that will open the portal.

As Captain Vidal leaves the labyrinth, he's met by the rebels and the sight of his headquarters in flames. The hell that this ogre has visited on so many others has come to call on him. He hands the child to Mercedes. "My son." He looks at his watch and clenches it in his fist to break it, so his son can one day know the time of his death. "Tell my son...Tell him what time his father died. Tell him that I..." Mercedes cuts his speech short, and delivers a verbal blow that hits the Captain harder than any bullet. "No. He won't even know your name." They execute him, a single shot to the head, like his own fascists favoured, and he dies knowing his son will never know of him, that it was all for nothing, that he never truly existed. It was better than he deserved.

Mercedes is heartbroken when she finds Ofelia, and cradling her in her arms, sings

to her the same lullaby she sang to the lonely girl in her bedroom.

But while Ofelia's body has died in our world, he spirit has been reborn in the otherworld. A majesty voice tells her. "Arise my daughter." Ofelia is in a magnificent throne room (The red shoes she wears a loving homage to the ones Dorothy wears in *The Wizard of Oz*, one of the most wonderful fantasy films ever made). She sees to her joy, that's her beloved true father who is king here (another homage to *The Wizard of Oz*, where characters from Dorothy's existence in our world, also exist in a different guise in Oz). "Father." He is proud of her following her heart, even to the sacrifice of her own life, which is as it should be. He tells her. "You have spilled your own blood rather than the blood of an innocent. That was the final task and the most important." Ofelia's mother is alive here too, holding her brother (Ofelia has kept her promise and he's become a Prince), and all the fairies, including those killed by the Pale Man, are her too. She tells her daughter. "Come here with me and sit by your father's side. He's been waiting for you for so long." And all the inhabitants of the otherworld happily applaud, their brave princess has finally returned home!

And in our world, Mercedes sadly cradles Ofelia's dead body, not realising she has been born again in a better place. In a mirror of the narration at the beginning, the narrator tells us. "And it is said that the Princess returned to her father's kingdom. That she reigned there with justice and a kind heart for many centuries. That she was loved by her people. That she was loved by her people. And that she left behind small traces of her time on earth, visible only to those who know where to look..."

And in our world, in the forest where Ofelia first discovered the magic, her insect alights on a beautiful flower blossoming on an old tree....

The Spanish Civil War

"At times to be silent is to lie. You will win because you have enough brute force. But you will not convince. For to convince you need to persuade. And in order to persuade you would need what you lack: Reason and Right."

Miguel de Unamuno debating with fascist General Milan-Astray, on October 12 1936, at the University of Salmanca. Milan-Astray famously spat back the following answer. "Death to intelligence. And long live death." He then had the elderly Unamuno driven from the university he was rector at by gunpoint. Miguel de Unamuno had a heart attack as a result of his brutal treatment and was dead within a week.

"It is not sceptics or explorers but fanatics and ideologues who menace decency and progress. No agnostic ever burned anyone at the stake or tortured a pagan, heretic, or unbeliever."
DANIEL BOORSTEIN

The roots of the Spanish Civil War go back to the turbulence of the 19th century, where there were several civil wars and revolts. The Spanish Constitution of 1812 was liberal and sought to abolish the absolutist monarchy of the old regime. The old regime in turn, tried to preserve itself and repress these reforms. From the 1850s, Socialism in various forms began to take hold, and also anarchism, which was more popular in Spain than elsewhere in the European countries.

Spain remained neutral in World War I (1914-1918) and profited from selling industrial goods to the warring nations. But the war's end caused widespread unemployment in Spain, and those Spaniards who had jobs earned low wages. These conditions added to an already growing discontent with the rule of Alfonso XIII.

In 1912, Spain gained control over parts of Morocco. But the Moroccans would not submit to Spanish authority. In

1921, they revolted and killed more than 10,000 Spanish troops. This disaster caused bitter disputes in Spain, and these disputes became more intense as the fighting continued in Morocco. Coupled with the nation's political unrest and poor economic conditions, the Moroccan situation led to strikes and violence throughout Spain. In 1923, General Miguel Primo de Rivera headed a military revolt to take over the government and restore order in Spain. Alfonso supported the rebels and Primo became prime minister with the power of dictator.

Primo restored order in Morocco and Spain. He also promised to re-establish constitutional government in Spain but repeatedly postponed the move. The army finally turned against Primo in 1930, and he forced to resign.

Meanwhile, a political movement for a republican form of government gained strength in Spain. The movement consisted of liberals, socialists and other people who did not want Spain to be a monarchy. Early in 1931, Alfonso called for city elections to be followed by provincial elections, and then a general parliamentary election. In April, the people voted overwhelmingly for republican candidates in the city elections. Alfonso then left the country, though he refused to give up his claim to the throne.

Republican leaders took control of the government after Alfonso left Spain. They called for a parliamentary election to be held in June, 1931. Liberal, socialists and other Republican groups won a huge majority in the Cortes. The new Cortes immediately began work on a democratic constitution, which was approved in December, 1931. That same month, the Cortes elected Niceto Alcalá Zamora, a leading liberal, as the first president of the republic.

The republicans had won control of the government, but political unrest continued in the country. Many Spaniards still favoured a monarchy. In addition, the various republican groups were only loosely united. Radical leaders agitated for the overthrow of the government and created uprisings in various sections of the country. The worldwide economic depression of the 1930's added to these difficulties as Spain's exports fell and poverty spread among the people.

A number of controversial reforms were passed, including the Agrarian Law of 1932, which distributed land amongst the poor peasants. Millions of Spaniards had been suffering the yoke of poverty, their lives under the control of their aristocratic landlords, who operated a quasi-feudal systems. There were also military cut-backs and reforms, and strong moves were made to separate church from state.

With the benefit of hindsight though, it is seen that the Second Republic in 1931 created huge hopes and improvements for Spanish peasants, workers and women. In the 1931 Constitution, women received both the right to vote and the right to elected to public office. In 1931, laws on divorce and civil marriage were introduced that were the most progressive in Europe at that time, recognising the right of women to custody of their children and divorce by mutual consent. Workers were given the right to freedom of association and the right to join a union. An eight-hour work day was introduced and night work became regulated, compelling business owners to grant eight hours of rest, and the Sunday Rest Law was granted to all workers.

But the greatest opposition was created when the new government decreased the power of the Roman Catholic Church (a move which was condemned by the Pope) and gave greater power to the trade unions. It took over many of the great estates held by aristocrats and greatly increased the wages of farm workers. In 1932, the Cortes yielded to demands from nationalists in Catalonia and granted the region limited self-government. Other regions then demanded similar freedoms.

The action of the republican government created opposition among increasing numbers of Spaniards, especially conservatives, who supported the Roman Catholic Church and wanted

Spain to become a monarchy again. The government called for a parliamentary election in 1933. In the election, a newly formed conservative party emerged as the most powerful political force in Spain. This party was the Confederacion Espanola De Derechas Autónamas (Spanish Confederation of Autonomous Rightist Parties), called the CEDA.

Late in 1934, socialists and Catalan nationalists led an uprising against the government. The uprising quickly spread throughout Spain, Government forces put down the revolt, but they killed more than a thousand persons in doing so. The political division in Spain then widened. Army leaders, monarchists, and Roman Catholic groups made up the Right. Communists, socialists, trade unions and liberal groups formed the Left.

President Alcalá dissolved the Cortes in February, 1936, and called for an election to try to unite the republic. Forces on the Left joined in an alliance called the Popular Front and won the election by a slight margin. Their victory touched off increased violence in Spain. Rightists and Leftists fought in the streets. Armed bands dragged opponents from their homes and murdered them. Political assassinations become common.

In July, 1936, Spanish army units stationed in Morocco proclaimed a revolution against Spain's government. Most army units in Spain then rose in revolt, and they soon won control of about a third of the country. The rebels hoped to overthrow the government quickly and restore order in Spain. But Popular Front forces took up arms against the military. In October, the rebel leaders chose General Francisco Franco as their commander-in-chief. They also made him head of the revolutionary government. By this time, the revolt had developed into a full-scale civil war.

Franco's forces became known as Nationalists (nacionales) or Rebels. They were supported by Spain's fascist party, The Falange Espanola (Spanish Phalanx). The forces that fought to save the republic were called Loyalists or Republicans (republicanos). Both sides killed civilians and prisoners in a violent, bloody conflict that raged across Spain for nearly three years.

Like all civil wars, family members and friends fought each other. The rising was meant to take over the country quickly but mistakes were made which let the government retain control of parts of Spain, such as Valencia. Franco stated that if necessary he would shoot half of Spain. The irony that those in revolt were declaring the elected government to be rebels is not lost. Republican soldiers taken prisoner at the front could expect to be executed, sometimes even the wounded. For instance, when Málaga was conquered by Franco's forces in February of 1937, over 5,000 were executed without trial for Republican sympathies, particularly any prisoner considered to be intellectual. Franco was waging war on reason as well as the Republic.

The Spanish Civil War drew international attention. Nazi Germany and Fascist Italy supported Franco's forces, as did much of the Roman Catholic clergy and Communist Russia aided the Loyalists. Mexico also came out in support of the Republicanos. In addition, Loyalist sympathisers from the United States, Britain, Ireland, and many other countries joined the International Brigades that were formed to fight in Spain (Republican sympathisers saw the war as a struggle between tyrannical fascism and democracy, they also saw the Spanish Civil War as the opening salvo of the coming devastating war with fascism).

The fascist leaders generally came from a richer, conservative, pro-monarchist, landlord background, that favoured the centralisation of state power. The Republicans consisted mainly of much of the educated middle class (particularly those who were not landlords or businessmen), most peasants, and most workers.

The Spanish Civil War is notable for the large amount of non-Spanish citizens involved at various levels in combat

and 'advisory' positions. Franco's fascists received a huge amount of support, wheras the Republicans were very seriously hampered by the arms embargo declared by Britian and France. European Governments were aware that a second Great War was imminent, while Germany and Italy were prepared to further provoke it with their involvement in the Spanish Civil War, other countries foolishly tried to appease it by burying their heads in the sand and leaving Spain's legally elected government to its fate.

As always, just like its current incarnation the United Nations, the League of Nations was useless, good only for watching the carnage unfold, while doing little or nothing, a 'proud' tradition upheld by that organisation to this very day.

Both Nazi Germany and Fascist Italy sent aircraft, guns, tanks, and troops to support Franco. Mussolini provided The Corps of Volunteer Troops (CTV), and Germany sent in its now infamous Condor Legion. The CTV reached a peak of approximately 50,000 men, with as many as 75,000 Italians going to Spain to fight. The Condor Legion reached a peak of approximately 12,000 men, and as many as 19,000 Germans fought in Spain.

The Soviet Union ignored the League of Nations embargo and sold arms to the Republic. The Soviet Union was the Republicans main source of tanks, artillery and aircraft. It should be noted though, that the Republic has to use the official gold reserves of the Bank of Spain to pay for these weapons. The arms were often of inferior quality and were sold at a cost beyond their true value. To put this in perspective. The cost to the Republic of Soviet weapons was in excess of 500 million US dollars, or two-thirds of the gold reserves that Spain had at the commencement of the war.

The soldiers of the International Brigades made up the largest contingent of foreign troops fighting for the Republicans. Approximately 30,000 foreign nationals from up to possibly 53 nations fought in the various brigades. The Mexican Republic publicly supported the official Madrid government, and refused to follow the French-British Non-Intervention proposals, recognising immediately that offered a huge advantage to the Fascists.

Contrary to the United States, Mexico did not believe that neutrality between an elected government and a military junta was correct policy. Mexico's stance gave the Republic great moral support, particularly when you consider that the bulk of main Latin American governments gave their sympathies to the Fascists. Mexico gave some material assistance including a small quantity of American made aircraft.

In November 1936, the Republicans repulsed Franco's attack on the capital, with the International Brigades forming a major part of Madrid's defence. Franco was to have Madrid bombarded from the air and made several attempts to take the city

On April 26 1937, the German Condor Legion committed one of the worst atrocities of the war at Guernica, the massacre of hundred of civilians including women and children (the subject of Picasso's famous painting).

By the end of 1937, the Nationalists clearly held the upper hand in Spain. They had taken most of western Spain in the summer of 1936 and were gradually pushing the Loyalist forces to the east and north. Russia ended large-scale aid to the loyalists in 1938, and Franco launched a massive offensive against Loyalist armies that same year.

Franco entered Madrid, one of the last Loyalist strongholds, in March, 1939. The remaining Loyalist forces surrendered on April 11. Several hundred thousands of Spaniards had died in the war, and much of Spain lay in ruins. A dictatorship under Franco replaced the short-lived republic.

The war increased tensions in the lead-up to the Second World War, and can possibly seems as war by proxy between the Communist Soviet Union and the Fascist Axis of Germany and Italy. Tanks and the aerial bombing of cities would be distinct

features of the Second World War. Franco took a bloody revenge on the Republicans, having thousands executed, and many killed by his concentration camps or by being used as forced labour. Many were sent to concentration camps such as the one in the disused monastery of San Pedro de Cardena near Burgo. Here, prisoners were held under terrible conditions. They were threatened with being burnt alive. They suffered from the cold and foul diet. There were daily beatings and tortures for offences such as not genuflecting in church. They were subjected to indoctrination and obligatory attendance of mass.

Such treatment was a deliberate attempt to dehumanise and demoralise the prisoners, some of whom compared such behaviour to that of the Inquisition. Bob Doyle, one of the International Brigade was held in this concentration camp. He describes his treatment in his autobiography 'Brigadista': "Our treatment as prisoners was a deliberate strategy to demoralise us and make out that we were subhuman and could not be normal to have come and fight in the international Brigades...All international prisoners were subject to immediate execution up to then, what did the democracies care, we were now in fascist hands. No Red Cross functioned for us, we were not prisoners of war under the Geneva Convention and most of our governments considered us criminal because we'd broken their non-intervention agreement since we had come to fight for an elected government against a revolt by military generals...The morning after we arrived, we were given a special display of brutality. As the Spanish prisoners assembled in the patio below us for their breakfast (oily water containing a few crumbs), they were attacked with sticks and rifle butts, scattering them in all directions as they tried to form the lines the Fascists demanded."

Bob survived the camp to return home, and indeed he devoted the rest of his life to fighting courageously for causes large and small. Many Spanish people fled abroad to escape Franco. Vichey France sent 5,000 Spaniards to die in Mauthausen concentration camp.

The rise of mass media led to a huge focus on the Spanish Civil War, it was covered by such famous names as Robert Capa, George Orwell, and of course, Ernest Hemingway, all of which has helped to embed the tragedy in the consciousness of history.

The Spanish Civil War still has huge resonance today, because it speaks of the perils of burying our heads in the sand, and turning a blind eye to injustice. This can be on the big scale of the Spanish Civil War, or the small scale in the every day 'small wars' we witness like turning a blind eye to bullying in the workplace or school. No man is an island. The quote below, sums up the danger of turning a blind eye better than anything I could write, and could apply to any similar circumstance of cruelty and injustice.

"First they came for the communists,
But I didn't speak up because I wasn't a communist.
Then they came for the Jews,
But I didn't speak up because I wasn't a Jew
Then they came for the trade unionists,
But I didn't speak up because I wasn't a trade unionist
Then they came for the Catholics
But I didn't speak up because I was a Protestant
Then they came for me, and by that time,
There was no one left to speak up"
PASTOR MARTIN NEIMOELLER

The last word in this piece can be summed up eloquently in the quote below.

"It was in Spain that men learned that one can be right and still be beaten, that force can vanquish spirit, that there are times when courage is not its own reward. It is this, without doubt, which explains why so many men throughout the world regard the Spanish drama as a personal tragedy."
ALBERT CAMUS

Pan's Labyrinth - Analysis

Pan's Labyrinth is a companion story to *The Devil's Backbone*. Events in the real world had a big effect on Guillermo's concepts for a follow up film. He explains. "...from 2001 to 2006, in five years the world changed completely after September 11, and everything I had to say about brutality and innocence, childhood and war changed dramatically. So, *Devil's Backbone* being set in 1939, I was curious to do a movie that was set exactly five years later...in 1944...in Spain. This particular period of time would mirror in some way how much the world had changed there and how much the world had changed today. I felt if the ghost story in *The Devil's Backbone* was to enunciate the microcosmos of the Spanish Civil War, this movie should be about choice and disobedience which were themes that I felt were as urgent today as they were in 1944."

The opening image in *Pan's Labyrinth*, that of Ofelia's nose bleeding in reverse (showing the cyclical nature of death, also reflected in the use of the Celtic spiral motif on the Faun and other aspects of the film, which means exactly the same thing), was gruelling for Guillermo to develop. "This image, the blood going back to the girl's body and the writing of the first ten minutes of the film was the hardest thing in the screenwriting process. I was stuck in this for months and months, and the moment I saw the image of the blood going back to her nose, I understood the rest of the movie was not about a girl dying but a girl giving birth to herself the way she wanted to be , and the movie went through many permutations... Then I realised if this was going to be a movie where two stories intersected, then I needed to have this beautiful fairy tale prologue in the narration, but I needed to see images of a destructed Spanish city, torn by the by the war, as a contrast to the fairy tale narrative, so they would start to juxtapose from the very beginning."

I feel one of the masterful touches of *Pan's Labyrinth* is now the violence of the real world, and the fantasy of the other world begin to impose on each other. Again, this was carefully thought out by Guillermo. "The idea in the movie is to try and juxtapose violence and fantasy... and how the 'real world', the material world, scuffs the girl's interest in the fantasy world and the magic, starting with the mother. Somebody said in the 19th century, it was our duty to deal with children as though they were the ambassadors of a higher culture and not the other way around, not like we want to educate them, we want to learn from them. I believe that children have a perfect personality and then we ruin it with our intelligent decisions to educate them."

Ofelia and her mother arriving by car is a direct connection, a parallel with *The Devil's Backbone*. Guillermo says. "This is a direct quote to *Devil's Backbone*, the visit of the boy arriving for his first day at the orphanage, to the collective bedroom of the orphanage. I constructed the two movies to be similar, I wanted to have a circular opening and closing type of structure with a narration on it. I wanted to have a child arriving at a new building through a car with an adult and then be visited on the first night by a magical or fantastic creature, and then have to solve a mystery the creature would pose that night, throughout the movie. Amongst other similarities...there are similarities between the two antagonists in the movies, and the two protagonists in the movies."

"The children in *Devil's Backbone*, one of them writes stories, another one draws pictures and illustrates the stories, and this girl is a combination of the two characters...and the fact the protagonist in *Devil's Backbone* is really a proto-fascist, a guy who is not intellectual enough or political enough to be really called a fast, but Captain Vidal, the villain in this piece is a fully-fledged fascist...Now the two movies are intended to be companion pieces, to link them by the fact that they needed to occur in a single building because to me the essence of the Civil War, is to make it a household war, a war that occurs within the walls of a building and amongst members of a family."

Captain Vidal's watch has the same significance as Hellboy's crucifix, or as the Cronos Device does to Jesús Gris, an item of

totemic character defining importance, that they never want to let out of their sight and feel incomplete without. "The introduction of Captain Vidal was done through his watch, which we understand is...the only memory he has of his father, really pressing him to be a really famous, really large man. This watch was given to him by his father, he is sort of oppressed by that."

Guillermo's love of the works of Charles Dickens comes to the fore in the scene where Ofelia attempts to shake her stepfather's hand. "...a direct quote to Dickens, to *David Copperfield*. Where the first time David Copperfield meets his stepfather in the cemetery outside the church, the stepfather grabs his hand when David Copperfield offers it and he says 'it's the other hand, David', because David Copperfield is offering him the left hand to shake."

In *Pan's Labyrinth*, Guillermo has also created a fantasy movie about fantasy movies and books. "The movie's completely peppered with references to other fantasty movies and to other fantasy worlds like novels or short stories. Han's Christian Anderson's *The Little Magical Girl*, *The Wizard of Oz*, *Alice in Wonderland*, Oscar Wilde...I have been fascinated by fairy tales ever since I was a kid...The true power of a fairy tale is the fact that it is very simple and very brutal." As has been stated elsewhere in this book, Guillermo is not a fan of the Hollywood-scriptwriting tradition of literally explaining the life out of a story.

"We shy away from magic that is not explained, a Hollywood upbringing of story-telling where you have to explain every piece of magic and therefore castrate and destroy it. I think that characters can be types and still have an emotional reality."

For instance, the rebels in the forest are woodmen, the Captain can be seen as the Big Bad Wolf, with Ofelia was Little Red Riding Hood. A fairy tale Guillermo is fond of proves his point. "One of my favourite fairy tales is called *The Three Hairs of the Devil*. The wolf says when the Devil is asleep, if you pluck one of his hairs, he has to answer any question you want to ask him. Why ? Because the rules generate themselves. They give you a magical universe in the sense of a world that is inaccessible to you but fully formed but that is an act of simplicity...The hardest thing to pull off in art is simplicity...Fairy tales actually externalise conflicts that are intrinsically human and make them manifest...In fairy tales, monsters need to exist, to be a manifestation of something you need to understand, they need to represent, much like the Angels represent the beautiful eternal pure side of the human spirit, monsters need to represent a more tangible, a more mortal side of being human, aging, decay, darkness... and I believe that monsters originally, when we were cavemen sitting around a fire, we needed to explain the birth of the sun and the death of the moon, and thunder, and we invented creatures that made sense of the world. A serpent that ate the sun, a creature that are the moon, a man on the moon living there, things like that. All the things we were repressing needed an explanation. Monsters are here in our world to help us understand it."

In fairy tales, the rule of 3 is important. A knight on a quest may have to carry out three tests, to undertake three tasks, as Ofelia is set by the Faun. We see in fairy tales that there are 3 little pigs, a man who had three daughters, a genie grants three wishes, there are three Billy-Goats Gruff, three ugly sisters in Cinderella. Thus, Ofelia has 3 doors to choose from, and three tasks to reveal if she truly is the Princess, at the climax of the film, there are three thrones and a trinity of mother, father and daughter (Mercedes can be seen as an older version of Ofelia, while Carmen can be seen as what Ofelia will become if she doesn't choose from the heart no matter what the cost. In Celtic mythology, there is a triple aspect to the Earth Goddess), there are three fairies (a red one, a green one, and a blue one), three women in the story, three fascists (Vidal and his two officers).

As Guillermo himself comments. "The movie's full of the rule of threes. The reward is it will expand the movie with each viewing. It's not an addition of elements, it's multiplication. It's almost like a game of interpretation, with this movie or *Devil's*

Backbone, and *Cronos*. It's actually worth going through them...in *Cronos*, alchemy. In *Devil's Backbone*, repetition and rhyme, and in this one, there's a lot of layers carefully built." Of course, *The Devil's Backbone* is described by Guillermo as the brother movie to *Pan's Labyrinth*, the male energy to its female energy. *The Devil's Backbone* is the microcosm of the civil war interpreted though the filter of the gothic romance.

In Guillermo's own words. "I tried to use an orphanage as the classic haunted building in the gothic romance." The Civil War is a household war, brother against brother, and both films share all too familiar monsters, a point Guillermo's films frequently make. "The only real monsters are the human monsters, the only thing we have to be afraid of is people, not ghosts but people." Sad but true. "I thought it would be really interesting to take a period after the Civil War and create a companion piece to *Devil's Backbone*. This would be about fairy tales but applied to a rough context, a rough period which was around '44 in Spain, five years after the civil war was officially over. The Resistance in Spain is expecting the Allies to look back. I thought the fairy tale occurring at this crossroads in the history of Spain would be a tale about choice and disobedience. The girl who needs to disobey anything but her own conscience. Her own soul."

This is the prime theme in *Pan's Labyrinth*, that you only become immortal if you lose your fear of death. Think about what that would mean in your own life, if you woke up one morning and decided that you weren't going to be afraid anymore, if would change everything. This is also interesting from a Catholic perspective, as Guillermo has pointed out, part of being a Catholic is feeling guilty all the time, and part of losing fear is coming to terms with guilt. We also spend our lives trying to avoid pain. A person may stay in a horrible relationship or job out of fear, the same fear that prevents them making a change. We also live in a cynical time, where we worship celebrity, reality TV has replaced intelligent debate. Surely our ambitions, our hopes and dreams, can rise above the prison-like 'comfort' of the known and accepted. We should be driven by love, optimism, intellect, instead we are driven by fear.

Another very Mexican element to Guillermo's work is a distrust of institutions or uncaring authority, and an embracing of the pain of life which is refreshing. We are conditioned by chat shows to believe that everything we want should be ours, not so, how could it be? Yet so many people believe it should be thus. So many people believe they shouldn't get older or sick but that's as much a part of life as breathing. You can no more avoid pain than you can avoid breathing, so why is so much energy wasted in a futile attempt to do so? Look at your television, adverts brainwash you that you will be popular if you buy this car, the opposite sex will flock to you if you drink this drink, you will never grow old if you buy this cosmetic. All lies, and it's the hardships that we face in life that make us human, that make us grow. If I was going to take just one thing from Guillermo's films if would be that

Pan's Labyrinth is also full of symbolism, such as Ofelia finding the statue's eye in the forest. No one else would have noticed it. Moreover, Ofelia knew that she replaces it on the statue. It symbolises her eyes opening to the magical world. It is at this point the insect comes from the statue's mouth. Symbols in Celtic mythology connect us to states that otherwise lay dormant (the Celtic spiral is a fine example of this, it can be seen to represent that there is no death, only a cycle of birth and rebirth).

Symbols communicate with a part of is that understands instinctively that there is a deeper meaning to life than the world we see around us. This meaning is transcendent and transforming and cannot be expressed in words. Trees, water, and the Moon were all important symbols to the Celts and influenced the sacred geometry of their places of worship. Trees are special in the Celtic calendar, they conveyed symmetry, balance, and complexity of form. It's no coincidence that the Faun sees to be composed of the same material as the forest itself. To the Celts, Oak was a spiritual wood, the Rowan tree represented the life, and the Elder and the Hawthorn were sacred trees. Symbols are also a universal language.

The symbols of the Celtic peoples evolved from their interaction and contemplation of the world around them, not only what they could see, but what they could feel in their hearts. Carl Jung summed it up well. "Because there are innumerable things beyond the range of human understanding, we constantly use symbolic terms to represent concepts that we cannot define or fully comprehend."

As we have seen in *Cronos*, entomology is a major fascination of Guillermo's, *Pan's Labyrinth* is no exception, with an insect serving to introduce Ofelia to the magical world. "I wanted to emphasise with the camera how important the insect was, so the camera very often favours the insect. I think of insects like I think of persons. It was very important that this creature was the guy to take the girl into the labyrinth the first time. It was also very important like in *Devil's Backbone* that the first discovery of the labyrinth and the first discovery of the ghost occurred in daylight. This is something I really wanted to do with both movies, to show the fantastic in a mundane context from the get-go, because one of the things that I think makes the fantastic tangible...is to treat it like any other subject."

If the insect represents freedom in nature, (there are no straight lines in nature, it is self-organising chaos), then the Captain represents a desire to crush that freedom. Guillermo shows him wanting to control at all costs, control through fear because of his own fear. "It was important to show this captain being obsessed with little detail. For him the rebels are just a concept, little pin-points in a map that he has to look at with a magnifying glass. He's a guy that is so focussed on the small stuff, I show him with a magnifying glass, and I show him with a magnifying glass a little later on when he's fixing the watch. I wanted him to be a guy who's so obsessed by the little things, how shiny his boots are, how well his watch runs, how neatly he pinpoints his strategy on the map. He loses perspective of the larger stuff. He truly loses perspective of life and people. He is a sociopath who is completely focused on his own little details."

On *Pan's Labyrinth* we see the further development of a camera technique that started on *Mimic*, and features a lot in this film. The camera is kept slightly mobile at all times if possible. There is never a completely settled frame. The camera drifts with great subtlety. It doesn't shout 'hey, look at me', rather it's something the viewer is subliminally aware of. It's reminiscent of the ultra-fluid camerawork of Dean Cundey on the classic early films of John Carpenter, like *The Fog* and *Escape From New York*. Also the warm colours of the fantasy scenes are highly reminiscent of the work of Terence Fisher, one of Guillermo's major influences and inspirations.

The camera work is important because Guillermo dislikes lengthy exposition, he would rather show than tell. "It's story-telling without words that interests me the most. I hate dialogue and I love story-telling with the camera."

I feel that the rose at the top of the mountain in the tale Ofelia tells her unborn brother mirrors the Captain, not in it's beauty, but in it's isolation, the Captain is so isolated, he is 'forever alone, until the end of time.'

One of the indications of an auteur is the repetition of certain themes (in the same manner as an alchemist). Thus, when we see the devoted care the Captain puts into cleaning his watch, it works on two levels. One, to show the obsessive level of control that exists in his world, whether it's a speck of dirt in a cog of his clock, or a group of rebels, they must both be removed to fit his narrow world view. Two, they reflect the directors own gentle obsession with gears, cogs, and clockwork, not in the same way as the Captain, in Guillermo's case, it with a sense of wonder at their beauty, construction and operation.

One of the most beautiful components of *Pan's Labyrinth*, that is both pleasing to the eye and essential to the story are Guillermo's carefully thought out use of colour. "The colour palettes in the movie are meant to reflect that these two worlds are completely opposite. I wanted to contrast the fantasy with the reality...the fantasy is very warm, very rounded, uterine, because I felt it should echo the belly of the mother, and the reality's all in cold, rust, grey, blue colours, very cold greens and so forth. And straight

lines, no rounded lines, except for the gears on the Captain's set, or round elements that appear only on sets that are related to the girl and the fantasy. So, other than the gears of the mill and this wheel, the rest of the world outside is straight lines."

One of the most forceful scenes in *Pan's Labyrinth* is the Captain's brutal, almost off-hand murder of the two unfortunate rabbit poachers. It was deliberately chosen to be "the first act of violence, because the intention was for the violence to make you more susceptible to fantasy. And for the fantasy to make you more vulnerable to the brutality of the violence of the movie."

Worse again, for this scene, Guillermo was inspired by a true-life atrocity of the Spanish Civil War. "This particular episode is unfortunately based on an oral account from a post-war occurrence in a grocery store where a fascist came in. A citizen was there and he didn't uncover himself, he didn't take off his hat, and the fascist proceeded to smash his face with the butt of his pistol, and then took his groceries and left. I read this account and I wanted to put it in the movie, and the detail of the bottle actually came from a personal experience unfortunately. Where a friend and I got into a street brawl and I was being beaten with a chain and he was being beaten with a bottle, and while I was being beaten with a chain, the only thing I noticed was that the bottle they were beating him with didn't break like in the John Wayne movies. In Westerns, they always break, in life they didn't."

The almost off-hand violence of the Captain is synonymous with the brutality of the Spanish Civil War, where the death of two innocent men would go unnoticed amongst the slaughter of so many. As always the world keeps turning, no matter what sorrow it sees. Guillermo describes it thus. "It's that inconsequential, the death of these two guys and that is a fact, violence and death of civilians in civil war Spain and post-civil war Spain was completely inconsequential. He just shot these two guys, killed these two guys, and you know, the crickets are chirping, the train is moving in the distance. It's not a big deal. I thought that was important to show this in a war, that out of the approximately 500,000 people that died in the civil war, approximately 250,000 of them were either summarily executed or killed in cold blood without battle engagements. We have to take brutality in this movie and articulate it very carefully. That first act of violence is the most violent act in the film. After that the violence gets more and more simple in the way it's staged until the final few deaths and final few violent moments occur in a single shot, in a very throwaway way."

The point where the insect takes on the form of a fairy is pivotal, using as it does the illustration in Ofelia's book as a point of reference, it shows the world of the Faun impacting on our world. It's significant that not until Ofelia tells the insect what she feels it should look like, does it change shape. I believe that on a subconscious level she is reacting to the powerlessness of her situation in our world, and realises at a very subliminal level that the path to salvation, escape, call it what you will, relies on her following her own intuition, her own certainty the otherworld exists, and through her belief, allowing it to filter through. This is an important theme in *Pan's Labyrinth*. In our own lives we far too often feel powerless, at the mercy of those who are stronger or wield more power than us, we fear them. Only by losing that fear, and listening to our own inner voice do we become free. "We see where the girl's fantasy becomes material. This is my favourite magical moment in the film...and it's done in a very objective way."

Guillermo makes a very clear demarcation between the two worlds. "You have the blue outside world, you have the golden magical world, then you have this netherworld which is the pit, which technically belongs to both."

The look of the faun and fairies were to be believable, it was too look like something real rather than something antiseptic and unfeasible. The faun will get progressively younger as the film progresses (shades of Wilde's *The Picture of Dorian Gray*. At the beginning he is very mossy, with white hair and almost blind eyes. Guillermo has a strange take on the fairies. "The fairies were

in the meantime the girl is going to become a princess for the first time in her life through the book the Faun gave her. She is now going to find out that what the Faun told her is true. So you have the girl becoming a princess for real in the bathroom and the mother outside with her little green ridiculous dress, 'Alice in Wonderland' dress outside."

designed to be like little monkeys, that were dirty and scratching themselves, that were like little carnivores. I wanted this magical world to feel used, like somebody left it out in the rain completely unkept." Doug Jones puts in a magnificent performance as the Faun, it's not just the dialogue, a far greater proportion of the performance is in the nuances and patterns he invests into the creature.

When watching *Pan's Labyrinth*, you can see the two stories are very separate, but also on a collision course where they will merge. Guillermo went to great efforts to keep the two stories in harmony until they gradually begin to merge. "The movie is constructed with two stories that start completely separate. You have the real world and the fantasy world, and they seen to be completely independent, completely parallel. No relation to each other, and as the movie progresses, these two worlds start to intertwine amongst themselves and eventually they will lead inevitably, eventually, to a single outcome....the two worlds starting to contrast each other....the mother is there with her mundane idea of what the girl needs to be. She needs to be a princess only in appearance for the mother. She has to have this dress and please the captain, and she has to wear these shoes and be feminine. And

As I have discussed earlier in this book, books are an important part of Guillermo's inner and outer world. They formed an escape from the unhappy parts of his childhood at school for example, his inner world if you would, and then in parallel with Ofelia in *Pan's Labyrinth*, what he had read began to permeate the real world and make the magical manifest in our world. Look around you for proof, when you meet someone with an imagination, it's like the sunlight suddenly poured into a drab room. It's only through imagination, the power of belief that things can change and get better, and Guillermo's achievements not only as a film maker but a human being prove this. John Hurt (Professor Broom in the *Hellboy* movies) paid a lovely tribute to Guillermo when he said the reason the director is so big is because he needs the room to house his big heart. The naming of the book is significant too. "This is called The Book of Crossroads... the idea was to create crossroads. For every character in the film is at a crossroads in his or her life."

The similarity between the bathroom scene in *Pan's Labyrinth* and *Cronos* is deliberate on Guillermo. "I did a scene similar to this before which also involved a green dress, in *Cronos*. Federicco Luppi is getting younger and younger in the bathroom while

his wife is talking about a green dress that doesn't fit her anymore, and they are both reflections on immortality and time and age. But one is very venal and the other is much more subtle and deep."

When Ofelia sees the moon sign on her shoulder, she knows (and so do we), that she is a princess in fact. It's not a figment of her imagination. This leads us into what I feel is the most important message in all Guillermo's work, particularly *Pan's Labyrinth* and the *Hellboy* movies: that your true identity comes from you, not imposed from the outside. "I think that you are who you think you are. For as long as it comes from a genuine place in your heart...it doesn't matter materially what the world tells you are, you can always believe in your true essence. This is something I try to do in *Hellboy* too, where Hellboy knows he is human, or knows he is more than a human, even if everyone else tells him that he is a monster, he is a creature, and he is a freak."

The scene where Mercedes tells Ofelia that she used to believe in fairies when she was a child, but mostly doesn't believe in anything anymore, the horrors of the world have driven out her hopes and dreams, the sleep of reason has produced nightmare. This reflects a lot on Guillermo's own beliefs. "Of course we know she believes in freedom, in the Republican government and so forth, she doesn't believe in fairies. To me, politics or religion, organised politics and organised religion are much more fairy tales than fairy tales, they're fantasy. I don't believe in geography. I don't believe in borders. I don't believe in religion making us different. I believe in spiritual conceits making is equal not different."

Three other images that mirror each other in *Pan's Labyrinth* are those of keys and knives, and dining rooms. The knife Ofelia takes from the Pale Man's banqueting hall in the otherworld has its mirror image in the knife that Mercedes keeps on her person. The key that Ofelia retrieves from the toad mirrors the second key to the storeroom that Mercedes keeps concealed from the Captain, and the banquet that the Captain hosts is paralleled by the sumptuous tempting feast at the table of the Pale Man, both tables feature a monster at the head of them.

Again this is an important element that Guillermo has very deliberately placed in *Pan's Labyrinth*. "The key becoming an important element in the fantasy world and a key being an important element in the real world and later a knife will become an important element in the fantasy world and the real world... And a dining room will be a common element in both worlds...It is important that some of the elements in the real world have fantasy resonance to them... The Pale Man, the faceless thing that devours children, can either be the Captain or the priest at the table, the organised church, the organised politics."

There is also a parallel with elements in Guillermo's other films, for instance, the tale Ofelia reads in the Book of Crossroads is very similar to the one Professor Broom reads to the young Hellboy on Christmas Eve, 1955, in *Hellboy II: The Golden Army*. "Again we have a fairy tale being told by the girl reading her book...the Book of Crossroads about how harmony was destroyed but harmony was beautiful in the beginning. Under a magical tree all the creatures of the forest lived together." (This is interestingly the root of the Grail story, the idea that the world was perfect, but is now broken by the acts of man, and can be restored if only certain magical elements can be put back in place).

The two story lines begin to creep closer through transitions, though at the this point they are still very divergent, contrast the innocent Ofelia reading the Book of Crossroads with the Fascists reading off in the forest with murder in their hearts. Guillermo sees this as being part of the fairy tale themes of the story. "There transitions are not just eye candy, they are eye protein, they are helping to tell the story. They are also reminiscent of a book page being turned and wiping in front of your eyes...They are there to be storytelling with camera and sound."

Guillermo uses the pollen you see floating around Ofelia always signposts the presence of the magical world. "You can see the magical pollen floating around her. I introduced that element earlier on in the movie, in the insect scene where she first sees the insect and it will be present every time a magical creature is outside in the daylight world. It becomes a magical little element visually that I will quote at the end of the movie for a dramatic purpose."

To that end, the creation of a magical effect, the colours of the film are very saturated. Nowhere is the contrast between the two world more apparent than the warm inside of the frog's lair inside the tree, and the cold outside world. I have to say it's a tribute to Guillermo's story-telling that the two stories could well stand alone, the real-world story and the magical world story both wield their own fascination, but it's the combination of the two that is magical.

A theme of Guillermo's that has not received much discussion, yet most certainly is worthy of it, is the use of umbrellas in his films, think of the mournful Hellboy looking on at his beloved father's funeral, the hearse surrounded by agents carrying umbrellas like black flowers of mourning, yet unable to join them because he is a monster. *Pan's Labyrinth* too features the judicious use of umbrellas. The arrival of the diners to Captain Vidal's banquet is made more ominous by the use of umbrellas (something we see at Professor Broom's funeral in *Hellboy*). Guillermo has 'them opening in an almost ballistic way, like black explosions, or bat-wings expanding."

In this dining sequence, we can see how Guillermo deliberately intended it as a mirror image of Pale Man's dining room. "Here, you have the dinner table with the chimney that is all square, all straight lines.... and a monster sitting at the head of the table. You will see this dining room perfectly echoed in round forms and a different colour palette...in the Pale Man's dining room. It will be perfectly echoed a little later in the Pale Man sequence."

It's also important to realise that this banquet makes a statement on the state of post civil-war Spain, because in *Pan's Labyrinth* the context of the environment in the country around the table they are dining on, is as crucial to the story as the room's layout. "It's very important to see this banquet in 1944...people were literally boiling the roots out of trees, making almost stone soup for dinner. In a time where nobody had food, these guys are not only hoarding the food to make the rebels come...and hoarding the medicine...but also he's throwing up a huge a party. He sees himself almost like an overlord, a feudal lord over his subjects...the banquet has that spirit."

As with the previous brutal murder of the unfortunate father and son, Guillermo was inspired to write the conversation at the table by real-life events. "The priest, when he says. 'God doesn't care about their bodies, he's already saved their souls', is verbatim what a priest used to say when bringing confession to a Republican concentration camp."

While we see the Captain as a monster, it's important to realise that, like a lot of people that cause hurt in the real world, he has utterly no empathy with anyone else. He thinks he's the good guy, it's everyone who won't do his bidding that's wrong. It's a lack of empathy that makes monsters in the real world, because it's empathy that makes us feel other's pain as if it were our own. Thus when the Captain tells everyone that he wants to be there, and that he wants to destroy everyone that would stand in his way, it tells us everything about both him and fascism. He is the real monster because he is always right, everyone else if always wrong, and as we will see, he doesn't care for even poor Carmen.

His love for his son isn't even love. It's a form of narcissistic self-love, a means of perpetuating and glorifying himself. When he tells the Doctor to save his son even at the expense of his wife, or when he tells the rebels to tell his son how he died (he dies when they tell him his son will never know of him, not just from their execution). The truly wicked always need someone to hate, someone to blame, and someone to justify their actions. Human beings do not like to own their own negative emotions, they prefer to reflect them on someone else. Guillermo understands this. "This speech the Captain says is important...because the Captain really needs to believe he's doing everything he is doing for the good of the community."

It's a deliberate choice on Guillermo's part for Ofelia's true father to have been a

tailor. "...Because most of the fairy tales were told by tailors and cobblers travelling from town to town in the old days, and therefore have tailors and cobblers as main characters." That the father of Ofelia was a tailor is important because it provides a link with that storytelling. There is also a hint that perhaps Captain Vidal may have murdered Ofelia's father to free the way to his marrying Carmen. "It's never revealed but I like stories with loose ends like that. Compared to Hollywood screenplay writing, I love to leave threads for the audience to speculate and talk about." Not surprising from a director who loves to talk about movies himself, Guillermo has much in common with his own audience, which is why his work strikes a deep chord.

The Captain's reaction to the story about his father is significant because the Captain lies when he says his father never owned a watch. This is a special trait of Guillermo's here. "I do another thing here that rarely is done when I'm working on a Hollywood movie. I cannot have a character lie without making a whole scene about it. Here the character just off-handed, says 'no, my father never had a watch.' He makes the watch more important by him denying it...when somebody denies something, it's so much more important than when somebody affirms something."

As with *Hellboy II: The Golden Army*, Celtic myths and themes are an important inspiration to Guillermo. "...The design of the pit and the design of the fantasy world was done all around circles and curves like the Faun's horns or like the labyrinth to echo each other, and it was meant to be very Celtic in the feel of it, very simple traces, but very elaborate patterns that are the essence of Celtic art...Most people link Celtic with Ireland and the UK...but the Celtic culture actually came through the north of Spain into the islands above."

The Faun and his fairies are drawn from mythological archetypes and thus, their

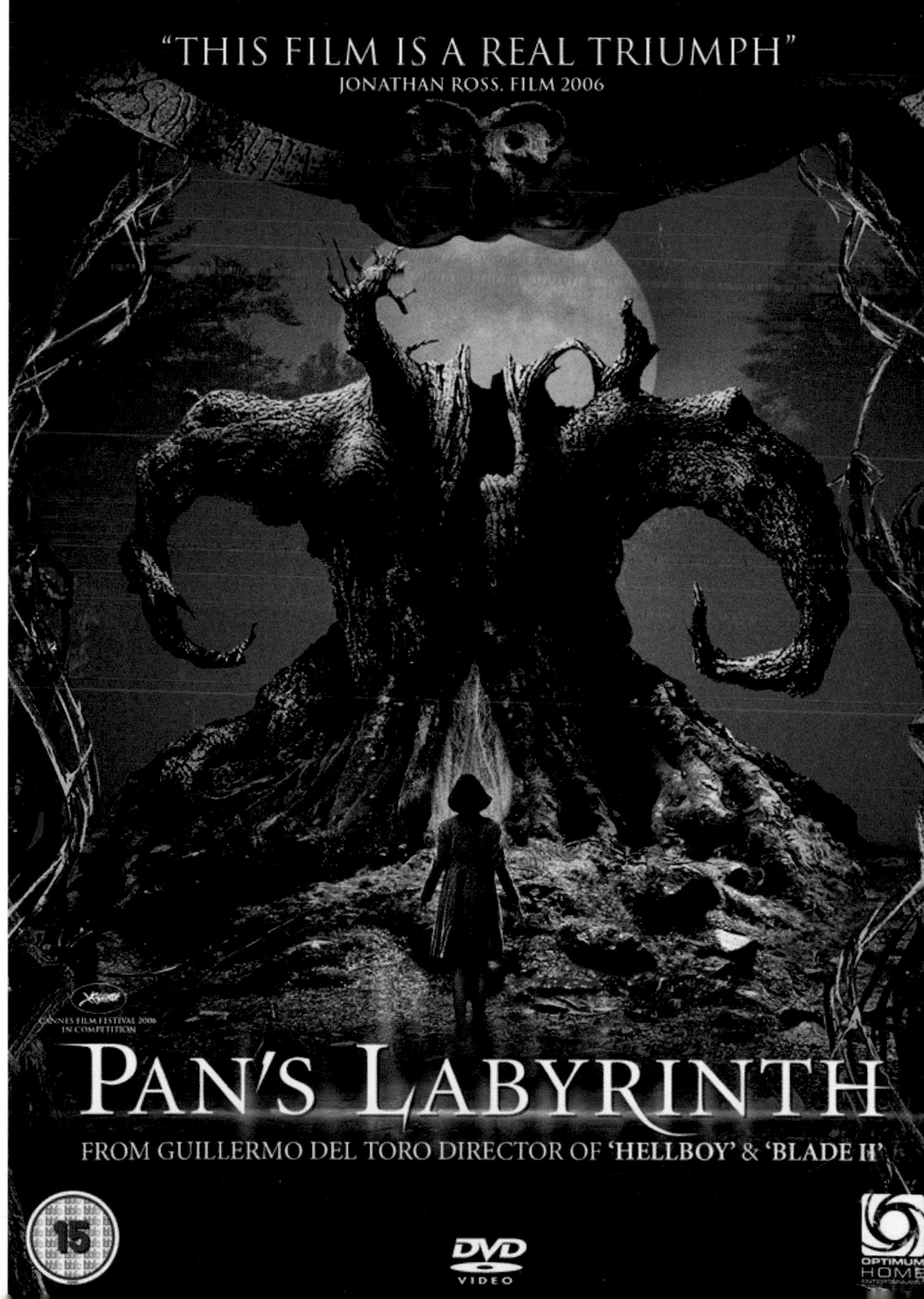

nature is never completely straightforward, something Guillermo places great emphasis on. "I wanted to have ambiguity in the Faun and ambiguity in the fairies. Are they good or are they bad? Very important that they're never fully good or never fully bad. A faun in classical mythology is a creature that is neither, it's a neutral creature that represents nature.

Only in America is the movie called *Pan's Labyrinth*, it was originally the *Faun's Labyrinth* in Spanish. The Faun is meant to be a force of creation and destruction, and therefore I wanted the Faun to be very ambiguous and I use his index finger like a dagger almost...Then I have him say 'why would you be afraid of me?' and smile with the most wicked smile you can ever imagine...so that you keep the girl guessing. I didn't want the girl to have a safe choice in the movie. In essence the tests are not important in terms of her failing or passing them, she actually fails two out of the three tests in theory. The important thing is how she goes about these tests, how brave and how self-reliant her spirit has remained intact."

The scene where the Fascists distribute the bread to the people is also drawn from reality. Something that made a deep impression on Guillermo. "The legend that the civil guard reads is printed on the outside flyers that contain the bread. This was based on reality, because these pieces of bread with the legends printed outside were thrown from planes into occupied cities, into the resistance cities of the Republicans and what the Captain is reading is exactly what is printed outside on the bread package. It was propaganda with bread, trying to tell the rebels 'surrender, there's no hope, we're winning and everything is good.'

The scene where the pages of the Book of Crossroads bleed are heavy with symbolism, as is the crescendo female scream that accompanies it in the background soundtrack. Guillermo's inspirations here come from interesting sources. "The Fallopian tubes here and the Faun's horns are echoed... in this incredibly ominous blood pattern, and the montage grows into a soundtrack that is very much inspired by one my favourite engineering in pop music which is Pink Floyd, it's actually an echo of a moment in Pink Floyd's 'The Wall'"

The Book of Crossroads, which is a magical book from the Otherworld, predicts the haemorrhaging of Ofelia's mother, showing that the two worlds are beginning to have an impact on one another. And to match this, Guillermo has the colour palette of the film will change subtly and slowly "Now the fairy tales and the real world start affecting each other...We see the magical book predict the semi-miscarriage, and therefore the magic seems to be effecting the real world. It really occurs."

From an emotional point of view, Ofelia's world is getting worse by the day. One of the messages of *Pan's Labyrinth* is that when the outside world turns most against us, we need to fall back on our inner world, not as an 'escape' from reality, but as a way of understanding it and coping with it, and perhaps like Ofelia to make it more like we feel in our hearts it could be. This is a very positive message, a million miles away from aggression or the passive-aggression of becoming a victim. The Vikings had a very wise saying, 'lift up the self by the self.'

The true tests in *Pan's Labyrinth* are those that tests Ofelia's courage, decency and self-reliance, just in real life. The importance of this cannot be understated, how many times in life do we all ignore our own inner voice and go ahead and do what we know is wrong for us anyway. In the 21st century our inner voice is even more likely to be drowned out by TV, the internets, iPods, all to our own detriment, because within us, our inner voice is withering through sheer loneliness and lack of use. This one of the pivotal points for Ofelia in *Pan's Labyrinth*, where she sees the magical world and is real and knows her fate depends on her courage and her following her own heart, a trait she shares in common with Guillermo. "Here, it is important to keep in mind that the girls has not eaten since the day before, the mother punished her, the mother said you will go to bed without supper then there was the near miscarriage." So by the time the next night comes, Ofelia is very low indeed. "The girl is in a moment where everything is going wrong and she's hopeless, lost in an attic...I love this idea of a princess in an attic...just realising the power of magic in her heart, while the world around her is collapsing. She's just realised 'there is a giant frog, ''I am a princess'.

The scenes were the rebels appear to the Doctor and Mercedes also is constructed by Guillermo to have its dark mirror image later in *Pan's Labyrinth*. "We have this scene two times in the movie, much as we repeat two scenes in two different places in the movie. We echo them exactly because I think there is an advantage in rhyming images. It creates a sense of rhythm. I believe the viewer registers these things. But here, instead of the Captain, the rebels appear, it will be echoed."

Writing *Pan's Labyrinth* was an extremely difficult process for Guillermo, because he knew that in creating it, "it was going to be about juxtaposing the fantasy and magic to the most mundane concerns and brutality....It took a long, long time to sort the tasks and elements of magic in the film because...there is magic or a magical element every other scene in the movie, almost like a chequerboard. You see that it may be the mandrake, it may be a fairy, it may be an insect or a magical book but I patterned very carefully so that every two scenes more or less, you get a magical scene and a reality scene and this started to get more and more complicated as the structure advanced because the two worlds were melding...I had to write and reorganise the tasks again and again and again, to mirror each other, and the mandrake needed to echo the unborn child of the mother."

Guillermo intended the cave the rebels use as a base is intended to be magical in its own right. "The cave of the rebels reminds you of the cave of the Faun-the pit, the centre of the labyrinth. I wanted the rebels to feel like magic creatures of the forest, so every time we meet them they are coming out from behind trees, or there is pollen floating around them and there is this sort of linkage between them and the magic. It is a romantic view. This is a romantic movie at the end of the day to me. A hopelessly melancholy romantic movie but nevertheless full of the spirit of hope and despair at the same time."

That *Pan's Labyrinth* is deliberately set in 1944 by Guillermo as he sees that year as crucial both in the context of the rebels and the greater war in the world outside. "1944 was important also because we hear about the Normandy beach occurring, and how the rebels were fighting in favour of the Allies to upset the balance of World War 2, and they were for example sabotaging the mining of tungsten in the mines of Galicia, that was mined and sent to Hitler for the construction of panzer tanks, and if it hadn't been for the sabotaging of those mines by the Spanish rebels, the World War 2 outcome would have been very different, but they were repaid by being abandoned to Franco's dictatorship for decades."

The violence of *Pan's Labyrinth* is not that of a typical horror film. For example, the unfortunate Frenchie's amputation is not shown. It is fair to say there is absolutely no gratuitous violence in *Pan's Labyrinth*, which gives what violence there actually is a huge weight and impact. It also makes our own imagination work, which is good as with the bulk of Hollywood's output this is done for us, we contribute nothing to such films, and we bring nothing away, we are the same person when we leave the cinema as we were when we go in (except perhaps a little poorer and more jaded than before).

Also if the violence was graphic it would totally unsettle the elements of the magical world in the films, the transition from one to another would be hard to accept. The frog in the tree is the least violent of the magical tests. It is in the banqueting hall of the Pale man that the violence of the real world will manifest itself. In *The Orphanage*, the question of doppelgangers arises. I feel that the Pale Man in some respects not only mirrors the Captain, but is what the Captain could become. He is the face of fascism. Expressionless, incapable of showing any emotion-that is surely the most frightening monster of all. For we cannot read its feelings and thus, we project our own. His eyes are the most scary feature of all-the Pale Man only uses his eyes to see one thing, a victim to satisfy his appetite. This is a very deliberate on Guillermo's part that the Pale Man reflects 'the facelessness of the fascist, or of organised politics, or organised religion, whatever you want....The geometry is the same as the dining room. The long table with the food, the chimney at the back and the faceless monster at the head of the table."

Ofelia's point of view is crucial, it is important to realise the magic comes through her, she is its portal. The world outside is cold while the magical world is warm, you can really see this in contrast when Ofelia enters the realm of the Pale Man, and the door she's made with the magic chalk is open.

Like much of imagery in Guillermo's films, particularly *Cronos*, the Pale Man was inspired by experiences of the church when he was growing up. "The original design for the Pale Man was that of an old man who had lost a lot of weight...I really didn't like the sculpting. It seemed a little mundane. So I ordered them to remove the face of it, and place the little eyes on a plate, like St. Lucy, which was a statue I saw as a kid in a church, that had her eyes on a platter and had blood pouring out of her eyes, and I wanted to a echo a sort of church-like feel, a sort of concentration camp feel with the shoes piled up in a corner, so I'm telling you this ogre, which is a classical element in a fairy tale, this ogre eats children. It's a perverse creature that has a lot of food in front of it, but only eats innocents."

"You can see the three doors, which again is an element in fairy tales, three doors that are completely distinct and the girl disobeys, disobeys the fairies that are pointing to the middle door, and goes with her instincts and opens the left door, which does contain the dagger. I think it's very important that disobedience has different incarnations in the film. The girl disobeys and gets it right with the dagger, and then...because she's hungry, she will disobey like a 10 year old would, and eats two single measly grapes, from a huge banquet table, and she thinks it is not important. She learns a lesson there but she learns to trust herself. At the end of the movie, the important thing is that no matter what danger she went through, she still does not distrust her nature. She does not distrust her instinct. I think it's really important that she chooses for herself, regardless of danger, regardless of influence, she remains true to herself."

The work of many painters Guillermo has admired from an early age influenced *Pan's Labyrinth*. The scene where the Pale Man devours the fairies is a direct quote from Francisco Goya's *Saturn Devouring His Sons*. Other artists whos work influenced Pan's Labyrinth include Arthur Rankin, Edmund Lachman, Arnold Shwaub, Arnold Bucklin, and obviously some of more romantic pre-Raphaelite period painters, and the symbolist painters. Guillermo believes that "the power of the of the symbolist painting is that it puts spiritual origins in absolutely pagan motifs, archetypes that are universal in a Jungian sense, archetypes that are universal but also unique to each of us. The power of this is that I think it taps directly into the subconscious and the spirit, and it makes fantasy and magic a very spiritual experience."

Originally, *Pan's Labyrinth* was intended by Guillermo to be a very different film. "The origins of the film were a very different story. It was the story of a pregnant woman who arrived to a big mansion in the north of Spain and her husband was working for a Fascist captain restoring the mansion. And the woman fell in love with a satyr, with a Faun in the Labyrinth...they fell in love and he asked for the blood of her first born in return for the labyrinth to open and for her to go to the magical kingdom with him, and the end of the movie was her sacrificing her son to go with the love of her life, that happens to be non-human. It was a very different story...The evolution of the story included a daughter of the pregnant woman, and little by little I realised that it would be more interesting to talk about the magic through the eyes of the girl, and toss out the love story completely."

When Ofelia follows the Faun's instruction with the mandrake and it comes to life, it's one of the most beautiful moments in the film, particularly in the way it imitates the movements of Ofelia's unborn brother. Guillermo says it also marks the point where we can see the magic is real. "Here we start

seeing the fantasy affect the real world because the mother starts healing magically. So objectively the mother gets better for real, therefore the magical world starts affecting the real world."

However, at this point, the magic's source is still ambiguous. "The mandrake is actually visible in the kitchen scenes when they're chopping vegetables, and actually the vegetable Mercedes is chopping is a peeled mandrake if you will. So I wanted it to go both ways, it could be fake, all in her head, or it could be real. As the movie progresses though, it becomes more and more apparent to me, writing and directing the story, that it is real, that the girl is truly going through that transformation, and truly has encountered these magical creatures. Whether objectively everybody sees them or not, is not important to me, the Captain for example could not see the Faun...Mercedes may not be able to see Faun. Only those that know where to look, only those that have the right gaze will see that world. It's part of the movie's idea...the movie's thesis."

One thing that should be bourn in mind when watching *Pan's Labyrinth* is that it very nearly didn't get made. More than once while setting up the film financing collapsed. Guillermo started pre-production with $100,000 of his own money, and Alfonzo, his producing partner, committed to half of that, a terrific commitment for what could have ended up being the world's most expensive collection of pencil drawings had the film not eventually have been made. "In the eyes of many people I should have given up, but I wanted very much to do it because I felt that it had something to say about the moment in which we put away our toys, we put away our fairy tales and we put away our soul, and became just another adult. That crossroads we have all gone through, and the moment of the loss of childhood is a profoundly melancholy moment in our lives."

This wasn't the only financial sacrifice Guillermo would make to commit his heart's vision to celluloid. "The shoot in the forest cost $500,000 dollars in SFX, which came from the producers' salaries...The idea of the financing of this film was if we went over we would give our producer's salaries and we did. Now as the visual effects account grew because of various mishaps, I also ended up giving up my director's salary, but I think that it was worth it, and it always will be."

Once Carmen recovers through the intervention of Ofelia using the mandrake, it marks the point, in Guillermo's opinion, where "we see the mother fully recovered which makes the magic fully objective in the real world."

The scene where the fascists shoot the wounded rebels, is drawn by Guillermo from real life events, including the rebel being shot through his hand as he tried to push the officers gun away. "This account of being shot through the hand is also based on an aural account that I read of the Civil War."

After the Captain has taken a wounded rebel prisoner, one of the most harrowing scenes Guillermo wrote for *Pan's Labyrinth* occurs, "the torture scene. One of the earliest things I wrote from the movie. I wrote it in 1993, more or less. I had an interest in doing a civil war movie back then, but I wanted to do a war movie that took place in either the Civil War or the Revolution in Mexico. And I thought it would define the character that did it, by making him an absolute control freak. This guy, the way he combs his hair. The way he carries himself. The way he shines his boots. The way he fixes his watch. The way he sews his own lip, all of it tells you of a type of character that is an absolute control freak."

Guillermo believes there is a particular psychology to fairy tales that makes them extremely hard to integrate into a real world setting, like a dew on a spider web that will evaporate in the harsh light of day. "This is a thing in fairy tale story telling that is very difficult to actually make a decision for, because there is a simplicity to the way fairy tale characters have to work...that makes them types...is not so much psychologically three-dimensional fully-nuanced characters as it is types. Little Red Riding Hood and the Big Bad Wolf, which this guy [the Captain] is in my mind.

Now you can preserve the structure of the fairy tale and go at deconstructing the

In the magical world, Ofelia becomes an outcast, the Faun tells her she's failed, she will never see the other world, she will grow old and die and mortal, trapped in a world she does not fit in with until she dies. For a kind imaginative child like Ofelia there can be no worse fate. At the same time, in the 'real' word, with the capture of the rebel, and his torture, it seems inevitable that the Captain will find out all he needs to know and crush his enemies. It is the worst possible situation in both worlds, as Guillermo describes it. "It all seems to be going really wrong, even more against the girl ever seeming like she can conquer the odds, that was very important... the need for the girl to feel hopeless...It's the absolute final test of when she has no other option. She actually has the option to tell the Faun, "No, I am not giving you the baby...I am not giving you the baby in order to save myself'."

characters or you can try and deconstruct the fairytale structure to preserve the simplicity of the characters. You cannot do both, because then the fairytale essence becomes, I believe, unrecognisable. I knew I was gonna be juxtaposing fantasy and reality making the anecdotal elements of the fairy tale very against the grain. So, I wanted to keep the simplicity of this character, though I wanted to make them seem like memorable types and give them a reason to be. The girl loves books to the point of having internalised the fantasy, not only has she read books, as the mother says...but she is also capable of inventing a tale like the story of the rose than is incredibly moving."

Guillermo found the co-production of *Pan's Labyrinth* to be much more effective than some of his previous directing experiences. "The fact that this movie had to happen as a co-production was very difficult to deal with in putting it together because I wanted very much to use Mexican talent...I had tried that in the past with *Devil's Backbone* and it backfired terribly and with this one we applied the lessons we learned, found a great partner in Telecinco in Spain. Much to their credit they were the best partners we could ever hope for, and I really believe the future of Spanish language cinema lies within co-productions, and not just lonely efforts of each of the countries."

If we take away any message from *Pan's Labyrinth* it is that. If we lose our fear of disapproval, discomfort, punishment and even death. Then none of those things have power over us, and only then will we be free. All the things we fear are transitory anyway, 'this too will pass' as the wise saying goes. It is this mindset that informs the Doctor's decision to give a mercy killing to the rebel prisoner even though he knows it will cost him his own life. Guillermo sees this as being a part of the film's theme of choice. "This decision of the girl is the essence of the film there. Crossroads-the choice. We have here another character, which is the Doctor and in this rapid succession we see the Doctor choosing to kill to disobey the Captain, to kill the rebel and risk his own life,

and I always wonder if those 18/25 paces the Doctor takes outside in the rain, right before he is killed, I always think those are probably the absolutely most amazing moments of his life, where he is at his highest, where he feels the best...where he feels the most alive, and if that is so then the choice of the Doctor is validated."

Ofelia's mother's situation mirrors that of her daughter, in that she too has the option of making life-changing decisions, if only she is prepared to pay the price. Guillermo sees the root of Ofelia's mother's woes as being in the choices she has made. "The idea of the film was also to show the mother of the girl at a threshold, she could disobey the Captain and be a mother, tell the girl 'magic is real...you are valuable, your stepfather is crazy', but no. The mother who has given up on magic, chooses to tell the girl 'magic is not real, magic does not exist, leave it alone, you are to become a woman, you are not a girl anymore...' And by defining that choice, by not believing in magic, then she kills herself by throwing the mandrake into the fire, and miscarries one more time with fatal results, so I'm always interested in these characters that in making one choice redeem or doom themselves to become something tragic, a tragic result of their choice or to become immortal."

The mandrake itself symbolises ambiguity in *Pan's Labyrinth*, this is not a typical Hollywood film where everything is laid out in a simplistic way, with all Guillermo's films, and this one in particular, you have to engage with the work, let it get inside your head, in much the same way as Ofelia does. It also shows how adults often don't believe what children tell them even when it's true. Guillermo has constructed the scenes with the mandrake to be ambiguous.

"I think it is very important to show the mandrake with the Captain because objectively that root is there but it is not moving. But if you have so far the belief that it's all in her head, the fact that the mandrake is there but it's not moving, proves that it could be one of the many roots that they're peeling in the kitchen. The mandrake becomes alive only at the end of the scene, when the mother burns it and it is dying, but only the girl sees it. It is a crucial scene to see the mother give up her hopes, give up the crossroads, all of Spain was at a crossroads, all the world was at a crossroads in 1944."

"Everything was changing, and I think that of the essential meaning of a labyrinth is that its full of twists and turns to the left, to the right, in a convoluted way to reach an evitable centre. I believe that life is like a labyrinth. The universe is like a labyrinth and there is an inevitable centre, and we're right in the transit of it, and I also believe as a symbol, the labyrinth can mean the labyrinth inside the girl's head where the Faun lives, or the historical labyrinth where the Captain is trapped...The labyrinth, like a symbol, like any other symbol, cannot be closed to a single meaning, because the symbol becomes a cipher and the tale becomes an equation of an exact value. I love symbols because of their ambiguity and I think that is very important to keep them as open as possible and at the same time knowing what you want to do with them because instinctively there is a level with working with symbols where you know where you're going with them."

The Doctor's death scene is one of both tragedy and triumph. We are sorry to see the death of a man who is both gentle and brave, and yet to die in defiance of evil is surely fine way to die. Guillermo affords this courageous man a death of great dignity. "It's an almost serene death, if there is such a thing, it's a beautiful, tragic, and poetic, and fragile death....We came to create a sense of death being less and less important as time goes by. I think what is important at the end of the film is the birthing of the girl into a world where she will become herself."

When Mercedes decides to bring Ofelia with her, she returns to her hiding place in the kitchen, as before, and when Ofelia and Mercedes reach the forest, instead of being met by the rebels, this time they are met by the Captain and his men. Here, the Captain's umbrella acts as a reveal, like a conjurors trick, echoing the umbrellas of the Captain's dinner guests arriving.

Now, it seems the captured Mercedes will suffer the same fate as the previously

captured rebel. Because we care about this brave and decent woman, our tension is high. This genesis of the scene where the Captain appears beneath his umbrella is scene goes a long way back. This is a scene Guillermo has wanted to use for a long time. "It's the prelude of things going apparently very wrong for everyone...actually story-boarded for another movie in 93/94. I had it in my notebooks."

So, understandably, we fear Mercedes will not survive, something Guillermo has carefully constructed. "The staging of this scene is staged exactly the way we staged the stuttering guy's torture...not only to mirror each other, but its important you feel the two interrogations are gonna go equally wrong. In other words, if this is the moment of the film in which the girl is absolutely lost, and this is the moment of the film where Mercedes is absolutely lost. You should never expect her to come out of this alive."

But come out of it alive, she does, with the knife concealed in her dress (that mirrors the knife Ofelia took from the room of the Pale Man), she not only frees herself, but wound the Captain physically, and worse, wounds his massive pride. She literally cuts the smile off his face, a scene that Guillermo loves, one that marks a turning point in *Pan's Labyrinth*. "I love the way it hurts his vanity, to me, it's almost like a castration."

This is the one of the worst possible things that could happen to the Captain, defeated, injured and humiliated by a woman, and one he barely acknowledged existed. The glee with which Guillermo orchestrates his just deserts drips from the screen. "I actually love torturing this guy, I must say, I hate him so much. I love for him to pay...From now on the idea is the movement starts to turn in the film....This is where the tables turn, everything that seemed to be hopeless is now hopeful."

It is at this point that the Faun returns to Ofelia. Guillermo sees this as being part of Ofelia's destiny. "He comes back because hopefully we see he was meant to give her another chance no matter what. The tests needed to continue. He is the Pale Man, the reason why Doug is playing both roles is because the Faun is controlling the frog. The way to prove that is that at the end of the movie, the three fairies (including the two that were devoured in Goya-fashion by the Pale Man), they return, they come back at the end, so the Pale Man never ate them...the real test...is not so much the results of the tests as how the girl goes at them and its very important that he says 'I'll give you another chance, but you have to obey me without ever contradicting me', and of course, she disobeys him and that's important.'

It's in the scene where the Captain sews up his own cut cheek, that he becomes, in a sense, larger than life himself. Note how the flames behind him form almost a pair of wings or horns. It's here that Guillermo sees the Captain as becoming more of a myth than a man. "It's the moment where he transforms himself into the ogre....the Big Bad Wolf, a thing that will not stop." It's entirely in character, that a control-freak like the Captain will attend to his own injury. "He shines his own boots, he fixes his own watch... he's gonna sew his own cheek." And the scene where he takes a shot of drink to kill the pain, but causes more, defines him "the moment where he drinks the alcohol and burns his cheek...defines his character, because after it burns through the wound, he pours another one."

Guillermo feels that it's in the very real threat of the Captain that Ofelia shows her courage in refusing the Faun's request. "In order for her to be truly afraid at the end of the film...In order for her to truly need to say no to the Faun...with a huge loss, she really needs to believe this guy is gonna kill her, and he already said if somebody comes for her-kill her."

Now, the magic chalk, already an important part of the tale, becomes more important again. Guillermo sees this as a sign of the magical world's growing impact in the real real world. "The element of the chalk, which up to now has been an imaginary element, crosses over...now the magical world becomes real...How did the girl get from above to the Captain's lair? There were guards outside the door, her door was locked, she was in the attic. So the answer is, she drew the magical door in the wall. To me, there is no other tangible way of getting down there.

The final thing in the movie that proves the magic is real is the fact that the chalk is there, the fact that the flower blooms at the end and the insect is watching it. It's a tiny thing but it's very important."

This also marks a point in the movie where the story is increasingly told by events rather words. The magical world is intruding ever more, and the real world becomes magical. Guillermo has often expressed a love for the silent movie-style way of story-telling. "Now this is what I think is beautiful. I would like to do a movie that is all like this, no dialogue, the camera and the objects, and the music and the sound design doing the story-telling for it, and let the marriage of word, and set design and camera angles, tell the story...Here, the tables start turning the otherworld starts gaining."

Guillermo has placed a message on the entrance to the Labyrinth. "The engraving there in Latin is a saying that essentially means 'In your hands is your destiny', or 'In your decisions is your destiny', 'In our judgement lies our destiny.'

At this stage of the film, the Faun is at his youngest, "his hair is now reddish, his eyes are completely unclouded, his chest is clean and free of roots and moss, and his teeth are straight and beautiful." This is significant, because when the Faun asks Ofelia to sacrifice her brother, he asks her to commit the most evil act imaginable to her. This is very significant, because in life, appearance unfortunately counts for far more than a kind heart, how many times have we seen evil committed by people considered to be beautiful, more so now than ever, in this cosmetic age (not for nothing was glamour an old word fro a magical spell). How much happier we would all be if we could see past surface experience and judge by deeds and not by looks, sadly such blindness is endemic to being human (and we consider ourselves superior to every other creature on this planet, when only a virus behaves with the same level of violence, stupidity and self-destruction as humanity).

Again Guillermo is inspired by his exposure to religion in his youth. "An almost biblical moment where he has her several times deny herself the rite of passage to the magic kingdom...she has to be that sure to pass the test, now that we know that the innocent blood was required to open the portal...from her. This is full circle to the opening of the film and the first time we see her. The first time we see her, she's dying. The second time we see her, she is being reborn."

Like Jacinto in *The Devil's Backbone*, the Captain has a moment of humanity, when he's well past the point of no return. Guillermo sees the two characters as mirror-images of each other. "I tried to build the character of the Captain like the antagonist in *Devil's Backbone*. I tried to build them so that at the end of the film, they may get their most human moment. In *Devil's Backbone*, it is the moment where Jacinto looks at his photographs as a child...If this was the story of the Captain, and the Captain was the good guy, this would be his climatic scene, beautiful speech...the watch...the music rises, he dies heroically, you can see him. The phrase she [Mercedes] says, 'he'll never know your name', kills him before the bullet even touches his face."

The origin of that fatal shot that takes the Captain's life, goes back to an early experience of Guillermo's in Mexico. "When I used to work in a mental institution as a volunteer...I used to go through the morgue in order to have my lunch in the cemetery next door, which is a strange place for a lunch, when I went through the area where the corpses were. There was a guy that had been shot in the face and his eye had rolled back...had actually rolled toward the wound. The forensic guy told me that's the way these injuries occur.

Ofelia's dying in our world is the calm after the storm, its part of Guillermo's giving the viewer a chance to reflect on what has occurred. "It's such a magical moment when the blood just drips, it's a serene moment. But I love the way it creates a quite after all that horror."

Through her sacrifice and courage, Ofelia may die physically in our world but is reborn in the otherworld, there is a sense of her having returned to the womb to be thus reborn. I feel she knows she is immortal when she realises the blood is gone. Guillermo fits in a nice film reference here. "Here we come to the point where I think the girl becomes immortal, and there is a quote to *The Wizard of Oz* there...And we see the fantastic world... completely like a womb, rounded with womb-like patterns. We see the pollen appearing magically and she's transported there."

The inverse nature of the ending of *Pan's Labyrinth* reflects the film's beginning, and the film's nature of balance, of each element having a similar but opposing element. It also reflects with great depth Guillermo's inspirations and personal philosophy. "This is a quote of Hans Christian Anderson's *The Little Matchbook Girl* but the fable she says at the beginning of the movie is essentially what I think immortality really is. Is there real immortality? And is there real magic? I believe there really is, if they are a spiritual reality, that they are as tangible and as real as the objective world, as the material world. I think that we have no problem believing in them when they are disguised as religion. When people say, I feel Buddha, Jesus, or Mohamed in my heart, people nod their heads and allow it to be true, but when we seek that solace, that refuge, in fantasy, people mostly deny us that licence and think it's a childish conceit, but I think that immortality is the act of refusing death, of refusing to give any importance to death."

"The fable of the rose says there was a rose that grew at the top of a mountain that gave immortality to those that dared to pluck it, but in order to pluck it, you had to go through a forest of thorns that were full of deadly poison, so only if you dared to die, you would reach true immortality and people in town talked about death and no one ever said anything about immortality, and everybody's so concerned with immortality, transcendence, and eternal youth, and I believe that these things are only achieved when you don't care for them. I think that the girl really becomes immortal and the legacy she leaves behind, it's a tiny, tiny, legacy, that is a flower, a fragile white flower that's blooming next to a dead tree, and escorted by an insect. And this flower, like the beauties in this movie, which is not a blockbuster movie, a massive movie, but a delicate little film done from the heart. The flower and the film are there for those who know where to look."

Like the Labyrinth of its title, *Pan's Labyrinth* takes us all on a very different journey, with a very different destination to each of us. A sign of good art is that we all bring our own experiences to it, we create out own interpretation. *Pan's Labyrinth* is a magical film in many senses of the word. That it opens up our own world and let's the magic back in may be its most magical trait of all. As the world grows ever darker, and as our own hearts run the risk of becoming harder, a film like *Pan's Labyrinth* that lets magic back into the world is vey special indeed. Guillermo sees *Pan's Labyrinth* as his coming of age film. "The most personal movie I've made. It changed my life." Story-telling is like alchemy, it takes base material and changes it to something transcendent and beautiful. Guillermo Del Toro is a 21st century alchemist and *Pan's Labyrinth* is a cinematic *Philosopher's Stone*, and those brave enough to open up to it's magic will never be the same again...

Goya

"Francisco Goya, whos paintings have become very important in my life from an early age..."
GUILLERMO DEL TORO

As well as being an influence on The Devil's Backbone, the scene in Pan's Labyrinth, where the Pale Man devours the two fairies is described by Guillermo as "an almost verbatim quote of one of Goya's most famous paintings which is *Saturn Devouring His Son* (which featured on the cover of The Obsessed's fine *Lunar Womb* album).

Francisco Goya (1746-1828), a Spanish painter, was one of the first masters of modern art. His free brushwork and brilliant colours make him a forerunner of the impressionist movement of the late 1800's. His skill in capturing a fleeting, dramatic moment influenced the romantics of the early 1800s. His fantastic imagination and his search for a deeper reality in man's emotions and subconscious inspired the expressionists and surrealists of the 1900's.

Goya was born near Saragossa. His full name was Francisco José de Goya y Lucientes. Aged 14, he entered an apprenticeship with the painter José Luzán. In Madrid, he studied with Anton Raphael Mengs. Unfortunately the two clashed, and Goya's examinations did not prove satisfactory. He submitted entries for a place at the Royal Academy of Fine Art in 1763 and 1766, but was denied entrance. He went to paint in Rome, and in 1771 he won the second prize in a painting competition organised by the City of Parma. He would go on to study with Francisco Bayeu y Subías. This marks the point of the emrgence of his own distinct style. He also went on to marry Bayeu's sister in July 25, 1773. The marriage, and Bayeu's membership of the Royal Academy of Fine Arts, certainly helped his employment prospects.

In 1774, he was appointed painter to the Royal Tapestry Works in Madrid, where he designed 42 patterns over a 5 year period, which gave him access to the royal court. His tapestry designs are typical of the late rococo style in elegance of line and colour. Yet their recording of everyday events anticipates the realism of the 1800's. Between 1780 and 1792, Goya reached the height of his material success. He painted a canvas for the altar of the Church of San Farncisco El Grande, which helped him to be admitted to the Royal Academy of Fine Arts in 1780. The pleasant nature of his painting reflected his optimism. In 1783, the Count of Floridablanca, a favourite of King Carlos II, commissioned him to paint his portrait. After the death of Charles III in 1788 and revolution in 1789, during the reign of Charles IV, Goya's popularity with royalty was at it's height.

In 1792, Goya became ill with cholera and a high fever, and lost his hearing. His art became more imaginative after his illness, and he became more introspective and withdrawn, no longer merely looking out at the world, he looked within to interpret it. During the half-decade he spent recuperating, Goya read much about the French Revolution and the philosophy behind it. While he recovered, in the period 1793-1794, he created a set of eleven small paintings on tin known as Fantasy and Invention , such as the terrifying, staring into the void loneliness of Courtyard With Lunatics (this, you must remember, is from a time when the mentally ill were to be punished and incarcerated as criminals, something Goya wanted to see reformed, and it would be consciously or sub-consciously, the subject of many of his paintings, he himself was suffering a mental breakdown to accompany his physical ill-health, this particularly manifested itself in his Black Paintings, especially *Saturn Devouring His Son*, a paean to self-destruction by devouring your own immortality).

Also in this period, he produced his best religious painting, plus a series of biting social satires in his etchings The Caprices. Goya said they portrayed "...the innumerable foibles and follies to be found in any civilised society, and from the

common prejudices and deceitful practices which custom, ignorance, or self-interest have made useful." The darkness of the visions depicted in these prints is aptly summed up in his (now famous) caption: "The sleep of reason produces nightmares." He reached his peak as a portrait painter with *The Family of Charles IV* and two Majas (ladies).

In 1799 he was made First Court Painter with a salary of 50,000 reales and 500 ducats for a coach. He did work on the cupola of the Hermitage of San Antoni de la Florida, and painted the King and Queen and many nobles and royals. One of the most interesting things about his paintings is that Goya was not inclined to flatter his subjects. Théophile Gautier decribed the subjects Goya's *The Family of Charles IV* as having the appearance of 'the corner baker and his wife after they won the lottery.

Napoleon's invasion and occupation of Spain from 1808 to 1813 inspired Goya's some of most powerful paintings such as *The Charge of the Mamelukes* and *The 3rd of May 1808*, and his print *The Disasters of the War*. These works depict the horrors of war. More amusingly, his Majas nude caused great controversy, but instead of giving into pressure and painting clothes on the lady that was the subject of his painting, he simply painted another painting of the said lady, in the same pose, but this time with clothes. Nevertheless both Majas were confiscated by the Inquisition as being obscene (ironic, considering the real obscenity was their persecution of innocent people), who doubtlessly kept them under lock and key lest they be distracted from their persecution by "impure thoughts"!

After the war King Ferdinand VII returned to Spain, but relations with Goya were no friendly, nevertheless, Goya worked constantly, like any true artist, he had to express what he felt within.

Goya retired to a country house near Madrid, known as the Quinta del Sorda ('House of the Deaf Man', named after a previous owner and not Goya) where he painted other imaginative, violent pictures, on canvas and the very walls, now known as the Black Paintings, the most famous of which is *Saturn Devouring His Son (sometimes known as Devoration or Saturn Eats His Child*. The painting portrays a Greco-Roman mythological scene of the God Saturn consuming a child, which may well be a reference to Spain's ongoing civil conflicts. Fred Licht described the painting in 1979 as "the most essential to our understanding of the human condition in modern times, just as Michaelangelo's Sistine ceiling is essential to understanding the tenor of the 16th century."

This painting is one of 14 in a series known as the Black Paintings. After his death the wall paintings were transferred to canvas and are a monument to the dark period of Goya's life, where deaf and suffering mentally, he looked deep within to see the world with his silent soul as well as his eyes. He liberated himself from the painting convention of the time. Many of the Black Paintings can see seen in the Prado museum in Madrid. Unlike his war paintings, the fantastic horrors of these pictures are relieved by touches of morbid humour, delicate beauty, and realistic observation.

In 1810's, Goya created a set of aquatint prints titled *The Disasters of War* (los desastres de la Guerra), which show events from the Peninsular War. The events depicted are both disturbing and macabre in their depiction of the horrors of the battlefield, and can be seen to represent Goya's disgust and outrage at limitless extent of man's inhumanity to man. The prints were not published until 1863, 35 years after Goya's death.

In 1823, Goya moved to France to escape the harsh rule of King Ferdinand VII. His last work became even more freer and more dazzling.

He returned to Spain, but despite being warmly received, he returned to France, where he died in 1828.

Goya's work was inseparable from the man himself, that is as it should be, for a true artist must have the courage to listen to his inner voice, and use it to reproduce what he sees and feels of the

world within and without himself. Some modern doctors believe the lead pigments in Goya's paints may have poisoned him and contributed to his health problems. The style of the Black Paintings prefigures the expressionist movement. Goya often painted himself into the background of his pictures. A true artist, he was as much a participant as an observer, something which gives his work a unique and lasting intensity.

Chapter Seven The Orphanage

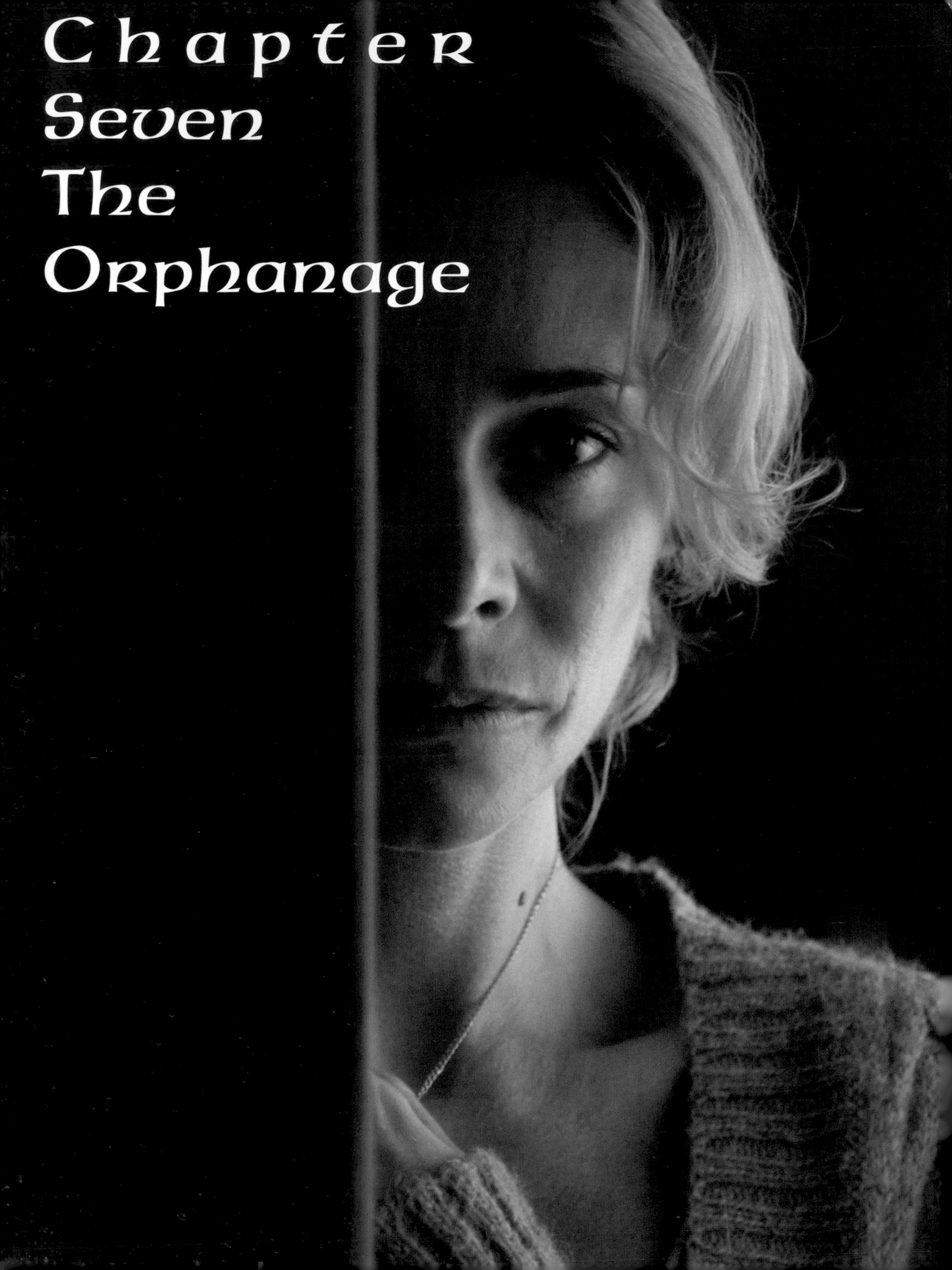

THE ORPHANAGE/ EL ORFANATO

"...to die will be an awfully big adventure."
Peter Pan

The story begins in 1970s Spain, at the Good Shepard Orphanage. A young girl named Laura (Mireia Renau) is playing happily with her friends, a game of chase that begins- "One, two, three, knock on the wall." The only incongruous object in this otherwise perfect scene is a sinister scarecrow, it face formed from an old sack. One of the staff at the orphanage takes a phone call. They've found a home for Laura, who is told: "Your friends will miss you a lot."

The present day. A seven year old boy, Simón (Roger Princep), calls for his mother, Laura (Belén Rueda) in the middle of the night. As we shall discover, this is the Laura from the start of the film, now a grown woman in her thirties. She comes quickly the frightened child, who tells her. "They're coming. Listen." It's clear she adores her son, who asks her. "Weren't you scared here, when you were little?" Laura and her husband, Carlos (Fernando Cayo), have bought the same orphanage she spent her formative years in, intending to turn it into a home for special children. Laura assures Simón. "You couldn't be afraid. There was a gang of us and there was the lighthouse." On the shoreline close to the house, is a majestic looking lighthouse. Laura explains that the lighthouse protects them with an invisible light.

Simón has imaginary friends, Carlos believes he will grow out of them when real children arrive to stay with them.

Laura and Simón go to the nearby beach, in the caves, Simón tells her he's found another friend, a boy. He asks if he can come home to play and lays a trail of seashells for his new friend to follow.

An old woman named Benigna Escobedo (Montserrat Carulla) turns up at the house, introducing herself as a social worker, she's wearing a rather old fashioned photo-locket. Laura tells her the house used to be an orphanage, where she grew up. She wanted to return, so she thought of running a home for special children, which is why she assumed Benigna is here. But she's actually here for Simón. She produces an old file and says "There are new treatments. An experimental program." With a mother's instinct, Laura knows there's something not right about this woman. She tells her. "My husband is a doctor. We're aware of all treatments for Simón's disease. Now please leave. Simón doesn't know he's adopted or about his illness, and I'd rather deal with it with my husband."

Once the old woman makes her welcome exit, Laura glances at old file she's left behind. It reveals the unfortunate Simón is HIV Positive (due to his biological parents drug-addiction). She locks the file in a drawer, as though locking it away could change the truth, a forlorn hope. Simón is drawing pictures of his imaginary friends.

That night, Laura wakens Carlos, she's heard a noise in the garden. He replies. "I'll go. It's my turn." He promptly falls back to sleep. Laura goes to investigate, she enters a storage shed, full of clutter from the old orphanage. She sees Benigna, the social worker, in the shed with a shovel. She runs from Laura. She tells Carlos, who decides. "Sleep with Simón tonight. If she shows up again, we'll call the cops."

The following morning, she finds a pile of seashells outside the front door, as though someone actually followed Simón's trail, gathering the shells as they went.

Simón is reading *Peter Pan*, he asks Laura. "Wendy gets old and dies?" "Wendy gets old, but Peter Pan takes her daughter to Neverland." "Why doesn't Wendy go too? If Peter Pan came to get me, would you come too?" "I'm too old to go to Neverland." "How old are you?" " Thirty-seven." "At what age will you die?" "What sort of question is that? Not for a long time. When you're much older. " "I won't get older. I'm not going to grow up." "Like Peter Pan?" "Like my new friends." "There's more than one?" "Six!" "They won't grow older either?" "They can't."

Laura sees a drawing Simón has made of his six friends, including a disturbing-looking one, his face obscured by a scarecrow-like mask of old sackcloth, wearing a whistle around his neck. "What are they holding?" "Treasures to play with." "Your friends play together?" "Sure. They steal your treasure, something you love, and you have to find it." "That's the game? Finding treasure?" "Yes, but following the clues. If you find it they grant you a wish." "And you have a treasure?" "Special coins. An old man left them in the park. I think they're gold and very valuable. Want to see them?"

Simón takes Laura to his room and shows her his treasure box. She's impressed. "Where'd you get all this?" "I found it." She indicates a wrapper. "The first ice cream I had after my tonsils operation." (The things children value!). He shows her the box that he says contain the special coins but, creepily, it's full of tiny teeth. She says. "They're not coins, they are milk teeth." "They're the first clue. They've got my coins." "You want to play treasure hunt." "The game's already started. Remember where you kept my milk teeth. If I find my treasure, I can make a wish."

Laura goes to a drawer in her room and opens the box that should contain the teeth and finds only...sand!" Simón says. "Sand. Where do you find sand?" "You set this up, right? The beach?" "No. It has to be at home."

Laura follows Simón into the garden, in the rain. They dig in a sandy flower bed, where Laura finds a thimble. Simón realises the next place they must look is a sewing box, where he finds a small piece of ornate metal that comes from what was the orphanage's chapel. There they find a Russian stacking doll, a Matreshka (woodcarvers makes these dolls to be hollow and fit inside each other, this one comes in a set of six to represent Simón's six friends). They reveal all the dolls and the smallest one contains a key. Simón recognises it. "That rings a bell...the key...to the kitchen." In the kitchen the key opens the drawer that Laura locked Simón's file in. He opens the drawer, coins fall out of the file. He's delighted. "I can make a wish." But she recognises the coins as Carlos's. "There are Daddy's...Leave that alone. Those are our things, you shouldn't touch them." "I didn't. It was them." "Don't lie to me." "I'm not lying. You're lying. You say you're my mother, and you're not!"

Laura's world begins to fall around her. She thinks he must have heard Benigna talking. "What?" "You're not my mother!" "Who told you that?" "My friend told me." "What friend?" "Tomás. Tomás said I'm just like them. I have no mother and father. And I'm going to die. You're not my mother, you're a liar."

Later, Laura and Carlos try to explain things. Carlos says. "We wanted you to be a bit older to talk about certain things." Laura tells him. "If you want to ask us anything." "Is Father Christmas a lie, too?" Laura is trying for damage limitation. "Simón, you heard Mummy and that lady, saw the envelope and invented the game, because you were afraid to ask about it." Simón looks at his medication, the two tablets in front of him. " What if I don't take them?" Carlos replies. "Nothing would happen." Simón is no fool, he persists. "If I don't take them, how soon would I die?" Carlos admits. "It would take many days, even weeks. Don't worry, we'll take care of you.

The imposing Orphanage of the title

You won't get sick or die."

Laura and Carlos are throwing a party to celebrate the opening of the home. All the kids are wearing masks. The garden is beautifully decorated. Simón is upstairs whispering. "You don't love me. It's a lie."

Laura goes upstairs with big tray of food to collect Simón. "Hurry, the first kids are here." "We can't go yet. I want to show you something." "What is it?" "Tomás' little house." "Not now, darling, you can show me tomorrow." "No"" "Go downstairs right now!" "I don't want to! Come to see Tomás' little house." He knocks the food she's carrying and shocked, she slaps him in response. "If you don't want to go downstairs, don't. No one is forcing you."

Outside the kids are enjoying the party, except for one child wearing a mask made of sackcloth that seems apart from the rest. Laura returns upstairs for Simón. He isn't in his room and she searches the corridors. She hears a whistle and it's the masked child from the party is at the end of the corridor. She tries to take off the mask, its Simón wearing it, and he pushes her into the bathroom savagely, hurting her and locking her in.

Carlos forces open the door, frantically checking all the masked kids, he could be anywhere. They check the store cupboard beneath the stairs, where a load of iron scaffolding stored from the house renovations falls against its back wall.

Frantic in way any mother would be at her son being missing, Laura tears off the masks from the kids at the party. People are staring. The caves! She fears he's gone to the caves, and runs to the beech. The tide is coming in and she injures her leg as Carlos catches up with her. She sees a shadowy figure in the now water-logged cave, but no one else can. "He's over there, Carlos." "There's no one, Laura, come on. We can't stay here."

That night divers search the water, the police search the caves, but they find no trace of Simón. Laura has been taken to hospital to have her injuries attended to. Carlos tells her that Simón wasn't in the caves. Laura insists she saw someone there. A woman says. "You must have imagined it in all the confusion. Believe me, he wasn't there. I'm Pilar. I know it's hard, but you must know we're doing all we can to locate your son." Carlos explains who this woman is. "Pilar is a psychologist. She works with the police. They're working hard to find Simón." Pilar (Mabel Rivera) has some questions. "Your husband told me about the adoption and your son's illness. As he was adopted, there are possibilities we must consider." Laura doesn't understand. "What possibilities?" "That he was kidnapped by a relative. I heard you recently found a woman intruder on the grounds." "Benigna Escobedo, a social worker, came a few days ago." "We can find no social worker with that name, can you describe her?" "She was about seventy, with white hair, pale eyes, very thick glasses." "We will find her. You can be sure of that."

Later, the police search the grounds of the orphanage. Temporarily wheelchair-bound, while her leg injury heals, Laura is distraught, she wonders if anyone would ever trust them with their kids after this. Carlos gives her his grandmother's Saint Anthony medal to wear, "to bring us good luck." "You don't believe that." "Exactly. But you do. Take it now. Give it back when we find Simón."

That night, Laura dreams she is swimming underwater. She hears the whistle and wakes up. She hears noises overhead, lights flicker. Even Carlos hears it and they enter the room the noises have been coming from. It looks like a child might be sleeping in a bed, but when they pull back the covers, there's only a doll there.

Months later, Carlos and Laura attend a group therapy session. The group therapist (Enric Arquimbau) himself explains to all those present. "Simón Sanchez's parents feel more and more forsaken. The seven-year-old boy disappeared from his home six months ago. The situation is even more desperate because Simón is ill and needs daily medication." Laura says. "My son disappeared six months ago. His name is Simón. There are posters everywhere. You may have seen them. We've tried everything, but not one clue, not even a trace. My son had imaginary friends. We never paid much attention, but...I have a feeling they're in the house." A woman

(Bianca Martinez) shares her feelings. "I saw my daughter a year after her death. It was at night, we were asleep. I woke up, and without knowing why, I went to her room. And there she was. Smiling. Calm. It was her way of telling me, 'I'm fine, I'm safe, don't suffer for me.'."

The Group Therapist sees this as a normal way of coming to terms with the grief of a child's death. "It is not unusual to feel, in some way, the presence of a loved one after their death. All of us in this group could tell you similar stories." The majority of those present raise their hands in agreement.

Laura is not one of them. "You don't understand. My son is not dead. His friends took him, I saw one of them. He was at home. I'll do whatever it takes to recover my son. I'm not crazy. Believe me. I know what I'm talking about."

Later, Laura and Carlos are driving through a mountainous area, perhaps hoping to get some respite from their worry and torment, but even here, there are reminders, posters with Simón's face. As they drive through a nearby town, Laura forlornly looks at Simón's medicine, the tissue in her hand shows she's being crying. Suddenly Carlos has to hit the breaks as an old lady pushes a pram in from of them. It's Benigna! Laura gets out and calls to her. Benigna turns and is cut down by a speeding ambulance. Laura hobbles over to the pram, now caught under the ambulance wheels, terrified that it might have been Simón in the pram. To her relief, it's not Simón, it's a doll. To her horror, the doll is wearing a sinister sackcloth mask.

She makes her way forward to where Carlos is trying to give the kiss of life to Benigna. Wiping the blood from his face, he shakes his head, it's hopeless, her injuries are too severe, even her jaw has been torn off. Laura notices a whistle around Benigna's neck, as she reaches for it, the dying woman grabs her hand, then finally dies.

Later, Laura and Carlos have a meeting with Pilar, who tells them. "We went to Benigna's house. We found some pictures and old Super 8 film. I'd like you to see them." She shows Laura a black and white photo. "Are any of these faces familiar?" They certainly are. "Antonia, the principle, and the orphans. My friends. Martin. She liked to be called Martin." Laura indicates with her finger. "Rita. Victor. I think his name was Guillermo. That's Alicia, she was blind. And this is me." She points to an unhappy-looking woman standing behind the children. "Benigna?" "The woman you saw worked at the orphanage." Pilar plays one of the Super 8 films. "That's impossible. I'd remember." "She wasn't there very long. She had a son. Tomás." The masked child appears on the screen. "The child was deformed. He was kept away from the others. No one knew."

On the film, the unfortunate Tomás is waving to his mother, but he's dragged back in. We cannot imagine the horror and loneliness that constituted his 'life'. Pilar continues. "It was a shock when they found the body." "What do you mean?" "It seems he disappeared while playing." Pilar opens a paper dated 20 May 1976. The headline reads: 'Child's body found on a beach near Good Shepherd orphanage.' "Shortly after your adoption. One of the orphans confessed that they had played a trick on him. They went into the caves with Tomás and took his mask off to see if he'd come out. But he never emerged. They found the body at low tide. The children weren't blamed. They were only playing." Pilar shows Laura a photo of Tomás, which Laura recognises. "That boy was at my house." But Pilar does not believe her. "We asked everyone at the opening party. No one remembers a child with a sack mask."

At home, Laura watches another of Benigna's Super 8 films. She sees Tomás writing his name. The luckless child, his face terribly disfigured, turns and looks straight at the camera. In another room, Carlos is coming to terms with his own grief, a metronome ticking in time with his tears, while he plays a few forlorn notes on the piano.

That night, Laura is restless and unsettled. She talks to Carlo's sleeping form under the blankets beside her. "I can't sleep through the night. I can't stop thinking. Remember what we called Simón when we first met him? 'Two Little Kilos'. 'My two little extra kilos'. That's all he weighed. The doctors said it wasn't enough. But it was plenty for

us. Although we knew there was little chance he could ever be normal. But when we first saw him, saw his smile for the first time, his eyes, his bright eyes...Simón made us strong, Carlos. Together, we're strong. Together. Forgive me if I get upset, but it's hard..." She stops. She's has seen a shadow move in the light beneath their bathroom door. "Carlos, someone's in the bathroom" The light goes off. The handle turns and Carlos comes out of the bathroom. So who has been in the bed with Laura? She turns to see but the bed is empty. She tells Carlos but he doesn't believe her. A gulf is growing between them.

Laura attends a lecture by a man called Leo Balaban (Edgar Vivar), who tells an auditorium. "That's what Jung means when he says it's in the subconscious that the living coexist with the dead. The Germans have another name for 'the herald of death'. Dopelganger." Behind Balaban are slides showing medieval images of death. "A being that appears in one's own image. Death facing Death. A double. To glance at him, or any of the others I've shown you, means, without the slightest doubt, a passport to the other world."

After Leo's lecture, Laura speaks to him in private. He asks her. "How long has your son being missing?" "Nine months. Strange things are happening. Things linked to his disappearance. I don't know who to turn to. It's not that simple." "You won't find an exorcist in the yellow pages." She gives him a piece of sackcloth. "This is from my son's kidnapper. The police say he's been dead for over thirty years." Leo puts on his glasses to scrutinise the scrap of cloth. "There's someone in this field, someone I trust. I'm talking from the heart. Would you allow a medium to visit your home?"

At the house, the medium, Aurora (Geraldine Chaplin), examines a room and says. "This wasn't a children's room in the orphanage." Laura indicates another part of the house. "The bedroom was back there."

Aurora decides that's where they should start. Carlos is sceptical but Enrique, Aurora's assistant goes to set up closed circuit television cameras and other recording equipment. Aurora asks for "...and old object from this house. Something related to its history. And if possible, some clothing from the past." They are joined by Pilar, this has been arranged by Carlos, who clearly doesn't believe any of it. He also didn't tell he had invited Pilar, the gulf between them grows ever wider, a chasm their love may not be strong enough to bridge.

After Enrique has set his equipment up, Laura, Carlos, and can see Aurora, holding an old doll, in a room upstairs. Leo is upstairs too Pilar asks. "What does she need that doll for?" Enrique explains. "To facilitate her trance. Clothing and objects help her get into it and begin the regression." "Regression?" "A psychic summoning." "Past, present and future are superimposed and cross. Like a sort of time travel. It may sound like witchcraft but you mustn't fear parallel perception. If there's anything, Aurora will see it." Carlos is cynical. "I hope we'll all see it."

Over a radio link, Aurora says everything is ready. Leo leaves her and joins

Laura faces every mother's worst nightmare

Overleaf: everyday is Halloween in The Orphanage

the others watching below. Enrique activates the recording equipment. Leo speaks to Aurora over the radio link. "Everything around you is beginning to fade. Darkness is forming a circle around you. It's closing in on you. Everything is fading. We're no longer here. Now you're alone in the darkness, and the darkness begins to disappear. I'm going to countdown, from ten, and once I've finished, you can go wherever you want and will be able to see anyone who is hiding in this house. Ten, nine, eight, seven, six, five, four, three, two, one. You can open your eyes."

Aurora can hear a noise, she walks around trying to find the source. Downstairs, the microphone picks up faint voices saying "...all alone." Laura says. "Children, I'm sure its children." Aurora walks towards the door at the end of the hall. "I can't open it. It's closed. But there's someone. Why aren't you crying? 'We're sick.' Who's sick? I won't hurt you. Open the door. Don't be afraid." The door opens, and things really go mad, there are screams being picked up by the microphone. Aurora asks "What have they done to you?" Leo asks her what she sees. She walks over to the empty beds "Five children. They're very sick. They're crying. What happened? They're dying. Who would want to poison you?" Laura and Leo ask if Simón is there. Then, one by one the monitors go down. Leo says. "Aurora, can you hear me? Let's get her. Aurora, stay in the middle of the room. I'll count from ten. Ten, nine, eight, seven, six..." A monitor comes back on. "Five. Four." Another flickers back to life. "Three." Another monitor reactivates. "Two." Another. "One." And on the last monitor, we see Aurora sitting in her chair.

Afterwards, Aurora explains. "I was in the house but everything was different. The beds, the toys, the décor, everything was much older. The light from the lighthouse came through the windows." Laura asks. "You didn't see Simón?" "It was too dark. I'm sorry. I couldn't recognise anyone." "But the children were there. You saw the children. Is that right?" "That's right." Carlos doesn't want to hear this. "You're talking about ghosts." Leo, however, believes. "And what is a ghost, Carlos? There's something here, and we all saw it." Aurora explains. "When something terrible happens, sometimes it leaves a trace, a wound that acts as a knot between two timelines. It's like an echo, repeated over and over, waiting to be heard. Like a scar...or a pinch that begs for a caress to relieve it. (We see Aurora's hand is wasted terribly from some disease). Laura, we who are close to death...we are more receptive to these messages." "You mean my son could see those children because..." Carlos isn't listening to anymore. "That's enough. Please take your things and leave." But they're Laura's only hope. "We can't let them leave like this." Pilar agrees with Carlos. "Laura, this is a farce, a sideshow trick." "I can't believe this. Why? For what reason? They're right...They don't want money." "Not yet." Laura is at her wits end. "What should I do. The police haven't found a single clue as to whether he's dead or alive. What do I do? Just sit and wait? Can it hurt to listen?" Carlos tries to stop her, but she's in full flight. "Pilar, how many similar cases have you had in this damned village? Get another distraction. I didn't invite you here."

As Aurora prepares to leave, Laura asks her what she should do. Aurora tells her, "My dear, you are a good mother. Your pain gives you strength, it will guide you. But only you know how far you are willing to go to find your son." "I don't know what to do." "You hear, but don't listen. Seeing is not believing. It's the other way around. Believe, and you will see."

Carlos begins to take down the press-cutting and map-sighting of Simón. ""We can't stay here any longer. We should go, at least for a while." "The children are here. Aurora saw them. I can't leave. You heard the voices." "That Enrique could have faked it all. Can't you see it could be a set-up?" "That's Pilar's theory, a set-up? Her rational theory?" "She's protecting us." "From what?" "Things like this evening..." "They just want to help." "Help. Didn't you hear them? Did they mention finding Simón? They just want to contact the dead. I can't see how they can help us. If he's not, they won't recover him. I can't and won't take this anymore. Please, let's leave this house." "You can't ask me to give up. Neither you nor Pilar." Only a man could tell a mother: "We can survive this. Many couples lose a child and pull through." "I want to be with Simón, don't you understand? If you want to go, I can't stop you. I just want to know where he is."

The following day Laura enters the children's dormitory. "Where are you? I'm not afraid."

As though in reply, the open window slams shut so hard, it shatters its pane of glass. The glass falls on a cushioned seat. Laura pulls aside the cushion, revealing wooden boards, each carved with a child's name, beneath them, corresponding with the names on the boards, are dolls. She takes a doll from a cupboard and places it with the others. Beneath the doll of a little boy, she finds a picture of herself and Simón. "You want to play? Are you playing with me?" She gets out a photo album and takes a dried rose from it. Looking in the rose bushes, she finds a piece of patchwork cloth. This clue leads her to a patchwork quilt inside the house. Inside the quilt, she finds a wrapper from an El Dorado, one of Simón's treasures. This clue leads her to Simón's treasure box, where she finds a brass door handle. She searches the house trying to find the door it fits, but she has no luck. She goes to the shed in the garden that's been used for storage.

Inside the shed, she sees the photo locket Benigna was wearing stick out from beneath a pile of sacks. She must have lost it the night Laura surprised her in the shed. She frantically pulls the sacks aside, revealing a padlocked door. Breaking the lock, she finds the chamber within is full of sacks. One bursts open as she drags it out, it's full of ash...and a child's jaw bone. Laura is horrified. "Please, don't let it be Simón." She opens another sack and a skull topples out. These are the children Benigna poisoned in revenge for her son's death. Laura calls in the police.

That night, Laura watches one of Benigna's Super 8 films. Carlos brings her a drink. Luara says. "There are five...All my friends, Martin, Rita, Alicia, Guillermo, Victor. Benigna killed them. That's why she went to the shed, to recover their bodies. I've thought it out. Their game killed Tomás and now they're playing with Simón and me. Simón's in danger, and I don't know how to play." Carlos is unconvinced, despite all he's witnessed. "Laura, you're making it up." "I saw it myself. And this afternoon? Who laid out the clues?" "Simón made it all up." "Who? Tell me! Who?" "I've packed. I don't want us to stay here." "I can't leave yet." "I won't live here, and you're not staying alone." "I can't leave, there are too many memories. I have to say goodbye. Two days. Please, I need this."

Carlos agrees and leaves while Laura stays. Once Carlos leaves, Laura frantically sets to work, washing linen, preparing the children's beds. She even manufactures a scarecrow to resemble the one that stood in the garden when she was a child. She then dressed in the uniform of an attendant. Taking a hand full of pills, she rings the bell that was used to summon the children to dinner when she was in the orphanage. He has set a beautiful feast, and has sat a doll to represent each child at the table. She says grace. "Please bless what you have given us. Thank you for letting us gather once again and be together."

But there is no response, she's understandably frustrated. "What else do you want? What more must I do? What? I have no time, I have no time. You want to keep playing? Is that it? Let's make a deal. I'll play a while, then you tell me where Simón is, okay?"

Later that evening, she starts to rap on the wall, repeating her own childhood game of chase. "One, two, three, knock on the wall." No response. Fighting back her tears, she repeats the chant again. Still no response. Just as she's about to repeat the chant, she hears a sound. The door of the room has opened. She repeats the chant. The children are there. They tip her on the shoulder, she is on to chase them, and they run away. "Wait, I won't hurt you. I just want to find Simón."

A child disappears into the cupboard beneath the stairs. The door shuts behind her. She reopens the door, which shuts again, this time locking her in. She turns on the light to reveal she's trapped. She begins to move the scaffolding from the far end of the room, revealing a door, that had previously being blocked by the scaffold it's the one that fits the handle she found. She opens the door and she's a set of stairs. She descends downwards entering a huge cellar. Switching on its flickering light, she sees it was used a child's den at one point, the walls are covered with children's pictures. As Laura examines one of Benigna and Tomás, a noise captures her attention. It's Simón, huddled in a blanket, who asks her why she is crying. Laura is overjoyed and embraces her son. "Oh, my darling. Are you okay? You're freezing. Don't worry about a thing. Don't be afraid, I'll get you out."

There are more noises, the sound of children. Simon asks Laura to stay and play with them, but his terrified mother's priority is to get him out. She picks him up. "Listen to me, Simón. Imagine it's just you and me here...Think about before we came to this house...Think about Daddy, think about next Christmas, and all the things we'll do together...Close your eyes tight, shut them really tight and think about what you'll be when you grow up. What would you like to be, darling? Think about the schools you'll go to, the friends you'll make. And just believe for a moment that Tomás and the other children aren't real. This is a fantasy, my darling, like a nightmare. Do it for me, Simón. When you open your eyes, make them go away."

When she opens her eyes the noises have stopped, but the blanket is empty. In a far corner of the room, Laura sees a child's body. With the mask removed, that head of hair is unmistakable. It's Simón. Her mind flashes back the day of the opening party, when Simón wanted her to come with him to see 'Tomás's little house'. She realises that Simón had been going down there to play. On the day of the party, when he'd ran away from her, he'd gone down there to hide, and became trapped when the scaffolds fell against the door as they searched for him (The horrible irony, that in trying to help him, they accidentally helped him to die instead), there, he starved to death. It had been Simón wearing the sackcloth mask on the party. It's a heart-breaking scene. Every mother's nightmare. Her screams of despair echo through the house. She carried his body upstairs to the children's dormitory. "I found you. This isn't fair." She takes the remaining pills in the jar.

The house creaks like a living thing. Laura says. "I want Simón back." The lighthouse outside suddenly starts working again, its light illuminating her. Outside the window, she sees her younger self in the garden. Simón is alive again. He asks. "Mummy, can I wake up?" "Of course you can, darling." "Mummy, I found the special coins. Now I just have to make a wish. I wish you'll stay and look after us." All the kids are there, they are overjoyed to see her, including Tomás. The blind girl Alicia (Carmen Lopez) touches Laura's face, and they realise it's their childhood friend. "It's Laura. She's grown old. Like Wendy in the story." Simón knows it's just like in *Peter Pan*. "The house, the beach, the lost children." Laura begins to tell the story. Not only to her son Simón, but to all the lost children. No longer lost, they are her family.

Laura has finally come home.

Later, we see a plaque that reads. "In memory of Laura and Simón and of the orphans. Martin, Rita, Guillermo, Alicia, Victor and Tomás. Carlos leaves red roses on it. He finds Laura's locket, he knows what it means, she doesn't need it now, and she wants him to know all is well. The doors open, and Carlos smiles.

He knows he is not alone.

The Stone Tape

One of the major influences on both *The Orphanage* and *The Devil's Backbone* was Nigel Kneale's famous teleplay, *The Stone Tape*.

Manx born Kneale became well known in the nineteen fifties for his work with the BBC, especially for his three massively popular *Quatermass* serials and an acclaimed adaptation of George Orwell's seminal Nineteen Eighty-Four, starring Peter Cushing in a career best role as Winston Smith. Going freelance, Kneale went on to produce scripts for Hammer films including *The Abominable Snowman* (again starring Cushing), and a fine adaptation of his BBC *Quatermass* serial *Quatermass And The Pit*, for Hammer films, starring Andrew Keir as Professor Quateramass.

In 1972, Christopher Morahan, Head of Drama at BBC2 (he had directed Kneale's 1963 script *The Road*, and a remake of Kneale's adaptation of *Nineteen Eighty-Four*), asked Kneale if he would be interested in writing a play to be broadcast the coming Christmas. Kneale was indeed interested, deciding that a ghost story would be most appropriate for Christmas, but a ghost story with a difference, he would drag the ghost story howling and moaning into the modern age! Phantasms encountering the cutting edge of modern science. Kneale's passion for blending technology and the occult had long been a signature theme of his work, as early as his 1952 radio play-*You Must Listen*, which told the tale of a telecommunications engineer who discovers that a telephone line has somehow preserved the last conversation between a woman and her lover, before she takes her own life.

The most famous example of the collision of the science and supernatural in Kneale's impressive body of work is *Quatermass And The Pit* (first broadcast as a highly atmospheric BBC serial starring Andre Morel as the titular character). In *Quatermass And The Pit*, a strange object found in a London building site (a tube extension in the latter Hammer version), turns out to be a kind of supernatural birth machine, left behind by colonists from a dying Mars five millions years before (Hence, the American title of the Hammer version, *Five Million Miles To Earth*). Unable to survive our atmosphere, they genetically manipulate the primitive ancestors of man, a kind of 'colonisation by proxy' as one character calls it. Thus, many of present-day mankind have dormant Martian characteristics, when the object is unearthed it activates, spreading it's influence amongst us, causing the descendents of those subjects of Martian manipulation to behave like aggressive insects, mercilessly destroying all those that are different to themselves. (*Quatermass And The Pit* was a huge influence on Kneale fan John Carpenter's *Ghosts Of Mars*).

It's a fantastic ambitious story, and a fine study of our inhumanity to each other. In the story, much of our mythology is a race memory of the Martians (the location Hob's Lane, is a reflection on the sighting of demonic creatures that have taken place whenever the ground has been disturbed). *Quatermass And The Pit* shares many elements in common with *The Stone Tape*, such as the abandoned house reputed to be haunted, the collection of past documentary evidence of haunting, and the sensitivity of some of the characters to the unexplained phenomena.

Kneale was also influenced for the 'Taskerlands' location of *The Stone Tape* by a trip he made to the BBC's research and development facility which is based at an ancient country house at the Kingswood Warren in Kings wood, Surrey. The researchers employed at Kingswood Warren would also influence the portrayal of the members of the research team in *The Stone Tape*.

Kneale delivered his script, at that time titled Breakthrough, in September 1972. Selected as director was Peter Sasdy, who had done *The Caves Of Steel* and *Wuthering Heights* for the BBC and *Taste The Blood Of Dracula* for Hammer Films.

Production of *The Stone Tape* began on 15 November 1972 with the exterior

shots of the 'Taskerlands' house taking place at Horsley Towers, East Horsley in Surrey. This was once the home of Ada Lovelace, the daughter of Lord Byron and sponsor of computer pioneer Charles Babbage (of 'Difference Engine' fame). Production then moved to the BBC Television Centre.

THE STONE TAPE-PLOT

Peter Brock (Michael Bryant) heads a research team for an electronics company called Ryan Electrics. His team are working on developing a new recording medium that it hopes will give the company an advantage over its Japanese competitors. The research team plan to move into a new facility at Taskerlands, a Victorian mansion that has been renovated to serve as their research facility.

Once they arrive, they discover from foreman Ray Collinson (Iain Cuthbertson) that one of rooms in Taskerlands remained unrefurbished. The builders will not work in that room because they believe it is haunted. The researchers investigate the room. They hear the sounds of a running woman, followed by her scream. One of the research team, Jill Greeley (Jane Asher), is unusually sensitive to psychic phenomena (Like Barbara Shelley's character in the Hammer film version of *Quatermass And The Pit*), and she sees an image of a woman running up the steps in the room and then falling, presumably to her death. Inquiries with the local villagers reveal that a young maid died in that very room in the Victorian era.

Brock believes that the stone in room has somehow recorded an image of the unfortunate girl's demise. He believes that this 'stone-tape' may be the key to the new recording medium that his team are attempting to develop. Brock moves his team into the room with their equipment, in the hope of being able to unlock the secret of the 'stone-tape'.

Alas, having become desperate under increasing pressure to come up with results, they only succeed in erasing the image from the 'stone-tape'. Brock's failure is compounded when he is informed by his paymasters that they have lost faith in his skills to oversee the project and thus, the Taskerlands facility is to be transferred to a rival research team working on a new washing machine.

While clearing up, Jill discovers that the recording was concealing a much older recording, left thousands of years ago. Returning to the room she is confronted by a powerful evil presence, and, like the maid in the erased recording, she too falls to her death trying to escape. Following the inquest, Brock destroys all of Jill's records, and makes a last visit to the room, where he discovers the 'stone-tape' has made a new recording, this time of Jill screaming his name as she dies.

The Stone Tape made it's television debut as a rather dark Christmas present on Christmas Day 1972, where it played to an audience of 2.6 million, and was well-received by viewers and critics alike.

So great is *The Stone Tape*'s influence, that following it's broadcast, the hypothesis of residual haunting, that ghosts may be recordings of past events made by the physical environment, has come to be known as the 'Stone Tape Theory' by parapsychological researchers.

The Stone Tape was also a great influence on John Carpenter's fine 1987 film *Prince of Darkness*, in which a group of scientists investigate an ancient evil concealed in a church crypt, that seeks to extend it's influence into the wider world. Carpenter wrote the screenplay under the pseudonym Martin Quatermass (producing a mock-biography for his pseudonym that suggested that Martin was actually the brother of the more famous Professor Quatermass!).

The Orphanage - Analysis

"The time is out of joint-O cursed spite.
That ever I was born to set it right."
William Shakespeare, Hamlet, Act 1, Scene 5

The Orphanage incorporates some strong concepts into its story, adding strength to its emotional core. In some respects it concerns a time loop. Balaban leaves a clue when he explains that seeing your doppelganger means your imminent death, and just before Laura dies, she sees her young self in the garden. There is also the notion that an evil act leaves a mark on a place,

As in *The Stone Tape*, a strong influence on Guillermo's own *The Devil's Backbone*. In common with *The Devil's Backbone*, the characters are given great depth. There is none of the one-dimensional simplistic quality that exists in a typical Hollywood movie. Benigna, for instance, while she has committed unspeakably evil acts, the combination of the suffering of bringing up her unfortunate deformed child, coupled with his tragic death, drives her into the realms of madness. And again in common with *The Devil's Backbone*, there is the burning question: "What is a ghost?"

But the beating heart of the film is a mother's love for her son. Belen performance is breath-taking, at the end of the film I realised I had actually thought of her throughout as Simón's mother (I also liked the fact that her character was not Simón's biological mother, as in real life, what does biology have to do with love?). In fact her success at following the ghost's game is proof of this, as Simón tells her at the beginning of the film, they take something you love, and they took what she loves most in this or any other world.

Once the films ends, your stomach and mind are churning. It takes time to fully digest and lingers in your mind afterwards, surely the sign of a great work of cinema, feeling both elated and sad at the end of a film is a sadly increasingly rare experience these days.

The Orphanage's theme of duality is also reflected in the film not only being a very human, emotional tale, but a fine horror film, one that actually succeeds in making the audience jump, that puts the proverbial hair on end. That it does so, with a very modern take on old school horror, without gore, is very much to the credit of the film's creators.

The suspense is embedded in the story itself, the script is very developed, one of the elements that attracted Guillermo. "There is sort of a lack of rigour in the European film genre. So I was pleased that it moved me... The nicest thing in a film script...when a script moves you this much, that's just the best. What I liked when I first saw it was that there was within, this will to create, an almost magical potential to change reality...*Pan's Labyrinth* and *The Orphanage* both share that idea. Because, for me, will-power is magic. I don't mean tangible magic which opens real doors, but it does allow you to see reality differently. And I like the idea of this woman, who, when faced with the horror of that day, changes her reality."

"In that way, it's like *Pan's Labyrinth*, maybe because of the fairy tale references or children's literature like *Peter Pan*. I think there was a tone which you could feel in the script, and which is in the film. I think it's in the atmosphere, in the sounds and from presences which aren't necessarily obvious, and I'm very attracted to that. Not just in Pan's Labyrinth but in the films I like doing. It's the only time I've read a script and said: 'I'd like to make this film.'" He joked. "If Bayona gets injured somehow...and believe me, I tried to make that happen, I'd love to make this." Bayona shares Guillermo's love of the script. "The writing in the script is so powerful. That's not always easy to find in a script. From just one sentence or dialogue you get the character's whole psychology. That's what Sergio's script is like, it has a nice theme: deep down, we all act like children when faced with adversity. And children need fantasy to understand the world. Fairytales are attempts to help children to understand reality."

The Orphanage shares the theme of the search for truth with Guillermo's own canon of films, he says. "For me, the landscape of cinema is subjective...And when the viewer doesn't relate to that subjectivity, he rejects

Fear is the key in The Orphanage

it, saying:' This is false'. But that's wrong. Nobokov once said; Drama isn't about the contact between characters but the contact between narrator and listener. What a film is, is not reality, but truth. The truth in the story. I'm not interested in reality. I'm interested in truth. So if the sky for this house is right and if the noises are right, that's truth. This was something we came up against early on. In the sense that when I arrived, there were already ideas for producing the film...And I think those ideas were going to be too small for the film Bayona need to make. Bayona is like all little guys, they need to be more and more bigger. What fits in his little head is a giant world, like fat guys, we need to devour the whole universe. And this insatiability that short guys and fat guys have, was reflected in the production when we changed the skies, put in a lighthouse, built the set...We said that we needed fantasy to understand reality, and cinema is the only art form that allows you to get so immersed in how you see the world in order to share it with others."

Bayona shares Guillermo's feelings. "I said it has to told this way. It's about psychological truths...something people understand." When you reflect on the fact that in the world we live in today, full of spin-doctors, corruption and worse, truth is an under-valued and yet essential quality, and in *The Orphanage*, the viewer is instinctively responding to that truth, truth is not always what we hear, one could say anything, that does not mean it is true, it is action and belief that make truth. It's like someone saying, "I love you", but with out being backed up by actions, and crucially, without the belief of the person saying the words, it is a falsehood.

One of the things that lifts *The Orphanage* above the level of so many horror films is its script. It has a very well written script, with very powerful characters. Its ending in particular is incredibly haunting, and stay with the viewer long after the films has ended. Guillermo was particularly impressed with the script. "The script was very intelligent and complex from the beginning. It's the best Spanish film script I've ever read in this genre."

Avoiding excess, there is instead the clever use of suggestion, in the vein of classics like *The Others*, or *The Sixth Sense*. The use of sound, of the house being almost a living entity itself, is reminiscent of *The Haunting*. With so many American horror films awash with gore or special effects, (at this stage, the weary audience of such films knows it is being patronised, such tricks are the horror equivalent of 'canned laughter', except instead of 'laugh now', it's 'scream now'), this is a refreshing contrast.

Nine months after Simón has vanished, Laura finds him. That nine months have passed is no coincidence. For nine months she has undergone the emotional roller-coaster and pregnant woman does. It is Laura, not the disbelieving Carlos, that brings Simón back into her world, a different plane of existence, but still a rebirth nonetheless.

The Spanish-speaking parts of the world have a much healthier attitude to

death than those in English-speaking world. Wheras in the English-speaking world, death has become an ever-more taboo subject (something that was not always so), leaving us less able to cope with the inevitable deaths we must encounter in the course of our lives, the Spanish-speaking world wake their dead, and do not speak of it in hushed tone.

There is also a healthy degree of humour. Bayona's inclusion of a beautiful meal prepared by Laura for ghosts is not unintentional. The Spanish-speaking world has a different sense of humour and a different attitude to death, unlike our youth-obsessed world where we live in terror of the inevitable aging process and death, they have a much more realistic attitude, and surely if we did not age and die, our lives would lose all value, something masterfully explored by Guillermo in his debut *Cronos*.

The sound tells you a lot about the story (something in common with *The Devil's Backbone*). It sparks your imagination, no monster, ghost, or devil, can ever match the human imagination. Think of the pounding on the door in *The Haunting*, no Hollywood monster could ever match the creatures our own subconscious can cook up.

The Orphanage keeps a strong balance between emotion and horror. The central character of Laura regresses back to her childhood. Something we all do to an extent as we get older. When our lives become unpleasant, there is a temptation to retreat back to an earlier, happier (whether real of imagined) time. While we may find it a pleasant means of escape, to daydream thusly, if we could really do this, would it be a good thing? Would it not be a worse nightmare? The past is a distant land indeed.

Director Bayona has his own take on *The Orphanage*. "When asked about *The Orphanage*, I say it's *Peter Pan*'s story but told from the mothers view. Some of the children are kidnapped and taken to a special place, and I thought 'How terrible for their mothers.'" Again, Bayona shows himself a kindred spirit to Guillermo, how many Hollywood directors with their concerns full of 'audience demographics' and 'movie tie-ins', even care about such things.

Bayona sums *The Orphange* up with the kind of concise empathy that will become a byword to his name in years to come. "I wanted people to be deeply scared by a horror film and deeply touched by a drama."

THE GENESIS OF THE ORPHANAGE

The Orphanage is masterfully directed by first-timer Juan Antonio Bayona. Bayona had known Guillermo for 15 years. Guillermo understood the film, and decided to finance it. Bayona pays tribute to Guillermo's vision. "In Spain, no production company got the point, except Guillermo del Toro, who's Mexican." One of the characters in the film is called Guillermo as a tribute.

Bayona is none to impressed with the current crop of horror movies. "In the cinema, most of the stories don't tell you anything. When I was a child I was very afraid of scary movies."

He speaks highly of his friend, Guillermo, who he first met at a film

Off to Never never-land

festival fifteen years ago, Stiges, where he was presenting Cronos, Bayona was then a journalist. Guillermo granted him an interview and, impressed with Bayona's questions, the two kept in touch. Guillermo was always encouraging Bayona to send him his work after he'd been to film school. "So, when he knew about *The Orphanage*, he wanted to be there immediately. He read the script and when he read the script, he decided to present the story which is a special commitment to the project because his name would be together with the title...Guillermo supervised the whole project."

Guillermo described their situation thus. "Producing a movie is like dating but presenting a movie is like marriage." So this was a marriage made in heaven. He is impressed with the finished result. "There are scenes which are true cinematographic moments. Pure cinema...Bayona demonstrates great cinematographic intelligence."

Bayona describes Guillermo's input thus. "Guillermo is a great guy. He's very sensitive. He's also very generous. For me, he's an example to follow, as a filmmaker, even more so as a human being. He's so generous. If you watch him talking about his colleagues, the Mexican filmmakers, he's an example to follow. And if you think about it, the perfect producer will be another director, because he will understand perfectly what you are going through shooting a movie. And he was there just to protect us, he read the script, plus a few suggestions ,like five or six...without Guillermo's great support, we couldn't have done it...We wanted a kind of Hollywood cinema that is not done anymore...Things used to be filmed in a studio and so we did the same. The scenery was immense, it was a director's dream."

If you can't beat them...join them

It says a lot for his character that Guillermo would give so much to another's debut: "He told me all the things needed for the film to be what he wanted. I told him, "As it's your debut, we'll do it the best possible way."

At Cannes, when the film got a standing ovation, Guillermo lifted the director up in the air. That sums up Guillermo's character as a man as well as a film maker. Whether it be the audience or his fellow film makers, Guillermo wants to raise them up on his shoulders, not stand on them to take the rewards.

THE CAST OF THE ORPHANAGE

Another element that lifts *The Orphanage* above the element of so many humdrum and mediocre films, is the huge level of commitment and enthusiasm the cast showed for the film

Fernando Cayo (Carlos) gave a performance of great control and nuance, he explains the significance of his character finding the locket at the end of the film. "That feeling of Calm and happiness, from knowing that his wife had sent him a sign from the other side telling him that everything was okay, and not to worry about her or them. Because the pendant tells us that Laura has found Simón. This is what we were showing in the grieving scene. In the scene where Laura and Carlos are grieving and someone comforts them by saying he had seen his own son's ghost." He continues. "It's all intrigue, machinery set, where all the clues are linked and lead the audience into a labyrinth that

turns into a roller-coaster, which all of us want to experience when we watch a film... What happens in this story is that characters go to the past in order to solve a problem in the present. The past is the orphanage."

But by far the most outstanding performance is that Belen Rueda (Laura), she is the beating heart (and it's a big heart) of *The Orphanage*, its pulse and its driving force. She gave herself totally to the character in a performance that is utterly mesmerising and emotionally engaging, she says. "I was fascinated by the fact that there were no loose ends in the story, like there usually is in this film genre and everything happens for a reason...There is no relief. When you think it's over, it begins again."

Sergio Sanchez, screenwriter believes Belen brought her own dimension to the character. "Laura is childish and mature at the same time, between the child and adult worlds. She clings tooth and nail to childhood. And when the moment comes, it drives her mad." He had a lot of input in the crucial character of Simón. "Simón is completely based on me as a child. In fact he has the same invisible friends that I had, Watson and Pepe. My mum was sick to death of them , because I even moved things around to prove to her they existed."

Bayona speaks highly of Belen. "Belen is childlike in some way. I was 100% sure about her, and she gave a 1000%."

Belen loved the way Bayona had the film lit. "It looked like a magic light and it was specially for this film." Like Guillermo, she sees the magic in the script. "I like how in the script, this character is like a child, and how, after returning to this house, she wants to become a child and has to use this fantasy to be able to understand the horrible trauma that occurs. We need fantasy to understand reality, and cinema, which is fantasy, is more real."

Fernando Cayo sees the dynamic between Laura and Carlos thus. "Laura represents the emotional and Carlos the rational, he's pragmatic. He wants to solve things in a scientific way. Carlos begins to hide things once Pilar appears on the scene."

Pilar is played by Mabel Rivera, who also found The Orphanage's concept fascinating. She asks. "Is reality just what we see or what we touch, or is there something else?"

Geraldine Chaplin (Aurora), discusses her character. "She is a woman who has a gift. She can receive messages from the afterlife." The fact that, like Simón, she is close to death, gives her performance great meaning and pathos.

THE U.S. REMAKE OF THE ORPHANAGE & FUTURE PLANS

Guillermo is going to produce the inevitable American remake, which was offered to Bayona, who understandably (and sensibly), declined. Bayona says. "He's not going to do exactly the same thing. He'll get the right director to boost the story in a different direction."

Bayona also intends to direct an adaption of the novel Hater by David Moody, with Guillermo producing. So for Guillermo and Bayona, *The Orphanage* marks the beginning, as a wise man said in *Casablanca*, of a 'beautiful friendship."

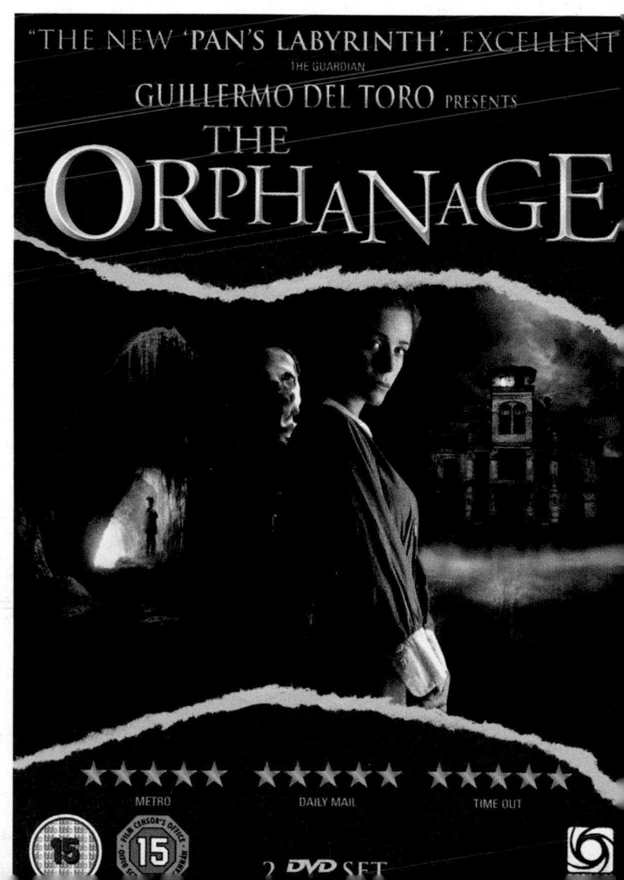

Chapter Eight
Hellboy II: The Golden Army

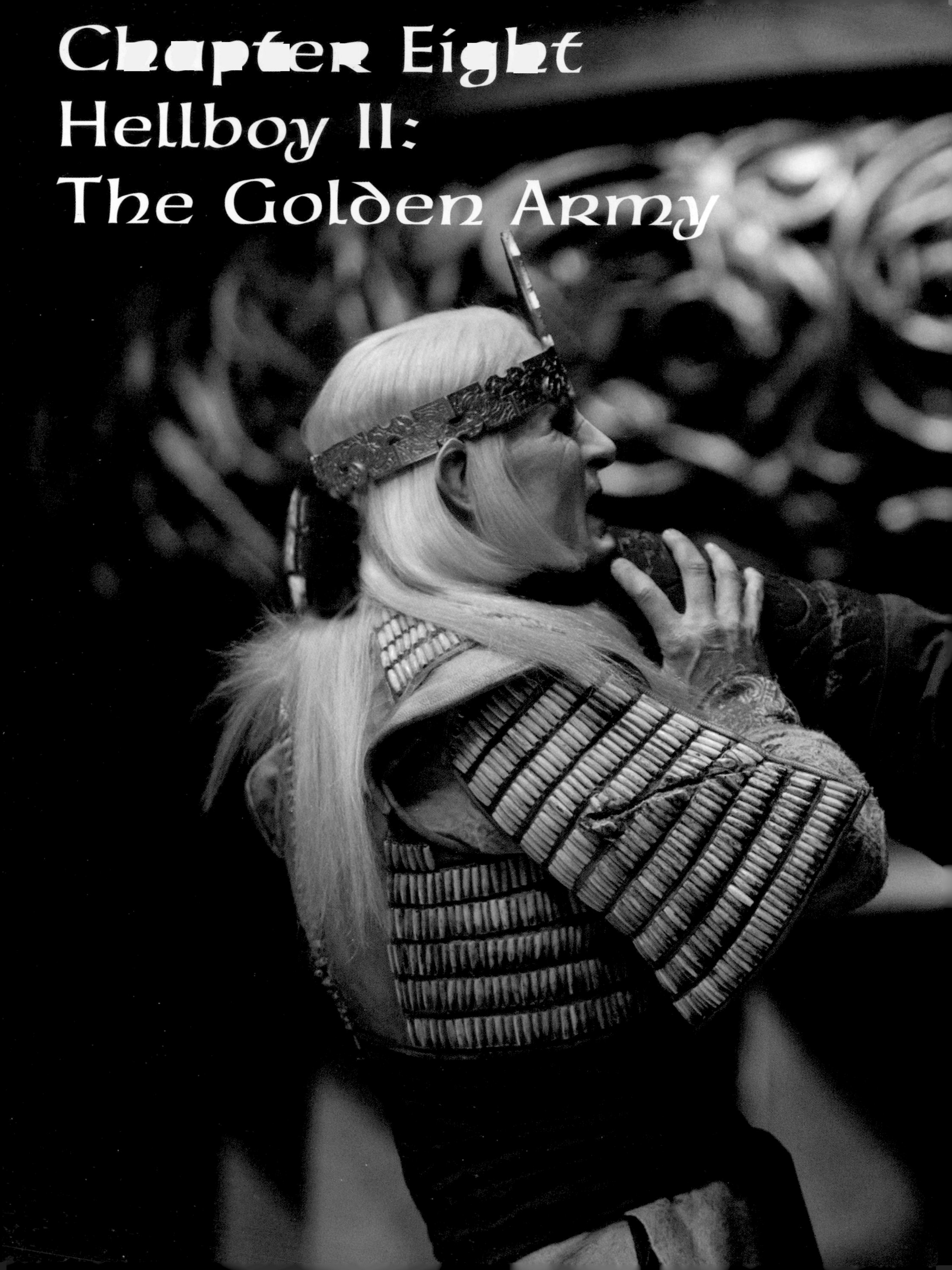

Shannongrove Gorget, found in the 18th century on the banks of the Shannon, close to Limerick City. It was constructed in 700BC, and the skills of the metal workers that created are so high that it many respects they haven't been surpassed today. Only eight similar items exist. It is currently in the possession of the Victoria and Albert Museum in London).

The rich and powerful bid for a variety of artefacts, all of which will be displayed out of context in the cabinets of curiosity of the idle rich. (The statue eventually goes for $375,000. It was worth much more than money to the people that worshipped her.)

Prince Nuada enters the auction room bearing some very fatal bids, as the auctioneer announces the nest item on the table. "A piece of the royal crown of Bethmora, coming to us from a long lost culture." Nuada would beg to differ. "Lost? Not at all. Forgotten by you perhaps, but very much alive."

Nuada puts one of the box he earlier showed Mr Wink, and a clockwork mechanism begins to open them, "I am Prince Nuada, Silverlance. Son of King Balor, and I am here, sir, to claim what is rightly mine."

Mr Wink's detachable metal hand takes care of security and he brings the other box which also begins to open. A man tries to get Nuada to leave, and receives a strange spore like creature that smothers him as a reward. "Be quite!" Nuada spits as he retrieves the crown piece. The bidders disgust him. "SIT DOWN! Proud. Empty. Hollow things that you are. Let this remind you why you once feared the dark." And the boxes release their deadly cargo...

TRENTON, N.J.
22:08 HRS

BUREAU FOR PARANORMAL RESEARCH AND DEFENCE.

Tom Manning (Jeffrey Tambor), Hellboy's chief has gone to visit Abe Sapien (Doug Jones), listening to classical music in his tank. Manning presses a file against the glass. "Fishstick, we have to talk."

Manning shows Abe a dossier of sighting of Hellboy. "Undercover. Can't he get the meaning of the word? Look, we are still government funded. We are still a secret, although a dirty secret if you ask me. Officially we do not exist. So that's the problem, when we get these...subway...highway...." Manning takes a photo from Abe. "And he posed for this one, and gave an autograph...I suppress each photo. Cell phone videos! They cost me a fortune, and then they end on You-Tube. God, I hate You-Tube."

Abe tries to explain, he knows how much Hellboy wants to be accepted by the outside world, after all, he's the good guy, he fights there monsters, surely they'd love him if they only knew. "He just wants the world outside to know what we do. What he does." Manning thinks it's a lot more personal than that. "He loathes me." "I don't think so." "No?" Manning shows Abe a target with his face on it. "Target practice. Then he posts them around. You know how that makes me feel?" He continues his self-pity as they walk past a group

Princess Nuala was pleased with her new makeover... because she's worth it

of agents trying to subdue a monster. "I tell you, Fishstick, he hates me. He's out to destroy me. My street cred is low." "Street cred?" "My mojo. Washington...they're wondering if I've got the stuff. Do you think I have an easy job? Do you think that I enjoy being a pain in the neck. I am medicated. This is not a candy, it's an antacid. Yes, it's an over the counter medicine...I worry because, I am, we are, after all, just humble public servants." Abe attempts to reassure Manning. "It's not about you, he's acting out. Things are a little tense with Liz." "Tense. How tense? Tense, how?" "You know, the usual. New couple making adjustments. They argue?" "How bad?" "Sometimes, like everybody else. They have good days and bad days." This must be one of the bad days! Liz uses her powers to fire Hellboy through the steel door of his apartment, sending the door flying past Manning and Abe.

Hellboy gives Abe a friendly greeting, like nothings happened, and when he sees Mnaning, gives him a very cold one. He warns them. "Watch it boys, she's on fire." Abe comments wryly. "Then again, there are the really bad days."

Hellboy returns to his smoking apartment, telling Liz (Selma Blair), "I'm not afraid of you, you know." Liz is not getting through to him, flames are not far away. "We, you should be. Look at this mess." "I have one rule, don't touch my stuff." I get it, that's your rule...How is that possible. Everything is your stuff. The same L.P." Hellboy has taste. "Al Green." "On 8-track?" Which shows how old Hellboy really is, but he's unrepentant. "One day the world's gonna realise its mistake." Liz melts his CD in fury. Hellboy lets his cats out from under the bed, where they've been sheltering from the domestic storm. "That's alright, kids. You can come out now, it's all over."

Liz is still trying the fruitless task of trying to get through to Hellboy. "What about me, Red? I need some space. At least enough to find my toothbrush." That strikes a chord with Hellboy. "Toothbrush? Wait a minute. It's right there." Sure enough it is, Liz removes her toothbrush from a tin of cat food. "Red, I can't live like this." An alarm goes off, Hellboy is literally saved by the bell, and he's delighted. "Damn, gotta go. We all gotta go. It's an emergency, right?"

Manning stops Hellboy before he leaves. "Red, listen, we're going to downtown Manhattan." "Yeah, it'll be fun." "Very dangerous, for you, and for me. I know you dream of the outside world, but trust me, it's not that great. It's savage as a matter

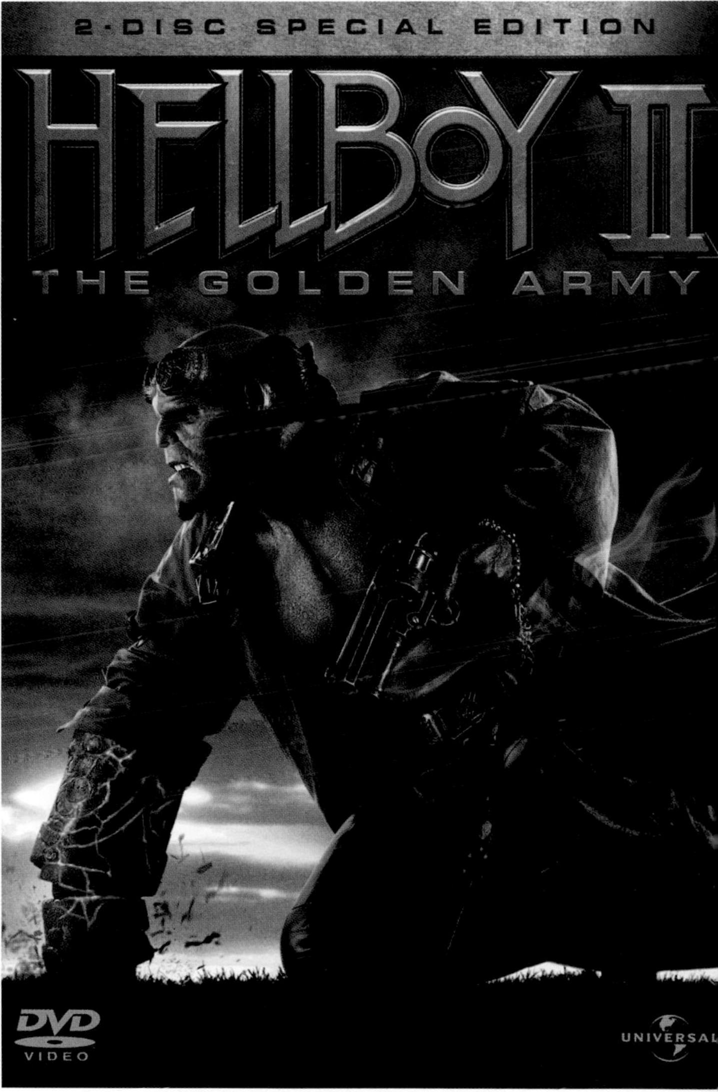

of fact." Manning offers him some expensive cigars as a bribe. "These on the other hand are good. Being seen...bad!"

Hellboy takes the bribe, promising to be invisible (Oh, Manning, trust not the promises of demons!). Liz, being a woman, is far wiser than Manning and doesn't believe Hellboy, who is indignant. "Hey, I can be

discreet. I followed you and Myers, didn't I?" She can't argue with that, but..."Then you had him transferred to Antartica." "Ah, he said he liked the cold." Hellboy again assures Manning that he'll be invisible, like a shadow in the night.

MANHATTAN 23:37 HRS

Manning tells the crowd outside the auction rooms that U.S. Customs discovered a few illegally imported artefacts, "a minor infraction", and for good measure that a 'gas pocket' has been detected, which FBI agents are going to investigate."

Inside the devastated auction rooms, Hellboy comments to Liz. "Stinks in here, worse than my rooms." "Whatever they called us for is over. Over seventy guests reported, we have no survivors, no bodies." Hellboy tells Abe Liz is still mad at him. He tells Liz when they get home, he'll clean up, but she tells that isn't the problem, and this isn't the place or time to tell him what it really is. Abe has found the two boxes that Prince Nuada unleashed the contents of on the bidders at the auction.

"This is interesting. Both boxes have the royal seal, only delivered in a time of war." Abe can see something moving behind the walls. He radios Hellboy. "Red, we have company." Abe looks up one of his bestiaries. "Burrowing creatures..." "How many?" "Many, there are no corpses because there are no leftovers...you notice the floor." Hellboy raises a sticky boot. "Ah, crap!" "Precisely all these things do is eat and eat, then poop and poop, then do it again." Liz cuts in wryly. "Remind you of anyone?" Hellboy asks. "Abe, what are these things?" "They're tooth fairies. Third century, Black Forest. Feed mostly on calcium, bones, skin, organs, but they do go for the teeth first, hence the name Tooth Fairies." Liz observes. "Actually, they don't leave money either."

When Abe accidently touches Liz, through his psychic powers he discovers..."Oh, my God, Liz, you're pregnant." "No, I'm not!" "Yes, you are." If Abe says she is, she is, Abe was able to discern the late Professor Broom's fatal illness.

One of the agents spots a tooth fairy. "He's kind of cute." Hellboy warns him. "Don't go near it." It attacks the agent. Hellboy crushes it with his red right hand, but then all the Tooth Fairies swarm and attack. Hellboy pushes the statue of the Earth Goddess down on top of some of the ferocious creatures (like a cross between the fairies of *Pan's Labyrinth* and *Piranha*). Liz flames up, telling Abe, and surviving Agent Steel to run for cover. The Tooth Fairies get Agent Steel, and Abe barely makes cover in a safe.

Liz warns Hellboy to stay away from the window, as the blast of her flames is strong enough to hurl him out. Mischievously, he deliberately stands right in front of it, commenting. "World, here I come." Liz's fireball incinerates the Tooth Fairies, and it sends Hellboy flying through the window, to crash land on a police car below. Hellboy is no longer a secret, no longer an urban myth but a reality. His wish of being out has finally come true, and he'll soon learn you should be careful what you wish for,

"Put the gun away Liz, my hangovers not that bad."

you just might get it. Like a gunfighter in a Sergio Leone Spaghetti Western, he shoots two Tooth Fairies that hitched a ride down with him. Manning is horrified. "What have you done?" Hellboy is delighted, as the press crowd in on him, in a sea of Guillermo-approved umbrellas. "Guess we're out."

EASTSIDE RAILYARDS. MIDNIGHT.

Prince Nuada and Mr. Wink enter a derelict building, the proposed site for a shopping mall. An unctuous creature, the Chamberlin (Doug Jones, the James Brown of Guillermo's world, definitely the hardest working man in showbusiness), complete with retinue of masked guards, greets Silverlance. "Your royal highness, Prince Nuada, you honour us with your return. Before entering the council chamber, you must surrender your weapons." You will remove Prince Nuada's silver lance only from his cold dead hand, he is outraged. "I will not."

As he reaches for his weapons, so too do the guards reach for theirs. The Chamberlin simpers. "It is protocol, Sire. For peasant and prince alike." Prince Nuada puts his Blade to the Chamberlain's throat. "It will be my pleasure to finish you off, Chamberlain." He is prevented in doing so by the arrival of his sister, the beautiful Princess Nuala (Anna Walton). "Please, brother. Surrender it." "For you, sister, anything." He bows respectfully and hands her the silver blade.

Back at the B.P.R.D, Hellboy is watching news reports about himself. One says HELLBOY: HELPING OR HINDERING. Some of the reports ask if he's really on the side of humanity, or is he endangering lives. He tells one reporter he just wants to be an ordinary person.

Liz, meanwhile, is taking a pregnancy test, one of many. Abe is hovering outside the bathroom door (A favourite location of Guillermo's as seen for example in *Cronos* and *Pan's Labyrinth*, while Hellboy does something as banal as watch himself on television, Liz is not only contemplating motherhood, which is daunting for any woman, but with her fire-starting abilities and Hellboy's origins, her situation is truly unique, plus Hellboy isn't exactly the most responsible man in the world).

"I knew there was something fishy about you, Abe."

Abe gives Liz a reassurance she doesn't want. "You don't need to do that, you can trust me..." "Shut up, Abe, get your damn hand away from the door." Still, like any true friend he persists in the thankless task of trying to help. "You have nothing to fear. In spite of appearances, Red would make an excellent father figure." (I agree, he had a good father figure himself, he has a good heart, and likes cats, you couldn't go too far wrong with that).

On television a reporter asks about Abe. "What about this guy, walking around with a toilet seat on his head." Abe is indignant. "It's quite obvious it's a breathing apparatus." Hellboy is feeling more image conscious. "I think we gotta lose the garbage truck. Sends out the wrong signal." Liz is wiser, she sees the big picture, Hellboy has been selfish, exposing his friends to the harsh scrutiny of the outside world without their permission.

"I hate it when people stare at me, makes me feel like a freak. You had no right, Red." As Hellboy laughs at Manning's uncomfortable explanations, the man himself walks in, telling Hellboy. "You have murdered me, you have ridiculed me. You have brought this onto yourself. Washington is sending down a new BPRD agent." "A new guy, why?" "To look after you."

Nuada has entered his father's chambers. Sad autumn leaves fall. It's reminiscent of the pollen that accompanies the magic in *Pan's Labyrinth*, but here it's a sad magic, like autumn leaves, the magic is waning, Aeglin the Father Tree has been poisoned by man's greed. It's like looking at a photo that's so faded by the ravages of time you soon won't be able to make out what it is. King Balor (Roy Dotrice) cannot believe his son has declared war on the humans (That isn't a crown that King Balor is wearing but natural antler like growths forming a crown-shape. It has the effect of an organic halo).

"Why? Why have you done this? Why?" "To set us free. All of us, Father." "You have broken an ancient truce between our people and mankind." "A truce based on shame. The humans have forgotten the gods. They have destroyed the Earth, and for what? Parking lots, shopping malls, greed has burned a hole in their hearts that will never be filled, they will never have enough." "What humans do is in their nature. To honour the truce is in ours." "Honour? Look at this place. Where is the honour in it? Father, you were once a proud warrior. When did you become their pet? I have returned from exile to wage war and reclaim our land, or birthright, and for that I will call upon the help of all my people, and they will answer. The good, the bad..." Nuada holds us the crown piece he took back at the auction house. "And the worse."

King Balor recognises what his son holds, and his hand moves instinctively to his part of the crown. "The Golden Army! You cannot be that mad." "Perhaps I am. Perhaps they made me so." Princess Nuala gives a woman's wiser perspective. "Awaken the army...but our green fields cannot grow out of all that blood. Let the army sleep. If our days have ended...let us all fade." But Nuada is determined. "We will not fade." King Balor makes a final appeal to his son. "For the last time, my son. I ask you...is this the path you wish to take?" Prince Nuada is adamant. "It is. I am sorry, father." King Balor raises his hand to signal his warriors. "Then you leave me no choice...Death!" Nuada asks Nuala. "And you, sister, are you happy with your King's verdict." I am, brother, I am." When Nuada realises the price she is prepared to pay, he accepts his destiny. "Then, very well. Death it is."

Joined by his ever loyal friend, Mr. Wink, Prince Nuada takes on his father's warriors. It is an incredible fight, balletic in both its beauty and brutality. We see too, that when Nuada's nose bleeds during the fight, so too does Nuala's. They are literally bonded by blood. Finally, Nuala kills his father, the act he did not intend to do, fratricide. So long has King Balor reigned over Elfland, that his body petrifies as he dies. Tearfully, Nuada tells him. "I always loved you, Father." He takes his father's part of the crown and it magically links to the piece Nuada retrieved from the auction room. He looks for Nuala. "Now for the final piece, my sister." But Nuala has fled crying from the scene of her father's murder, and more especially from the murderer himself, her dark mirror image.

BUREAU FOR PARANORMAL RESEARCH AND DEFENCE

Hellboy and the other agents are awaiting their new arrival. Hellboy doesn't think they need him, predictably Manning disagrees. "Evidently this guy is quite the big shot in Washington. His name is Johann Krauss. Top man in ectoplasmic research. Comes highly recommended by our European liaison. Hellboy isn't impressed, he remembers who brought him to Earth. "I don't like Germans. Germans make me nervous." Manning continues reading. "Dossier says he has a nice open face." An understatement, when Krauss (the actors that play Kraus are legion, John Alexander and James Dodd, with the fabulous vocal talents of Seth McFarlane, the voice of Stewie in Family Guy) arrives, he is literally a ghost in a suit, with a glass-bowl like helmet, full of ectoplasmic mist." Abe sees something in common with a creature that needs special apparatus to walk around. "I like him!"

Krauss examines the body of a Tooth Fairy on a special autopsy table (another Guillermo favourite, the autopsy scene). "Look at that poor little thing, bought and sold on the black market, crammed into cargo containers, smuggled, abused." Manning is impressed. "He has very expressive hands." Abe tells Kraus. "The seal on the box worries me also." Kraus recognises it. "A warring emblem." Abe confirms this. "From the Bethmora Clan, the Sons of the Earth." "Your file says you're the brains of the operation. I must admit I'm impressed."

Manning, desperately to bask in Abe's reflected glory, telling Kraus. "If you look at his file, you'll see I worked very closely with Abe in his training." Kraus isn't impressed with Manning however. "Let's see what our little friend here can remember." Hellboy interjects sarcastically. "Memory gets a little sketchy after you burn to death....He produces a reliquary. "...Maybe Saint Malachy can help." (St Malachy was a 12th century Irish saint, while in Rome in 1139 he had a vision which he transcribed as 112 short Latin phrases that describe all the Popes until the end of the world.).

But Krauss is having none of that! "No amulets...teleplasty." Abe explains. "Teleplasty...by which an ectopalsmic medium such as Dr Krauss can control inanimate things." A spectral mist arises from the finger of Dr Krauss's suit to enter the dead Tooth Fairy. "Organic, mechanical. Dead or alive." The reanimated Tooth Fairy is not pleased to see Hellboy, and the feeling is mutual. "Chewed off the tip of my tail." Krauss translates the Tooth Fairies agitated rant at Hellboy. "He says you're rude, brutish, and not very bright." Something that anuses Liz. Kraus continues. "It seems our little friend here remembers market sounds and voices... the Troll Market." Liz has heard of it but, "no one has ever found it." The Tooth Fairy expires for the last time, James Cagney-style. Krauss announces. "Now we know where to begin. Trolls dwell under bridges." Hellboy says sarcastically. "Wow! You're a genius. By the way, there's over 2000 bridges in New York City." Abe says a 19th century occult historian placed the market directly under the east end of the Brooklyn Bridge. Hellboy isn't impressed, they already looked there. That means nothing to Krauss. "Not with me...we're moving in."

BROOKLYN BRIDGE 03: 30 HRS

Hellboy is not having a good start to his evening, passers-by tell him, he's ugly, and Liz tells him he's intimidated by Krauss. Manning picks up a strange pair of glasses taken from the auction rooms. Liz explains what they are. "Normally we can't see fairy folk or trolls, they generate a cloaking aura of glamour. But in 1878, Amael Schuftain designed and built these, four crystal dioptres that penetrate that effect and reveal the true nature of things." Abe loves them, he goes into full fan-boy mode.

"Oh, Doctor Krauss, they're more beautiful than I imagined." "You must try them on then." Hellboy interrupts. "Uh, Mr Kraus..." "Krauss, Agent, there's a double 's'. "S.S. Right, right, these gizmos? How do you know they work?" They do, Abe sees Hellboy

The tooth, the whole tooth and nothing but the tooth

as Anung un Rama, in his full demonic form, halo of fire, glowing red eyes, and full horns. (An interesting sublimal message in these scenes is a sign on a building with a picture of a woman who looks very like Liz, bearing the legend: 'A big decision').

UNDER THE BROOKLYN BRIDGE 04:57HRS

Abe, Hellboy, and Krauss follow what look to all the world looks like a bag lady with a trolley full of cats. She is actually a Fragglewump (again a fine Brian Steele performance, the man is a natural comedian), an ugly Scottish troll, that has a fear of canaries (so they've brought one along), and feeds on kittens. Can a fouler creature exist? Hellboy is indignant. "She's gonna eat the cats!" Krauss doesn't want Hellboy to stop her. He wants to follow her to the Troll Market. "You will make her aware of our presence. " Hellboy repeats. "She's gonna eat the cats." "You will stay put..."

Hellboy, wearing the Shuftain glasses isn't having any of that. He approaches the Fragglewump, he can see past the glamour, she truly is disgusting, Hellboy's approach just prevents her eating a cat. "Oh, yes, dearie, can I help you?" "We're looking for the Troll Market." The Fragglewump won't help, so Hellboy produces the canary. The Fragglewump is terrified. "Not the canary!" "What? You're afraid of this little guy? Who would know?" The creature gives in. "No more. No more. I'll take you there." "Come on, you dirty old troll."

She leads the agents to a meat packaging plant. Krauss radios Liz and Manning, telling them they're going into the Troll Market, and to keep radio contact to a minimum. Manning is enamoured with Krauss, telling Liz he's efficient and precise. Liz isn't so sure. "Add resistant to that and you got yourself a new watch."

The Fragglewump leads them to a huge door with an incredible -looking clockwork lock. Krauss examines it. "It's a complex combination lock. What do you think, Agent Sapien?" "Not good. With the number of symbols of the combination, we'll be here for days." Hellboy doesn't agree, and tries to use the canary to get the Fragglewump to open the door. But the troll won't comply, so Hellboy punches the foul cat-consuming creature across the room. Krauss is disgusted. "Is that your investigating technique?" Hellboy asks him. "Are you gonna show us how it's done, Mt 'By-The-Book'?" "Yes, I think I will."

Krauss's ectoplasmic form leaves his suit and enters the lock to open it from within. Returning to his suit, he announces. "Gentlemen, welcome to the Troll market."

Inside the Troll Market is a market of unearthly delights. You could see it a thousand times and still see something wonderful you have never noticed before. It's like looking into Guillermo's vast imagination, and for this alone, Hellboy II is an incredible achievement.

In one corner of the market there is a huge medieval-looking garbage grinder, while Abe is horrified by a creature selling fish. In the air fly fairies like the ones from Pan's Labyrinth. Hellboy is amazed and radios Liz. "You should be here. You'd love it. Nobody's looking at us. We blend right in." Krauss interrupts. "Agent! I said keep communication to a minimum." Abe sees Princess Nuala and before she can conceal it, he spots the symbol on her bracelet. "The Royal Seal." Abe follows the princess.

Kraus approaches a creature that has what looks like a baby growing out of it, another creature is shaving it. Krauss shows them a photo. "Excuse me, gentlemen. Have you seen anyone purchasing this type of Tooth Fairy?" The shaver tells him. "No one sells them down here, pal. Jersey, maybe." He shows them another photo. "This then, do you recognise this seal?"

The creatures get very agitated, and Hellboy steps in and sends the shaving creature flying. Hellboy then gets the information from the creature with the baby, who tells them that Prince Nuada bought the Tooth Fairies. "They say Prince Nuada broke the truce and now there is talk of war, a war with the human world." Hellboy pats the baby on its head. "Sorry, kid." "That's alright." Krauss follows suit. "Nice baby." It corrects him. "I'm not a baby, I'm a tumour."

Abe follows the Princess into a map shop. Mr Wink spots him in turn. Inside the

map shop, a creature called Cathedralhead (Once again Brian Steele, if he joins forces with Doug Jones, the two can play their own cast of thousands. Originally there was going to be lots of tiny humans running around the ramparts of the cathedral but the budget didn't allow for it.) meets the Princess. "What do you want? Tell me your name?" She shows him her bracelet. He recognises it. "Follow me...your father left you this map. In it he said lies the secret to the location of the Golden Army."

Abe enters the room. Cathedralhead asks Abe. "Can I help you with something?" "No, thank you. I'm just looking." Princess Nuala cuts to the chase. "Sir, why are you following me?" "I was just hoping to find an old map of Algiers." She's too smart to buy that. "Why are you following me? Did my brother send you to steal the crown piece?" "Brother? Oh, you're sorely mistaken, I assure you." She pulls a knife. "Then answer me truthfully. Why were you following me?" "My name is Abraham Sapien." She puts the knife to his throat. "There is no such name." "I don't like it either but..." "Enough, give me your hand." Their hands touch, she has the same psychic skill as Abe does. "You are an agent. The Bureau of Paranormal Research and Defence, and your name is...oh." "Horrible. I know." "I'm Nuala. Princess Nuala." "Yes, I know. Forgive me, your highness. But as you were learning about me. I couldn't help but learn a bit about you...I know that you need our help." She sees Mr Wink enter. "I'm afraid that it's the other way around."

Abe bravely gives the Princess a chance to get away, but it's pretty uneven fight and he quickly follows her through the window. Mr Wink catches up with Abe, and it looks like it's over for him, when Hellboy's bullets start to bounce off Mr Wink's retractable iron fist. Mr Wink retaliates by giving Hellboy a punch with the aforementioned fist. The two of them battle, demolishing chunks of the Troll Market as they go at it. Hellboy crushes Mr Wink's metal hand. "Now, stay down." Hellboy has in turn lost a tooth which he tosses at Mr Wink. "Happy?" Mr Wink angrily indicates his ruined iron fist. Hellboy advises against it. "Give it up, pal. I wouldn't do that if I was you." Mr Wink's metal hand flies out on its chain...straight into the garbage grinder, which begins to pull him in on his own chain, past Hellboy, who comments laconically. "Told you." Lights out for Mr. Wink! Krauss turns up with Princess Nuala and Abe. "Look what you've done, Agent Hellboy, now we have to leave."

As they go to leave, two headed creatures chatter (known as 'Bogarts', and voiced by Guillermo). "Wink is dead. A big red man killed him." One of them goes to tell the news to Prince Nuada, who's working on an intricate clockwork apparatus (very reminiscent of the Cronos Device). He is very upset at the loss of his friend.

At street level, Princess Nuala explains her brother's plans to the B.P.R.D agents. "To wage his war, my brother needs this." She indicates her part of the crown and the cylinder from the map shop. "The final piece of the crown of Bethmora and this map to the location of the Golden Army chambers." Krauss does not like the sound of that. "The Golden Army! The harbingers of death."

Hellboy remembers his father's story, that Christmas Eve all those years ago. "Howdy Doody!" Princess Nuala won't hand over the crown-piece. "Where it goes, I go. My father died to uphold the truce with your world. You must honour his noble intentions." Abe doesn't realise it, but he's fallen in love with the Princess, and one of the first signs of true love, is that you stick up for the one you love. Loyalty goes hand in hand with love. "The lady's in dire need." Krauss is very officious. "I take it you're vouching for her, Agent Sapien?" "Most emphatically yes." "Even so...I am sorry. We cannot assume such responsibility on our own."

Hellboy is aghast and backs up his friend. "The lady just lost her father! What more do you want?" Krauss doesn't see it that way. "You may not care but there are procedures...rules." Hellboy definitely doesn't care about rules. "She's coming with us, you got that, Gasbag?" If he had ears, Krauss wouldn't believe what he's just heard. "What did you call me?" He's interrupted by the arrival of Prince Nuada, who accuses Hellboy. "You! You will pay for what happened to my friend down there." Hellboy draws the Samaritan.

"You take cheques?" Prince Nuada knows Hellboy's true origins. "Demon. Born from a womb of shadows. Sent to destroy the world that you still think you belong to." Hellboy isn't moved. "Are we gonna talk all night cos I'm really sleepy?"

In answer, Prince Nuada produces the Cronos Device style object he was previously tinkering with. Princess Nuala recognises it and begs him not to activate it. The device opens with a whirl of clockwork mechanisms, and Nuada removes a green foetus-shaped seed and orders it. "Kill him." He throws it towards them, and it hops along the ground, animated. Hellboy isn't worried. "It's just a jumping bean." The Princess warns Abe to stop it getting to water. But it gets into a drain. It germinates into a gigantic moving plant creature, bursting through the road, destroying cars. Nuada announces. "It's an elemental. A giver of life and a destroyer...a forest god."

Hellboy takes note of this, and goes to get a huge version of the Samaritan. "Forest God? I'm gonna get me Big Baby (a huge version of the Samaritan that fires shells with a baby bottle logo imprinted on them!)." Hellboy bravely rescues an infant from a car just before the elemental throws that same car at a helicopter. Leaping onto a building with the Big Baby gun in one hand, and the real laughing baby in the other (amusingly, his tail briefly catches the child for a second).

He admonishes the Plant Elemental. "You woke up the baby." He shoots it, but it's tragic seeing the wounded creature and he hesitates to deliver the killing shots despite Krauss's insistent order to do so. Prince Nuada asks him. "Demon, what are you waiting for? This is what you wanted, isn't it. Look at it, the last of its kind. Like you and I, you destroy it, the world will never see its like again. You have more in common with us, than with them. You could be a king."

On the street below, Krauss is still barking orders to Hellboy. Nuada tells Hellboy. "If you cannot command...then you must obey." Reluctantly, Hellboy delivers the killing shot and the creature dies in the manner of the classic black and white *King Kong*. It's a tragic death, more like a murder than a victory. It's dying body flowering into trees, and releasing seeds (again reminiscent of the pollen in *Pan's Labyrinth*, and the leaves in King Balor's throne room). It brings tears to the eyes with the tragedy of it all, and it is a beautiful representation of what so called 'humanity' is doing to the world. Nuada's methods might be wrong, but his reasoning is sadly all too true. It is in our nature too , to lie, hurt, deceive and destroy, even to ourselves. It is the nature of humanity to behave inhumanely, as though we have a built in self-destruct button. We behave more like a virus than a species of mammal. Abe observes the Elementals sad passing as seeds fill the air. "It's beautiful."

Hellboy returns the baby he saved to the infant's mother, but she's far from grateful, neither is an angry hateful mob. Why? Hellboy has just risked his life to save them, and destroyed a beautiful and unique creature in the process, one capable of contributing more positivity to the world in an instant than the entire mob. Why? A police officer puts his gun on Hellboy. "He's got a weapon in his hand."

Liz stands in front of the man she loves. Again the theme of loyalty, he will have to kill her to get to Hellboy "That is his hand. He was trying to help. That's all we do. That's all we've done all these years." But the crowd's mood is ugly, they thrown an object at Hellboy, and Liz begins to flame up. Hellboy takes her hand. "Let's go home."

Back at the Bureau, a report on the television tells of an "investigation into the B.P.R.D and its promotion of interspecies marriage, seen by many as a threat to traditional values..."

Liz tends to Hellboy's wounds, reassuring him. "You did a good job out there." Hellboy doesn't think so, all his life he wanted to be accepted, to be popular to belong, a very human desire, and one that has caused to much misery to so many. Belong to your own self before you belong to anyone else. "Tell me why I don't feel so good? I mean, I killed that thing and for what? They didn't even like me, what do you do with that?"

Liz has something difficult to tell Hellboy and then something even more difficult to decide. "Red, I don't want you to freak out...I'm gonna leave for a bit. I need time to think." "About what? Can't you do your thing right here? Look, I'll be really, really quite. I'll get rid of the cats." Liz doesn't believe he'd ever get rid of the cats, and she has a hard question to ask him. Hellboy needs to decide does he want to belong and matter to the whole world or to simply matter and mean the whole world to one person instead. "Red, why are you with me? Do you need everybody to like you, or am I enough? Think about it."

As she walks away, a classic monster movie plays on one of Hellboy's televisions. Frankenstein's monster announces forlornly. "We belong dead."

Princess Nuala is the library of the late Professor Broom. She has removed a parchment from the cylinder. It clearly shows Ireland, but there are no co-ordinates for the Golden Army. Abe has put in contact lenses in an effort to make himself appear more human (in the same way Hellboy files his horns). Nuala reads from a beautifully bound blue book. "When the heart is sick and all the wheels of being are slow." Abe recognises it instantly. "Tennyson, *In Memorium*, a beautiful poem. Forgive me, I didn't mean to startle you." "Oh, no, no. I borrowed this book. I hope you don't mind." He mirrors her answer verbally (another sign of being in love). "Oh, no, no. This is your home now. You are safe here." Princess Nuala knows better, despite Abe's noble intentions. "My brother will find me. He always does." "How could he, our location is a highly classified secret?" "But I know of it now, which means he does too. We're twins. Even as children, a link has bound us. One to the other. Something I cannot explain." Abe ties to reassure the Princess again. "No need." She notices something about Abe. "You look... different?"

Embarrassed at being so transparent, he makes a joke out of it, answering a question with a question. "Do I? Perhaps my hair." "No, it's your eyes. I can see your eyes. "Yes, I'm trying a new look" This is another significant act of courage by Abe, and yet another sign of how deep he's fallen in love. In many cultures the eyes are the windows of the soul, so to expose his eyes in this fashion is incredibly significant to Abe. In everyday life, you can observe it yourself, how rarely people truly look others in the eye, as though they're afraid of what they'll see reflected back. (It's also amazing that a romance between a fish-man and an elf-woman is more believable than any Hollywood romance, and far more moving, it's because it comes from a place of sincerity and we know in our hearts that it is real.)

The embarrassed Abe tries to change the subject, and indicates the parchment that the Princess removed from the cylinder. "Is that a map?" "Yes, it was in this cylinder. There are no co-ordinates." Abe holds it up to the light. "Perhaps there's a watermark." The Princess reciprocates Abe's feelings for her, telling him. "You were very brave, vouching for me. How do you know I'm not the enemy, bringing me here." He tries to explain, but love is something that isn't easily explained. "It's as you were saying just now, from intuition, maybe a link. Normally I'm able to read others quite quickly, but I've never met anyone quite like you." She smiles the sweetest smile at him. It must be as lonely and unique (one and the same thing) being an elf-princess as it is being an Icthyo-Sapian. This is their Bogart and Bacall moment. "Nor I like you.... Goodnight, Abraham." Love makes Abe very tongue-tied indeed. Everyone has been there. "Goodnight, princess, your highness, your majesty...Ma'am...ma'am?"

And in the background, a song plays aptly. "You're such a beautiful freak, I wish there were more like you."

In the locker rooms, Hellboy looks at himself in the mirror, there is a lot going on in his head, he is on the threshold of a very different way of looking at the world and himself. It's significant that he doesn't bother to file his horns, as if he's wondering is it worth going to the trouble to try and fit in with people who reward courage and kindness with bigotry and hate. Krauss is there too. "Good nacht, Agent Hellboy." Hellboy barely grunts in reply. Krauss tells him. "Look, Agent, I know you don't like me, but I could take away your badge." That doesn't bother Hellboy. "Never had one...kept asking though." "You will learn to obey me, follow protocol, and stay foc-yoosed at all at all times." Hellboy corrects his grammatical faux-pas. "Er, that word. 'foc-yoosed', with your accent, I wouldn't use it that much." Krauss isn't easily deterred however, in this he is much like Hellboy, neither of them can take a hint.

Then, Krauss tells Hellboy something surprising. "I knew Professor Broom, young man." Hellboy doesn't believe it. "You didn't know Professor Broom." "Yes, I did. After my accident, he designed this suit. A wonderful man, and even then he was..." Hellboy doesn't like what he's hearing. "Hey, Gas-bag, stop right now," Krauss to his credit isn't scared. "Or what? Are you threatening me? Because I think I can take you." "'Scuse me?" "You heard me." Hellboy comes closer to Krauss, his blood is up. I couldn't hear you from all the way over there." "I can take you because you have one fatal flaw." "Oh, I don't want to hear it." "No, you don't, you can't take criticism." He pokes. "Can't take it." Hellboy is really getting angry now. "What's my flaw?" "Your temper, it gets the best of you. Makes you weak, makes you vulnerable." Hellboy's fist shoots out like a jackhammer, proving Krauss's point for him, shattering the glass bowl of Kraus's helmet. . The suit collapses to the ground, like a deflating balloon, while the ectoplasmic essence of Krauss escape from it. Hellboy is guilty, like a bold child that knows he's going to get into trouble. "Johann, hang on in there, will you?" Freed from the suit, the ectoplasmic Krauss possesses the doors of the lockers and uses them to beat up Hellboy, in a very Three-Stooges-inspired fashion, one of the doors making a perfect impression of Hellboy's face."

Krauss's essence forms into a humanoid shape. Hellboy has proved his point for him, a lesson for us all, lose the temper and lose the fight. "There we are, your temper makes you sloppy. Try to control it, Agent Hellboy, before it controls you." Triumphantly, Krauss's ectoplasmic forms 'walks' off, singing German songs.

The battered Hellboy calls Krauss a 'glass-hole', and proceeds to get drunk. He hears music, 'can't live without you', and follows it to its source, the library, as he enters Abe quickly changes to classical music. "Hello, Red. You're up late." "What are you listening to?" "Vivladi." Hellboy spots Abe trying to hide a CD of popular love songs. "Oh, Abe, you fell for the Princess." Abe really has it bad! "She's like me, a creature from another world." "You need to get out more." "She's alone in the world. I want to help her." "You're in love. Have a beer." "No. My body's a temple." "No, it's an amusement park...shut up and drink it." The two pick track 8 on the CD. Abe says. "I can't smile or cry. I think I have no tear ducts." Hellboy still misses Professor Broom. "I wish Father were here. He'd know what to tell you."

Abe and Hellboy sing along with the song, they can be heard through the Bureau headquarters. Princess Nuala senses her brother's presence. Nuada is outside the gates where he's killed the guards. Nuala tries to destroy the map by throwing it and the cylinder it came in on the fire. Then she hides her crown piece in the book of Tennyson she had been reading from.

Abe and Hellboy are vey drunk by now (For a first-timer, Abe has taken to it like a fish to water, you could say he drinks like a fish!). Hellboy praises Liz. "She's my whole world. I would give my life for her...But she always wants me to do the dishes." Abe goes one better. "I would die and do the dishes." Hellboy knows something important is bothering Liz. "Why is she so mad at me? It's not because the room is dirty...something else." "Well, ask her." Hellboy gets deep with his reply. "No. Listen, Abe. When a woman's mad about something, but she's really mad about something else, you can't ask, cos then they get angry because you had to ask."

Prince Nuada has found his sister, and sees she has thrown the map on the fire. "Very quick of you." He reaches into the fire for the cylinder. "The parchment was of no importance. It's the cylinder. It's very interesting." He places the hot cylinder on a covered table and rolls it. As the cylinder rolls, it burns the co-ordinates of the Golden Army onto the cover, a map of Ireland, this time with the location marked. Prince Nuada is triumphant. "I will find the Golden Army there.

As for the crown piece. I know its here...it's in one of the books and I will find it."

Abe and Hellboy are with the sleeping Liz. Abe says. "Listen, Red, I know what's going on with Liz." She wakes up and tries to stop him telling Hellboy. Then, Princess Nuala sets off the alarm.

They follow the alarm to the library. Abe instantly moves to help the Princess, who tries to stop him. "Abraham, he'll kill you." Prince Nuada is astonished. "You talk to him like that?" He grabs his sister and holds a knife to her cheek, cutting it. His own cheek bleeds in the same place in response. "I will kill you, Abraham, and anyone else necessary." Hellboy is too drunk to fight, but he won't let that stop him. "Why don't you start with me?" Prince Nuada means business, he knows which buttons to push. "You move and I'll kill your Abraham first." Abe shouts a warning to Hellboy. "Red, you mustn't harm the Prince. If you hurt him, you hurt the Princess." So, not only does he have to fight in an intoxicated state, Hellboy also cannot kill his opponent, something Nuada will have no compunction about with him. Nuada scores a multitude of blows on Hellboy, with his lance at Hellboy's throat, he asks his sister. "Will you give me the crown piece?" She refuses, and Nuada stabs Hellboy, telling him. "You may have mused in the past. 'Am I mortal?' You are now." As he withdraws the lance, it leaves its tip behind. Nuada takes his sister prisoner and tells Abe. "If you want to save him and see her again, you will find the missing piece and bring it to me." And Nuada makes his escape with his reluctant sister.

In the Bureau's operating theatre, Abe discovers he can't remove the tip of the lance from Hellboy, every time he tries, it moves closer to Hellboy's heart. Abe knows the situation is deadly serious, which is exactly what Prince Nuada intended. "The wound will not heal until the spear is removed. We're running out of time." Liz will not let the man she loves die without a fight. "Then we go after the Prince and we make him take it out." Hellboy has decided what matters most to him. "I know what's important, it's you. I can turn my back on the world, all of it, as long as you stay with me." She will, telling him. "I'll stay with you, you're the best man I've ever met." A tear drops from Hellboy's eye. "Man." He's pleased he's a man to Liz, but is he a man to the rest of the world? It no longer matters, he's realised it's what he and Liz think that counts. If she thinks he's a man, then he is man.

Abe has discovered the crown piece the Princess hid. He brings it with him to a briefing Krauss is giving Manning and the other agents. Krauss says. "The cylinder yielded co-ordinates to County Antrim, Northern Ireland. The Giant's Causeway." Liz is delighted, it means they know where Nuada is . "Great, so we know where he is. What are we waiting for? We should get going." Krauss doesn't agree. "The Prince will demand the crown piece, Agent Sherman." "then we give it to him." Manning won't allow that, and Krauss agrees. "The Golden Army must not awaken." Liz cannot believe her ears. "So what? You're

They met with a stony reception...

crown piece and without it his army poses no threat." Liz asks Krauss. "So, we have clearance?" "Agent Sherman...Liz. Screw the clearance, we will take the plane."

ANTRIM, NORTHERN IRELAND 09:00 HRS

The B.P.R.D plane flies in. The Agents are met by the leg-less Goblin Blacksmith (John Alexander), who built the Golden Army. "I bid you welcome, strangers. How can I be of assistance?" Liz tells him. "We seek safe passage to Bethmora. We are looking for Prince Nuada." "Him I know. Trade me something and I'll take you to him." "Here, I have a shiny belt." Not much use to a goblin without legs. "And I have no pants." Liz produces a pair of binoculars. "A wonderful set of magic eyes."(This is an Irish goblin, Liz, he knows them by their proper name). "Ah, I already have binoculars. But I see something special." He's looking through Hellboy's dressings. "Something shiny underneath the bandages. I want that." Liz is aghast at the prospect. "No, you can't take it out. Not without killing him." "Maybe I know someone who can. Will you trade me then?" Liz agrees. The Goblin Blacksmith blows a whistle and a stone creature arises from the Earth. They enter through a hole in the stone that closes behind them. They enter a vast dead city, the legendary Bethmora.

The Goblin Blacksmith comments sadly. "You should have seen this city when it was alive." Abe asks him what happened to it. The Goblin Blacksmith explains. "Curse. As soon as the Golden Army was stored here, silence and death befell us. The world left us behind. They approach a cracked monolith, as the Goblin Blacksmith continues his tale. "For a long time I alone dwelled in the dust." He

"Okay, I'll give you one chance to surrender."

just gonna let him die." "I'm sorry, we called Washington. We have our orders." "I won't let him die." "Agent Sherman, may I remind you that I am the leader of this team." "Oh, there's no doubt about that, that is what you are, Doctor Krauss, and if you ever were human, that time is long gone." Liz has no way of physically seeing the reaction her words have had on Krauss, but they have cut him to the very core of his essence. One of the themes of Hellboy is not to judge by appearances. Krauss is as human as he wants to be...like all of us. He holds a small cloth bag sadly.

Abe doesn't tell anyone he's found the crown piece. Liz tells Abe. "Even without the piece, we have to get him out of here. We'll go to Antrim and we will find the Prince, Abe, just the two of us."

Abe warms up the B.P.R.D transport plane's engines. Krauss hears them however and asks Liz. "Do you have authorisation to take that plane?" Liz's hand sneaks towards her gun. "You're not gonna stop us, Johann." "On the contrary. I've been giving it some thought and we should be able to save Agent Hellboy." Krauss throws the cloth bag to Abe (it contains a ring). "You say I'm not human anymore, but you are wrong. I understand your pain all too well. A long time ago I lost the woman I loved, and that was in fact the source of my present misfortune. I will tell you about it one day but for now the tactical advantage is ours. Consider this, the Prince lacks the

pauses, and indicates to Liz and Hellboy. "The two of you come inside, the rest of you wait out here."

They enter the presence of the Angel of Death (the multi-talented Doug Jones again). The Angel resembles the legendary Banshee (literally 'female ghost' in Irish), a creature that is an omen of death and doom. The Angel of Death has no eyes on her face (like the Pale Man), but multiple eyes on her wings. She is one of the most awesome and frightening creatures ever to grace the silver screen. The Goblin Blacksmith greets this avatar of doom cheerfully. "Hello, friend, I have brought you visitors, and I have a favour to ask you." The Angel of Death barely looks up from the objects of fate she moves along the dusty floor and dismisses him. The Goblin Blacksmith sounds wounded by this (like I said, he's an Irish goblin). "But I have done so much for you. I have brought you many souvenirs..." Then he gets to the real object of his visit. "...And he has something shiny, something nice."

The Angel of Death calls Hellboy by his true name, Anung un Rama. With a terrifyingly sepulchral voice, the Angel of Death tells them. "I have been waiting for you both, many a winter moon...I am his death." Liz asks the Angel of Death if she can save Hellboy. The Angel of Death replies. "It is for you to decide that. It is all the same to me, my heart is filled with dust...sand. But you should know it is his destiny to bring about the destruction of the Earth. Not now. Not tomorrow. But soon..." The dust on the floors parts to reveal a mural of Hellboy as Anung un Rama.

The Angel of Death continues, her voice like honey-coated razor blades scraping across a blackboard. "Knowing that, you still want him to live? So, child, make a choice. The world or him?" Liz answers in a heartbeat, proof if any was needed, that Hellboy is the world to her. "Him." There is a saying: 'you cannot dance with the Devil, and expect to spin away with your soul intact'. The Angel of Death tells Liz. "The time will come, my dear, where you will suffer more than anyone." Liz doesn't care. "I'll deal with it, now save him." "It is done." The Angel of Death has Prince Nuada's lance tip in her hand. "I have done what I can, now give him a reason to live." The Angel of Death vanishes, leaving behind the 'shiny' for the Goblin Blacksmith. Liz tells Hellboy tenderly that he very much has a reason to live. "Listen to me, Big Ape. You have to get up because you're gonna be a father." And Hellboy does revive. "I become... father." Not only does he become a father, but I feel he's also referring to Professor Broom, his own father, that he has become a man, a responsible man like him.

The Goblin Blacksmith announces. "All this is very touching. If you want to beat Nuada. We have to leave now." The Goblin Blacksmith leads them to a huge cathedral-like chamber full of huge metal eggs (like the Cronos Device on a gigantic cyclopean scale). He stops at some steps. "There they are. Seventy times seventy soldiers. Sometimes I wish I'd never created them. Whoosh went the furnace...one those fires took my legs off. This is as far as I can go, I'm not very good with steps. If you're here to stop him...the Prince, I wish you luck. The Golden Army was never meant to awaken."

They confront Prince Nuada is an ornate rooms full of huge clockworks and cogs. He has Princess Nuala with him. Nuada is confident they have the final crown piece. "You are here, so I assume you brought the remaining piece." Krauss starts to answer. "Oh, we didn't..." Nuada cuts across him contemptuously (Guillermo gets a nice Wizard of Oz reference in here). "I wasn't addressing you, Tinman. Abraham, my sister is well, as I promised." Nuala pleads with Abe not to give Nuada the crown piece.

Hellboy is amazed, he never imagined Abe not only had the crown piece, but kept the knowledge to himself and brought it with him. "What the hell are you doing?" But nothing will stop Abe from trying to save her, telling Hellboy. "You would do exactly the same for Liz." Abe throws Nuada the remaining crown piece and the crown is complete. Nuada places it on his head and announces regally. "I am Prince Nuada, Silverlance, and leader of the Golden Army. Is there anyone here who would dispute my right?"

Vast cogs and gears clank into life,

reactivating the Golden Army (it's as though these clockwork robots have hatched from mechanical eggs). Nuada orders the Golden Army to kill the B.P.R.D agents despite his sisters protestations. Abe in his innocence is actually hurt. "He lied to us." Hellboy tells him laconically. "Abe, old buddy, if we ever get out of this, we've gotta talk."

Hellboy tears into action against the Golden Army, that deadly force of emotionless metal golems, blasting robots with the Samaritan, sending cogs and gearwheels flying and right. Krauss's ectoplasmic form leaves his suit to possess one of the Golden Army, which glows with an eerie blue light. The robotic Krauss rips through the nearest robots. He tosses a robot arm to Hellboy to use as a club.

Eventually however, the other robots destroy Krauss's ride and he returns to his suit. It gets worse, the robots that Krauss and Hellboy 'destroyed' reassemble themselves in a whirl of gears and cogs. The Golden Army cannot be destroyed. Even Krauss is out of ideas. Not Hellboy, who remembers the story his father told him that long ago Christmas Eve. "I've got one, I challenge Prince Nuada for the right to command this army." Nuada is contemptuous. "You challenge me, who are you to challenge me? You are nobody? You are royalty?" His sister Nuala begs to differ. "Yes, he is Anung un Ram, son of the Fallen One. He has the right, challenge must be answered." Nuada reluctantly agrees. Hellboy understands Abe's fears and reassures him. "I'm not gonna kill him, Abe, but I am gonna kick his ass."

The Golden Army draws back to let Hellboy and Nuada fight it out, they don't care who commands them. The two warriors fight an epic battle. Hellboy nicks the Prince's arm and his sister's arm bleed in sympathy, we see how closely their fates are woven. Leaping across the huge cogs and gears, Hellboy eventually defeats Prince Nuada, who begs him to kill him, because he cannot stop. Hellboy takes the crown, he has no wish to kill Nuada, but Nuada pulls a knife, meaning to kill Hellboy, but before he can Princess Nuala mortally wounds herself to stop him, they are as bound together in death as they were in life.

As Nuada dies, Hellboy holds Prince Nuada. A noble warrior who could not bear what we have done to the Earth. Nuada gives Hellboy a final piece of wisdom. "The humans, they will tire of you. They will turn against you. Leave them. Is it them or us?Which holocaust should be chosen?"

For me, the most heart-wrenching scene in any of Guillermo's films is the scene where Abe comforts his dying Princess. Words can't do it justice, it is something we have to feel and be brave enough to open our hearts to share. Abe tells Nuala sadly. "I never had a chance to tell you how I felt." She tells him to give her his hand. He does so, and for that instant a lifetimes love and experience flashes between them.

Surely there can be no truer, purer of more tragic love than these two unworldly creatures. Nuada speaks his last word. "We die, and the world will be poorer for it." Nuada and Nuala die together, dark and light of the same soul, one unable to live without the other, a dark dance that can only end in death. Like their father before them, their bodies petrify to stone, marble monuments to the beauty and magic mankind is wiping off the Earth.

Hellboy looks at the crown, tempted a little. "All that power, Liz." Liz takes the crown. "Don't even think about it." And melts it. The golden Army shuts down.

Leaving Bethmora, they find Manning waiting for them, he tells Hellboy. "You took that plane without permission, young man." He's stunned to find, Hellboy, Liz, and Abe quit, and even Krauss joins them in resigning.

As our heroes walk away into the sunset, Liz asks Hellboy. "So, what you said about us living anywhere?" He meant it, telling her. "Anywhere. You and me. We'll find a place in the country. Clean air. Green hills. A yard with lots of room to grow in, it'll be great for the baby." Liz has one last big surprise for Hellboy, she holds up two fingers. "Babies."

Ray Harryhausen

"One of the first things that came to mind was to make it more like a fantasy movie, a Harryhausen movie..."
GUILLERMO DEL TORO ON HELLBOY II: THE GOLDEN ARMY

Ray Harryhausen (born June 29, 1920), is famed for his incredible stop-motion animation. His characters appear incredible real, particularly in their interaction with human actors. Being animated in three-dimensions, they have an air of realism and believability CGI often doesn't have. They also have a special x-factor, something indefinable that makes audiences fall in love with them, I feel its Harryhausen's own belief, hard work and love of his characters coming through to the audience.

The young Harryhausen was inspired by the classic 1933 *King Kong* to learn all he could about stop-motion animation. He also gained practical experience working on George pal's Puppetoon shorts. During World War 2, Harryhausen gained further experience serving in the US Army's motion picture unit.

Following his demobilisation from the Army after World War 2, Harryhausen was eager to break into the motion picture industry, so he shot a scene showcasing what he was capable of animating. He took a scene from one of his (and mine) favourite stories, H.G. Wells' *War of the Worlds*, that of a Martian emerging from a cylinder. Alas, this project never came to fruition but Harryhausen did get work with Willis O'Brien, the animator of *King Kong*. Harryhausen was to work on *Mighty Joe Young* (1949) which was to win the special effects Academy Award.

Harryhausen's work really comes into the fore on *The Beast from 20,000 Fathoms* (Based partly on a story called *The Fog Horn*, by Harryhausen's old friend Ray Bradbury). Harryhausen began a partnership with Charles H. Schneer. Their first project was *It Came From Beneath The Sea* (1955). Harryhausen's work on *Earth Vs The Flying Saucers* was highly influential. He would also work on Irwin Allan's *The Animal World* (1956). In 1957 he worked on one of his all time classics *20 Million Miles to Earth*. Its creature, the Ymir, is not only awe-inspiring, but carries a great aura of pathos, this misfortunate creature is trapped in a terrifying world it doesn't belong to. Leaving aside Harryhausen's great technical skills and creativity, his greatest strength is the humanity he imbues his monsters with. We feel for them, even now years after I first saw the film, I still believe 100% in the creatures, I believed this is because their creator Ray Harryhausen did too, and this filters through to the audience.

In 1958, Harryhausen worked on his first Sinbad movie, *The Seventh Voyage of Sinbad*, which is a masterclass in how to create a beautiful fantasy world. He followed that up with *The Three Worlds of Gullivor* (1960), and *Mysterious Island* (1961). The labour that went into creating his dynamation effects is staggering, and I can only admire his prolific work rate during this period.

We have to remember, Harryhausen did not have a team working for him, he did it alone at this time. *Mysterious Island* is a particular favourite of mine, being a fine adaption of a Jules Verne tale, it was one of the first films I ever saw, and I'm pleased to say I enjoy it as much now as I did then. In fact the day that I don't will be a sad one. While Harryhausen's dream project of HG Wells' *War of the Worlds* never materialised (I cannot understand why no one has ever filmed the novel properly), in 1964, he did get to work on a adaptation of HG Wells' *First Men in the Moon*. A charming film and not one you could see getting green-lit today.

In 1963, Harryhausen created *Jason and the Argonauts*, a tour-de-force of fantasy, and probably his most loved movie. I covered this film extensively in *The Dead Walk* (Noir Publishing, 2008), so I will say no more save that in these dark times, watching *Jason and the Argonauts* will lift you to a better place.

In 1967, Harryhausen produced

some incredible dinosaur effects fro Hammers *One Million Years B.C.* An iconic film, what's not to like about Ray's dinosaurs and the lovely Raquel Welch in a bikini? (Even if the film did break the laws of evolution to get Raquel and the monsters in the same picture!).

In 1969, Harryhausen worked on what had once been intended as a film by his friend and mentor Willis O' Brien, *Valley of Gwangi*. This is my favourite of all Harryhausen's films. I love Weird Westerns, and this tale of cowboys and dinosaurs set in 1912 is an all-time classic. Beautifully shot, incredible creatures, well performed, and in *Gwangi*, the most sympathetic monster Harryhausen created since the Ymir. The filsm climax in the burning cathedral is unforgettable and moving. In *Valley of Gwangi*, the title creature is the innocent victim, not the monster.

The cinematic world was changing, becoming harsher and less-sympathetic to Ray's fantastic visions. He returned to Sinbad, producing two fine films. *The Golden Voyage of Sinbad* (1974), starring the beautiful Caroline Munro, features some incredible creations, including a ship's figurehead that comes to life, and a deadly Kali. *Sinbad and the Eye of the Tiger* (1977), starred the lovely Jane Seymour and features a fantastic battle between Sinbad and three ghouls which arise from a fire. Breathtaking doesn't cover it, it harkens back to Jason's fight with the skeletons but with a pleasingly insectile twist.

Harryhausen's final film was *Clash of the Titans* (1981), a fantasy tour-de-force, featuring an incredible Medusa and a very impressive Kraken. However, despite the film's success, Harryhausen had great difficulties in getting new projects green-lit. There was a follow-up to *Clash of the Titans* planned called *Force of the Trojans*, which was inspired by Virgil's *The Aenid*. It would have featured the three-faced, six-handed goddess Hectate, the flights of Daedalus and Icarus, a colony of Cyclops, Furies, and Scylla and Charybdis.

Alas, amazingly no one wanted to fiancé it, and this incredible film was never made. Around this time, he worked extensively on getting another monster film, *People of the Mist*, off the ground. This too, was never green-lit. (I recommend Harryhausen's fabulous book *An Animated Life* for more details of these, and many other projects that sadly were never made, such as *The Hobbit*, Dante's *Inferno*, *The Laberinthodon*, *Beowulf*, *Food of the God*, *Conan*, a project for Hammer called *Deluge* and *Sinbad on Mars*! Perhaps someday someone will finally realise some of these fascinating projects).

Sadly, Harryhausen decided to retire, he felt (not without justification), that the world of film making had changed. I believe that Guillermo Del Toro has picked up Harryhausen's baton of fabulous imaginative creature features, and I would love to see Guillermo attempt a stop-motion feature, perhaps with Ray Harryhausen involved in some capacity. While there are people in the world with an imagination , Ray's films will also live on in the hearts of their audiences.

Nuada & Balor

While the mythological Balor was not the benign leader we see in *Hellboy II: The Golden Army*, Nuada is pretty true to the myths. In any case, Guillermo is merely following in the footsteps of the bards, scribes and storytellers that came before him, who so vividly kept the Celtic tales alive. Plus a cursory glance at any two sources of Celtic myth will reveal many differences in interpretation. That is as it should be! The teller feels the tale in his heart as well as his head, and thus, is following his own vision, through his own experience, culture and imagination. In doing so, Guillermo passes on the story to others, keeping these great tales alive in their hearts in turn. Truth is not always what is recorded in stone, it is sometimes, like right and wrong, something we simply know in our hearts to be true.

Balor, in Celtic mythology represents the powers of darkness, death and evil. A god of the underworld, he was said to have come from the Land of the Dead. He was (among other names) known as Balor of the Evil Eye, for the gaze of his one eye could slay like a thunderbolt all those he gazed upon with anger. In old age, his vast eyelid had to be lifted by his servant via a complicated system of pulleys and ropes so that he could turn his power on his enemies.

Balor's people were the Fomorians, and their enemies were the Tuatha De Danann, the people of Danu, the Earth Goddess. They built four great cities, Falias, Gorias, Finias, and Murias. In these cities they learned from four great sages, one for each city, and from each city they brought a magical treasure. From Falias came the stone called the Lia Fhail or Stone of Destiny, upon which the High Kings of Ireland stood when crowned, and which was supposed to confirm the election of the rightful monarch by letting out a mighty roar. The stone previously stood at Tara, but legend has it that it was stolen in the 13th century and is now the Coronation Stone at Westminster Abbey, which might explain the stone's current silence!

The second treasure of the Dananns was the powerful sword of Lugh of the Long Arm, of whom we shall hear more of later, this weapon came from the city of Gorais. From Finias came a magic spear, and from Murias the Cauldron of the Dagda, a vessel which was famous for being able to feed a horde of men without ever being emptied. With these possessions, according to the version given in the "Book of Invasions", the Tuatha De Danann, the people of Danu, came to Ireland. Their arrival in Ireland was noted by the previous settlers, the Firbolgs, who discovered the Dananns at their fortified camp in Moyrain.

The Firbolgs sent one of their warriors, named Sreng, to parley with the Dananns. In turn, the Dananns sent out a warrior named Bres to meet him. They both noted that the Dananns weapons were lighter and of superior workman ship, whereas those of the Firbolgs were heavier, blunter and more primitive. Bres suggested that the two tribes divide the country between them, and defend it against any future incoming tribes. They then swopped weapons and returned to their respective camps.

THE FIRST BATTLE OF MOYTURA

The Firbolgs, however, were not in the least impressed by weapons of the Dananns, and didn't see any need to give half their country away to a group of strangers and decided to refuse their 'generous' offer. The battle was joined on the Plain of Moytura (the Plain of Towers, so called for the number of ancient dolmans and other monuments that then covered the area) in the south of Co. Mayo, near the spot now called Cong.

The Firbolgs were led by their king, mac Erc, and the Dananns by Prince Nuada, later to be known Silver Hand, who got his name from an incident in this battle, where he had his hand severed at the wrist by the aforementioned warrior, Sreng, who, while he took Nuada's hand, Nuada in turn, took Sreng's head. By dint of their superior fighting skills, weapons and magic, the Dananns gained victory, while the Firbolg King retained only the part of Ireland it took to bury his remains in. Happily though, reasonable agreement (for the Dananns at least!) resulted : the Firbolgs were allotted the province of Connacht for their territory, while the Dananns took the rest of Ireland. Truly, to the brave belongs all!

THE EXPULSION OF KING BRES

Nuada of the Silver Hand could not continue as ruler of the Danaans, his mutilation forbade it, for no blemished man might be a king in Ireland. The Dananns therefore chose Bres, who was the son of a Danann woman named Eri, but whose father was unknown, to reign over them instead. This was another Bres, not the envoy who had negotiated with the Firbolgs and met his death at the battle of Moytura. Now Bres,

though strong and handsome, had no gift of kingship, for he not allowed the enemy of Ireland, the Fomorians, to renew their oppression and taxation in the land, but he himself taxed his subjects heavily too, and gave no generosity to chief and nobles and harpers.

Then, as now, lack of generosity and hospitality was always reckoned the worst of vices by the Irish, particularly if originated from a wealthy prince, who could afford better. One day there came to the court of Bres, the poet Corpry, who found himself housed in a small, dark chamber without fire or furniture, where, after long delay, he was served with three dry cakes and no ale. In revenge he composed a satirical quatrain on his churlish host. This misery monarch would rue the day that he served such a stingy supper to so wily a wit as Corpry, for while the swords of the Celts were mighty, their sharp tongues were mightier still."

"Without food quickly served,
Without a cow's milk, wheron a calf can grow,
Without a dwelling fit fro a man under a gloomy night.
Without means to entertain a bardic company.
Let such be the condition of Bres."

Poetic satire in Ireland has a magical power, kings dreaded it then, a do corrupt politicians, bankers and businessmen now. This quatrain of Corpry's was repeated with delight among the people. The satire was virulent that it caused great red blotches to break out all over Bres's face. This in itself constituted a blemish that could not be allowed in a king, thus, the Tuatha Dé Danann called upon Bres relinquish his kingship.

Meanwhile, because Nuada had received an artificial silver hand through the art of his physician Diancecht, or because as some versions of the legend say, a still greater healer, the son of Diancecht, had made the veritable hand grow again to the stump, he was chosen to be king in place of Bres. He was also known as Argetlámh (silver hand in ancient Gaelic).

Amusingly, the same healer had replaced the blind eye of one of Nuada's servants with that of a cat. In the long run this was of little benefit to the man for the eye retained its cat's nature and, when the man wished to sleep at night. The cat's eye was always looking out for mice, while it could hardly be kept awake during the day.

The furious Bres went in wrath and resentment to his mother Eri, and begged her to give him counsel and to tell him of his linage. Eri then informed him that his father was Elathan, a king of the Fomorians, who had come to her secretly from overseas, and when he had departed had given her a ring, telling her to give it to the man whose finger it would fit. She now brought forth the ring, and it fitted the finger of Bres, who went down with her to the strand where the his Fomorian father had landed and loved his mother, and together the two sailed for Bres's father's home.

Fomor is a word derived from two ancient Gaelic words meaning 'under sea'. The Fomors were held to be more ancient than the gods, before whom they were, destined to fall in the end. They were known as the "Offspring of chaos and old night", they were for the most part huge and mutated. Some had but one arm and one leg apiece, while others had the heads of goats, horses, or bulls.

The most famous and terrible was Balor, whose father was said to have been Buaranineach, that is "cow-faced", Balor combined in himself two classical roles of the Cyclops and the Medusa. Though he had two eyes, one was always kept shut, for it was so venomous that it slew anyone on whom its gaze fell. This malignant quality of Balor's was not natural to him, but was the result of an accident. Urged by curiosity, he once looked in at the window of a house where his father's wizards were preparing a magic potion, and the poisonous smoke from the cauldron reached his eye, infecting it with so much of its own deadly nature as it make it disastrous to others. Neither god not giant was immune from its danger;

so that Balor was only allowed to live on condition that that he kept his terrible eye shut.

On days of battle he was placed opposite the enemy, the lid of the destroying eye was lifted up with a hook, and its gaze withered all who stood before it, The memory of Balor lives on. In Ireland 'the eye of Balor' was the name for the evil eye. Stories are still told of Balor Beimann or 'Balor of the Mighty Blows', and Balor's Castle is the name of a curious cliff on Tory Island. This island off the coast of Donegal, was the Fomorian outpost upon earth, their real abode being in the cold depths of the sea. Bres complained to his father Elathan, its king, asking him to gather an army to re-conquer his throne. The Fomors assembled in council, Elathan, Tethra, Balor, Indech, and all the other warriors and chiefs, and they decided to invade Ireland with a great host, so that the people of the goddess Danu would never be able to resist them again.

At the same time, another assembly was also being held at Tara, the capital of the Tuatha Dé Danann. Nuada was celebrating his return to the throne by a feast to his people. While it was at its height, a stranger clothed like a king came to the palace gate. The porter asked him his name and errand. "I am called Lugh," he said. "I am the grandson of Daincecht by Cian, my father, and the grandson of Nalor by Ethniu, my mother." After explaining he was the Ildanach or 'master of all arts", he joined the Dananns, Nuada was impressed by his numerous talents, he knew he would be of great help against the Fomors. (In Celtic mythology, Lugh, represents the powers of light)

The Dananns great men stated the assistance they would give in the coming battle. Diancecht the Physician said he would completely cure everyone who was wounded, lest it be a head or spinal wound. Goibniu the Smith, would replace every weapon with a new one, his lances will never fail to kill. Three blows of his hammer would make a spear or a sword. Ogma the Champion would kill the King of the Fomors.

The Dagda would fight with 'force and craft. Wherever the two armies meet, I will crush the bones of the Fomors with my might mallet. For my mallet is a legend, a national institution. Many are the Fomor heads I will crush with it. They will not be satisfied with such carnage, but I will, and that is the main thing!"

While Mathgan and his sorcerors cursed them. "The very stones of Ireland will be like razors beneath their feet, we will turn their sap to tar." And the Druids promised streams of fire to harass them. "No water for to satisfy their thirst, their throats will be like a bed of nettles

When the Fomors sent the tax gatherers to 'Balor's Hill' to collect tribute to the Danann, all were killed. That was as it should be! The two sides gave each other time to prepare, then met on Midsummer Day. The people of the goddess Danu appeared in a flaming line, wielding their 'red-bordered, speckled and firm shields." Opposite to them were ranged the Fomors

Then battle commenced. Great was the sound of sword song in the air, shields were beaten like bodhrans (an Irish handheld drum, still in use today) to create martial music, and the Danann women mocked the appearance and manhood of the mutated horde arrayed in front of them. Another weapon used was the fearsome tathlum, a concrete ball that Irish warriors used to make out of the brains of dead enemies hardened with lime. The battle is related with a marvellous wealth of incident.

"Fearful indeed was the thunder, which rolled over the battlefield; the shouts of the warriors, the breaking of the shields, the flashing and clashing of the swords, of the straight ivory-hilted swords, the music and harmony of the 'belly-dart' and the sighing and winging of the spears and lances."

THE DEATH OF BALOR

Then the Fomorians, seeing they could

not defeat such warriors as the Tuatha De Danann in fair combat, brought on their champion, Balor. Beneath his lethal gaze fell Nuada of the Silver Hand, and many other brave warriors. But Lugh, seizing an opportunity when Balor's eyelid drooped through weariness, approached close to Balor, and as it began to lift once more, he hurled a tathlum into the eye, the ball sank into the creature's brain, and Balor lay dead! This epic deed was recorded by the bards of the time.

"A tathlum, heavy, fiery, firm,
Which the Tuatha De Danann had with them,
It was that broke the fierce Balor's eye,
Of old, in the battle of the great armies

The Fomrians were then totally routed, and it is not recorded that they ever again gained any authority or committed any extensive depredations in Ireland. While Nuada had lost his life in the process, his brave sacrifice had allowed Lugh to liberate his people.

Celtic Mythology can be interpreted on more than one level, for instance, this tale could be seen as a variation of the universal solar myth embodying the concept of the eternal conflict between the powers of Light (Nuada, Lugh, and the Tuatha De Danann) and the powers of Darkness (Balor and the Formorians), and it could also be seen as a tale of great heroism and imagination, from which we can draw strength and inspiration in our own lives, just as Guillermo did for *Hellboy II: The Golden Army.*

Hellboy II - Analysis

"It's an extraordinary film, that makes you remember what it's like to have an imagination."
Anna Walton

"This is Hamlet and King Lear and all those things rolled into one."
Ron Perlman

It's important to remember that *Hellboy II*, is the follow-up film to *Pan's Labyrinth*, and is just as important to Guillermo, a film he describes as truly dear. It's a Ray Harryhausen movie for the 21st century, one where Guillermo del Toro and Mike Mignola's vision mutates to create something strange and beautiful. Guillermo feels he was able to up the ante on his second *Hellboy* outing. "I think the set pieces are more varied. The creatures are more varied. They're funnier. The fights are very different. So, all in all, there are much more flavours than in the first one."

Originally, *Hellboy II* was going to feature Hellboy and the B.P.R.D fighting the legendary four titans on the four corners of the Earth, but this was abandoned when Guillermo and Mike Mignola decided to tell the story of Prince Nuada declaring war on mankind, and his quest to control the legendary Golden Army.

The use of puppets to tell the story of the origin of the Golden Army at the start of *Hellboy II* is both practical and innovative, as Guillermo explains. "This sequence was originally budgeted to be done live action, with a lot of characters, with a Lord of the Rings type feeling, big massive battles...And the budget came back, and we needed to comply to cost $85 million. So I said to them, let's do it with puppets. I came up with that idea because the kid was watching Howdy-Doody."

"So, if the imagination of the kid is with puppets, and the designs done exactly match the designs that are in the film then we can make the leap of it being his own dream of what it would look like....Also another thing that was interesting about doing it with puppets, texturally, its artistically much more

fulfilling, it has more much of an old world appeal to it...It also allowed for brutality, we could be very ruthless with the puppets and it was less violent than doing it with humans. At the same time I thought it would be much more entertaining, more beautiful. It was designed only in three colours, red, gold, and black, Those are the only colours in the entire puppet sequence an those are colours repeated in the boiler room sequence that echoes the father's throne room." I

It also allowed for the appearance of the Golden Army while still allowing them to have an impact at the film's conclusion. "I was not ruining it, I was not springing it so early in the movie. All of these advantages made the puppet sequence ideal." You also have to bear in mind that with the average cost for a superhero movie at the time being in the $150 million dollar mark, *Hellboy II* is an amazing achievement for its budget. Its true what the old saying says, a lot more was done for love than money.

When it came to money, Guillermo's challenge was to make it go as far as possible. "The challenge was to make the movie the size we wanted on the budget we had. Because, obviously, the budget is big, but it's not as big as some of the gigantic summer , so we're trying to make it look as big, if not bigger than those movies, within that budget....By comparison, the first movie had few sets."

When the young Hellboy, having heard the tale of the Golden Army, finally turns in to sleep, Guillermo has him surrounded by many of the elements that will feature in his later life. "You can see around Hellboy, already, what will make him what he is, adventure books, a six shooter. So, Hellboy grows up to be this kid, just much larger. He has his Samaritan, his gun...I love this detail that he's going to sleep and smiling hoping to dream about the Golden Army.

This is a good set-up for the film, Because the movie wants to have the wide-eyed perspective of that 12-year-old." And in a sense, the movie is very much about Guillermo's own 12-year-old self. "The movie has many homages to Ray Harryhausen, John Landis's *American Werewolf In London*, Bernard Herrmann, and all the adventure movies that meant so much to me when I was a kid."

Make no mistake, this is a special film to Guillermo. "I can indulge in my fetish of gears, fetish of underground places, of creatures. And it is in so many ways, a much more personal film, visually and artistically, than the first one, the first one was very dependent on a storyline that existed in the comics...unlike the first one, where a monster was unleashed in our world, we have our heroes travelling to the place where these things live."

Guillermo has constructed *Hellboy II* to share similar artistic and design ideas with *Pan's Labyrinth*. "The human world is made of straight lines and very boring shapes, very cold colours." The auction room can be seen to represent the human world, so the humans the magical world is only a commodity, worth only its dollar value, not for its true intrinsic value. "It's very clear to me that this movie came from the same place as *Pan's Labyrinth*. I wrote *Hellboy II* during some of the production and post-production of *Pan's Labyrinth*. It took me about two years to develop the screenplay." There is also a tendency to tell the story without words wherever possible. "With the textures, tell the story with the colours, tell the story with the cameras."

Guillermo wanted creatures that are even more varied and imaginative than the first film. "When you design a creature, all I want to feel is that this creature exists somewhere...create creatures that you feel are beautiful and attractive." Only one rule was laid down to the creature designers. "No aliens. Nothing that resembles something that would be remotely sci-fi. It has to have a stance and a sense of fantasy, that is not reminiscent of sci-fi type things...These creatures are creatures that are surviving in the sewers."

Luke Goss, who plays Prince Nuada, is impressed by what Guillermo has created. "It's the attention to detail. You can't help but respect filmmakers that create that environment so wonderfully effectively so that the audience can enjoy it. You know that they care about their viewers. They're caring

about what people are experiencing. Because there's so much that won't be seen but maybe it would just create that extra percentage that you need to really believe that you're there. When I was reading the script for the first time, I was like, 'Okay, that would be CG'. How wrong was I? Most things that you see on the screen, as far as things that are living, are alive in the sense that they've been created and another actor is bringing them to life."

Guillermo has included so many more creatures in this *Hellboy* movie that in the first one, and because so many of them are practical, they have a great presence. "I think we did a total of five creatures in the first movie. Here we've done a total of 32 or 33 creatures. So it's a much bigger scope for the film. When Mike Mignola read the Troll Market, I think he was against the idea. When he read it, he was mocking me, he was doing the music from the Cantina. But I told him, 'I'm gonna shoot it completely different than that. I'm gonna shoot it in a way we design a creature, we can design a great set, and we're gonna treat it mike it's not important. You know, because in the Cantina, every mask, every creature gets a close-up. Each one is displayed. And I thought, 'well, you know, that would be too close. Let's do it like we're following the characters around a real market.'"

Paternity and fertility are a strong theme, seen in the statue of the Earth Goddess at the auction that symbolises fertility, Hellboy's Big Baby gun, and the baby Hellboy saves, at a time where he doesn't realise he's become a father himself. Many of these themes are subliminal, for instance, you could say that the walls of the auction house are pregnant with Tooth Fairies

Prince Nuada , I believe ,doesn't want to taint himself with the weapons of the humans he despises (with good reason). So he uses the Tooth Fairies, his silver lance, and of course Mr. Wink, a one man army.

The question of identity is a big part then of *Hellboy II*, if the first *Hellboy* movie established that you are who you think you are, Guillermo sees the second one is more about who you belong to. "At the core, Hellboy has more in common with the magical world than the human world. At the core, Hellboy is one of them...The first movie was about Hellboy deciding he was human, and the second movie is about him saying 'maybe I do belong to the other side'." Hellboy truly wants the world, but the world doesn't want him. He wants the world to look past his face, as we all do, but it doesn't work out that way.

The Tooth Fairies are inspired by the writings of Arthur Machen (of whom the library in which we're introduced to Sammael in the first *Hellboy* movie is named after), and also Algernon Blackwood (whom the auction rooms in *Hellboy II* are named in honour of). They were also inspired by a short story entitled *Tasty Teeth* that Guillermo co-wrote with Mathew Rawlins for a *Hellboy* anthology, "based on a belief I had as a child that Tooth Fairies were actually creatures that fed on calcium." It also came from a desire to do very different fights from the first *Hellboy* movie. "I wanted to stage this very brutal attack. The enemies and fights in the movie

"What is this 'goth-look' you speak of?"

are in very stark contrast with the first one. In the first one, it was always Hellboy versus Sammael, then Hellboy versus the giant Cthulu creature."

Another of Guillermo's favourite subjects, insects, also provided inspiration. "This essentially is 'how do we get rid of an attack of insects?' I have a proclivity for insects, and Tooth Fairies are basically a mixture of Praying Mantis and the fairies from *Pan's Labyrinth*....There are thousands and thousands of them that descend upon them to eat them. They are nasty, wild, savage, little creatures that feed on bones and calcium. So they need to eat the whole human to get to the bone. So they're not pleasant... they don't leave coins either....They land on Abe's arm, and they start chewing, and you should see them taking bites like a little Romero zombie."

Originally Guillermo wanted the inside National Bank of Hungary was going to serve as a location on *Hellboy II*. "We could not shoot inside the National Bank of Hungary, they were very afraid. It was like shooting in Fort Knox. We were joking that they may not have thought there was such a movie as *Hellboy II*, and that we were really trying to rob the National Bank. In my mind that was not a bad idea to make the budget a little bigger because we were urgent need for more funding."

This big exciting adventure at the auction room is treated by Guillermo with as much importance as Liz's dilemma with her pregnancy. "She doesn't believe Abe. She doesn't believe the pregnancy test. She really doesn't want to be pregnant because the father is a sort of irresponsible oaf. He may be a charming guy, but is he ready to be a father? I believe this is as autobiographical as it gets. *Hellboy I* and *II*, every moment Hellboy lives, I have somehow lived. And I live Abe's romance, Hellboy's romance with Liz, Hellboy's desire to be a public figure, and the way he has to decide as she says, being loved by everyone or just the woman he loves. Those moments come in the life or everyone who is an artist or a public figure, and I've gone through it in different ways. Ultimately, I identify with every single problem Hellboy has ever had."

Guillermo shows that Time has not been kind to the fortunes of King Balor. ""The throne room echoes in many ways the throne room in the puppet sequence, but it's now the king's last days, and the machines are the big statement, the fact that these guys are holding court in a disused steam engine repair area...I did the sketch for the machine behind the King many years ago." So serious was Guillermo about the importance of this ,that he paid for the pipes behind the King from his own salary as production would not authorise it. "I wanted them very much in the movie to keep saying all this is an industrial space."

Guillermo wanted King Balor's people to have a very distinctive look. "The look of the elves, which is represented very much by the Princess. I wanted it to be of beauty and remoteness. Those huge feline eyes like lion's eyes that are very expressive, very powerful, but their faces are cracked like ivory and they all have a marking across the face, the royalty has a line across the face that only they have, the other elves don't have it."

Guillermo sees Prince Nuada as very principled and very much a force of

"No sister, you're wrong, your mascara does look better on me."

morally ambiguous, basically we should not applaud intolerance. It's a movie very much about letting people live. Hellboy is used to destroying things."

To me, Johan Krauss's suit is a reminder of reading Jules Verne's *20,000 Leagues Under the Sea* with its fabulous diving suits. The mouthpiece of Johan's helmet was from a design that

nature, almost a personification of nature in humanoid form. "The Prince is the only character in the film that has ideals. The villain in this movie has ideals. The heroes don't; Hellboy is really aloof, really a rascal. He has no allegiance morally or ideologically to the human race. Liz and Abe do not think twice about sacrificing the world for the people they love, which I completely agree is the human decision, the emotional decision, and the unlikely decision in a superhero movie. I wanted very much for the superheroes to be flawed and act like regular people would. I'm tired of listening to superheroes that are do-gooders and always do the right thing...To create the contrast between their way and the way it should be done is why we brought in the character of Johann who is absolutely the by-the-book nobody, in the sense that there's literally no body in Johan's body, he's the perfect bureaucrat. He has no face he has no body. He's just a voice and a bunch of ideas taken from a rule book..."

"The problem with the Prince is the way he enacts those ideals. The way he goes at it is tragic, it's flawed. But the beauty of it is, it reflects politically what is going on in the world, where we are essentially having one holocaust after another, having to choose between destroying an entire religion, an entire race, an entire country, or have them destroy us according to the way we have things presented to us. I wanted Hellboy to be

Guillermo had created for a proposed *Halo* movie. It had the "insect like movement and the side rotation and the steam coming out because that's the only way you can do a close-up on a helmet...It's telling you how the character works without stopping to do so."

His helmet cleverly allows him to show emotion to a degree, something further articulated by keeping his hands and body constantly in motion. It's amazing to be able to feel empathy for what technically is steam in a suit, but that's the magic of Guillermo's universe. It appeals to the outsider in all of us. The helmet also has a very insectile quality. Johann is a marvellous creation, when he possesses the Golden Army warrior, he literally is the ghost in the machine, the *Deus ex Machina*.

Hellboy II also shares the imagery of a neon cross in the street with *Mimic*. The Shuftain Glasses are inspired by an old pulp that Guillermo read as a child." I'm obviously obsessed with that and I obviously have a fascination with Victorian machinery." It also demonstrates one of *Hellboy II*'s primary themes, "to reveal the true nature of things... Things that are hidden and come to the surface, revealing the true nature of things, which is a theme of the movie."

Hellboy's confrontation with the Fragglewump reveals the soft side of Hellboy's character without any need for unnecessary exposition. Hellboy hates trolls

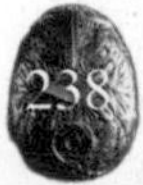

and she returns the compliment calling him a demon. Guillermo uses this scene to show us the kinder side to Hellboy's character. "We reveal the Troll bag lady...one of my favourite characters in the film. I wanted very much for this evil old lady to expand her mouth to eat a cat, which is the last straw in Hellboy's book. He will allow anything but not for a cat to be harmed. I think that's a really nice trait in the character of Hellboy...I want to try and define Hellboy in the first movie and in this one, and Abe and everyone, not so much by stopping the movie and having a character moment, as through showing their decisions and how they act. They are efficient enough to know the Trolls are afraid of canaries according to old European lore."

That the Troll market is hidden behind the 'Happy Cow' meat locker is in itself a subliminal message on Guillermo's part. "The idea of the Troll Market existing behind the corroded wall of a meat locker, and then descending by a ramp into this subterranean area, is something I was attracted to. Because humans in a strange way are happy cows for the Elf Prince. We are apes, we are not worthy of being the species that is the dominant species on Earth, and I wanted to show these things in the disdain he has for the human race, and part of it was, lets locate this entrance behind a sign that says Happy Cows."

When Johann opens the lock, he is not only showing Hellboy that brains are better than brawn in some situations, but it's also letting us know he control inanimate objects, something that becomes very relevant at the films climax when he possesses one of the Golden Army.

Hellboy is learning that how he imagined the humans would receive him and the harsh reality are two entirely different things, they lose no time in telling him he's ugly (from characters you couldn't exactly describe as oil paintings). Guillermo is showing us a 'be careful what you wish situation' here. "He thinks he hates monsters, and he thinks he loves humans. He has just been insulted by the humans he wanted very much to belong to."

The Troll Market – "All inhuman life is there."

"Then as part of a greater learning curve, he's shown a contrast, the world of the Troll Market, where no one calls him names, no one hates him, no one stares, and he fits right in. It's a huge contrast to the drab world of the humans. A great revelation for Hellboy, the world above is all straight lines, blue and cold colours, now all is round forms, arches, circles, and is vey much alive...We come into a beautiful living place, all teaming with things flying back and forth, all the colours of the spectrum, giant monsters in the background crossing the frames, the fairies literally from *Pan's Labyrinth* are everywhere. People are selling and buying, and talking and yelling, it's so great!"

Guillermo is setting the stage for an evolution in Hellboy's character. "He is still going to get into a couple of fights, but then as a character, he is going to have a big 'to be or not to be' moment with the elemental..." After which. "He is finally going to have a moral dilemma, and at the end of the movie, he says to the Prince: 'I win, you live'. And that in a character like Hellboy who is just used to destroying everything, is perhaps a modest arc, but an arc nevertheless. He does learn something, and I think its really important in superhero movie, instead of the destruction of the bad guy by the hero, is the hero allowing the bad guy to live...not having to choose one holocaust or another but give the chance for both to co-exist."

The tumour baby is also an image of paternity for Hellboy, and Guillermo was inspired by a character that appeared in Richard Corben's Fantagor. "I thought it would be nice to have a super-cute baby that was really a parasitic twin...like his own ventriloquists dummy." There is also a nice H.P. Lovecraft reference in the creatures you see plucking fairies from the air to eat. "The creatures in the background are from *Mountains of Madness*. There are the Old Ones, H.P. Lovecraft's Old Ones."

Eamonn Butler, animation supervisor at Double negative expands further on these Lovecraftian creatures. "Guillermo is a huge fan of H.P. Lovecraft, massive fan, and he's always trying to jam some kind of creature design for H.P Lovecraft into his movies. If you look at all of his movies, you'll see the influence is in there. So we invented a couple of shots where we start high looking up at a pixie coop in the troll market and two Lovecraftian creatures walk by. One picks one of these creatures out of the air, and eats it, then leaves, and you never see it again."

The Troll Market is an amazing creation, like a beautiful painting, every time you look at it, you see some previously unnoticed detail to delight the eye and entrance the soul (It reminds me of the underworld of John Carpenter's *Big Trouble in Little China*, re-imagined on a massive scale.) A lot of this is down to the wide variety of influences Guillermo used in its creation.

"The inspiration for the Troll Market came mostly from Moorish, Arabic architecture, Eastern European, Far East, and one of the things we did very consciously in the movie was take Celtic motifs, the things you usually associate with fairy tales and fairy folklore, and take these motifs and twist them into almost Hindu Japanese...twisting these motifs into different cultures, creating hopefully a unique look for the Troll Market. This beautiful set is almost like a shrine in which the characters stand and talk."

It's also amazing how much of the Troll Market, and *Hellboy II* in general, was shot for real, CGI being used when necessary (and then with as much skill and love as Ray Harryhausen did in his day.

The CGI on *Hellboy II* is outstanding, take a bow, Double Negative, for doing such a fine job). This is all for the better, because Guillermo understands modern cinema audiences are jaded by the over-reliance on CGI. "One of the challenges that was interesting was that we knew we wanted to create an entire troll market, which frankly, those sets alone, should have skyrocketed the budget thirty, forty per-cent, but we kept the movie controlled, and that was the big challenge, to keep an eye on the creative, and keeping an eye on the physical responsibilities of getting the movie to a good point."

The Troll Market is full of curved lines, whereas the B.P.R.D is straight lines and edges. In Guillermo's films, the human world is usually straight lines, while the magical world is curved. "The colour of the market was so uniform...From the earliest concept design, we knew that the depth was gonna be created by steam and colour and light, because otherwise you get no sense of perspective. If you lit it all the same colour, it would really muddle into a single place...From the moment of the conceptual drawings, we knew that we wanted air-conditioner units peppering the old European facades, because I think it was a really nice contrast to have modern AC units."

It's fair to say that on *Hellboy II*, Guillermo really let his imagination loose. "On *Blade II* or *Hellboy I*, I was self-censoring myself much more than I thought. But after *Pan's Labyrinth*, I said, 'let's let loose the hair'."

A trait in Guillermo's films is that he likes the monsters so much, it becomes infectious. Mr. Wink is a good example of this. "I very much wanted the character to be almost cute before he died. He's arguing about who's going to pay for his hand. Obviously the Prince underpays Mr. Wink severely and he's very angry. He must have a terrible dental plan, a terrible health plan, look at the gums!" There seems to be no limit on Guillermo's imagination, save perhaps that of budget. "The idea is to go more surreal. We don't want to do stuff that you feel you've seen. It's about what we can do with not so much money, but with a lot of creativity in doing and applying those things. Because I really think this movie could make a difference in the way that creatures are designed...Because I think the camera likes to see something real, and the audience, even if they don't realise, even if they think it's CG, or even if they think the CG is real, they get a sense that we're making it up. Mr. Wink is over seven-and-half feet tall, and he's massive and it's practical..."

"We are literally taking animatronics as far as I have seen them taken...If the creature is physically impossible to get with make-up and prosthetics and animatronics. If it's, in other words, too small or too large, then it goes to CGI. And even then, we try to keep an element or two. If the creature is the right size and it can be executed by performers, then we go physical."

Johann Krauss, while not being as in-you-face spectacular as say, Mr. Wink, is nevertheless a marvellous creation on Guillermo's part. "The idea was to have a character that was very much a guy that goes by the book. Johann is Prussian, very Teutonic, and Hellboy is completely the opposite, he's a disaster! Johann tries to direct his attention to the manual and the procedures, and obviously he fails miserably."

The casting of Prince Nuada and Princess Nuala was crucial, with both Anna Walton and Luke Goss putting in fine performances. Anna Walton gives her character a haunting otherworldly empathy, while Luke Goss brings great sympathy and weight to Nuada.(As well as enduring many hours a day in make-up, then putting in long days on the set, an actor of great dedication). Guillermo saw the right casting as crucial.

"The Princess was very hard to find. We needed an actress that looked otherworldly, and talked and behaved like royalty but not in a smug way, but that she seems so exquisitely fragile, and exquisitely raised, delicate, and exuded royalty without having an attitude. The brother and the sister, they are literally opposite sides of the coin... The Prince and Princess represent sort of one person, who is divided by their conscience. She is everything he isn't, she's sensitive and kind and has empathy...The Prince, essentially, is like Geronimo. He's like the last of a race, or the last warrior of a race. And the humans are pushing and pushing the magical creatures away into the outskirts of society, the underworld. And the Prince essentially says, 'no more'. He has the key to awaken the Golden Army. So, it's essentially like if Geronimo had the key to a nuclear bomb."

The look of the Princess went through many variations before Guillermo decided on the version you see in the film. "She was too spooky before. She looked like Bride of Marilyn Manson!"

Anna Walton has her own take on her role. "For Princess Nuala, it was important that she looked pure and clean in a way, because she's the antithesis of the Prince. The Princess can sometimes look very beautiful, but then also sometimes look quite frightening. I think that's exactly how it should be, because if it's otherworldly, and it just looked beautiful, then it would be too modern. It has to be more than that, and I think an element of danger is good."

Doug Jones, as you'd expect, has a unique insight into Guillermo's creations. "I think a trademark of Guillermo's is creatures that have an organic edge to them, and also an architectural edge to them." Doug's Cathedralhead character cleverly embodies both these traits.

Guillermo wanted the battle with the plant elemental to mark a turning point in Hellboy's life. "I always liked the idea of a council of elementals that governs the Earth. Imagine the creature's horror at seeing all the buildings smothering the Earth." Originally the idea was to have a beanstalk and a giant, in common with the fairy tale element of the story. But Mike Mignola hated the idea so instead Guillermo suggested, "why don't we make the bean stalk itself the elemental, make the beanstalk unfold and the elemental is essentially concealed in that beanstalk. It is one and the same and I like the idea of one thing that the bean has in common, is visually the bean has a central glowing vein...I think the elemental becomes a really moving creature that represents nature."

"This again goes against the grain of most superhero movies, Normally the superhero destroys the creature right at the time the creature is most dangerous and the hero saves the day and it becomes a big event...It actually grows into making the creature look defenceless at the end. Yes, he is destroying buildings, throwing cars. But he is the last of his race....Hellboy realises that the things that he is defending are, in the words of the Prince, 'shopping malls and parking lots', and the thing he is destroying is a magnificent old thing that never will be again."

"So the fact that we create an action scene that goes against the audience satisfaction of 'we killed the monster' is pretty insane, especially in a summer movie. I think it was very worthy to take these risks with this movie, more so even then the first one where we had a lot of things going against the grain. It's really almost an anti-superhero movie on this one in my mind, because I show Hellboy destroying not only a very beautiful thing but when he finally faces his 'beautiful' humans, they are not grateful at all to him, they actually catcall him and throw him a stone. It's a really sad humiliation for him...Hellboy learns a lot more in this movie than in the first one." Particularly he learns that wanting to be popular has the opposite effect, it's often the way in life, that what we most want, we either push it away, or if we get it, we find it's a poisoned chalice.

Many people, myself included, can see an ecological theme, but this may not have been intentional on Guillermo's part. Nevertheless, the Plant Elemental is "a very risky image to do in a summer movie, the fact that the creature that was destroying the city a few minutes ago is now blooming into a flower. It's a pretty insane, pretty surreal image. But I wanted to pepper this movie with surreal Dada-ist images as much as I would in *Pan's Labyrinth*, to keep the construction , the camera, the images very fresh, very risky, very edgy, very not regular summer movie, the aesthetics of the film. That is a political and a content stance that I was pretty happy with to do an 'anti-summer' summer movie..."

"The beauty of this creature is that essentially he was just doing what the Prince told him to do. Once he starts growing into the building with his blood, and his blood grows moss everywhere, you realise that with the pollen flowing in the air, which is another image the movie has in common with *Pan's Labyrinth*...hopefully in that scene you actually realise the world would be much more beautiful, if, instead of buildings the elemental had unleashed nature. But the movie's theme is not ecological. I think it is however in favour of saying the most mundane things...the most mundane concerns are destroying beauty, and they're destroying spirituality, and they're destroying ideas, and they're destroying magic, they're destroying nature...the things we're destroying with our mundane concerns."

"It's not just an ecological film for me. It's a film about how we can forget about anything sublime when we're worried about the most mundane and frankly forgettable things. I think the things that we defend, the

fact that we can go to war over oil, over gas mileage and our supremacy as a car culture and still go to the supermarket in a hummer to do the grocery shopping. These are things I just wanted to poise in what was not a single angle, ecological or political, just phrase them in a nice fairy tale. Because that's what I think *Hellboy II* is at the end of the day, pretty much defined by the prologue, it is like *Pan's Labyrinth*, a fairy tale for adults."

"It is a movie that nevertheless many kids can watch because they may not get all the supposed subtexts or the content or the idea. But if I was 11 years old and I watched this fairy tale, I would maybe not get the adult content or the ideas, but I would get the colours and the shapes and the monsters and the glee that goes into the creation of the monsters. It would be the biggest compliment of my life if this movie grows with some kids. I don't care if it's 10, 1, or a 1000...and they visit the world Mike Mignola has created so brilliantly and beautifully in the comics."

Liz's character grows greatly in *Hellboy II*, despite her own worries, she is willing to stand in front of a gun to protect the man she loves. For someone who hates being looked at, the fact that she's prepared to stand in front of a crowd and show her love for Hellboy shows great courage. Guillermo notes this change in Liz's character. "This is a beautiful moment, because in the first film, it was all about Hellboy defending Liz... Instinctively he does want to be with him. She knows he is the guy who makes the world make sense. More and more she becomes his saviour. It's a complete reversal of the roles from the first movie to the second."

The old black and white classic playing on the television in Hellboy's quarters as Liz dresses his wound is a very deliberate homage on Guillermo's part. "A beautifully nihilistic declaration of principle by the Frankenstein monster. 'We belong dead' because we cannot belong alive. It's one of the most beautiful films ever made, *Bride of Frankenstein.*"

The poem that Princess Nuada recites harkens back to *The Devil's Backbone*, with Guillermo making a poetic connection between the two films. "This is the same poem that the Professor recites to the dying Carmen in *Devil's Backbone*. It's Alfred Lord Tennyson. One of his most beautiful poems. It talks about love that would be undying, even when you're dying. There is a certain beauty and hopelessness to the poem that is inexplicable."

One of the most touching things in *Hellboy II* to me was the romance between Abe and Princess Nuala, which effects his character so profoundly, he goes from agreeing with Krauss to being a rebel with a cause. Guillermo has really expanded Abe's character arc, with his almost courtly love for the Princess. "He is so hungry for human contact, for others to like him...He has the most wonderful relationship with the Princess. The beauty of that romance is they don't need to know each other for weeks or years or decades. Their hands touched and they know each other the moment their hands touched. Obviously it's a platonic idealised form of romance. The purest form of romance, to know the other at touch."

Now, the fight between Hellboy and Krauss was designed by Guillermo to show how "beautifully silly it is everyday at the BPRD...like nothing is happening..." Even though "you have an invisible man made of gas and a red demon in the locker next to you." Johann wins the fight because he is in control and Hellboy is not, but even so when Liz tells Krauss that he is no longer human, it hurts him and he sets out to prove her wrong (there's also a nice humanising touch where we see him making miniature furniture and clocks).. Like Myers says in the first *Hellboy* movie, we love people for their defects. "If my movies are in favour of anything, it's fallibility. The characters that have the huge ideals, and act in a steamroller way, those are the dangerous ones. The characters that are more at peace with their flaws are the characters I love the most."

Guillermo has included a little reminder of the first movie that also points to the third *Hellboy* movie. "The Kroenen mask in the glass behind Hellboy that is later observed by Johann is seen because in case there is a third movie, there is a link between Johann and Kroenen. They did know each other. How, and how much, we may never find out if

there's not a third movie."

The sing-song between Abe and Hellboy has to be unique in this genre of movie...or indeed any movie, but in a film where you have a blue fish-man, a red demon, and a man made of gas, anything is possible. Guillermo cites this as one of the reasons he made the movie.

"Along with the elemental, this is one the reasons I made the movie...the idea that you can do a superhero movie where two characters have a beer and tackle a Barry Manilow song. These two guys are the most unlikely Barry Manilow duet, Abe is supposed to be cerebral and exquisite and he only listens to Vivaldi and Beethoven, and he would never sing Barry Manilow. Hellboy is a gruff tough 350 pound gorilla, listens to Al Green and Tom Waits, and he would never sing Barry Manilow, and yet, in my experience, with a couple of beers and the right sentimental frame of mind, you can't help but hum this thing!"

We have to give great respect to Ron Perlman, Doug Jones, Brian Steele and all the performers wearing SFX make-up, as well as the weight and discomfort, they often can't see or hear properly, yet they put in performances that would put Shakespearean actors to shame. Something Guillermo very much appreciates. "I'm very proud of my actors, because they really deliver. I love them, I thank them, and I salute them."

In the confrontation between Hellboy and Prince Nauda in the B.P.R.D library, we see Hellboy and the Prince are connected by the colours of their clothes, Hellboy has more in common with the world of the Prince than he does with the world of the humans. Like everyone Hellboy has always wanted to be accepted, now the world of the humans has scorned him, where does he go, the answer he eventually discovers is to Liz, the one who loves him. Here too we see in the colour blue the connection between the Princess and Abe, right down to the blue-covered book. That Hellboy can be mortally injured here is very significant to Guillermo. "In setting up the third movie, if there ever was one, Hellboy's mortality will come back."

In Guillermo's world it is the character's sincerity that counts. "I love them because they are written to be made of small gestures. Hellboy is a very coarse character, but he has a beautiful, beautiful heart." We see this when Liz tells Hellboy he's the best man, and a tear rolls down his cheek. "Because, A-he is not a man, and B-now he is realising perhaps that he doesn't want to be a man, he doesn't want to belong, it's theme that is sated throughout the film visually."

Johann and Manning's character is expressed by their betrayal of the hero that saved the day, Hellboy. Johann at least is capable of change, and proves it, whereas Manning is one of those all too common people with no empathy for anyone else, and an incredibly low-level of self-awareness. If anything he's devolved since the first *Hellboy* into a spineless character, even more selfish and obnoxious than in the first film. While Abe, as a result of being in love for the first time, is willing to betray everyone to save the woman he

Hellboy in action this page and opposite

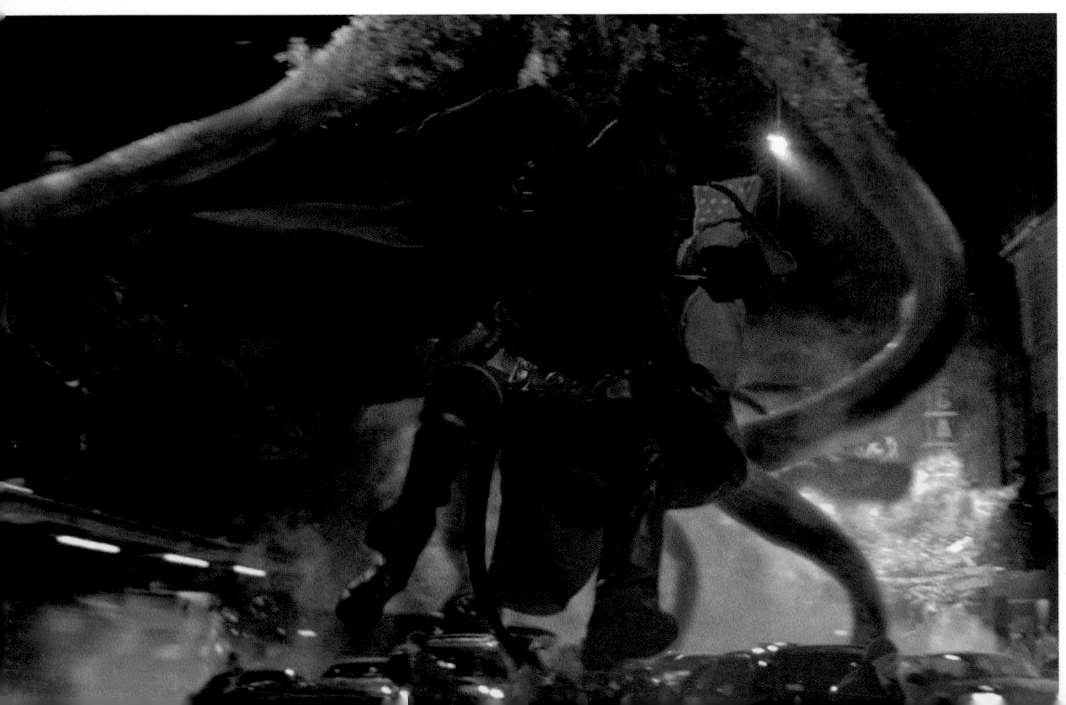

loves.

The Stone Giant in Ireland is what Guillermo describes as "the Harryhausen moment", specifically inspired by the awakening of Talos in *Jason and the Argonauts*. "Talos is perhaps by favourite Harryhausen creature ever, followed very closely by the skeletons in Jason, I wanted the wide shots, majestic shots of a Harryhausen picture." And the tooth fairy autopsy scene was inspired by the homunculi in the Sinbad movie "done in a similar way that Harryhausen would stage them" Danny Elfman was also inspired by Harryhausen musical collaborator Bernard Herrmann on scoring Hellboy II.

The colour scheme for the Angel of Death was specifically chosen by Guillermo. "Red and gold because this is the particular Angel of Death of Hellboy. I love that idea that each of us has an Angel of Death that awaits for us at the right moment. He meets us and says 'are you gonna go out this way? Or are you gonna go out that way?"

The Angel of Death has to be one of the most awe-inspiring creations in the entire fantasy genre as a whole. I feel she already knew what the outcome was going to be, and has been waiting for aeons to see it pass. Perhaps she was once beautiful but has over years become what we see now. The hard crescent of the Angel's face is reminiscent of the halo from an old Catholic religious painting. Guillermo is of course very inspired by Catholic imagery, particularly of the Mexican variety.

"The wings come from an old design in the early 1990s, the idea of the wings with the eyes. That comes in and of itself from medieval engravings and Mexican baroque carvings and Mexican baroque paintings, murals that depict certain cherub, certain archangels, certain seraphims with eyes or mouths in the feathers...And the idea that the Death is blind. Death does not care who it's gonna take or if he lives or not. Neither does the Goblin...the Goblin just wants his little trinket."

Liz has the hardest decision to make in the entire movie, as it not only effects her and Hellboy, and their unborn children, but the entire world. Liz makes the only decision she can make, she loves Hellboy and chooses him. Guillermo sees this as important in the set-up of a third *Hellboy* film. "It's essentially a Faustian bargain, that if there were ever another movie would come to a very tough conclusion."

Guilermo speaks very highly of Mike Mignola. "He is not only the most generous landlord of the *Hellboy* universe, allowing me to decorate his penthouse with colours that perhaps he would not like, but also as a partner, as a creative energy in the films, he is just very generous and giving."

The influence of *Cronos* comes to bear on the Golden Army and in response I see the Golden Army as a cross between the Golem and the *Terminator* endoskeleton as imagined by Ray Harryhausen). Guillermo explains his inspiration. "I wanted them to be like eggs. I love the idea of this eggshell container of massive proportions." And a myth also provided inspiration. "I always thought about them to have the physicality of a Golem...Mike Mignola and I fell in love with these little metallic golems that were sold in Prague"

The Golden Army robots look like they could actually work as well as look fabulous. "They had to actually mechanically work because you're seeing the naked skeleton. Sounds easy, but I assure you it's like designing a car. In other words, if there was actually an engine in those robots, they would work. They mechanically make sense. I think its one of the best pieces of animation in years. The ribs move down, and you see fire, and you see gears, red-hot gears, moving inside. The light pushes through, and it backlights the eyes." The Golden Army share a powerful languid reassurance of strength with the legendary golems.

"They are not in a hurry to get you because they will get you. They're not in a hurry to defend themselves because they'll put themselves back together." And they don't care who hold the crown. "The Golden Army was meant to be a form and function thing, where they are like living breathing weapons. That is, essentially beasts that serve whoever the master is at the time."

As part of Guillermo's hands on approach. "Everything in film is shot first unit."

Hellboy's refusal to kill Prince Nuada marks Guillermo's conclusion of his own personal story arc, "This is the moment where Hellboy learns his lesson and allows him to live, and it's a beautiful moment, and hopefully, the final sacrifice by the sister who knows her brother will never stop is hopefully more surprising and more moving because of that."

Here we have Guillermo creating small emotional dramas to unfold in a vast place, the scale is massive which makes the character look insignificant, "they look like music box figures' though they most certainly are not insignificant to those that love them. "The heroine dying and the lines on the floor are meant to echo *Pan's Labyrinth* in feeling." The moment where Abe and the Princess touch hands and share each others souls before she dies is utterly hearty-breaking. This is a moment, the most beautiful for me...romantic kiss in the history of these two little characters, they completely fuse with each other before she dies, they completely understand each other."

Guillermo uses the music to further open our wells of emotion. "This music cue, is perhaps one of my favourites that Danny Elfman created for the film. I find it moving and beautiful, at the same time very discreet, and it grows into this huge melodic unabashed, unashamed melodrama, to be shameless, and I encourage anyone working in the movies to be shameless."

To me, the sight of Abe crying really reaches a common emotional core we all share but are frightened to articulate. "And that little detail of Abe crying is significant because he said before that he didn't think he could cry: 'I don't think I have tear ducts'. And this is the first time Abe Sapian has cried and he cries for her, for the loss.' Interestingly in the mythology of the *Hellboy* comics, the tank Abe was originally found floating in was composed of a saline solution very similar to human tears...

Hellboy is tempted by the crown for a second but Liz takes it off him, part of what Guillermo sees as her growing strength of character. "She's the adult, he's the kid, and she destroys the whole crown. It's great that they didn't allow it to be misused or misuse it themselves."

Hellboy II, despite the momentous events that have occurred, and the portents of even great tragedies in the future (which very much reflects the uncertainty of the world we live in today), affecting the whole world, still

ends on an optimistic note. This chapter of Hellboy ends an era, who knows what the future holds (for us, as much as our heroes). Guilermo carefully orchestrated this ending. "I wanted the ending to be like an Alexander Korda movie. I wanted to have a sunset fell and a really golden feel to the finale of the movie. Hellboy has now taken a position. He knows he doesn't belong to the humans. He belongs to Liz. He does not belong to the monsters. He belongs to Liz. And he makes his vows to her, and his child, he doesn't know, children." He's not the only one to make a decision. "

Johann and Abe side with Hellboy and walk away. They walk away from the B.P.R.D, the institution, and start a nomad life...I wanted very much to wend the movie with one little surprise, a little touch of Hellboy learning he's going to be the father of more than one kid."

Hellboy II is important not just for the aforementioned reasons but because it sets the stage for Guillermo's future, being able to meld the personal vision of his small films with large scale big budget film making, creating work that is entertaining and beautiful.

Hellboy II ends with a nice little in-joke by Guillermo. "To end with Barry Manilow was pretty clear from the earliest stage of the screenplay...This ends a movie that is as close to my heart as possible. *Pan's Labyrinth*, *The Devil's Backbone*, and *Hellboy II*, those are my favourite movies that I've made. The experience of shooting this film was horrendous, nightmarish, horrible nights, horrible days, against time, against budget, freezing, coughing, getting sick...But the result is a movie I absolutely love and everyone that worked on it was a hero!"

To conclude, *Hellboy II* is a very special film, to Guillermo and his audience. It marks the point where his films start becoming seriously epic in scale and ambition, and yet marvellously, still personal to him, and us. That to be is true cinematic alchemy. Guillermo can see that magic and imagination are struggling for existence in the 21st century, and he is helping in to survive, finding a home in his films and from their into our imagination and hearts, where, as long as we live, the magic will too.

CELTIC MYTHS AND LEGENDS

The characters of Nuada and Balor in *Hellboy II: The Golden Army* are inspired by the tales of the gods and heroes of the Celtic people. Scholars have classified the myths and legends, according to their subject matter, into groups called cycles. These groups are the Mythological, Ulster, Fenian, and Historical cycles.

THE MYTHOLOGICAL CYCLE

This cycle tells how tribes of people from mainland Europe invaded Ireland. Irish myths describe the arrival of a tribe of people in Ireland, led by a chieftain called Partholon. This tribe introduced skills like gold-working and brewing. Later, other tribes invaded Ireland in turn. The most famous of these were the Tuatha Dé Danann (people of the goddess Danu), who had great skills in many areas. The Tuatha Dé Danann eventually became the gods of the Celts.

The most important of the Celtic gods were the Dagda and Lugh. The Dagda was a god of many skills. The word Dagda means 'good god', meaning good at many tasks. The Celts gave him titles such as All-Father and Lord of Perfect Knowledge. The Dagda was coarse and carried a huge club, and was very popular indeed with the ladies. He could kill nine men with a blow from one end of his club, and restore them to life with the other end. He also had a great cauldron, which was always full of food. For the Celts, a cauldron symbolised plenty. The Dagda's club and cauldron symbolised the basic qualities that the Celts sought in their gods, the power to protect them from their enemies and the power to provide them with food.

The god Lugh also had magical weapons. He carried a sling and a spear. He too had many skills, which he used for the well being of his people. Several places on the mainland of Europe, such as Lyon in France, have been named after him.

Manannán MacLir, a sea-god had a magic spear that killed any person it

struck, this spear would not return to him until it had tasted the blood of an enemy. He also had a magical boat that carried him wherever he wanted to go on sea. He helped to provide the Tuatha Dé Danann with pork from his magic herd of pigs that returned to life after being killed and eaten. The Isle of Man (Inis Manann in Irish) was named after him.

Unlike the Gods of the Greeks and Romans, a Celtic god did not, generally, have one specific function. The Celts, for instance, did not have a god of war equivalent to the Roman god Mars. But the Celtic god Goibniu was and exception. He was the blacksmith of the Tuatha Dé Danann.

THE ULSTER CYCLE

This describes the exploits of the Ulaid (Ulstermen), who were ruled by King Conchobar MacNessa from the fort of Emain Macha, near the present-day town of Armagh in Northern Ireland. The heroes of these sagas are called The Red Branch Champions. The heroes were a group of aristocratic warriors whose duty it was to defend their people. In the stories, they are described as essentially human, but they had superhuman powers. Many of them were sons of gods or goddesses, and they represent the Celtic ideal of a warrior.

The central figure of the Ulster cycle is the hero Cuchulainn, who is said to have been the son of Lugh (these Gods and Goddesses got around!). He had superhuman powers from birth and soon became the champion at the court of Conchobar. He travelled to many parts of Ireland and Scotland, and explored the world of the Celtic supernatural. When fighting he became filled with a berserker battle frenzy, and then he was invincible. Many of his exploits are described in the Táin Bó Cuailnge (Cattle Raid of Cooley), which is the tale of an attempt by the army of Queen Medb of Connacht to steal a brown bull from Ulster.

The goddess Macha had put a curse on the men of Ulster, so that in times of great peril they lay helpless for nine days. Cuchulainn alone escaped this curse, perhaps because of who his father was. He went on to defend Ulster single-handed against Medb's soldiers until the other warriors recovered.

Many heroes in Irish mythology were subject to obligation and prohibitions called geasa (singular, geis). In certain circumstances, the hero had to carry out certain acts, or had to avoid performing others. Generally, when a hero found himself in a situation where one of his geasa contradicted another, his life would soon be at an end.

For example, one of Cuchulainn's geasa forbade him to pass a hearth without tasting the food being cooked on it. But another of his geasa prohibited him from consuming the flesh of a dog. Travelling to what would be his last battle, he met three old women cooking a dog over a fire. One of the women gave him a shoulder of the dog to eat, and he accepted her offer, realising that his death was drawing near.

THE FENIAN CYCLE

Is named after Finn MacCool (Fionn Mac Cumhaill in Irish), the leader of one of the bands of roving warriors called Fianna. Fianna comes from the Irish word fian meaning a band of soldiers. The stories of the cycle describe the exploits of Finn and his men. Unlike the Red branch Champions, the Fianna lived, hunted and fought in organised groups. They protected the country against invaders, and in return, they received special privileges. A young man who wished to become a member of the Fianna had to undergo difficult tests to prove his strength and courage.

Many stories now included in the Fenian cycle do not refer directly to the Fianna. According to folk tradition, these stories were written by Finn's son Oisín. The cycle is also known as the Ossianic cycle.

Originally, Ossianic lore in its oral form was largely part of folk tradition, and it contrasts with the Ulster cycle, which had an aristocratic background. The

Ossianic stories contain many descriptions of the countryside and the pleasures of outdoor life. Many of these stories are noted for their power and beauty, and are similar to those of other cycles. The Pursuit of Diarmaind and Gráinne resembles the story of Naoise and Deirdre in the Ulster cycle. Gráine, who was bethrothed to Finn, caused Diarmaid, one of Finn's men, to elope with her. Finn and his men, pursued the two lovers and finally brought about Diarmaid's death.

THE HISTORICAL CYCLE

Is a group of stories mainly about various kings, but particularly about High Kings of Ireland, such as Conn of the Hundred Battles and Cormac Mac Airt. The cycle was an attempt to record genuine history. It describes the origins of dynasties, and battles and other incidents relating to kings and their families.

In Britain, traditions developed around a leader called Arthur, who emerged in the literature of Europe as King Arthur. These traditions were probably based in part on events in the life of a war leader who successfully led Celtic forces against the Saxons after the Romans had left Britain. To these accounts of actual events were added mythological material centred on one or more Celtic gods.

The fact that these stories are still being interpreted today in films such as *Hellboy II: The Golden Army* is a testimony to their power, beauty, and their essential truth, the truth we have in our hearts, not our heads.

Hellboy - Animated Films

"Mike[Mignola] is at a point in his life when he can chose what he wants, and trust me, having worked with him, we're gonna go on to some very strange places!"
GUILLERMO DEL TORO

"There's no upside to cutting the dead any slack."
HELLBOY

Following the comic books, text stories and live-action movie, animating Hellboy was a logical move, in fact at one point, frustrated by the difficulties of getting Hellboy the movie off the ground, Guillermo considered an animated version of the first *Hellboy* movie (An option once considered for his dream project *Mountains of Madness*). Thankfully we now have the best of both worlds.

The first animated *Hellboy* film is *Sword of Storms*. Guillermo Del Toro and Mike Mignola serve as creative producers, so we know 'Big Red' is in good hands. The film was directed by Phil Weinstein and Tad Stones, and scripted by Stones and Matt Wayne, based on a story by Mike Mignola and Stones. *Sword of Storms* was nominated for a prime time Emmy. Interestingly, Guillermo and Mignola once considered a Japanese setting for the second *Hellboy* movie.

After an exciting opening sequence with *Hellboy*, Abe and Liz fighting mummified zombies. The action switches to Japan, where a folklore expert Professor Sakai opens a forbidden scroll. He becomes possessed by ancient Japanese demons of Thunder and Lightning, who seek to return to this plain and summon their brothers, the Dragons, to destroy the world of humans.

The BPRD is called in to investigate, after the possessed Sakai attacks a sword collector he was previously friends with. When Hellboy picks up a fallen katana sword, apparently discarded during Sakai's rampage, he finds himself transported to a bizarre world of Japanese mythology. As he tries to return to his own world, he encounters a variety of mythological Japanese creatures, including a group of traditional Japanese vampires (nukekubi) that can literally lose their heads, a giant oni, and a mystical fox.

The animation is fabulous, particularly a huge battle Hellboy fights in which it looks like he's stepped into an ancient woodcut. In side plots, two other BPRD agents, Russell Thorne (a Cushing-esque psychic) and Kate Corrigan (Peri

Gilpin) pursue the possessed Sakai, and Abe and Liz find themselves stranded on an island following a plane crash where they have to battle a dragon. The Japanese mythology is superbly researched and adds a great authenticity to the movie. There's also a very good script with some great deadpan humour (the interplay between Hellboy and the fox is fantastic).

Hellboy: Blood and Iron is the follow up to *Sword of Storms*. The story is gain from Mike Mignola and Tad Stones, with a script from Kevin Hopps. Direction is provided by Stones and Victor Cook. As before, Mignola is joined by Guillermo Del Toro as creative producer. This time the inspiration is clearly from Hammer Horror and European vampire myths. There's a scene inspired by Hammer's *Dracula* (1958), when Professor Broom emulates Peter Cushing Van Helsing in pulling aside some drapes to destroy the vampire.

The film is also inspired by the *Hellboy* comic book *Wake The Devil* (All of Mike Mignola's *Hellboy* comics are well worth checking out. One of the beauties of his artwork is, unlike the majority of current comic artwork, a reader could actually teach themselves to draw from the beautiful black line-work within. The stories are very finely wrought, miles away from any mindless superhero comic. They are for anyone who likes a good tale well told, not for some narrow group).

After a dramatic opening in a sewer, where Hellboy and Abe fight a Minotaur (clever idea, a sewer is after all a labyrinth, also the Minotaur has a metal fist on a chain like Mr Wink, and can be seen as a dry run for their battle in *Hellboy II: The Golden Army*). They are being observed by Hectate, who would like to recruit or annihilate Hellboy. "Can this be him, the one I have waited centuries to see?" She cannot understand his working with humans. "Who are these mortals who would have you turn your back on your own kind?"

Then we are treated to the first of many *Momento* style flashbacks, featuring in the young Professor Broom in 1939 (Five years before he adopts Hellboy). Professor Broom destroyed a vampire called Erzsebet Ondrussko (inspired By Countess Elizabeth Bathory), who had sold her soul to Hectate, the goddess Queen of Witches. An event that will have consequences for Hellboy and the BPRD in the present day, when they investigate a haunting in the Hamptons.

Professor Broom himself joins the investigation, along with an inexperienced agent named Sydney Leach. Broom discovers that the ghosts are the victims of the aforementioned Erzsebet. Erzsebet's two harpy servants are planning to resurrect her. Whilst the others deal with Erzsebet's minions, a phantom wolfpack , a werewolf transformed from a priest that Broom met during his first encounter with Erzsebet, Broom deals with Erzsebet once and for all, proving that age and cunning beats a vampire queen any day of the week, when he adds a little something holy to her bath.

Hellboy battles Hectate, who would like Hellboy to embrace his destiny to destroy mankind, something he refuses to do. Hellboy defeats Hectate, but her spirit makes its way back to the underworld, to return to fight another day. You don't kill a goddess that easily. It's an immensely ambitious movie, particularly with its constant flashbacks. It's also very dark indeed. The relationship between Hellboy and his father is particularly well handled.

The sense of redemption when the priest is released from his curse is very poignant. It also shows the strength of Hellboy's character when Hectate tries to tempt him. "Why do you walk this lesser world?" Mortals? They don't know you, we are greater beings than they could ever be." Hellboy replies deadpan. "I'm doing just fine."

These two animated films are a fine addition to the *Hellboy* cannon, you can tell they are part of the *Hellboy* universe but separate from the comic books and motion pictures. So, we see that Professor Broom and Agent leach are alive in this particular animated universe. The return of original cast members, Ron Perlman (Hellboy), Doug Jones (Abe Sapien), Selma Blair

(Liz Sherman), and John Hurt (Professor Broom), adds a great sense of authenticity to proceeding. A welcome addition to the cast is the character of Kate Corrigan (well voiced by Peri Gilpin). Kate appears in the comics but not in Guillermo's films. The animation is very good, and the stories would put many live-action features to shame and are highly recommended.

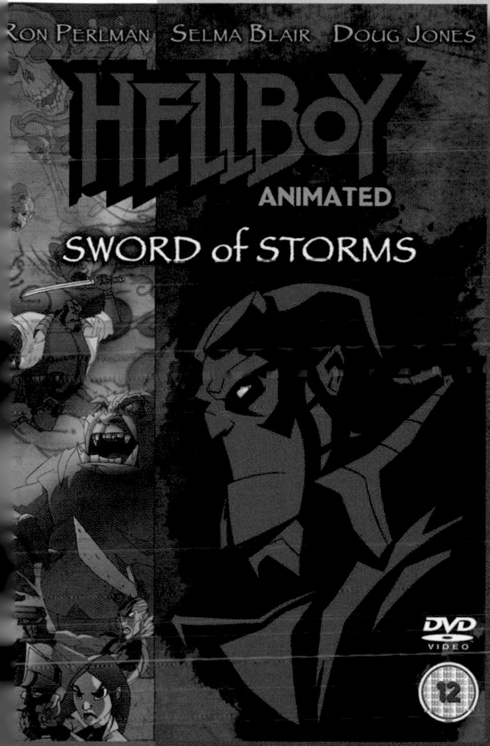

RON PERLMAN SELMA BLAIR DOUG JONES
HELLBOY ANIMATED
SWORD of STORMS
DVD VIDEO
12

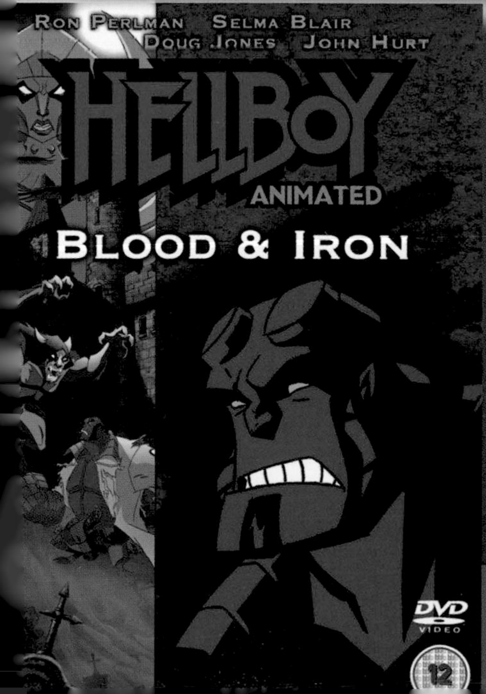

RON PERLMAN SELMA BLAIR
DOUG JONES JOHN HURT
HELLBOY ANIMATED
BLOOD & IRON
DVD VIDEO
12

Top Pic: Hellboy - Sword of Storms
Middle & Bottom: Hellboy - Blood & Iron

SWINDON COLLEGE

LEARNING RESOURCE CENTRE

Index of Films

(*bold indicates picture from a film*)

Noir Publishing titles should be available from all good bookstores; please ask your retailer to order from:

UK & EUROPE:
Turnaround Publisher Services, Unit 3, Olympia Trading Estate, Coburg Road, Wood Green, London. N22 6TZ
Tel: 0208 829 3000 Fax: 0208 8815088
www.turnaround-uk.com

USA:
SCB Distributors, 15608 South New Century Drive, Gardena, CA 90248
Tel: (310) 532-9400 Fax: (310) 532-7001
www.scbdistributors.com

SOUTH AFRICA
Stephan Phillips (Pty) Ltd, Unit 3, Old Brewery, 6 Beach Road, Woodstock, 7925, Cape Town
www.stephanphillips.com

Other titles available from Noir Publishing:-
Necronomicon Book Three, Necronomicon Book Four,
Necronomicon Book Five - All edited by Andy Black
Once Upon A Fiend - By Ratfink & Pete McKenna
Shocking Cinema of the 70's - Edited by Xavier Mendik
The Last Snake Man - By Austin J Stevens
Flowers From Hell - By Jim Harper
The Dead Walk - By Andy Black & Steve Earles

NOIR PUBLISHING 1999-2009

CELEBRATING 10 YEARS OF TRANSGRESSION

Necro[illegible]
ISBN: 97809[illegible]400

The Dead Walk
ISBN: 9780953656424

Once Upon A Fiend
ISBN: 9780953656417

Necronomicon 4
ISBN: 9780953656431

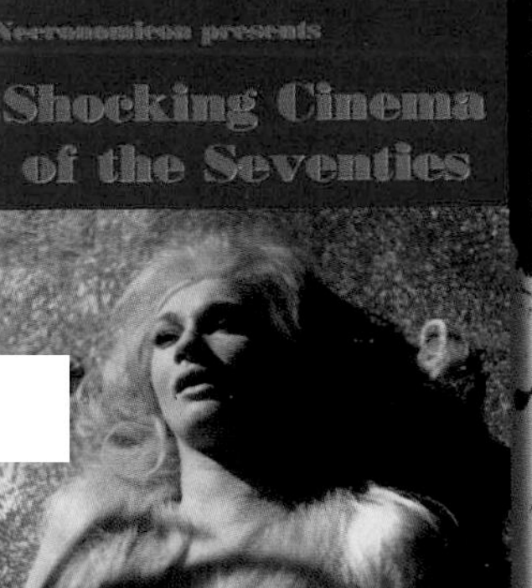

Shocking Cinema of the Seventies
ISBN: 9780953656448

The Last Snake Man
ISBN: 9780953656462

Necronomicon 5
ISBN: 9780953656455

Flowers From He[illegible]
ISBN: 97809536564[illegible]

The Dead Walk (New Edition)
ISBN: 9780953656486

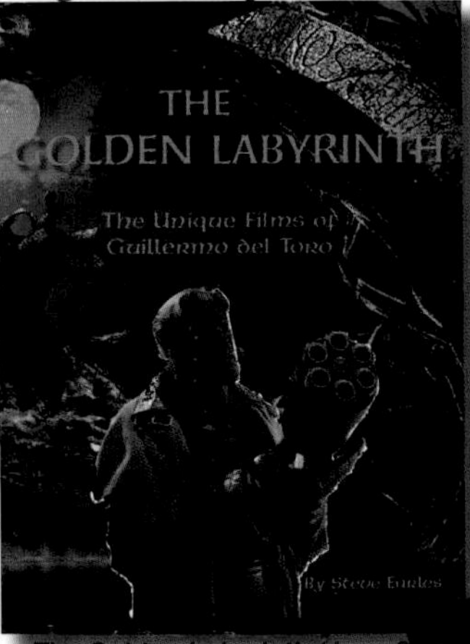

The Golden Labyrinth (June 0[illegible]
ISBN: 9780953656493

Dark Dreams (Nov. 09)
ISBN: 9780956192509

Noir Publishing
10 Spinney Grove
Hereford
Herefordshire
HR1 1AY
UK
www.noirpublishing.co.uk
e:noirpub@dsl.pipex.com

DISTRIBUTION - UK & EUROPE

Turnaround Publisher Services, Unit 3,
Olympia Trading Estate, Coburg Road,
Wood Green, London. N22 6TZ
Tel: 0208 8293000
Fax: 0208 8815088
www.turnaround-uk.com

U[illegible] CANADA

[illegible]stributors
[illegible] S. New Century Drive
[illegible]ena
[illegible]0248-2129 USA
[illegible]10 5329400
[illegible] 5156692
www.scbdistributors.com

SOUTHERN AFRICA

Stephan Phillips (Pty) Ltd
PO Box 12246, Mill Street
Cape Town, 8010
South Africa
Tel: +27 21 448 9839
Fax: +27 21 447 9879
www.stephanphillips.com